PHOTOGRAPHING *the* ELEMENTS

First published in the UK in 2012 by
I L E X
210 High Street
Lewes
East Sussex BN7 2NS

Copyright © 2012 The Ilex Press Limited

Publisher: Alastair Campbell
Associate Publisher: Adam Juniper
Creative Director: James Hollywell
Managing Editor: Natalia Price-Cabrera
Specialist Editor: Frank Gallaugher
Editor: Tara Gallagher
Senior Designer: Kate Haynes
Designer: Andrew Milne
Colour Origination: Ivy Press Reprographics

British Library Cataloguing-in-Publication Data
A catalogue record for this book is available
from the British Library

ISBN: 978-1-907579-76-9

Printed and bound in China

10 9 8 7 6 5 4 3 2 1

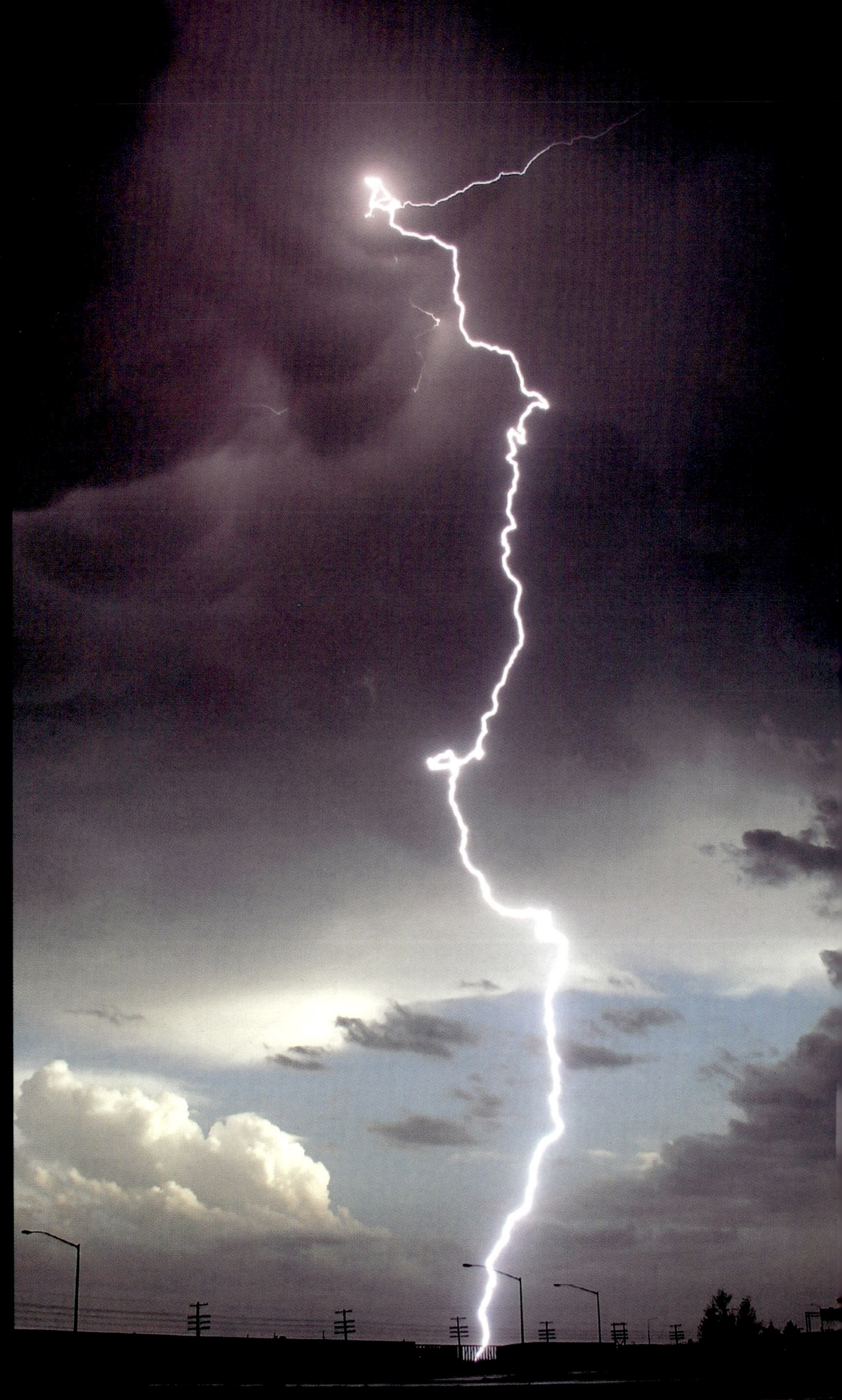

PHOTOGRAPHING *the* ELEMENTS

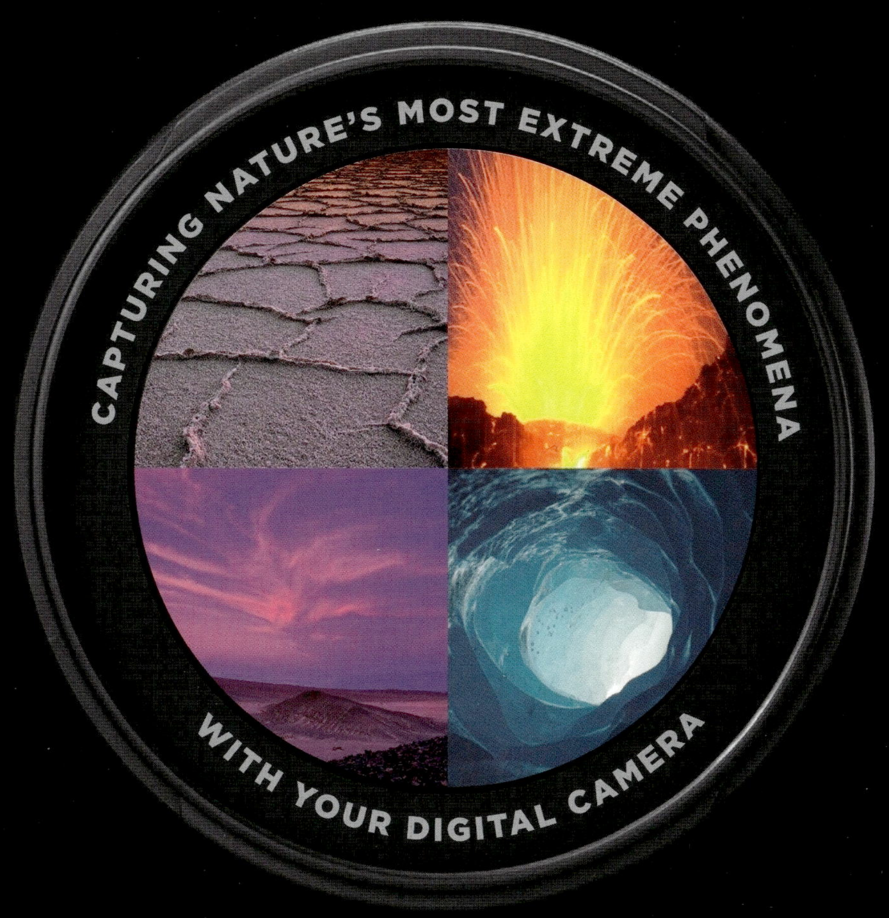

JOSEPH MEEHAN and **GARY EASTWOOD**

ILEX

Contents

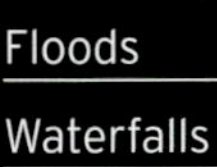

Introduction

This planet is extraordinary. The drive to capture the stunning natural phenomena it exhibits is felt by everyone who travels to exotic locales, but it is particularly suited to photographers, who can capture and showcase its visual qualities, all the while benefiting from the thrill of engaging these powerful forces head-on. It's one thing to appreciate at a distance the aesthetic qualities of a photo of a volcano erupting in the night, or a twister ripping through an open field (and the destruction left in its wake); almost everyone recognizes the value of such imagery. But it's quite another thing to be the person who captures those images in the first place, to venture out into the world with a keen eye for the best possible angles and composition, and return home not only with fantastic images to display and sell, but also with the enviable ability to say, "I was there. I captured that. Here's the proof." Such is the unique domain of extreme nature photographers.

In describing the particular geological and ecological systems that encapsulate the Earth's exceptional subjects, there is no shortage of precise, scientific terminology. While this book does contain an abundance of scientific information (as the knowledgeable nature photographer is all the more likely to get great shots), it is not a textbook. Toward that end, the subjects contained herein are categorized into the ancient elements in order to represent the basic, fundamental qualities that encompass the full stretch of nature's awesome incarnations. You may call it an alchemical approach to extreme nature photography. The elements of earth, air, fire, and water are deeply rooted in our collective unconscious, and they resonate with our most primal instincts to impart awe, mystery, inspiration, and even fear. The extreme nature photographer seeks from the viewer precisely such reactions to their images, and so approaching these various and diverse subjects in elemental terms can help them focus on the most effective means of capture and representation.

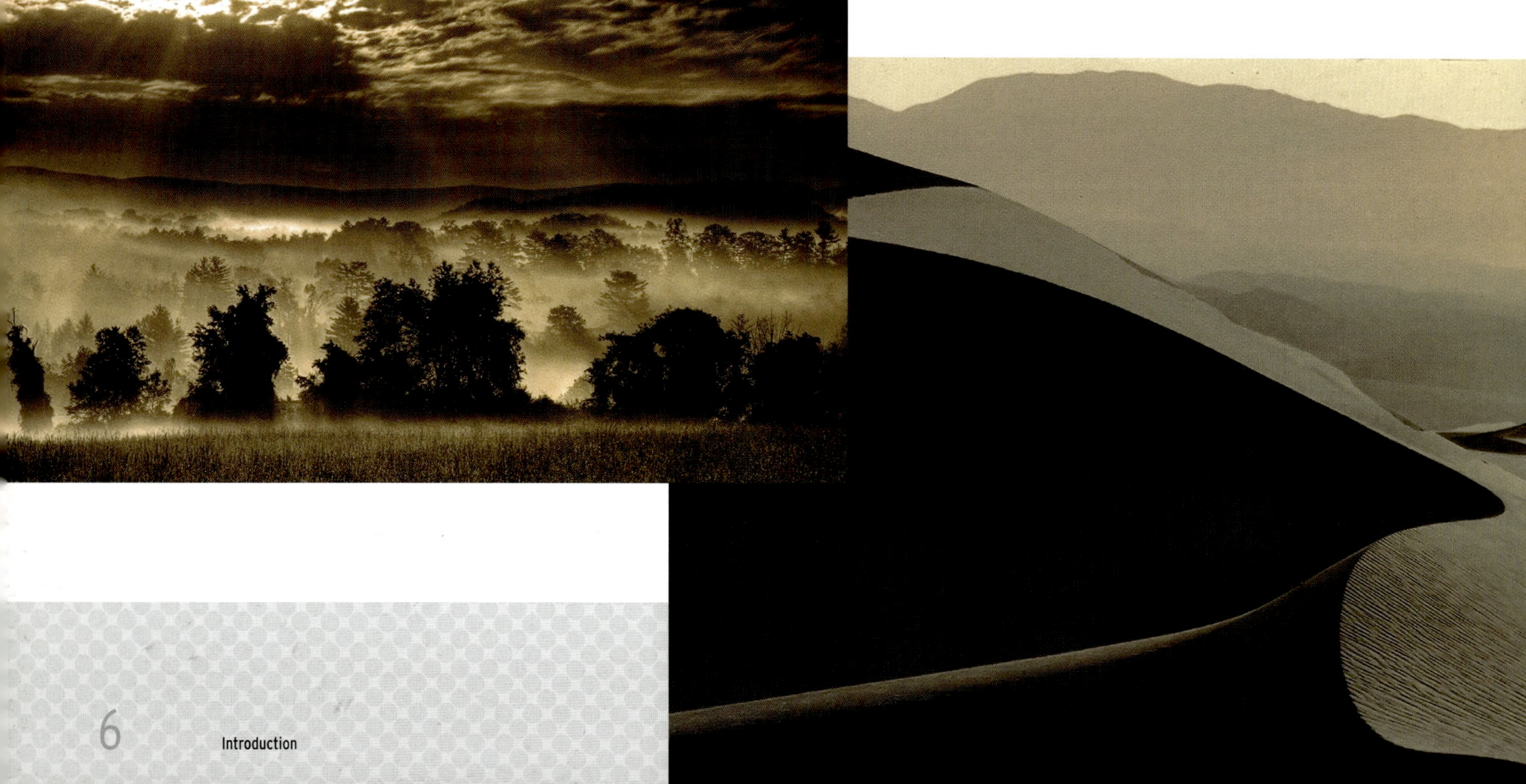

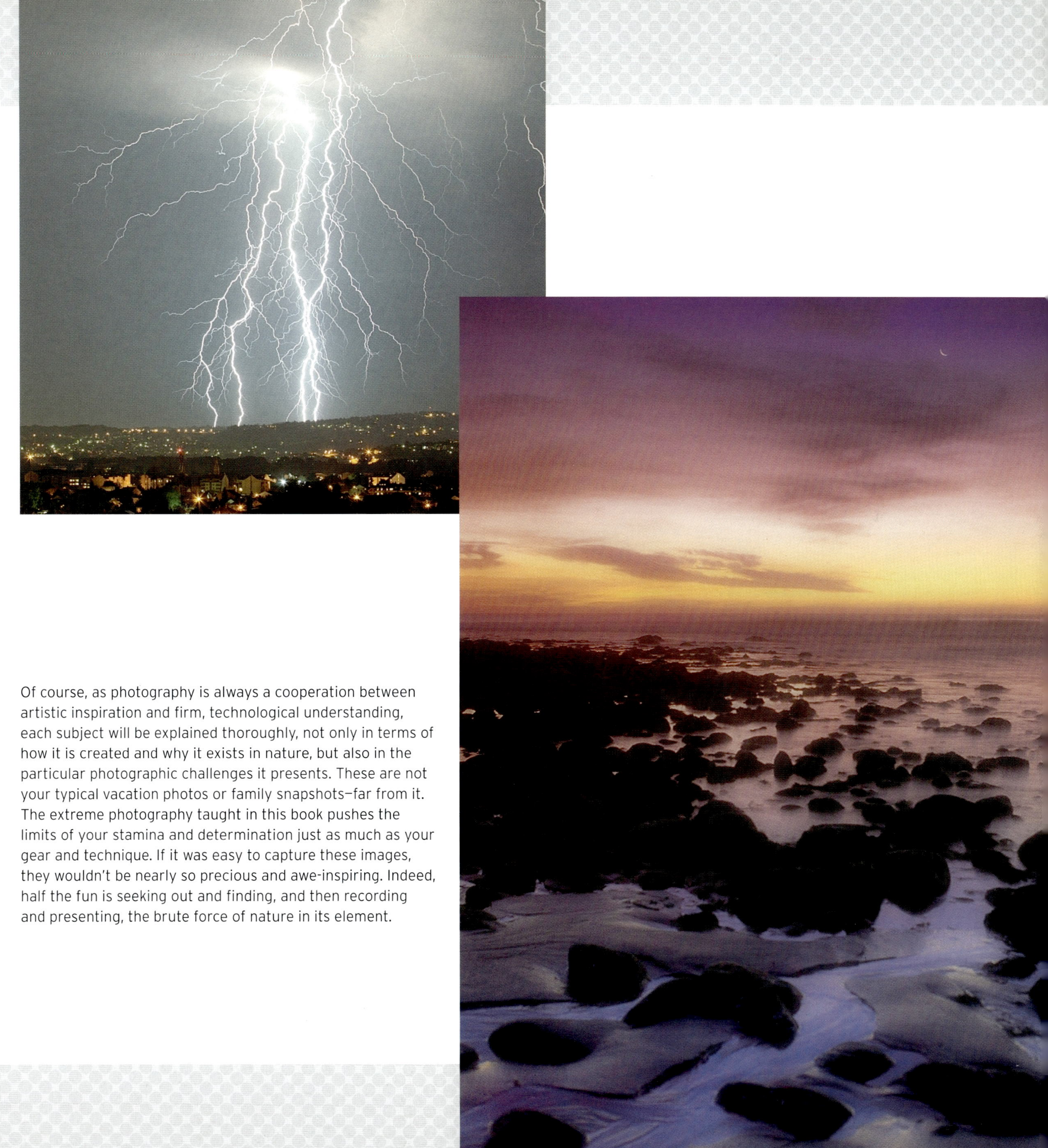

Of course, as photography is always a cooperation between artistic inspiration and firm, technological understanding, each subject will be explained thoroughly, not only in terms of how it is created and why it exists in nature, but also in the particular photographic challenges it presents. These are not your typical vacation photos or family snapshots–far from it. The extreme photography taught in this book pushes the limits of your stamina and determination just as much as your gear and technique. If it was easy to capture these images, they wouldn't be nearly so precious and awe-inspiring. Indeed, half the fun is seeking out and finding, and then recording and presenting, the brute force of nature in its element.

Earth

Unless you manage to snag a ticket into space, you'll likely be taking all of your photographs here on planet earth. Of course, for the purposes of this chapter, earth has a more narrow definition: the land, and all the stunning geologic formations in which it presents itself. We begin with a discussion of that most classic of photographic genres, the landscape, whose photographic and compositional rules apply largely to every other topic throughout the book. Learn how to balance the exposures of the sky and the land, and how to incorporate foreground, mid-ground, and background elements into a harmonious whole, and you will have the basic approach to a great many other elements. This chapter also embraces one particular earthen feature: the desert, and all the challenges (and opportunities) that this extremely hot environment presents to the adventurous photographer.

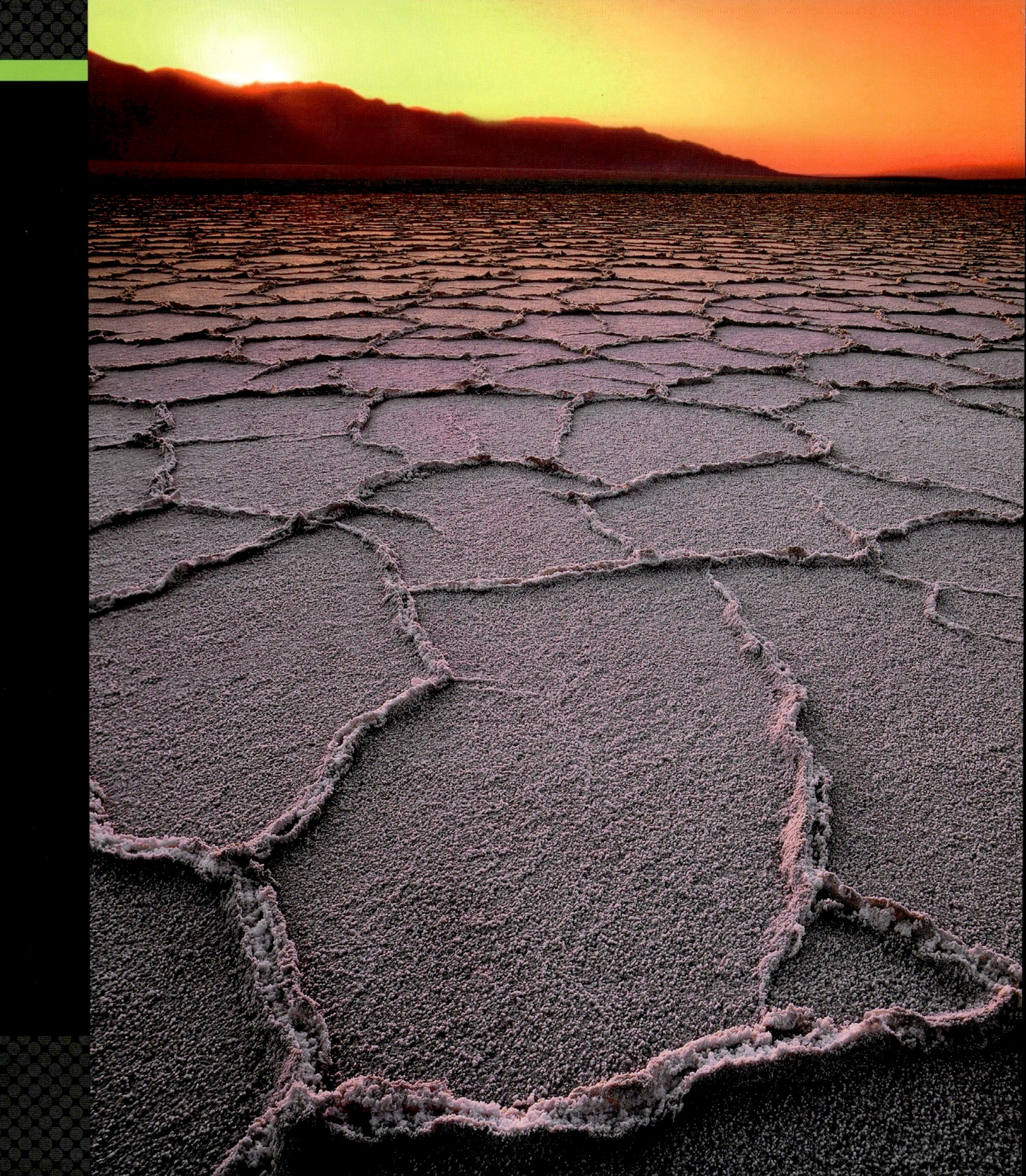

Landscapes

Landscapes are one of the most popular and rewarding genres of photography. It has enjoyed a real renaissance in the last decade since the introduction of sophisticated, affordable DSLR cameras, which allow amateur and professional photographers alike to create high-quality landscape imagery. Yet the masters still have the ability to raise the standard of their landscape photography well above the average. Good landscapes require planning, dedication, and strong photographic technique.

The evolution of humankind is inextricably linked to our environment, and the joy we gain from viewing a stunning landscape image is arguably a subconscious acknowledgement of our ancestral past. Whether it's a coastline, mountain range, mist-shrouded peak, river, forest, you name it—a powerful landscape image has the ability to stir strong emotions within us.

Historically, landscape photography was the preserve of the large-format field camera, which required long treks with heavy equipment, making prior scouting of locations essential. The need for exemplary technique was also paramount in order to avoid costly mistakes with 5x4 sheet film. The work of Ansel Adams, performed mainly in America's Midwest, is a perfect example of the craft, and continues to inspire new generations of landscape photographers.

Arguably, some of today's higher-end DSLRs—particularly those with an abundance of megapixels—can now match the resolution of the old field cameras without the expense of film processing or the bulk. However, there is no substitute for good technique. Many of today's top landscape photographers have made the switch from field cameras to DSLRs, and they apply the same rigorous techniques of the field camera to their DSLR work.

Without a doubt, quality of light is the transforming factor in landscape photography. Composition, technique, equipment, and mood are all important as well, but the quality of the light can transform even the most humdrum location into a stunning masterpiece. Almost without exception, the best landscapes are therefore captured during the golden hours—the hour leading up to sunset, and the hour following sunrise. At these times, the distinction between day and night is blurred (boundaries and edges have always made interesting photographic subject matter by adding a sense of tension to images). Rich colors, such as red, orange, pink, and magenta, are also most prevalent at these times—a result of the sun's rays having to travel farther through the earth's atmosphere, which has the effect of filtering out the blue end of the light spectrum. Bright sunlight also tends to bleach out colors.

Grand Canyon National Park

While the earth offers no shortage of stunning landscape subjects, some are invariably more photogenic than others. The Grand Canyon, for instance, has been photographed countless times over the years, but it still reveals itself in new ways, under different lighting conditions.

At the same time, clouds can be dramatically illuminated from a sun that is below the horizon from the perspective of an earth-bound viewer. Even when the sun is above the horizon, its intensity is much softer at these times than during the middle of the day. This makes exposure easier insofar as there is typically less dynamic range (or difference between the brightest and darkest areas of the scene), which is less demanding of your camera's sensor (which is capable of capturing only so much dynamic range before highlights get "blown out" to pure white, and shadows "block up" to pure black).

The low sunlight also provides modeling for the contours and details of the landscape. When the sun is high in the sky, the ground is fairly evenly lit resulting in flat, dimensionless images. But low sunlight during the golden hours creates dramatic contrast between shadows and highlights, illuminating edges and creating strong light patterns and shapes.

The golden hours also have implications for image composition. The best results are often obtained by shooting at an angle of 90 degrees to the low sun (with the sun to either side of the camera), which accentuates the modeling of the land, and creates rich, contrasty images by reducing the relative dynamic range of the scene.

Of course, rules are there to be broken. The presence of mist, for example, might allow the photographer to capture stunning images by shooting directly into the sun, often termed *contre-jour* (translated from French as "against daylight"). Placing foreground subjects, such as trees, rocks, and buildings, can also "damp down" the intensity of the sun, thus allowing *contre-jour* shooting.

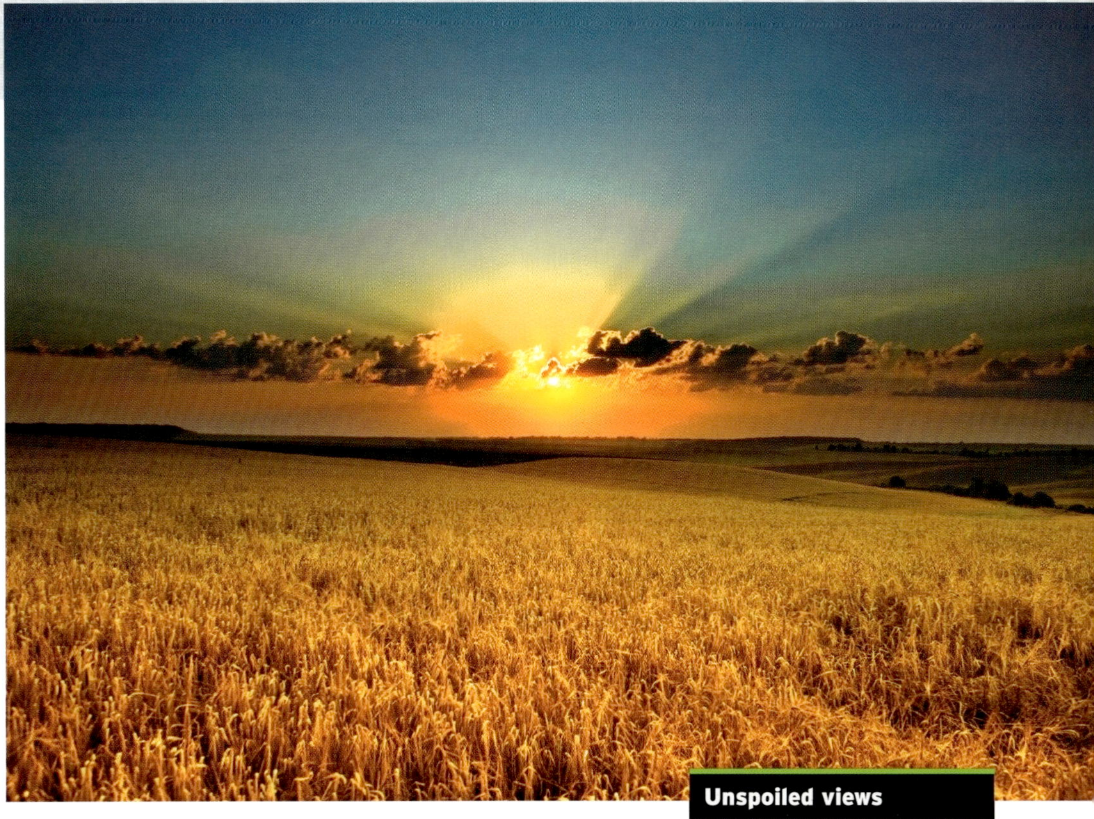

Unspoiled views

A key to photographing high-quality landscapes is finding a perspective that isn't obscured or contaminated by any elements of human civilization.

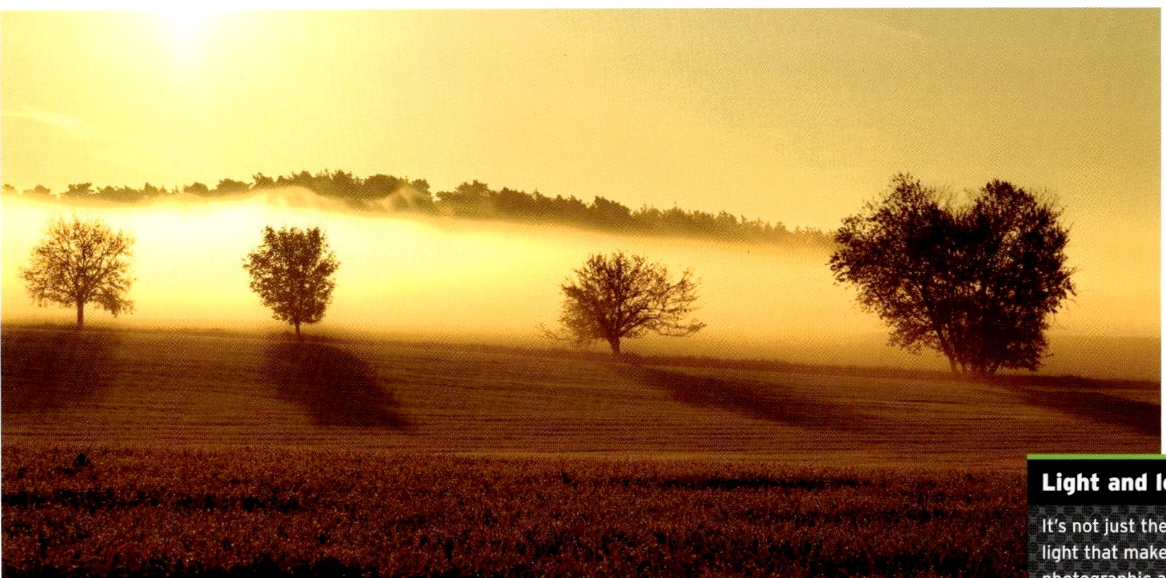

Light and long shadows

It's not just the warm, saturated quality of the light that makes the golden hours such a valuable photographic aide, it's also the acute angle at which that light strikes its subjects, casting them in stark relief against a rolling vista, accentuating their forms with long shadows that stretch out before them.

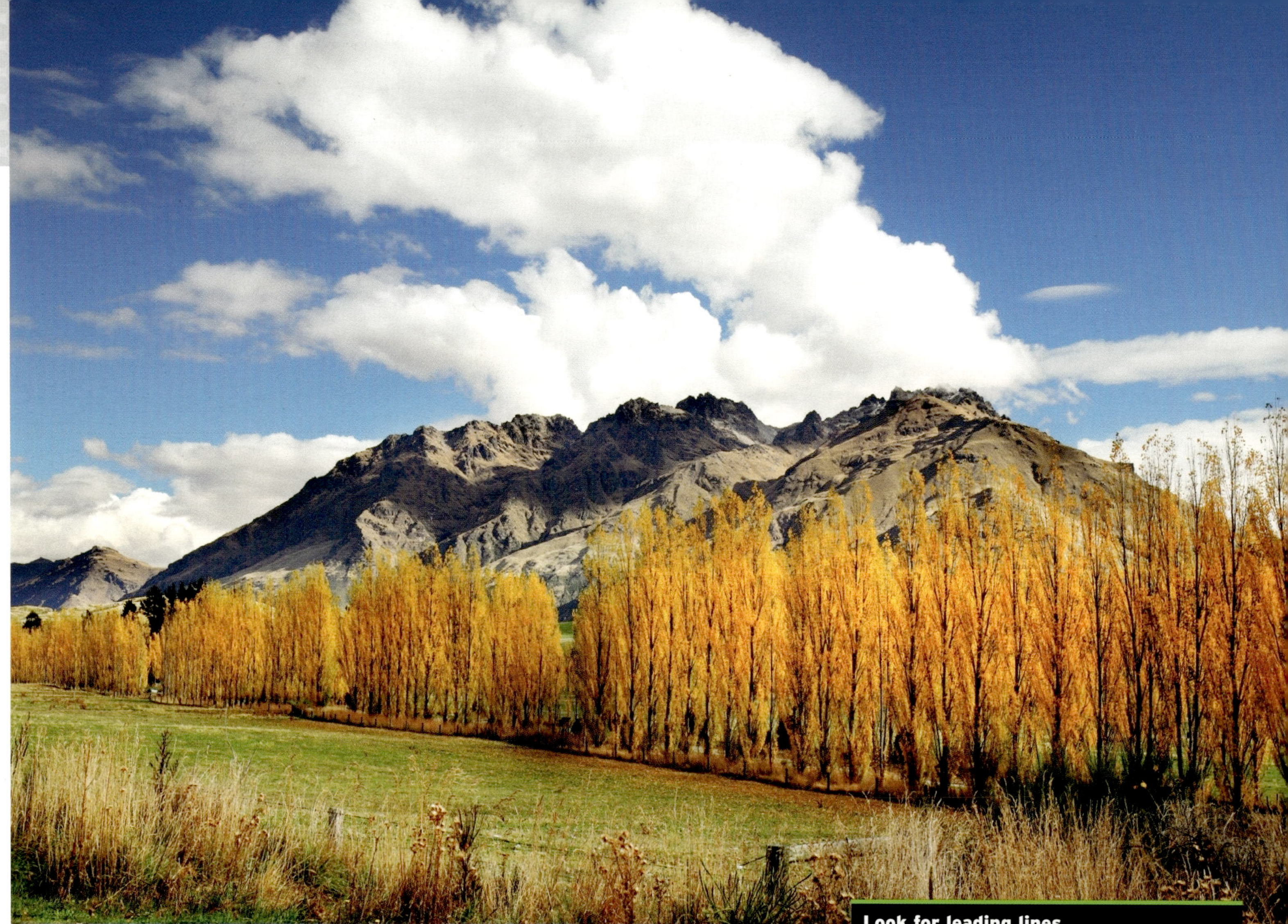

Commonly, landscape images adhere to the rule of thirds when it comes to composition. Compare the impact of a landscape image with the horizon placed in the center of the frame, with one in which the horizon is placed one-third down from the top of the frame. As well as adding more tension to an image, this compositional rule also allows the photographer to include foreground interest—waves, rocks, a line of trees, gates, paths, animals, and so on—and to create all-important leading lines.

Placing foreground interest in the frame, often at close quarters, creates a sense of being there for the viewer. The presence of textures, such as lichen on a rock, will add to this effect, hopefully making the viewer want to reach in and feel the surface of the subject. Foreground subjects also provide a sense of perspective for the sweep of a wide landscape or a towering mountain range.

Leading lines are used to add impact and interest, and to literally lead the viewer into the image or toward the intended focal point. A line of trees, a path, a sequence of rocks, a mountain ridge, clouds, even shadows and shapes can be placed in such a way that they draw the viewer's gaze toward the main point of interest, which could be the rising sun, a cliff, a lone tree, or a distant mountain enjoying the first glowing rays of dawn.

Look for leading lines

Though not exclusively artificial, leading lines do tend to originate from man-made setups, as with this row of trees planted in a perfect line. The order they instill in a scene is a powerful contribution to the composition. Besides guiding the viewer's eye into the scene, they can also organize an otherwise cluttered landscape.

Conversely, some of the most powerful landscape images are the simplest, drawing on mood, color, shapes, and balance to create graphic or contemplative images. Such creative decisions are of course down to the individual photographer.

Another consideration is whether to shoot landscapes in a literal fashion, recording the scene exactly as it appears, or to work more interpretively, using shapes, colors, forms, and textures to create a mood, feeling, or concept, while still retaining a sense of place.

Choosing a suitable location is one of the most challenging decisions for a landscape photographer. There is a temptation to travel increasingly farther afield in order to capture a new or previously un-photographed scene and location. However, getting to know a location by repeat visits can often yield better results, as the photographer becomes acquainted with the nuances of the location, such as direction of the sun, how the light models the land, microclimate (is the location prone to mist?), and the best vistas or compositions. Intimate knowledge of a popular location can elevate images from the average and provide a new interpretation of a familiar or well-photographed location or landmark.

If visiting a new location, there is no substitute for prior scouting trips. Understanding the location allows the photographer to quickly respond to changes in light, mood, and weather during what is often a small window of opportunity. If the sun briefly appears from behind a cloud, casting glorious golden light over a scene, the last thing a photographer should be doing is working out how best to use the light in context of the landscape before them.

Patience is key in landscape photography. Some of the best images are a result of repeat visits coupled with hours of patient waiting for the right light or weather. Atmospheric conditions will also have a strong impact on the mood of the final image. Arriving or receding weather fronts and storms can often produce dramatic lighting.

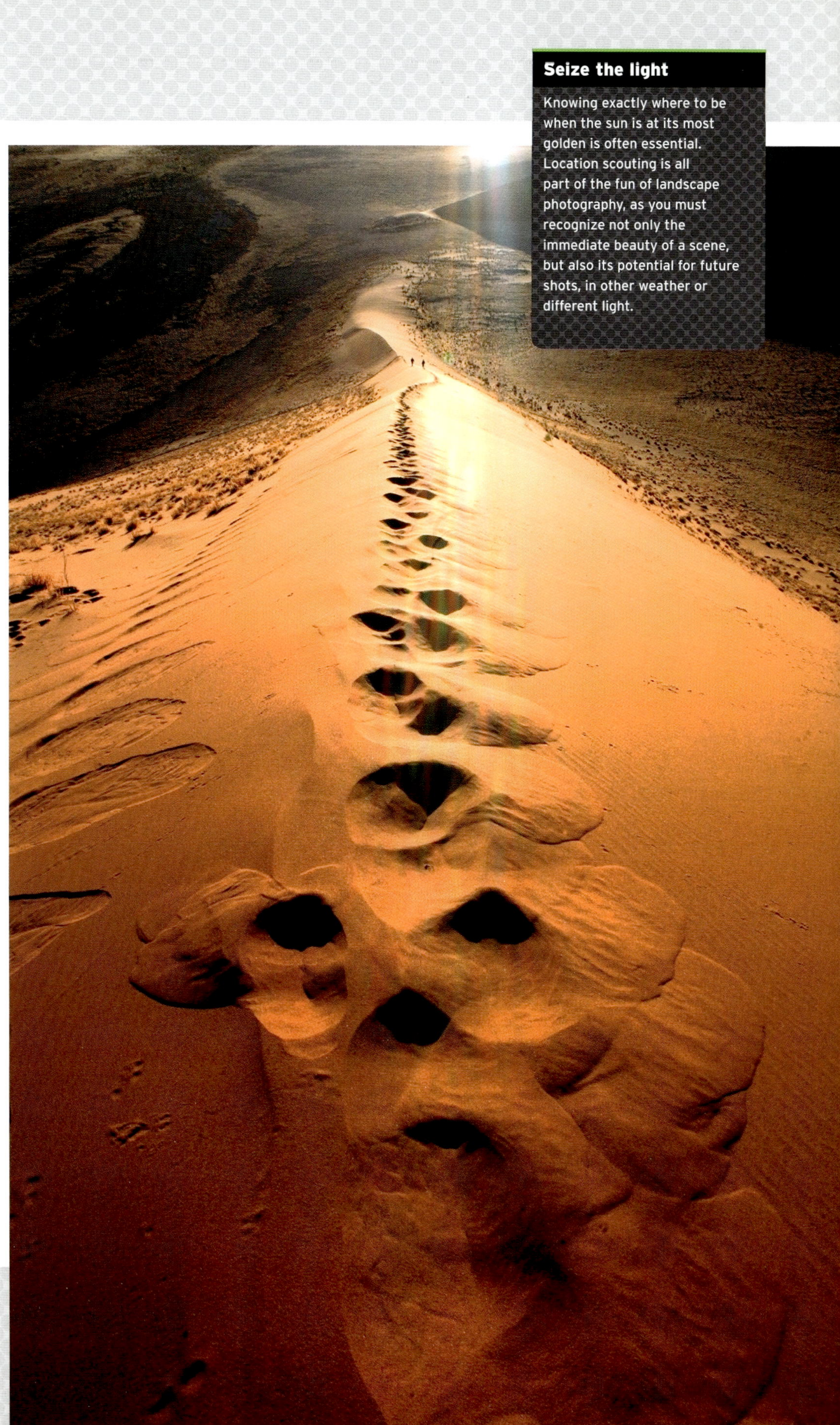

!

Shooting Tips:

> Treat your photo excursions like a camping trip, and pack everything you'll need for the day.

> Don't just take one shot and be done with a scene; see if there are passing clouds that will diffuse the light, or if the angle of the sun later in the day will enliven certain elements with long, contrasty shadows.

Setting the exposure will depend on the composition and whether strong light is included within the frame. For the best image quality, use a low ISO of between 50 and 200. Aperture settings of around f/16 and above are routinely used in landscape photography to ensure the greatest depth of field—the zone of sharp focus between which the nearest and farthest elements of the frame.

Such narrow apertures do, however, add the problem of diffraction, which degrades image quality; so balance is the key. One way to avoid this is to use hyperfocal distances to focus. A more general tip for focusing is to focus on a spot around one-third into the frame at a mid-to-narrow aperture, which will often yield good results (because at any given aperture, depth of field extends one third in front of the focused distance, and two thirds behind it). This combination of low ISO and narrow aperture will most likely require a fairly slow shutter speed, particularly during the golden hours—hence the need for a tripod.

As a rule of thumb, take an initial exposure reading from a neutral tone in the scene such as a gray cloud, rock, blue sky (away from the sun), or grass, and work from there, ensuring that both the highlight and shadow details are recorded by the camera's sensor by checking the histogram on a test exposure.

It is quite common for the dynamic range of the scene to be too high for even the best camera sensors, so graduated neutral density filters are used to balance the dynamic range between the brightness of the sky and sun, and the shadows in the foreground. ND filters are another essential item for the landscape photographer (see box opposite). Shooting in a Raw format does provide more flexibility in post-production, and in some cases can retrieve blown-out highlight areas.

In general, the exposure on a modern DSLR should be skewed as far to the right of the image histogram as possible without blowing out any highlight details. By dialing up exposure as far as possible (but not allowing the histogram to get "clipped" off at the far right) the photographer ensures the best possible image quality, as noise levels in the shadows are reduced, and the sensor is working in its optimal range. It is therefore able to capture more information and detail—exposure levels can then be dialed back down in post-processing, while retaining the optimal quality.

More extreme landscapes require the same adherence to technique, if not greater care. At the same time, they risk more potential for damage to both equipment and photographer. Waterfall or desert photography, for example, will require extra weatherproof protection for the equipment, while extremely cold conditions not only reduce battery life, but also bring the danger of condensation once the equipment is returned to a warmer, indoor environment.

More extreme landscape photography should also be performed in the presence of trained guides, or experienced fellow photographers. As always with landscape photography, careful preparation and planning is key.

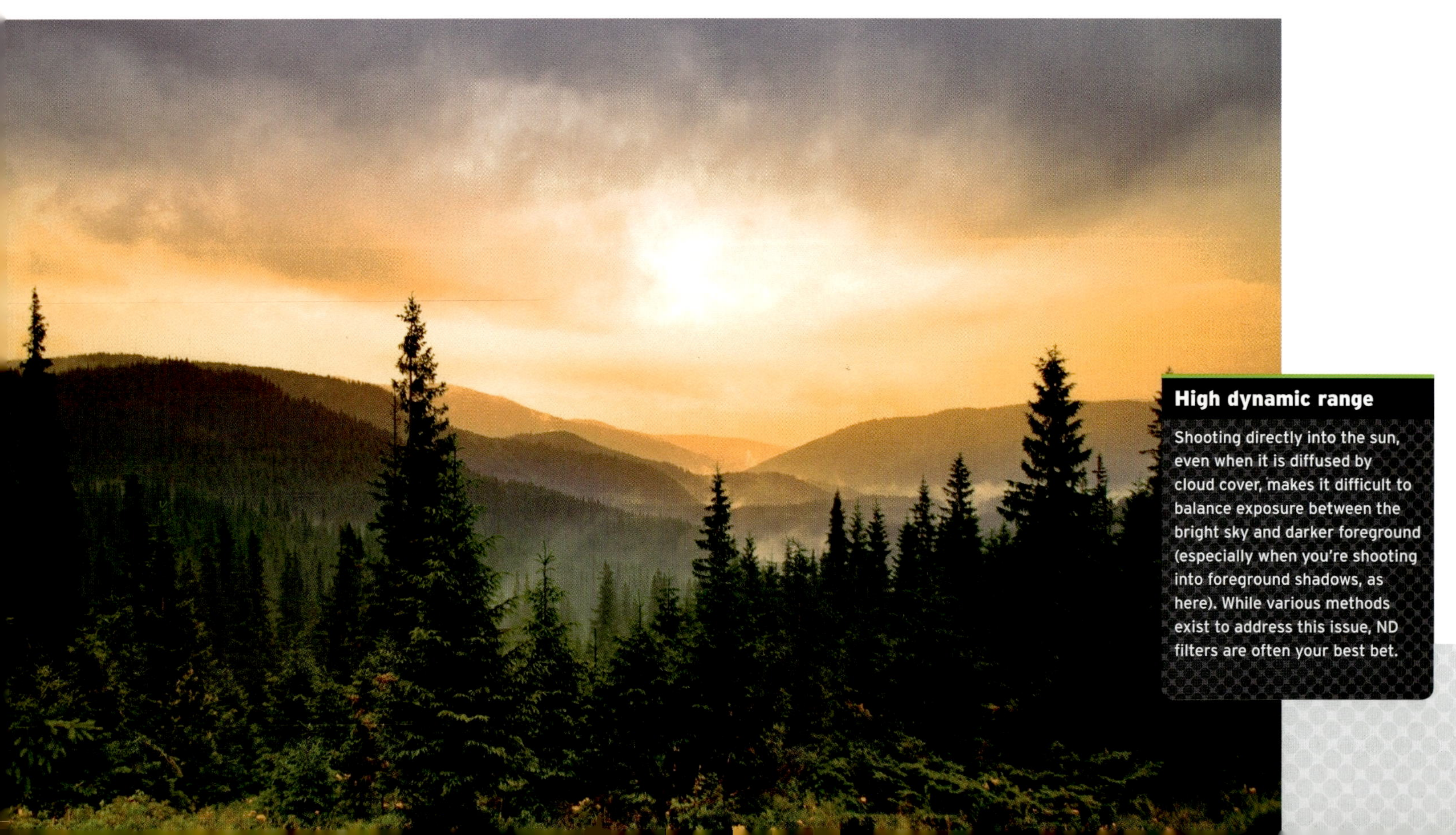

High dynamic range

Shooting directly into the sun, even when it is diffused by cloud cover, makes it difficult to balance exposure between the bright sky and darker foreground (especially when you're shooting into foreground shadows, as here). While various methods exist to address this issue, ND filters are often your best bet.

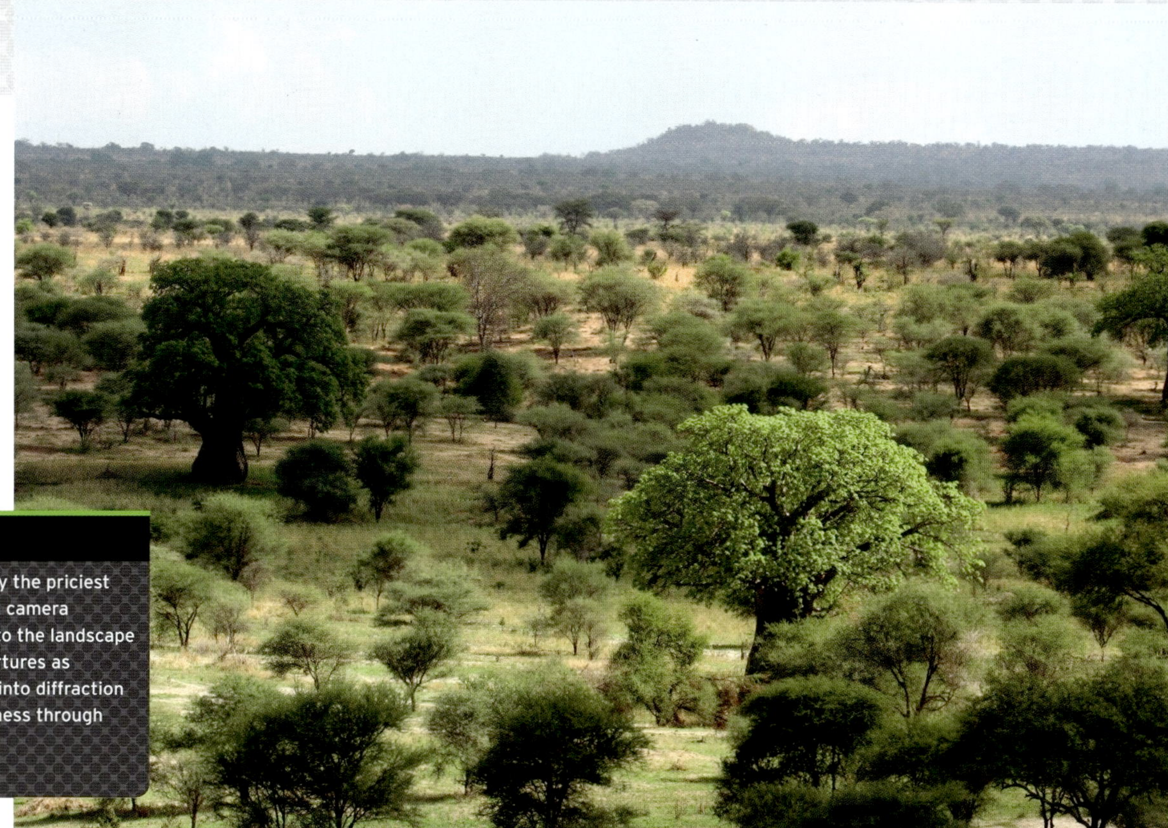

Focus from near to far

While wide-aperture lenses are usually the priciest and most desired lenses for any given camera system, they are of quite limited use to the landscape photographer, who tends to keep apertures as narrow as possible (without reaching into diffraction territory) in order to maximize sharpness through the full depth of their scenes.

Setting Exposure with Graduated Neutral Density Filters

Graduated filters are made of transparent material, with a darker area at the top half of the filter. This darker area reduces the exposure by a set amount, for example a 1-stop graduated ND filter, 2-stop, 3-stop and so on, only in the areas of the scene that it covers. The filters are slid into a filter holder on the front of the lens, with the transition from the transparent to the dark area on the filter positioned along the horizon as the photographer looks through the viewfinder. The effect is to reduce the exposure of the sky by the appropriate amount.

Take an exposure reading from a neutral tone in the sky such as a gray cloud, and a separate reading from a similarly neutral tone in the foreground. If the difference is, say, four f-stops, use a filter that will bring the difference down to one f-stop—in this case a three f-stop filter.

Graduated ND filters are available with a "hard" graduation—a distinct line between the dark and transparent sections of the filter, useful when the horizon is clearly visible and not obscured by subjects such as trees or mountains—or with a more gradual "soft" graduation, used when the horizon of the scene is not flat or is obscured.

Setting the Hyperfocal Distance

The hyperfocal distance describes the closest distance at which a lens can be focused, while keeping everything from there to infinity in acceptable focus. When the lens is focused at the hyperfocal distance, everything from half of the hyperfocal distance to infinity will be in focus. So, for example, if the hyperfocal distance is 1 meter, by setting the lens to focus at 1m, everything from 50cm (half the hyperfocal distance) to infinity should be in acceptably sharp focus.

The hyperfocal distance is always the same for a particular focal length, aperture and sensor size, so they can be found on many reference sites or charts, and simply printed out and placed in your backpack ready for the next landscape trip. Let us say that, having set up a 35mm camera and tripod and framed a composition at 24mm and f/11, the fixed hyperfocal distance (reading from a source chart) will always be 3.64m—so setting the lens focus distance at 3.64m will mean that any objects from 1.82m (half of 3.64m) from the front of the lens to infinity will be in acceptable focus. This method allows the photographer to use the smallest aperture number possible (i.e. widest aperture) and therefore reduce the risk of diffraction, an artifact of using high aperture numbers (such as f/22) that degrades image quality. A wider aperture also allows the use of faster shutter speeds.

Deserts

Desert areas of the world have many topographical structures that fascinate photographers, from the supple shapes of sand dunes to the starkness of barren mountains and other formations that can convey an otherworldly appearance. To the uninitiated, all this may appear to be stark and desolate, lacking the vitality of colorful vegetation, reflective bodies of water, majestic trees, etc. Those experienced in photographing the typography of the desert areas such as the American Southwest (the subject of these images) understand that there are many opportunities for impressive photographs by capturing the delicate aspects of these inhospitable places. One of the most effective ways to bring out these visual elements is to make use of the soft light of dusk and dawn and the angular natural light immediately after sunrise and just before sunset. Consequently, a photographer needs to be on location at least 45 minutes or more before sunrise and then remain for a similar time after sunset. These are also the coolest times of day when the blurring effect of heat waves coming off large surface areas are minimal and there is less concern about heat stress on equipment.

What one chooses to photograph is, of course, a very personal decision, rooted in the photographer's impressions of the scene, individual style, and level of skill. What follows are some suggestions that combine different forms of light with various themes as a way of demonstrating the variety of photographic opportunities that desert areas have to offer.

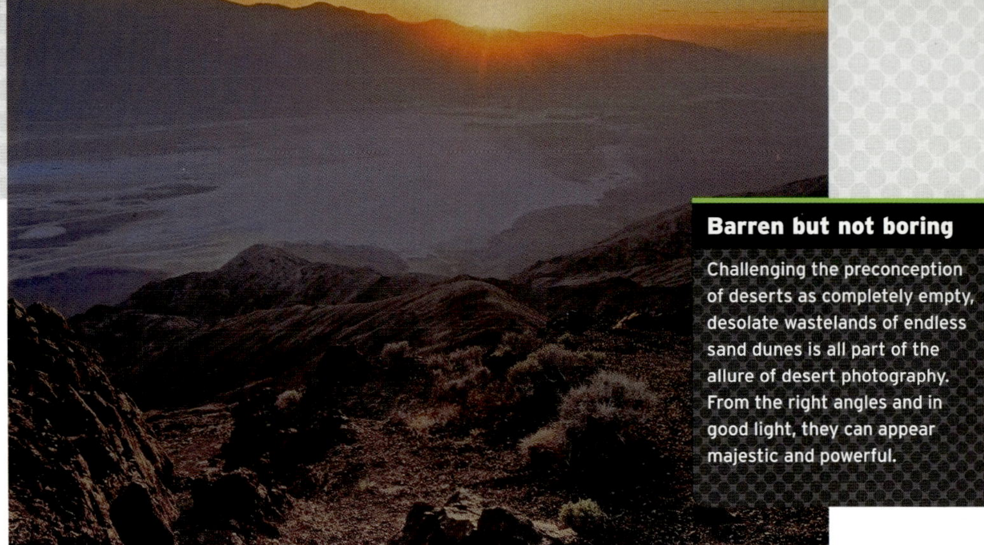

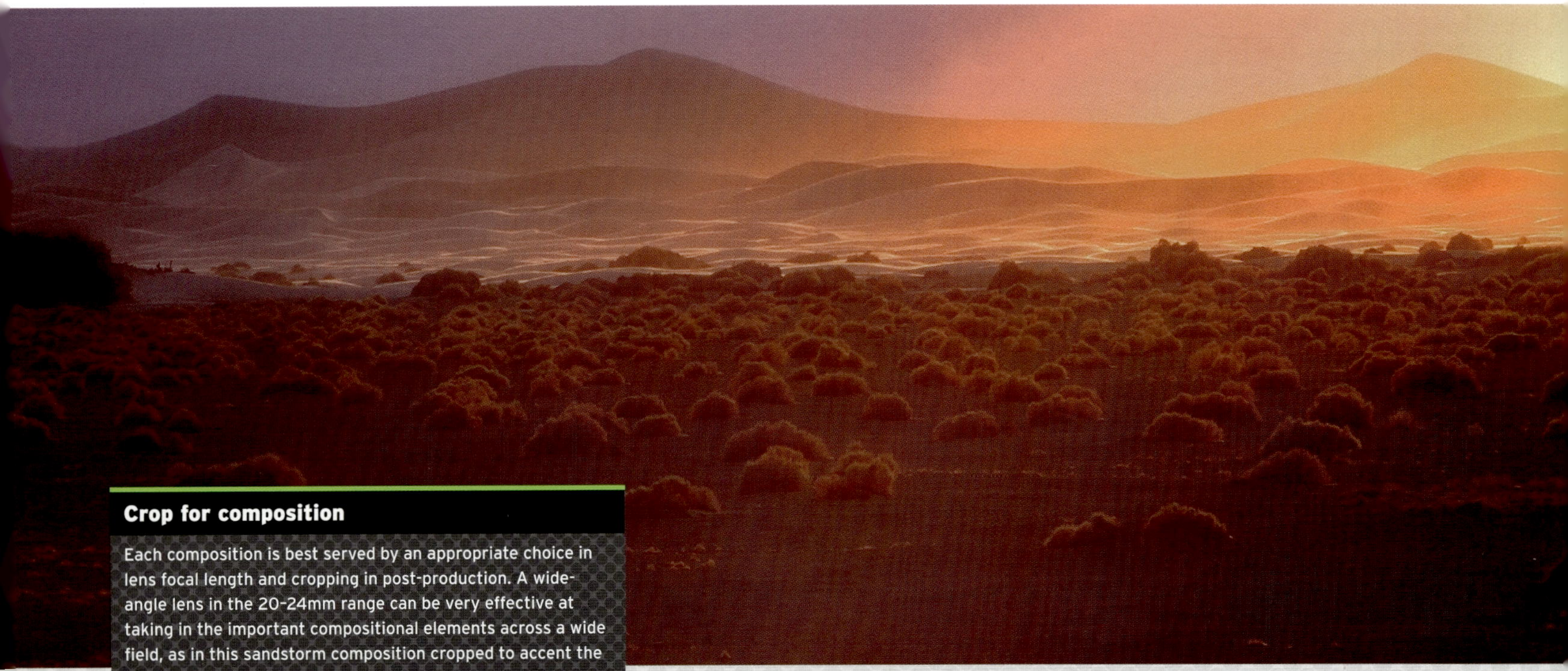

Barren but not boring

Challenging the preconception of deserts as completely empty, desolate wastelands of endless sand dunes is all part of the allure of desert photography. From the right angles and in good light, they can appear majestic and powerful.

Crop for composition

Each composition is best served by an appropriate choice in lens focal length and cropping in post-production. A wide-angle lens in the 20-24mm range can be very effective at taking in the important compositional elements across a wide field, as in this sandstorm composition cropped to accent the middle section of the scene.

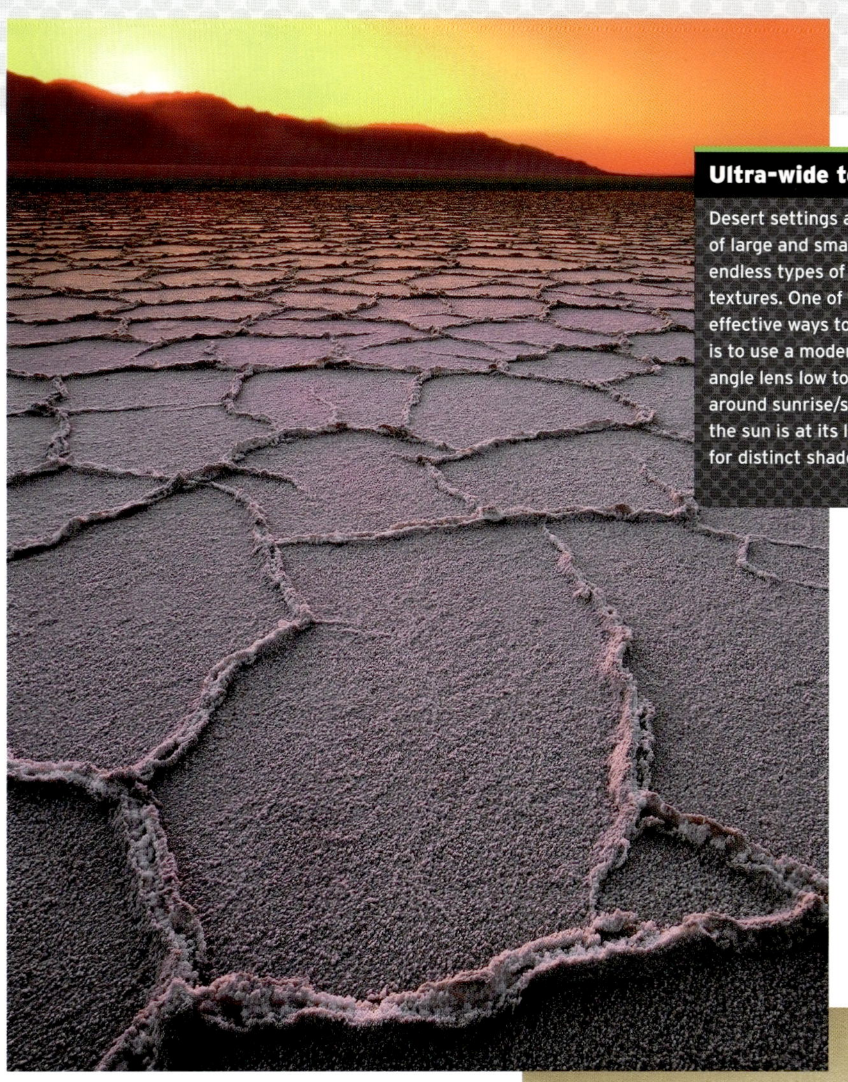

dried and cracked mudflats receding from the foreground. Setting the camera low and close to the foreground using a wide-angle lens is a very effective way of producing such a composition. The wider the angle, the larger foreground subject will appear in relation to the background.

A similar arrangement would be a shot containing layers of sand dunes with perhaps distant layers of mountains. An added sense of depth will come if the mountains appear subdued in contrast and color in the soft light of dawn or dusk. In general, as the relative size of the background is reduced with the use of a wider lens, it is more likely to serve as a framing element rather than a separate detailed structure. If the desire is to capture a much wider vista, taking in, for example, a long series of mountain ranges, this is best done using the panoramic approach—as described on page 148.

The Power of a Wide View

A typical first impression of the desert environment is that of a stark, even foreboding, expanse. To capture such an impression requires a wide-angle focal length or a stitched panoramic view. The key is to have some sort of organization for the visual elements present so they support the impression of a large open space while providing the illusion of depth. One of the best ways of accomplishing this is to look for receding layers within the landscape combined with details about the physical makeup of the scene. For example, capturing two layers of mountains in the background while having the strongly defined texture of

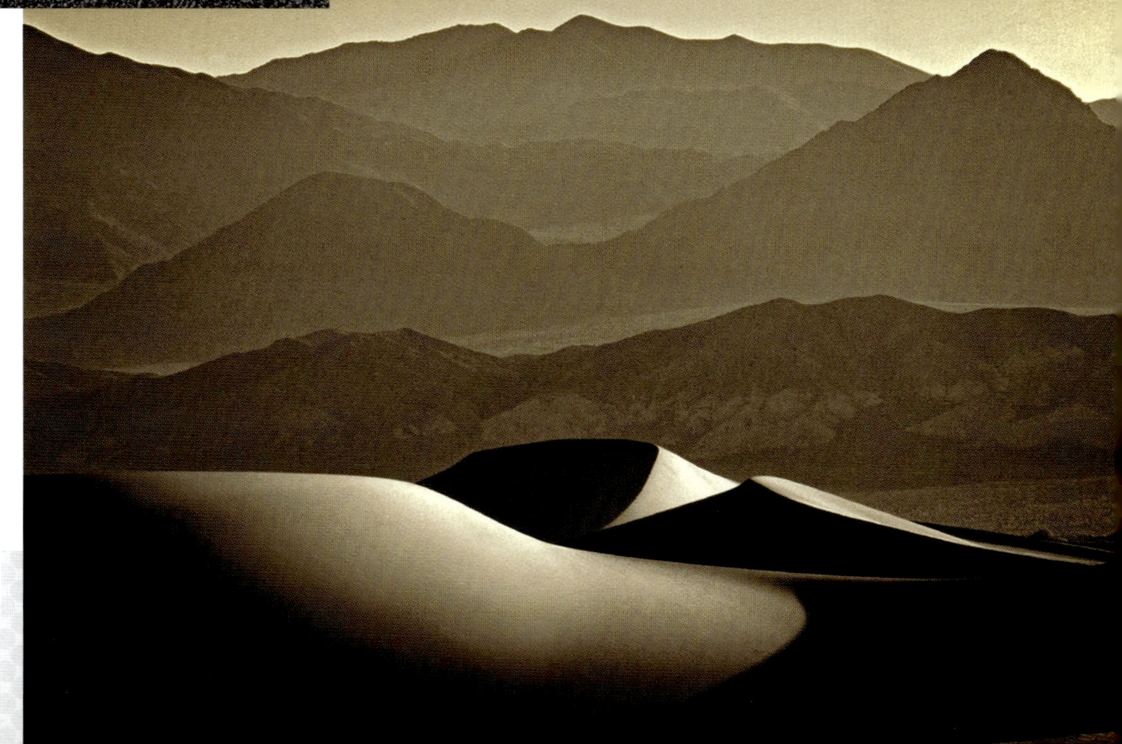

Shapes and Textures

Isolating and capturing the shapes and textures of the American Southwest in simple compositions can make for some interesting pictures. These elements can emerge out of the landscape in the delicate light of dawn and dusk, and especially in the more angular light at sunrise or just before sunset. This is because the shadows are pronounced but have not become so strong as to lose their delicate structure, as happens in the high-contrast light of midday. In general, the shadow-to-highlight brightness range of key subject matter in these early and late hour compositions is within the latitude of a digital camera.

Sand dunes are endless sources of subtle shapes, leading lines, and wind-sculpted waves. These shapes and textures can be captured in isolation, in layers, or in combinations thereof. An interesting approach is to find a location in which two or more very different textures abut one another. For example, the texture of dry cracked mud contrasted with the granular texture of sand. When capturing larger shapes such as mountain ranges or a very wide view of imposing dunes in a panorama, textures will be less prominent and may, in fact, not be visible. Such compositions will tend to emphasize a more grandiose impression of desert landscapes. Whatever composition is used, the light at the beginning and end of the day is quite short-lived, requiring the photographer to have the equipment ready and to work quickly.

Desert Skies

With all the variety of strong ground elements in the American Southwest, some consideration should be given to balancing this with a distinctive sky. For example, a deep blue color during the day perhaps enhanced by a polarizing filter or the warm color variations that occur very early and very late in the day. This is most effective when the warmest wavelengths of a low sun are in higher amounts and mix with the dominant blues of the upper sky. The result is layers of magenta that are at their strongest when the sun is just below the horizon. Any

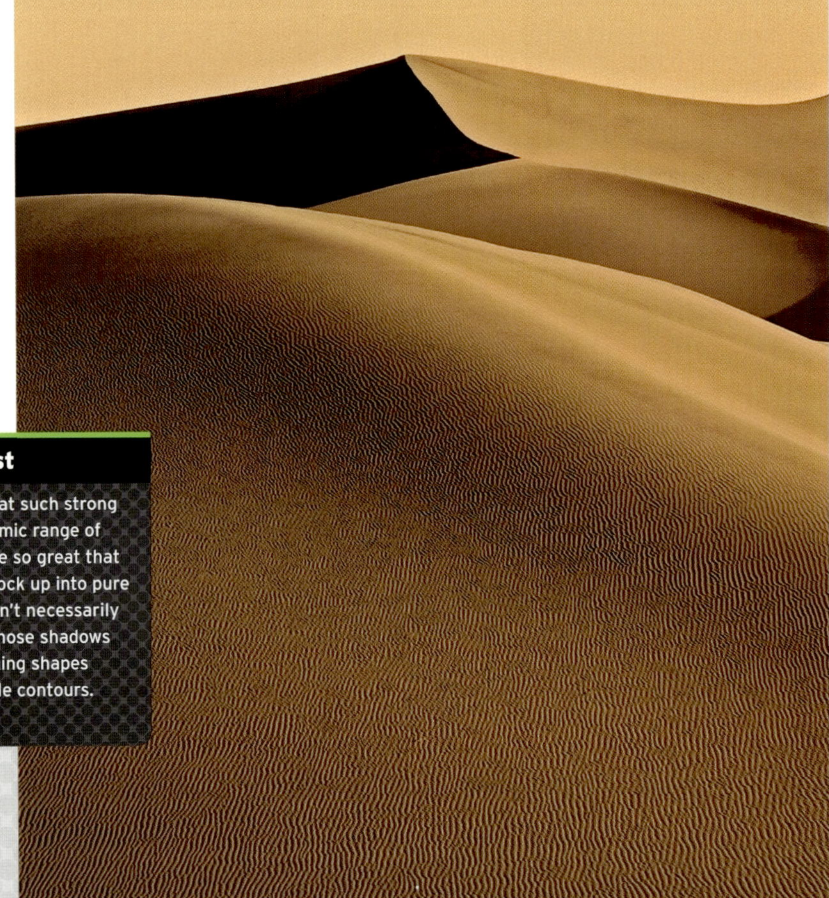

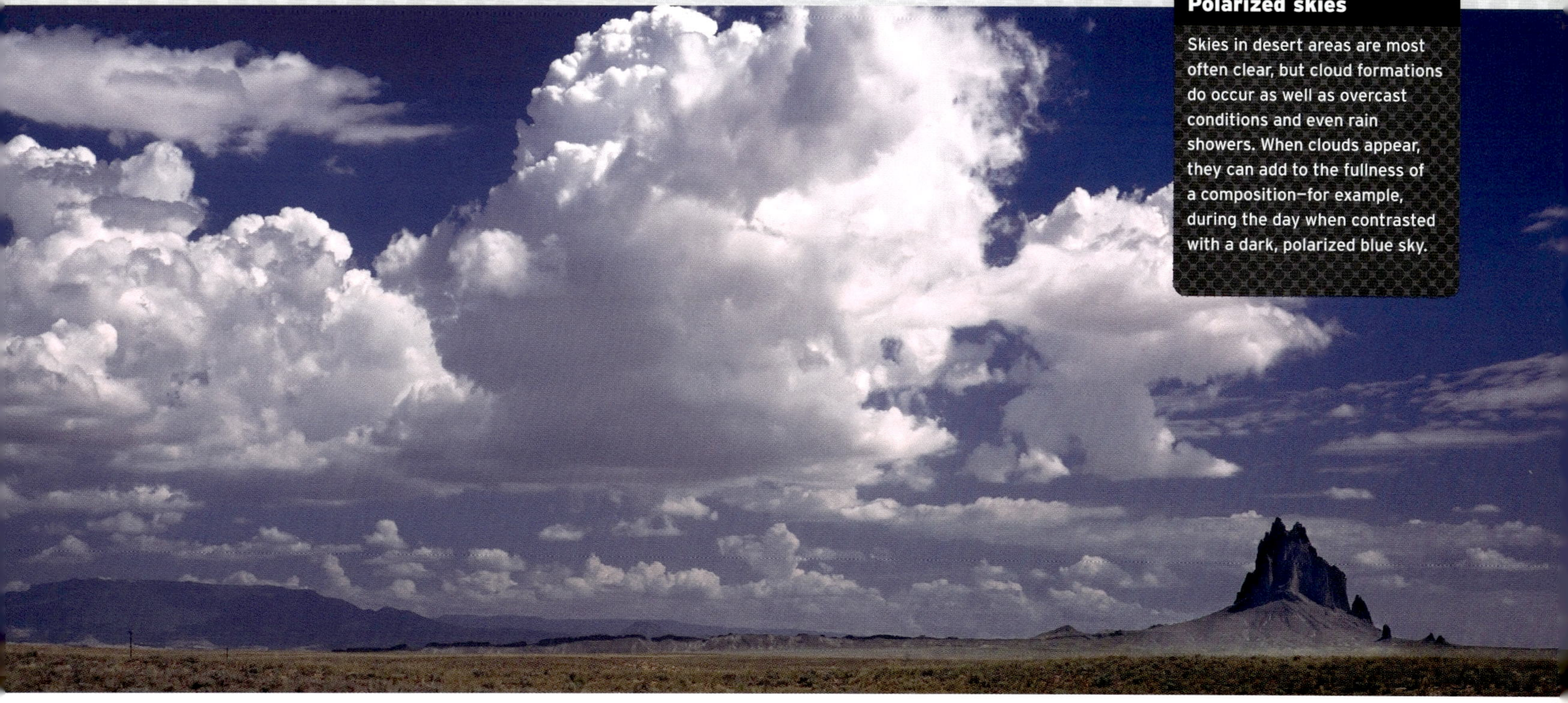

Skies in desert areas are most often clear, but cloud formations do occur as well as overcast conditions and even rain showers. When clouds appear, they can add to the fullness of a composition—for example, during the day when contrasted with a dark, polarized blue sky.

clouds in the sky can pick up and reflect these tones, adding colorful shapes to the sky. Then there is the gentle graduated look to a clear sky at dawn and dusk when cool and warm colors flow into each other like some natural graduated filter.

Desert settings are usually not associated with rain but areas of the American Southwest will occasionally have small patches of passing rain showers. These appear as splashes of white and gray in the sky. Their appearance is caused by the scattering effect on the light by water droplets that help to give the characteristic wispy appearance. Sometimes, these areas will pick up a warm coloration from a setting or rising sun.

In summary, the landscape of the American Southwest is rich with visual elements when organized in different ways using various lenses. Furthermore, complementary and revealing light at certain times will capture the mood and drama of this unusual topography. There is certainly plenty of opportunity for the photographer willing to get up and out early. Many desert photographers will then spend the rest of the day scouting locations, cleaning equipment, catching a nap, and then getting into position for the day's sunset pictures.

You will need:

> Plenty of water to stay hydrated
> Circular polarizers and ND filters, with step-up or step-down rings
> A bag in which to change your lenses to avoid getting dust on the sensor and lens elements

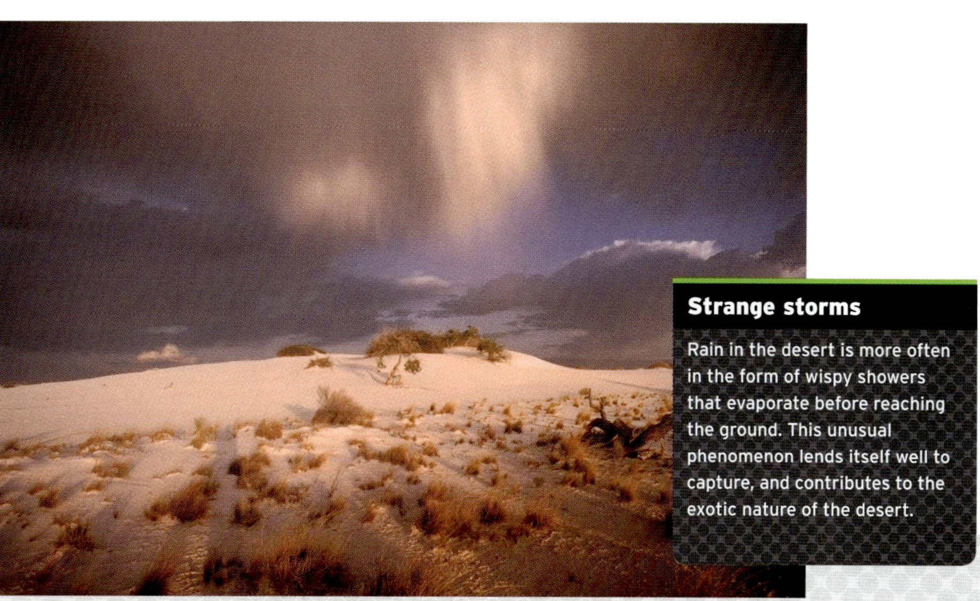

Strange storms

Rain in the desert is more often in the form of wispy showers that evaporate before reaching the ground. This unusual phenomenon lends itself well to capture, and contributes to the exotic nature of the desert.

The Earth in the Stars

Photographing star trails offers the opportunity to produce some truly eye-catching celestial images. Using very long exposures on clear nights, away from sources of light pollution, photographers can catch the amazing arcs and circles of countless stars as the earth revolves around its axis.

These stunning images are a result of exposure times that last hours rather than minutes, and which are recording the earth's daily rotation around its axis (rather than the movement of the stars), giving the impression that we are hurtling a dizzying speed through space. If one is lucky, such long exposure times can also capture other solar bodies, such as shooting stars and gaseous structures, that are unseen, or unnoticed, by the human eye.

There are a number of options when shooting the stars: static shots of the night sky, star arcs and streaks, or circular star trails—each as mesmerizing as the next. While static shots can be captured in a matter of minutes, it is the arcs, streaks, and circular star trails that we are concerned with here. These can only be captured using extended exposure times (star movement starts to be recorded at around 15 seconds). So a sturdy tripod and remote shutter release are therefore vital.

First, however, it is essential to choose the right location, and the ideal atmospheric conditions. A clear, bright, haze-free night sky is the only option for capturing dazzling star trail images. Ensure that the night sky is clear and forecast to remain so for many hours. At the same time, the location should be as far away as possible from all sources of light pollution, such as streetlights, house lights, and even air traffic.

Despite using such long exposure times, the light emitted by distant stars is still very dim, so any other present light source will have a significant negative impact on the star trails recorded. The moon, in particular, is such a strong light source that it can significantly decrease the number of stars in the image—choose to shoot when the moon is in a new phase, keep it out of frame, and ensure that it will not move into frame during the lengthy exposures required.

Stellar Composition

After deciding on location, next choose the composition. When choosing a composition, foreground subject interest is often the best option for star trail photography, as foreground subjects, such as trees, rocks and buildings, can provide some perspective to the size and majesty of the star trails recorded in the background.

Choice of lens is not critical when it comes to shooting star trails. Anything from fisheye to telephoto is fine, but bear in mind that a longer focal length will exacerbate the movement of the stars. Conversely, a standard or medium focal length, in the region of 35-80mm, is probably the best option for star trails, as zooming does not tend to have the same impact as sweeping, wide-angle shots.

Incorporating foreground interest also requires careful balancing of exposure between the long times needed to capture the dim stars and the relatively bright light near to the camera. If the location is truly free of light pollution, then this should be simple. But more often, avoiding light pollution completely is difficult. But if dynamic range is too wide between say, a building in the foreground and

the dim stars in the sky, it is wiser to move the camera and tripod away to a darker area than to spend a long time trying to balance the two.

As already mentioned, there are two options for the star trail photographer when it comes to desired effect: arcs and streaks; or circular star trails. This is quite simply a matter of where in the night sky the photographer points the camera. The earth revolves around a north-south axis, so by locating the North Star, or Polaris, and pointing the camera directly at it, the photographer can capture circular star trails—as the earth's north axis points directly at the North Star, making the stars appear to circle it.

Conversely, pointing the camera toward a portion of the night sky that does not include the North Star will result in arcs or streaks of star trails blazing across the sky. The creative choice is down to the photographer, but the exposure techniques are the same for both.

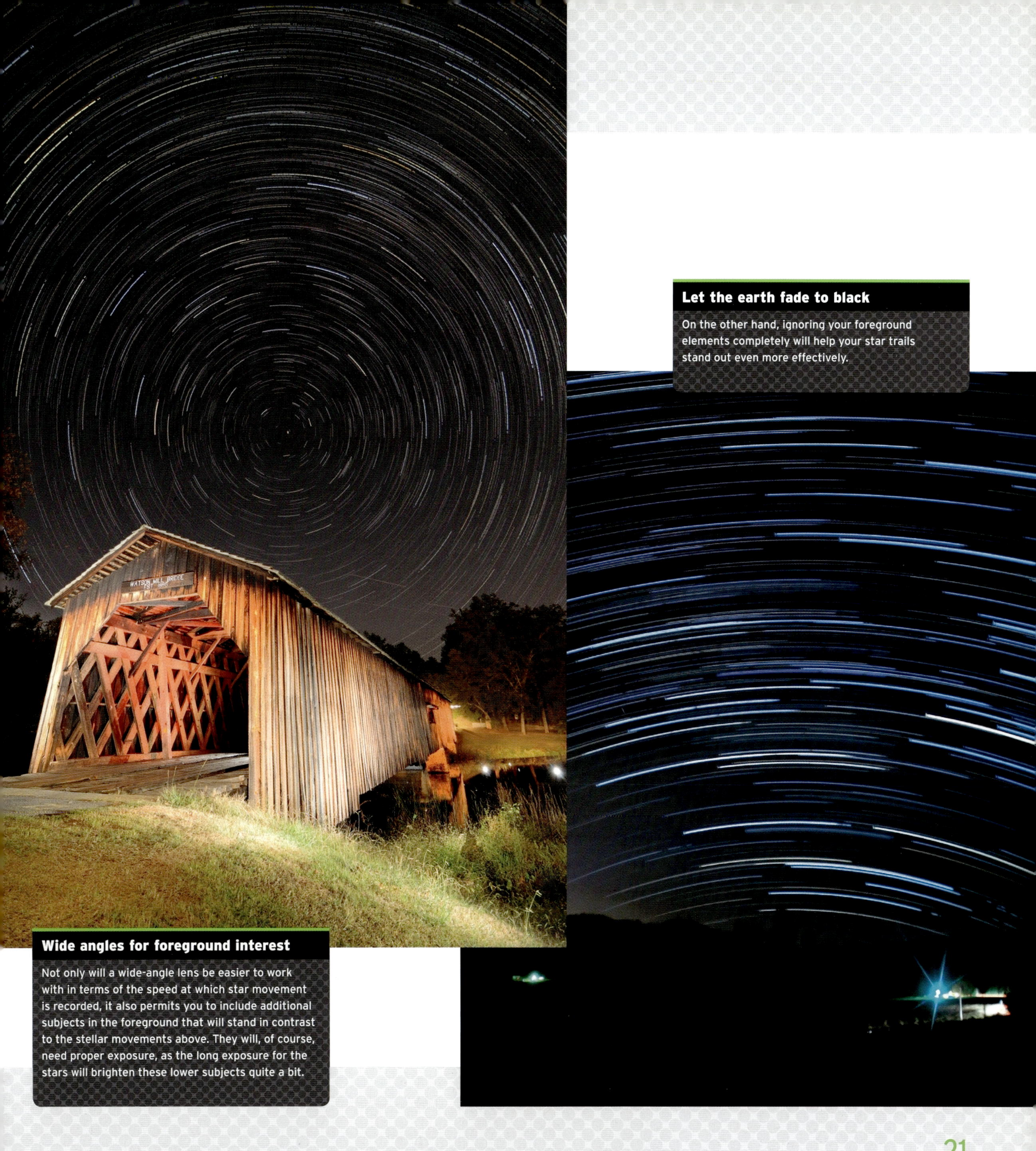

Let the earth fade to black

On the other hand, ignoring your foreground elements completely will help your star trails stand out even more effectively.

Wide angles for foreground interest

Not only will a wide-angle lens be easier to work with in terms of the speed at which star movement is recorded, it also permits you to include additional subjects in the foreground that will stand in contrast to the stellar movements above. They will, of course, need proper exposure, as the long exposure for the stars will brighten these lower subjects quite a bit.

However, there is one further choice to make when it comes to exposing for star trails, and that is between single exposure or stacking multiple exposures. The single option comprises one long exposure of an hour or more, while the stacking option requires a sequence of shorter exposures (each at 30 seconds) to be merged in post-processing to create the same effect. As discussed later, there are pros and cons for each technique.

If taking a single exposure, shutter times are likely to be in the region of one hour, or more. As most cameras have a maximum shutter time of 30 seconds, this means that Manual settings will be required, with the camera set to Bulb mode. This way, the photographer has complete control over exposure times—simply holding or locking the remote shutter release will open the shutter until the photographer decides it is time to close it again. The longer the exposure, the better the star trails.

In terms of execution, first set the focus to Infinity (or, even better, at the published hyperfocal distance for the focal length and sensor size being used), bearing in mind that tweaking may be required to ensure that foreground interest is also in focus. Exacerbating the challenge is the fact that the light coming from the stars is so dim that a wider aperture (smaller f-stop) is also necessary, reducing depth of field in turn.

Exposure-wise, a good base point is to use a low ISO of 100 or 200 in order to minimize noise, and a relatively wide aperture of f/5.6 in order to capture enough light from the dim stars, while balancing that with reasonable depth of field. Then take some test shots. Given that exposure times will be long, see Tips for Test Shots on the opposite page for an important tip on how to take test shots in a fraction of the time.

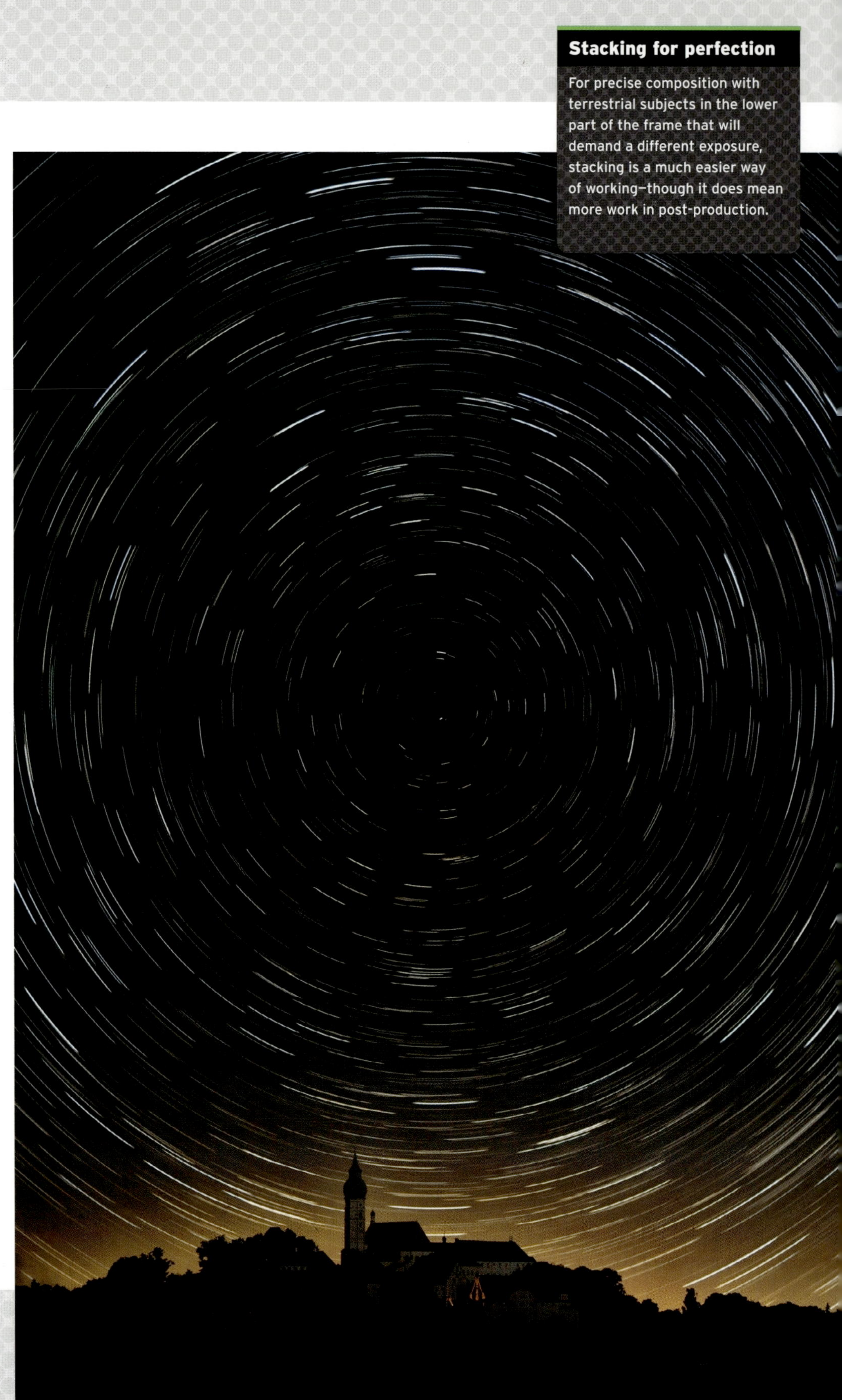

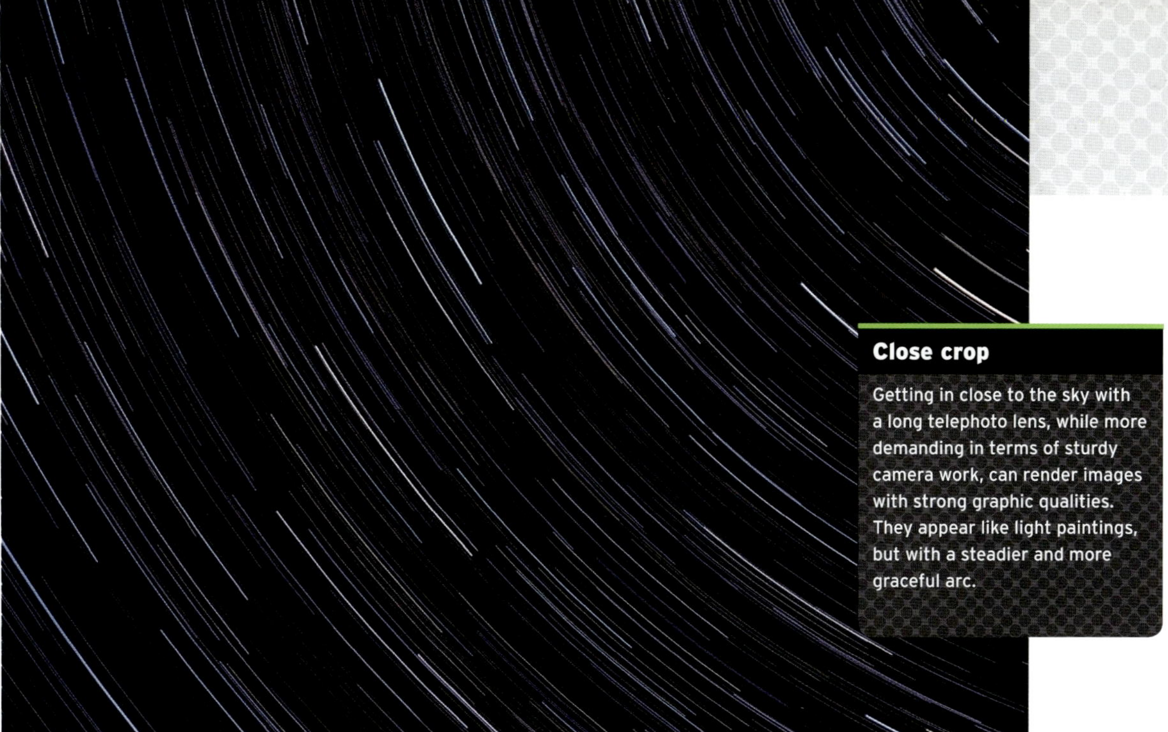

Close crop

Getting in close to the sky with
a long telephoto lens, while more
demanding in terms of sturdy
camera work, can render images
with strong graphic qualities.
They appear like light paintings,
but with a steadier and more
graceful arc.

Exposures will probably need to be tweaked from the starting point provided, but don't be afraid to go for a lower or higher exposure than the ideal calculated by the camera's metering system in order to achieve the desired effect. Set the correct exposure, fire the shutter, and settle back for the results.

The second way to expose for star trails is to use a series of shorter exposures—around 30 seconds—and then merge or "stack" the resulting images in post-production, creating what is effectively a time-lapse single image. Calculating exposure is the same as for single exposures, but is made easier by the much shorter exposure times involved.

The advantages of the stacking method are reduced noise levels in the final image (as exposure times are much shorter), and more eye-catching star trails (in some opinions, anyway). In addition, some cameras do not have a Bulb mode (the ability to expose for more than 30 seconds) so this method provides a simple workaround.

The downsides of the stacking method are increased time in post-production (although many free software packages are available to aid processing), and the requirement for a camera that can be programmed to take numerous shots at predefined times over a specific time period (through the use of an intervalometer). However, if your camera lacks an intervalometer, and you don't particularly want to stand by your camera clicking the shutter every 30 seconds for over an hour, there is a workaround: Set the shutter speed to 30 seconds, set the camera's shooting mode to Continuous, and then lock the remote shutter release with tape or a rubber band. Separate, accessory intervalometers do exist for certain camera models, though this adds to the cost of already expensive equipment. Trial and error, personal preference, or the limitations of available equipment should guide the choice between single exposure and stacking.

Some final considerations. Ensure that the camera has enough battery power and memory card storage (when using the stacking method) for such long exposures; keep warm and bring food and drink; carry a torchlight; and bring some form of entertainment for passing the time, or just lie back and marvel at the awesome beauty of the cosmos.

The Earth in the Moon

The moon has held humankind's fascination for centuries. It is the earth's nearest cosmic neighbor and exerts a strong influence on our daily lives, creating the sea's tides and marking the boundary between day and night. As the brightest satellite in the sky, it is no wonder that once dusk settles, the attention of photographers everywhere turns from the setting sun toward the rising moon.

Getting the technical aspects of moon photography right can yield stunning results: a close-up of the moon, revealing the minutest details of the ridges and craters that scar the moon's face; or a wide-angle shot of the moon in the sky as its earthly reflection sparkles across the surface of the sea or a mountain lake.

To our eyes at least, it should be a relatively simple task to capture stunning shots of the bright orb in the dark night sky. However, photographing the moon creates a number of challenges for a camera sensor. Few, if any, of today's cameras are able to cope with the wide dynamic range (the difference between the brightest and darkest areas of a scene)

created by the moon's relative brightness compared to the dark night sky. Careful exposure and manual camera settings are therefore the order of the day (or night).

At the same time, many photographers use a lens with too short a focal length, leaving the moon as an irrelevant dot in the wide night sky. As a result, moon photography can lead to disappointing results for the uninitiated; but by following a few simple rules, photographers can propel their images of the moon to another level.

Like any form of landscape photography, the first rule of good moon photography is to match the prevailing weather conditions to the

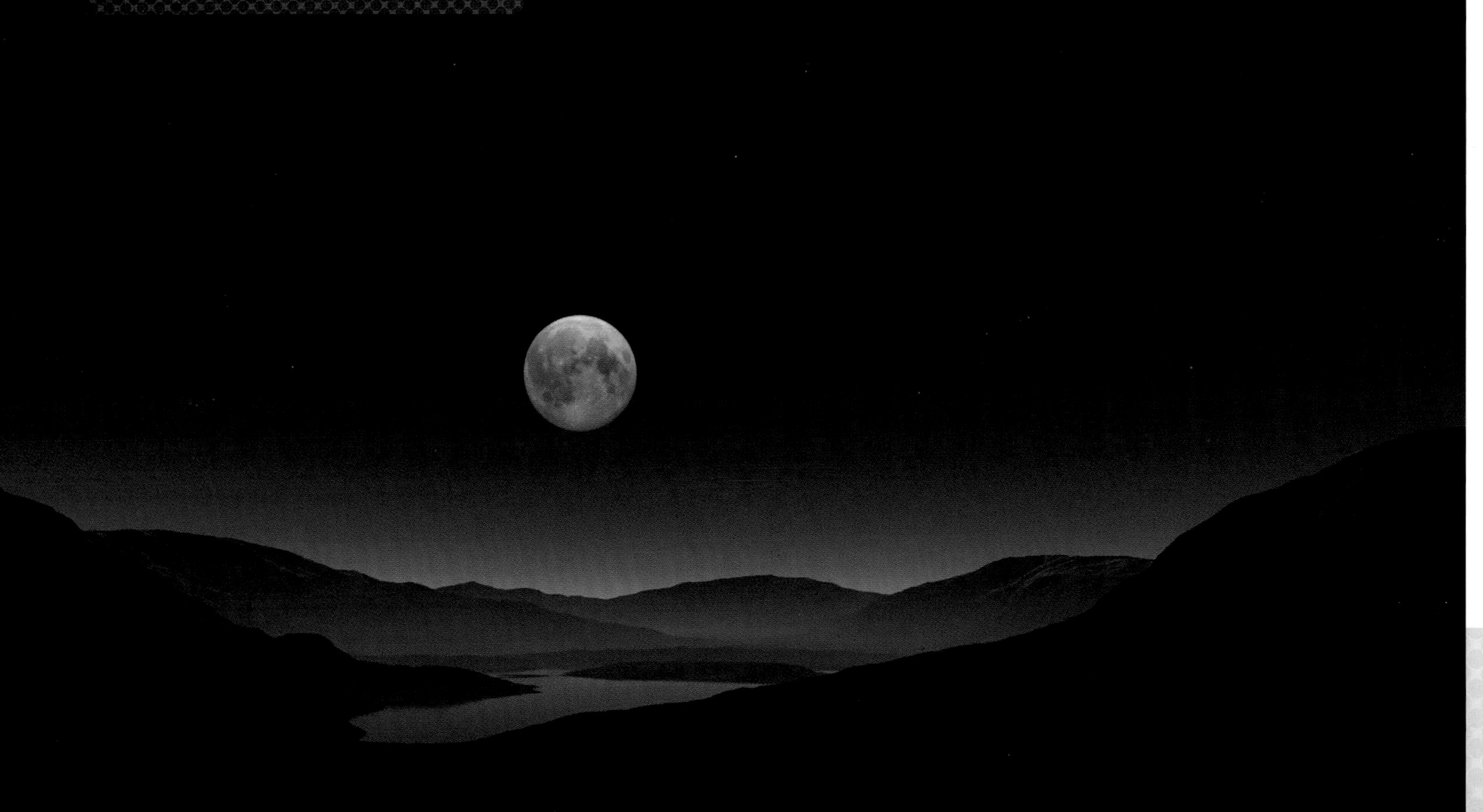

atmosphere of the previsualized image. Clear, cloudless skies are the obvious choice for close up shots. However, we have all seen nights where the Moon briefly breaks through dark brooding clouds, giving a more dramatic effect.

After choosing the desired composition—which may be a close-up of the moon, or a wider shot of the moon in its earthbound environs—set camera focus to Manual and focus by sight (the moon may be too dim for the camera's autofocus to lock on correctly), or focus at Infinity, tweaking if necessary. Some of today's cameras offer Live View, which when magnified can significantly aid accurate focusing.

One of the main challenges of photographing the moon is its relative distance from the camera (and the earth), meaning that all but the most powerful zoom lens will result in the moon appearing as a tiny white blob in a dark sky. For those wanting a close-up of the moon, a zoom or telephoto lens of at least 200mm focal length will be required to reveal the intricacies of the moon's surface. An alternative is to use a 2x tele-converter or extender on a medium telephoto lens, offering a much cheaper option to buying or hiring a high-quality telephoto lens.

The second main challenge of moon photography is getting the exposure right. As mentioned, the moon is very bright compared to its surroundings (i.e. the dark sky). This means that leaving the camera's exposure metering setting on anything other than

Manual will result in an overexposed moon—which will appear as a blown-out disc in the dark sky. The camera's autoexposure settings will average the exposure over the entire scene (which will be mainly dark sky and foreground), resulting in overexposure of the moon—much like a bright lightbulb in a darkened, or dim, room. Spot metering will not resolve the issue, as even a 200mm telephoto lens is unlikely to provide the sort of magnification required for the spot metering to isolate the moon's exposure from the surrounding sky.

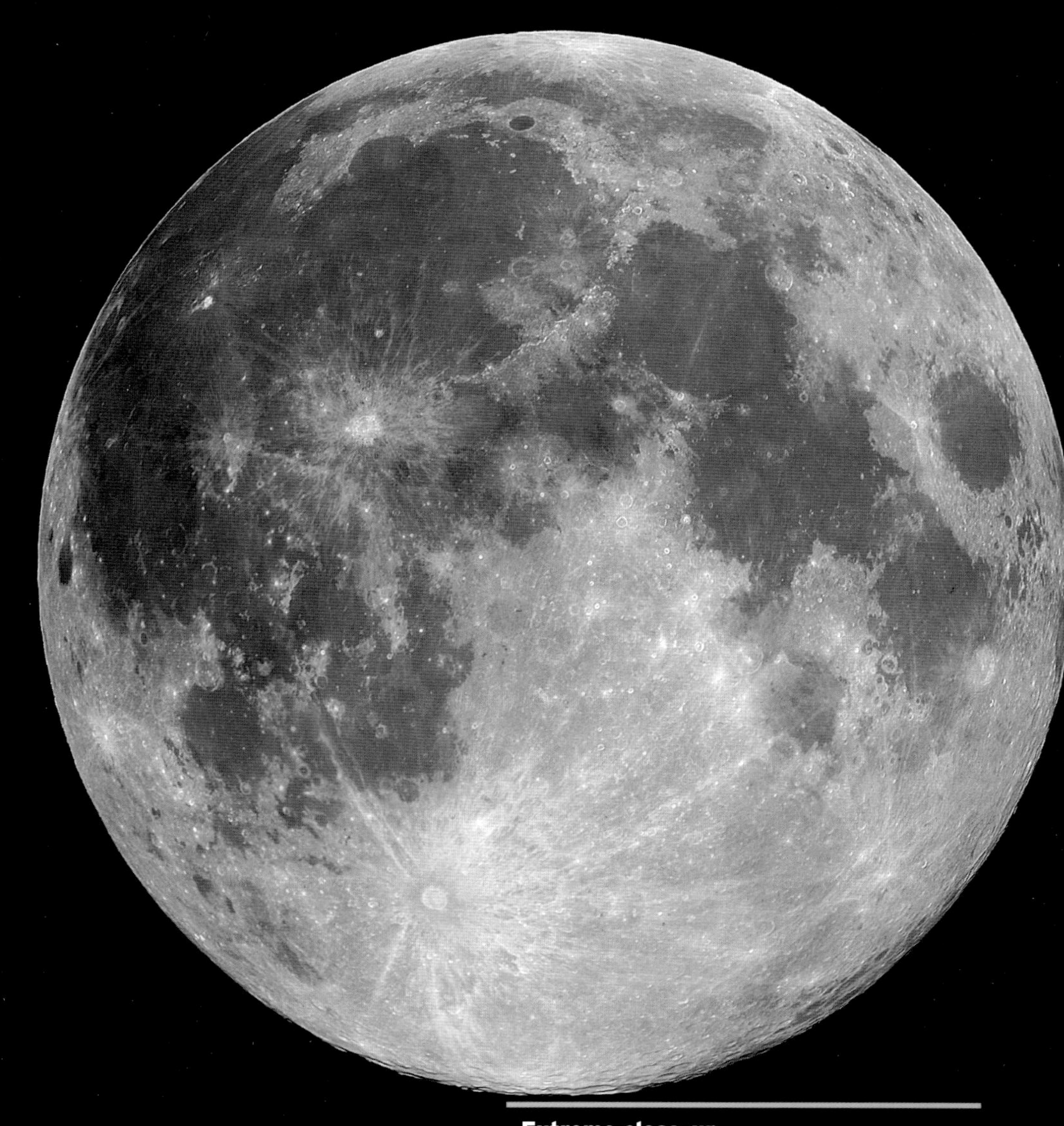

Extreme close-up

Unless you have an extremely high-resolution camera (allowing you to crop in very close), the only way to reach this level of detail on the moon is to attach your camera to a dedicated telescope. A wide variety of accessories exist toward this end, and the Live View feature (if your camera has it) makes focus and composition quite easy.

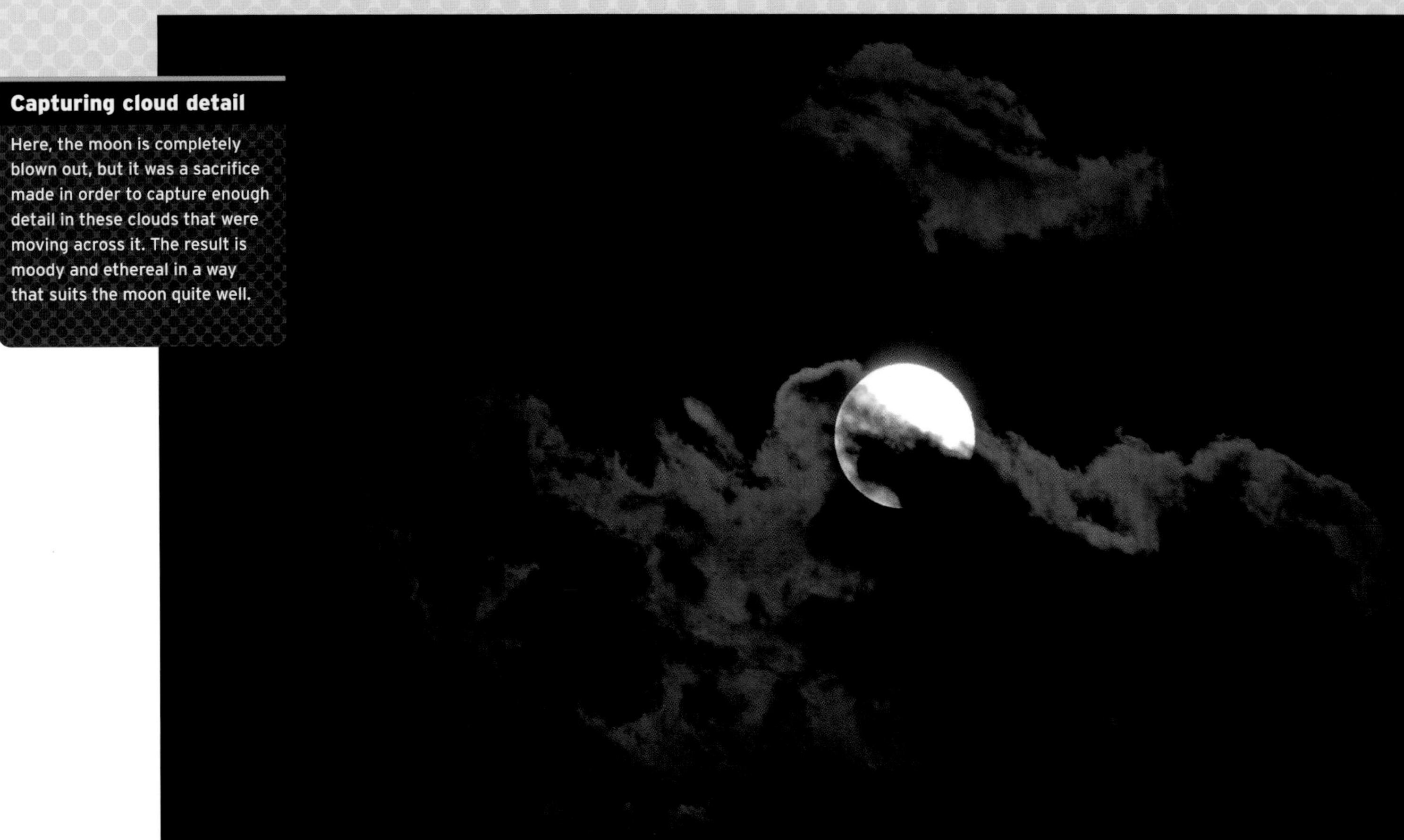

So how to expose for the moon? Start with a low ISO of 100 in order to minimize image noise (more of that later), and a medium exposure—as a rule of thumb, say, f/8 at 1/125 second. Don't forget that the larger the aperture number, the less sharp is the image due to chromatic aberration, so a medium setting (around f/8-f/11) is a good starting point. Take some initial test shots and, using the histogram on the back of the camera's LCD screen, tweak the exposure to get a well-exposed image of the moon. Highlight details should not be blown out as these may not be retrievable in post-processing—which is why shooting in Raw format is always recommended over JPEG shooting. But if one is shooting in JPEG it is even more important to retain highlight details.

For close-ups, it might even be more prudent to slightly underexpose—not too much though. This will leave room for altering Curves in post-production in order to bring out the contrast and details of the moon's surface contours.

Also bear in mind that the moon slowly moves across the night sky, and this can show up as movement blur at shutter speeds slower than about 1/8 second. Of course, a full moon will be brighter than a moon in a different phase, so one setting does not fit all purposes. Again, start at a base exposure and tweak according to the histogram.

This exposure balancing act certainly applies to close-ups of the moon. However, wider shots—where, for example, the photographer wants to include foreground interest such as rocks, trees, waves or buildings—require a slightly different approach. Again, start with a medium base exposure and dial exposure up and down, according to the histogram and taking care not to blow the highlight details.

However, in many cases, it may be that the dynamic range is just too wide—for example, the moon is well exposed but the foreground interest or clouds are just areas of dark blocks, or the foreground is well exposed, but the moon is blown out.

In this case, ND filters may be of limited use as they will add further noise to the image, due to longer exposure times. It might therefore be that two different images, and exposures, are required (one for the moon and one for the foreground), which should then be merged in post-production. The use of a tripod and remote shutter release should minimize the risk of moving the camera position between each shot, ensuring a final sharp merged image. Also, bear in mind that naturally, the foreground would appear darker than the moon to the human eye (after all, it is nighttime!), so don't overdo the foreground exposure.

Foreground subjects can add interest to shots of the moon—look for the reflection of the moon on the surface of water, such as the sea, a lake and so on, or for eerie shadows cast by bare winter trees.

Another challenge peculiar to night photography and/or long exposures is that

of noise. The longer the sensor is exposed, the more likely the impact of noise and hot pixels appearing, as the sensor works overtime to gather enough light for the exposure. Many modern cameras come with built-in noise-reduction settings. But be aware that turning on noise reduction usually requires double the time for each shot—time for the shot itself, plus the same again for camera noise-reduction processing. So if you're looking to capture foreground movement, for example, bear this in mind.

Also consider that moon photography does not necessarily need to be performed in darkness. The moon can often be seen in late afternoon or early evening, even before the sun has set, and shooting the moon during this transition from day to night can result in fantastic and unusual colors in the sky and clouds, while the reflection from the setting sun can make the moon glow in deep orange and yellow colors. As a bonus, shooting the moon in lighter conditions can overcome some of the challenging exposure issues discussed earlier.

The Moon in Transit

The phase of the moon can also impact the atmosphere of the images, for example, a full moon might be more suited to a close-up shot detailing the ridges and craters of the moon's surface, while a low-crescent moon can be offset by interesting foreground, or earthbound, subjects. The moon can also be front-lit or side-lit depending on its relative position to the sun and the earth: each will, of course, significantly affect the atmosphere of the shot. Many online sources will forecast the rising and setting of the moon, as well as its phases.

Also be aware of a well-known optical illusion that makes the moon look larger when it is closer to the horizon, compared to when it is higher in the sky. While no definite explanation has adequately described why this happens, it does offer great potential for dramatic moon "dawn" shots for the photographer who is willing to thoroughly research this fascinating subject matter.

Finally, most moon photography—particularly close-up shots—can benefit from some simple post-production work, with the main tools being Sharpen and Curves. Altering the Curves tool to boost contrast will enhance the details on the moon's surface, while desaturating color slightly, and adding toning effects to enhance the natural beauty of our nearest neighbor.

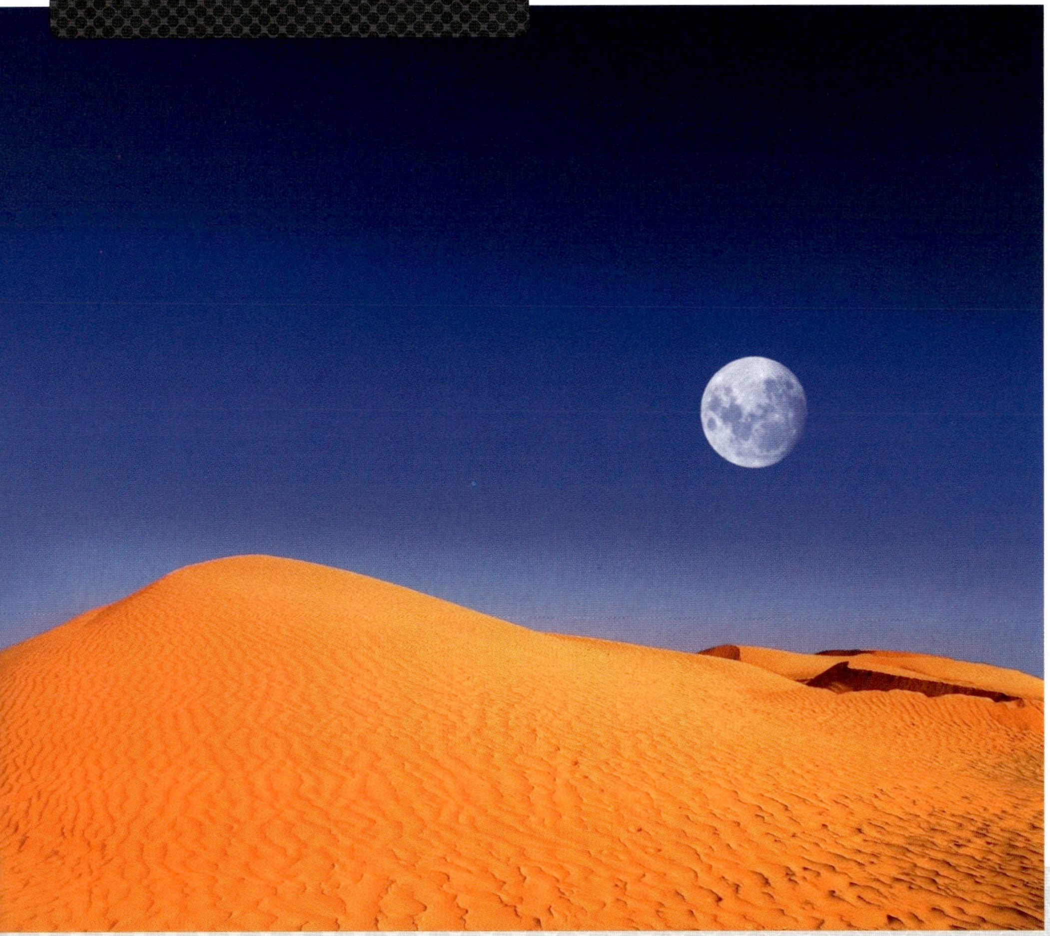

Caves

Cave photography is not for the faint-hearted, and the technical limitations it imposes can challenge the most experienced professional photographer. Those afraid of the dark, or even mildly claustrophobic, need not apply. Then, there are the technical challenges of working in complete darkness, confined spaces, and in wet and dank conditions. So what is the appeal?

Cave photography can transport the viewer into a subterranean universe inhabited by contorted mineral formations, colorful crystal growths, jeweled walls, crevice-like corridors, vast underground chambers, and bottomless, turquoise lakes. Furthermore, the intrepid photographer is likely to have this underground studio all to themselves, resulting in a unique set of images. The effort will be worth it.

Caves are broadly defined as natural, underground cavities or openings in the earth's surface that are wide enough for human entry and which are in some parts completely dark. Rock and water are commonly the two defining ingredients, but there are several different types of caves, including volcanic, glacier, crevice, erosion, and solution—each defined by the manner in which they are formed. In general, they are

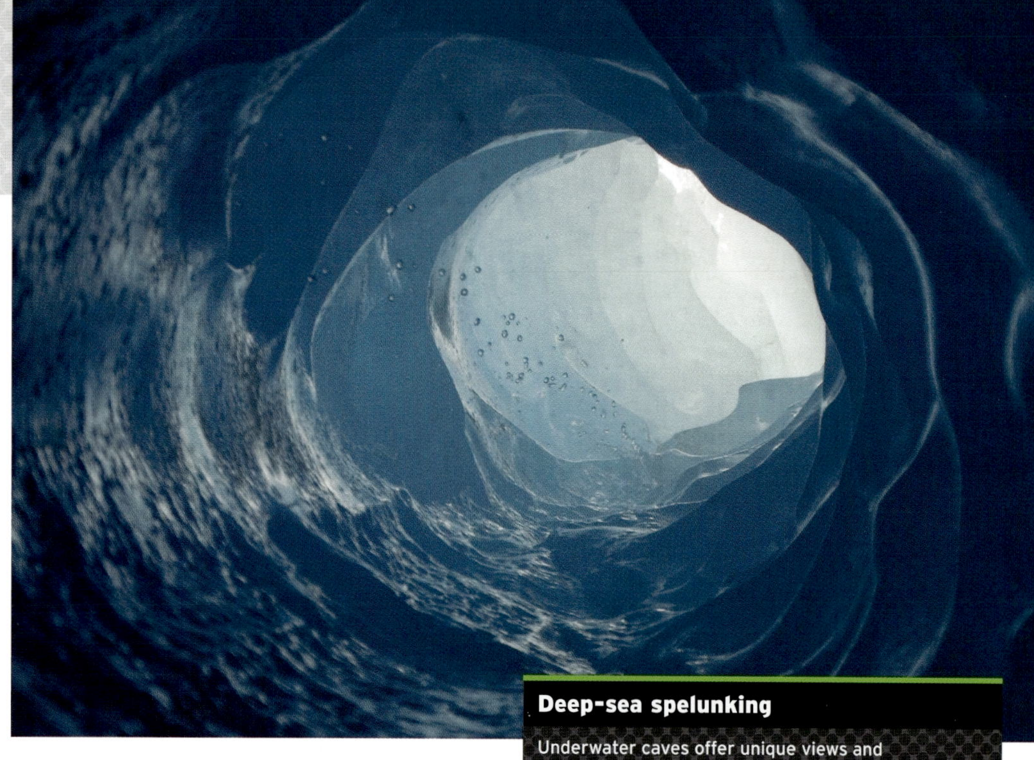

created by geological, mechanical, microbial, or chemical processes taking place over thousands of years.

Limestone caves are the most common, and are formed by the erosion of soft rock by acidic groundwater—these include Lechuguilla Cave in New Mexico and the nearby Carlsbad Cavern. Other cave types include lava tubes such as those found in the Canary Islands and Hawaii, and sea caves, such as The Painted Cave in California and Thailand's Phang Nga Bay.

Needless to say, safety is the upmost concern for cave photographers. Under no circumstances should an inexperienced cave photographer enter a cave on their own, particularly during or after heavy rainfall, and never without telling anyone of their whereabouts (communication devices will not work underground). Commercial caves, open to the public, are fine, but of course are unlikely to appeal quite as much to the adventurer.

When considering any underground trip, it is essential to get prior training in techniques such as pot-holing, abseiling and general

cave safety, and to ensure beforehand that one feels comfortable in such dark and confined spaces, and that panic will not be an issue. Of course, the possibility of getting lost or stuck in cave systems is very high unless the photographer has extensive experience of that system. So almost without exception, joining forces with experienced cavers, cave photographers, or other caving specialists is essential, to not only ensure a more pleasurable and enjoyable experience but also a safe return. Underwater caves present their own unique challenges and should not be entered without specialist training and local knowledge.

Safety aside, one of the main challenges is the damp, cramped conditions that can easily ruin camera equipment, either through moisture damage or impacts with rock and hard surfaces. The narrow confines of cave systems often mean dragging equipment on hands and knees through tiny crevices and

!

Famous Caves

> Longest: Mammoth Cave in Kentucky, USA (390 miles or 628km in length)

> Deepest: Voronya Cave in Abkhazia (7,188 feet or 2,191m in depth)

> Largest: Sarawak Chamber in Malaysia (one room opens up to an area of 2,297 x 1,312 feet or 700 x 400m)

mud-covered floors, leaving it open to both types of damage. A compact, waterproof, and padded shoulder bag or backpack is therefore essential, in order to cushion cameras and lenses from the worst impacts.

The use of watertight plastic bags in which to store equipment during transit is prudent. Another tip is to then place the bagged equipment inside plastic boxes, such as tupperware, to provide extra protection from moisture and impact—there is no need to rush in cave photography, so rapid access to equipment will not be required. A dry towel or lens cloth is another must-have in the bag.

Also bear in mind that equipment needs to be compact in order to squeeze through narrow networks, so pack as lightly as possible. A tripod and several flashlights or other forms of off-camera lighting will be required, so only take what is absolutely necessary—indeed, some public caves do not allow tripods, so check beforehand.

The final matter is what to shoot. Rocks, crystals, shapes, contours, chambers, corridors, people, action shots—the options are quite varied. If shooting people, try placing them in natural, action poses, climbing through narrow crevices or rappelling into vast chambers, as this provides much more dynamic shots. Or pose them in natural frames, such as a passage opening, or underneath a forest of stalactites. People always add perspective and scale to shots, the magnitude of which may be otherwise difficult to ascertain Mineral deposits and unusual formations and shapes also make good underground subject matter, so try experimenting with different lighting setups to make the most of the subject matter.

So what should the cave photographer pack? A DSLR with watertight or weatherproof casing—in fact, some cave photographers prefer to rely on older analogue, mechanical-based cameras, as they find them more reliable and resistant to the underground humidity. Of course, the downside is the expense of using film, and the lack of ability to immediately review shots.

As discussed later in this section, cave photography can involve a lot of exposure bracketing and experimentation, which is much easier with the immediate feedback provided by digital cameras, so there is no reason to not stick with a DSLR. However, if the photographer is unsure of the weather-sealing of their camera, it might be better to use an older DSLR, or a backup body, in order to avoid damaging high-end equipment.

The camera should also have the ability to fire an off-camera flash—many compact cameras, for example, do not have this facility. Caves are completely dark, and both the surface materials and the scale of some caves is said to eat up light. On-camera flash will not be powerful enough to light anything beyond a few feet or so in front of the camera. Taking an external flash unit—or, preferably, numerous flash units—off-camera also gives much more dramatic results in caves, particularly when it comes to modeling rock formations, such as stalactites and stalagmites, as discussed later in this section.

Likewise, the camera should have a Bulb mode for setting unlimited shutter times. Due to the complete absence of ambient light underground, a technique known as "light painting," whereby the camera is set to Bulb and an off-camera flashgun or strobe is used to fill in or "paint" light into the different parts of the image, will help to correctly expose and light larger cave systems and formations, particularly useful when the photographer can only carry limited lighting equipment.

One of the most important lenses in cave photography is the ultra-wide-angle zoom, such as a 10-22mm, 16-35mm or 17-40mm. Space will be at a premium underground, and so having a wide enough field of view to fit the subject, whether it be a crystal or a fellow spelunker, into the frame from a close distance will be essential. There will not be many instances in which a telephoto lens will be required underground, and they often add unwanted and unnecessary bulk and weight to the backpack. Most importantly, the lens (or the camera if not using an interchangeable lens system) should have the ability to allow Manual Focus. Again, due to low ambient light levels, the camera's autofocus system will be almost useless, unable to lock onto subjects in the dark, so manual focusing is an essential requirement.

As might be clear now, lighting is the fundamental requirement in cave photography. Remember that the entire lighting setup is down to the photographer,

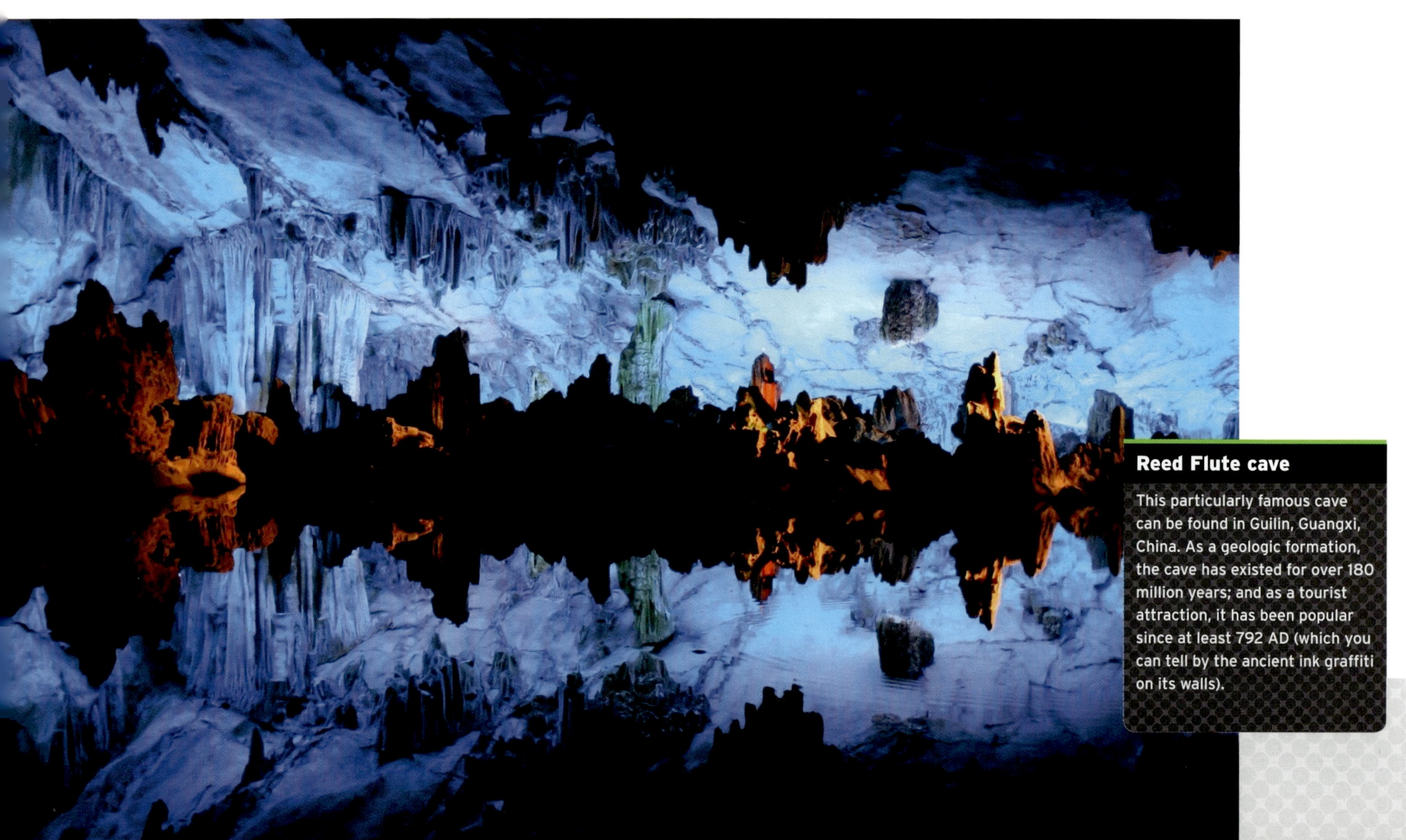

Reed Flute cave

This particularly famous cave can be found in Guilin, Guangxi, China. As a geologic formation, the cave has existed for over 180 million years; and as a tourist attraction, it has been popular since at least 792 AD (which you can tell by the ancient ink graffiti on its walls).

as there will be no ambient light. Off-camera flash will provide depth and dimensionality to the images, by creating shadows and highlights, which enhance the natural contours and textures of the cave walls and rocky formations. A simple, fail-safe setup would be to use two flash units, set up around 45 degrees to the camera on either side. Use one as a key light and the other as a fill light (set 1 or 2 stops lower than the key light).

In addition to a set of strobes, the photographer will need a remote trigger on the camera (either built in or connected to the hotshoe) to tell the strobes when to fire (i.e., on pressing the shutter), as well as a system to fire the remote strobes themselves—the flash receiver will usually be built into the flash unit itself. Otherwise, small, inexpensive slave units can be connected to the bottom of each flash hotshoe to instantaneously fire the flash whenever it senses another flash in the vicinity—however, the slave units will only trigger when they sense another flash, which in this case could be the on-camera pop-up flash.

Approaches to Cave Lighting

When considering how to light cave subjects, experimentation is key. In some cases, the walls of the cave may be reflective and allow for bounce flash, while larger chambers require multiple lights (which might still be inadequate) or the use of the Bulb setting and light-painting technique outlined previously. Traditional lighting techniques, such as one flash used as key light and another as a fill are applicable, particularly when including people in the shot. In this case, ensure that the main subject (e.g. a fellow spelunker) is the most brightly lit part of the image, otherwise attention will be drawn elsewhere in the composition.

Backlighting is another technique favored by cave photographers. Placing a strobe behind the main subject, but out of view of the camera, will make the subject stand out from the dark background, creating highlights around the edges of the subject. Often, mineral formations and growths are translucent in nature, so backlighting can really enhance this effect and showcase the nature of the subject. Take your time and experiment with different lighting setups and different numbers of lights.

Each cave exposure will be unique. As a very broad rule, there are three shutter speeds that the photographer could safely stick to: 1/30 second (used with flash, a tripod and wide apertures this should be enough to strike a balance between achieving a natural-looking exposure and avoiding noise in the image shadows); 1/200 or 1/125 second (i.e. the flash sync speed of the specific system being used, which will also freeze people movement); and Bulb (for techniques such as painting with light).

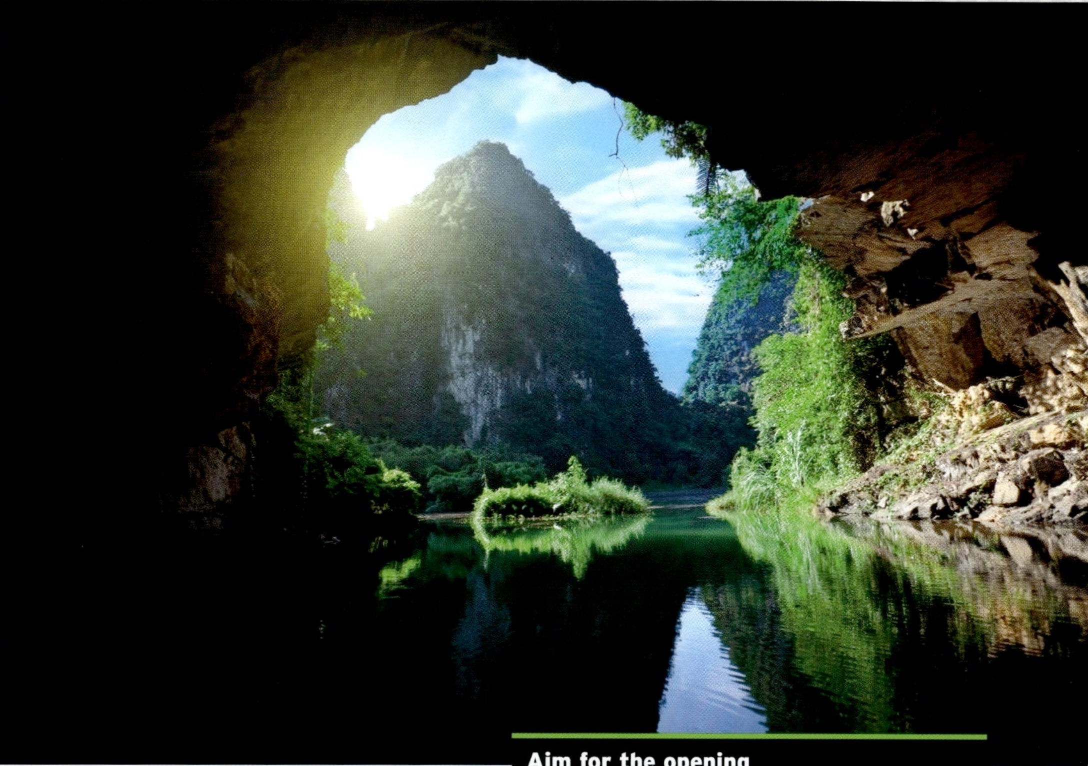

Aim for the opening

The entrance to many caves offers a classic setup for using frames-within-frames—that is, using the arched entrance to frame another subject farther away. Exposure is a challenge here, as the interior is typically much darker than the exterior. External flash on the interior walls may help, or you can bracket your exposures and combine them in post.

Bracketing is another useful technique, as the low ambient light will require experimentation and some lighting setups may cause small areas of blown or specular highlights. Bracket in stops up to two f-stops in either direction, although veering toward overexposure will probably be more useful. For the same reason, shooting in Raw will ensure that slightly off or noisy exposures have the chance of being fixed in post-processing, while pulling back slightly blown highlights. White Balance should be set to Flash, as this is the only light source present (apart from helmet lights), but again this can be changed easily in post-production if shooting in Raw.

Sinkholes

Sinkholes offer a wide range of landscape photography opportunities, and occur all over the world, on low and high ground, on the coast, or out at sea. While sinkholes caused by human activity (literally, where the ground collapses) offer a spectacular and newsworthy angle for photographers, this section will focus on natural sinkholes, which can appear anywhere at any time.

A sinkhole is a natural depression in the Earth's crust created by Karst processes. Karst is the geologic term for landscapes formed by the dissolving of bedrock such as limestone and dolomite. Karst landscapes are characterized by large springs, caves, sunken streams, subterranean caverns, and drainage systems. Sinkholes are also referred to as cenotes, shake holes, swallow holes, dolines, tiankengs (in China), blue holes, and black holes.

Sinkholes are normally associated with underground water sources that gradually dissolve bedrock layers such as limestone and then carry the dissolved sediment away, leaving behind a void.

Sinkholes can appear gradually or suddenly, and vary widely in depth and diameter—typically they are between 1 to 600 meters in diameter and up to hundreds of meters deep. They can be soil-lined bowls or rock-edged chasms, and are often filled with water depending on the level of the surrounding water table. Well-known sinkholes include the Teiq sinkhole in Oman, Ik-Kil Cenote in Mexico, Minyé sinkhole in Papua New Guinea and Cave of Swallows in Mexico.

When sinkholes form at sea—examples of which include Blue Hole in Egypt, Great Blue

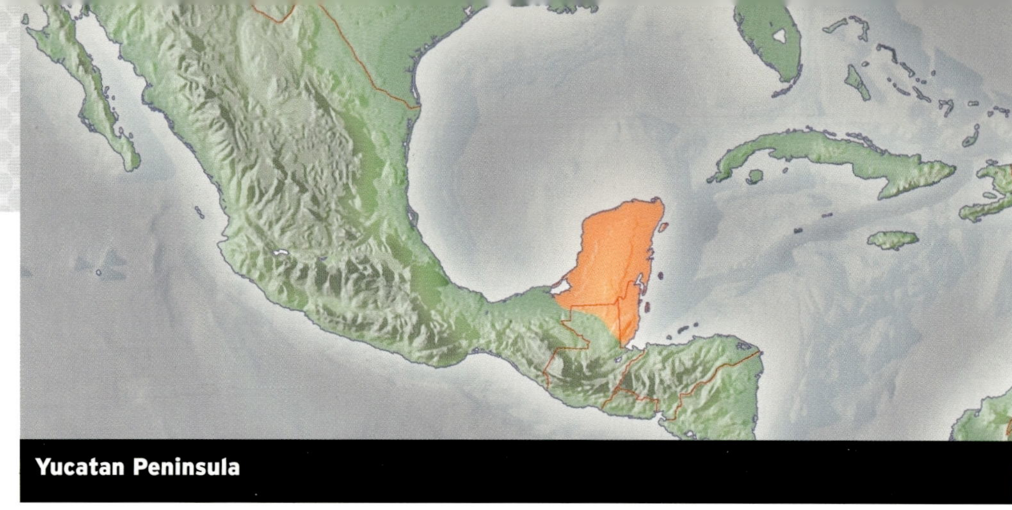

Hole in Belize and Dean's Blue Hole—the result can be spectacular underwater chasms of deep turquoise, most often visible from the air.

Equipment for underwater sinkholes will include diving or scuba gear, an underwater camera or underwater housing for camera equipment, a fisheye port as part of the housing (for minimizing water refraction and distortion when using wide-angle lenses), a macro lens, a strobe (if the housing allows, otherwise a high-powered underwater light of some kind), a high-capacity storage card (as changing cards underwater will not be possible), and a fully charged battery.

Sinkhole Exposures

As sinkholes appear anywhere in the world, the landscape, habitat, geology and appearance of each will differ, so prior research will help the photographer to pre-visualize shots and pack the right equipment. For deep, water-filled sinkholes, such as those found in Mexico, sunrise and sunset is unusually for landscape photography not the best time of day, as the angle of the sun will be too low to penetrate the natural well. Indeed, a bright sunny day, with sunlight piercing the darkness of the hole will provide far more dramatic images.

Expose for the brightest part of the image, and then check the histogram of a test shot on the back of the camera. Alter the exposure so that the brightest part of the image (the sunlit area) is as far to the right of the histogram as possible, without clipping the highlights (the highlights are clipped if any part of the histogram is off the scale, either too far right, or off the top of the histogram).

There should be enough reflected light from the sunlight to ensure that shadow areas are not in total darkness. However, if the dynamic range of the scene is just too much for the camera sensor, try either recomposing the image to include less shadow area, or preferably set up the shot with a tripod and take two exposures—one exposed for the highlights and the other for the shadows—and merge the two in post-production. Technically, this is what high dynamic range (HDR) photography and processing aims to achieve, but this two-exposure method has occurred for decades in film darkrooms going back to Ansel Adams for exactly this purpose, and does not induce the hypereal effect of over-processed HDR and Tonemapping (which one either loves or hates).

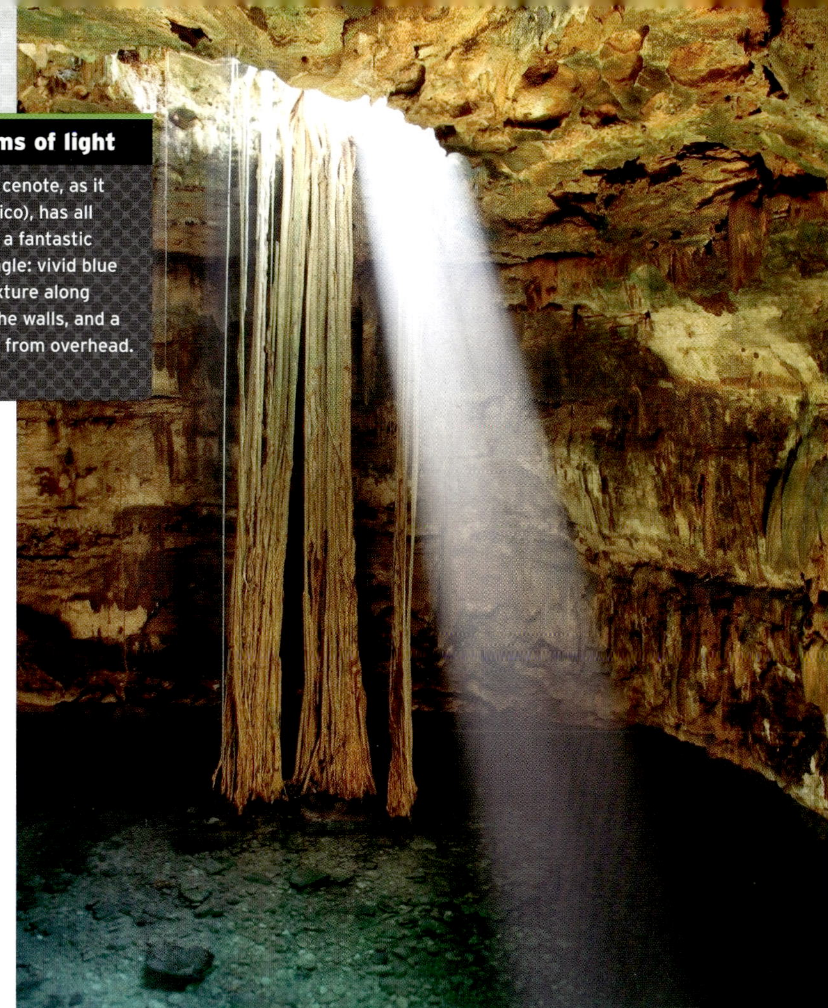

Radiant beams of light

This sinkhole (or cenote, as it is located in Mexico), has all the elements for a fantastic shot from any angle: vivid blue water, tons of texture along the surfaces of the walls, and a perfect spotlight from overhead.

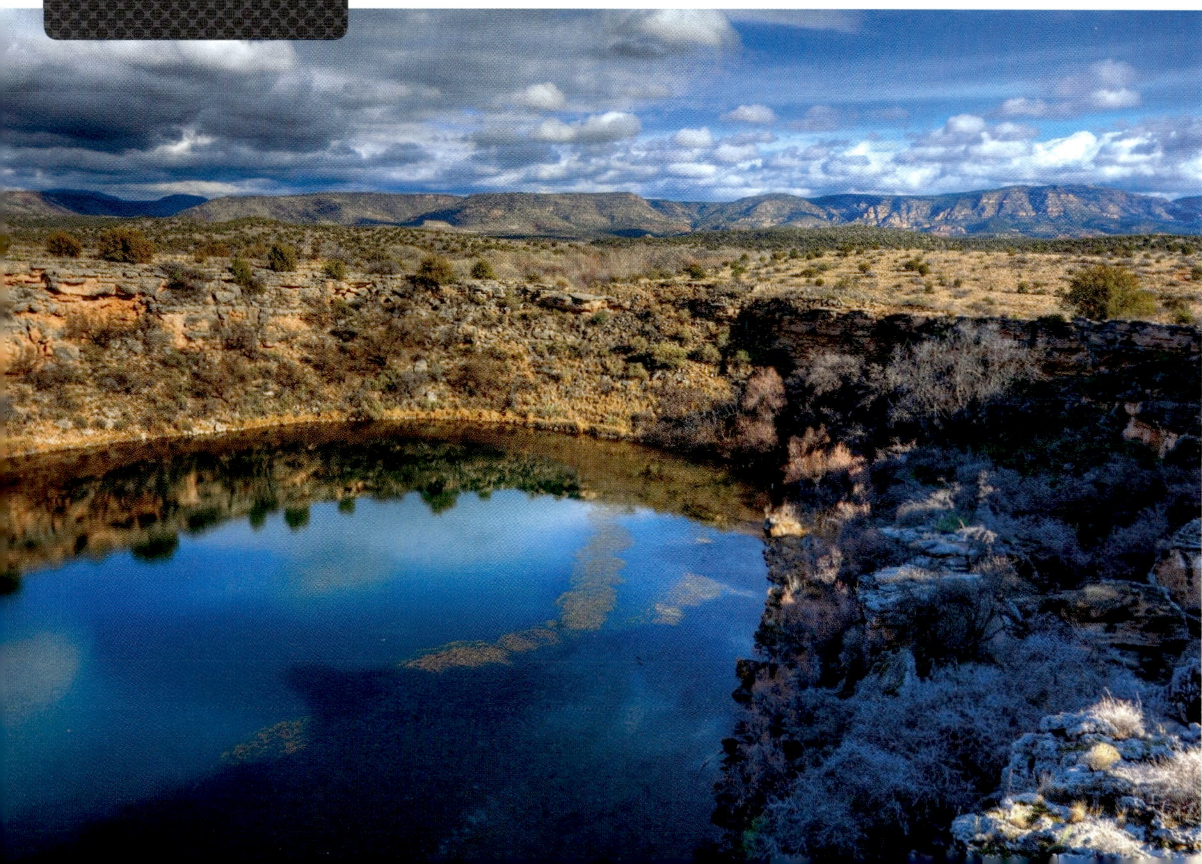

Montezuma Well

This well known limestone sinkhole is located in Arizona, USA, and has been used for irrigation for over a thousand years, as over 1.4 million gallons (5.3 million L) of water flow through it each day.

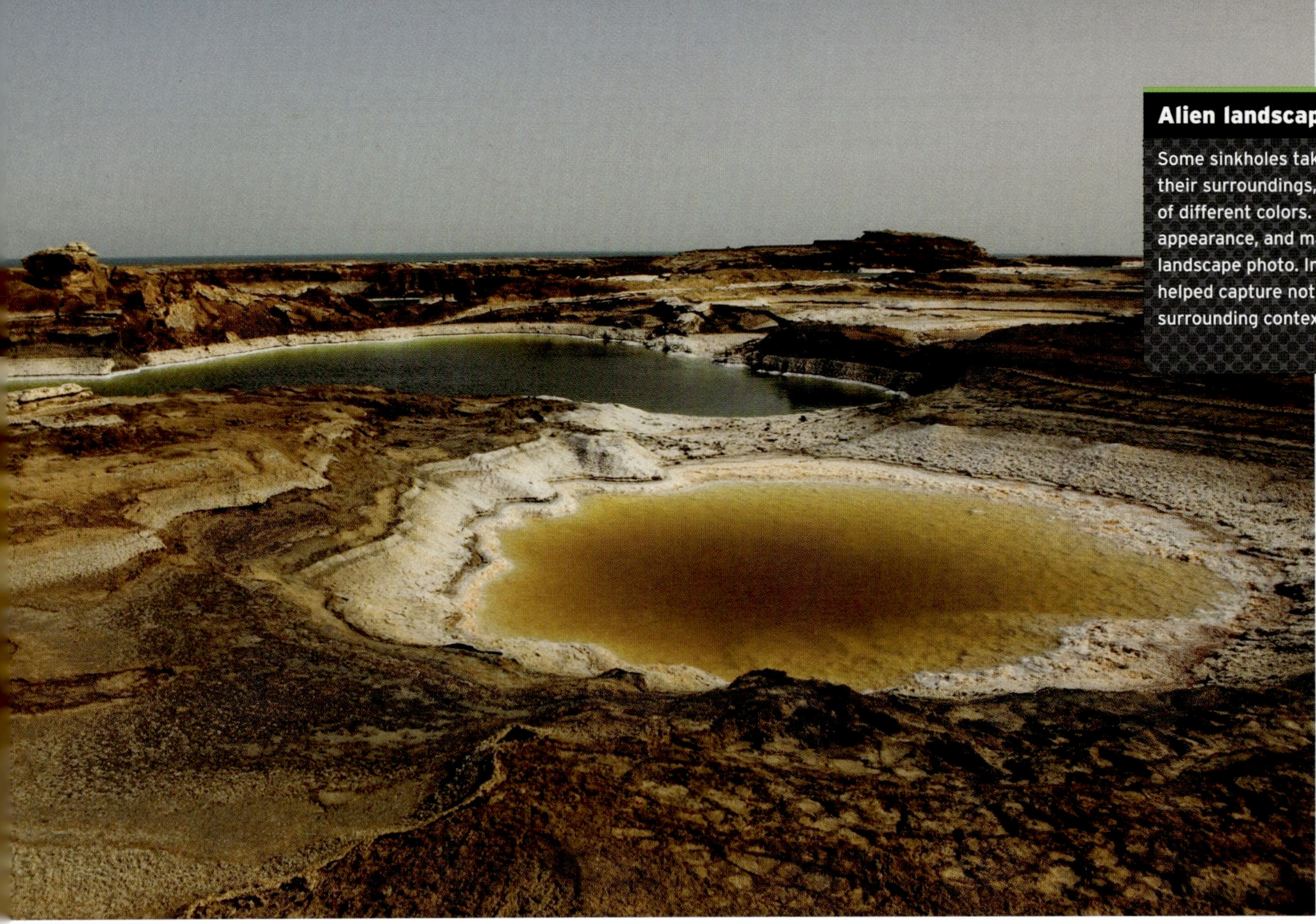

Composing a Sinkhole Shot

In terms of composition, where possible a location within the sinkhole will provide more interesting and balanced images. Images taken from the rim of a sinkhole, looking down, tend to be a little flat, probably due to the front lighting that will effectively come from the sun directly above the camera position. Conversely, taking a shot from the pit of a sinkhole, looking toward the sky, will create dynamic range problems, and possibly flare as the camera will be pointing directly up at a bright sky, or even directly into the sun. A position either halfway down or some way into the sinkhole is therefore preferable, where access is available, and will provide a more natural perspective to the view.

Sinkholes often require the use of a wide or ultra-wide focal length lens in order to encompass the complete circle of the structure. Taking a section of a sinkhole does not have as much impact as a full view. Given the limited space within a sinkhole, an ultra-wide, or possibly fisheye, will be the only lens that can capture the entire structure.

While arriving later or earlier in the day will mean avoiding other visitors to the attraction, having people behaving naturally in the shot—for example, swimming in the turquoise water of a cenote—will add scale and perspective, and can make a more interesting and dynamic image. Where water is involved, the use of a polarizing filter will also cut down on the glare and reflection from the surface, giving the water a deep, rich, and saturated look.

Where water is not a component of the sinkhole, look for interesting rock formations and mineral deposits. In this case, a portable flashlight or strobe may be required in order to add fill light, or provide backlighting, and to reduce contrast between sunlight and deep shadow. Again, using people can add scale and perspective to the overall structure—natural-looking action shots will look better than posed shots. Use natural archways and ceilings to frame the subject. If the cavern is deep and large, dynamic range may be a problem, so the use of a tripod and merged exposures in post-processing can once again help.

Glacial sinkholes bring forth a different proposition again. It is vital to join a trained or experienced guide or team. For example, abseiling into a sinkhole or crevice may be required, so specialist training or guidance is necessary. Pack lightly and appropriately.

The benefit of shooting in a glacial sinkhole is that light from the opening will be reflected and bounced around by the icy walls of the hole, improving exposure levels and reducing contrast. Reflected light from ice is usually blue in hue, so shooting in Raw will allow more flexibility to enhance or reduce this lighting effect in post-processing using the White Balance control, according to personal preference.

One of the most spectacular ways to photograph sinkholes is underwater. Often with vertical or steep sides, and a large mouth that allows sunlight to pour in from above, sinkholes are filled with deep, aquamarine water that is penetrated by rays of light, making underwater photography something special.

As well as requiring the right equipment, underwater photography requires specialist training, so attending a course and gaining appropriate qualifications is necessary before attempting this type of photography. For those experienced and trained, underwater sinkholes provide spectacular opportunities to capture stunning images. Use marine life or fellow divers for scale and place them so they are illuminated by pools of light or underwater rays of sunlight against a dark blue background.

Another option for sinkhole photography is to shoot from the air. Hiring a local plane or helicopter may not be as expensive as expected. The Great Blue Hole in Belize is an obvious example, but sinkholes over land can be just as spectacular. For aerial photography the best times of the day are likely to be when the sun is lower in the sky. Over land in particular, midday aerial photography will result in dull images lacking in contrast and saturation, so aim for the hours after sunrise and before sunset, or as near as possible. Use a polarizing filter to cut down glare and reflections and to increase color saturation, as well as fast shutter speeds to reduce camera shake and vibration.

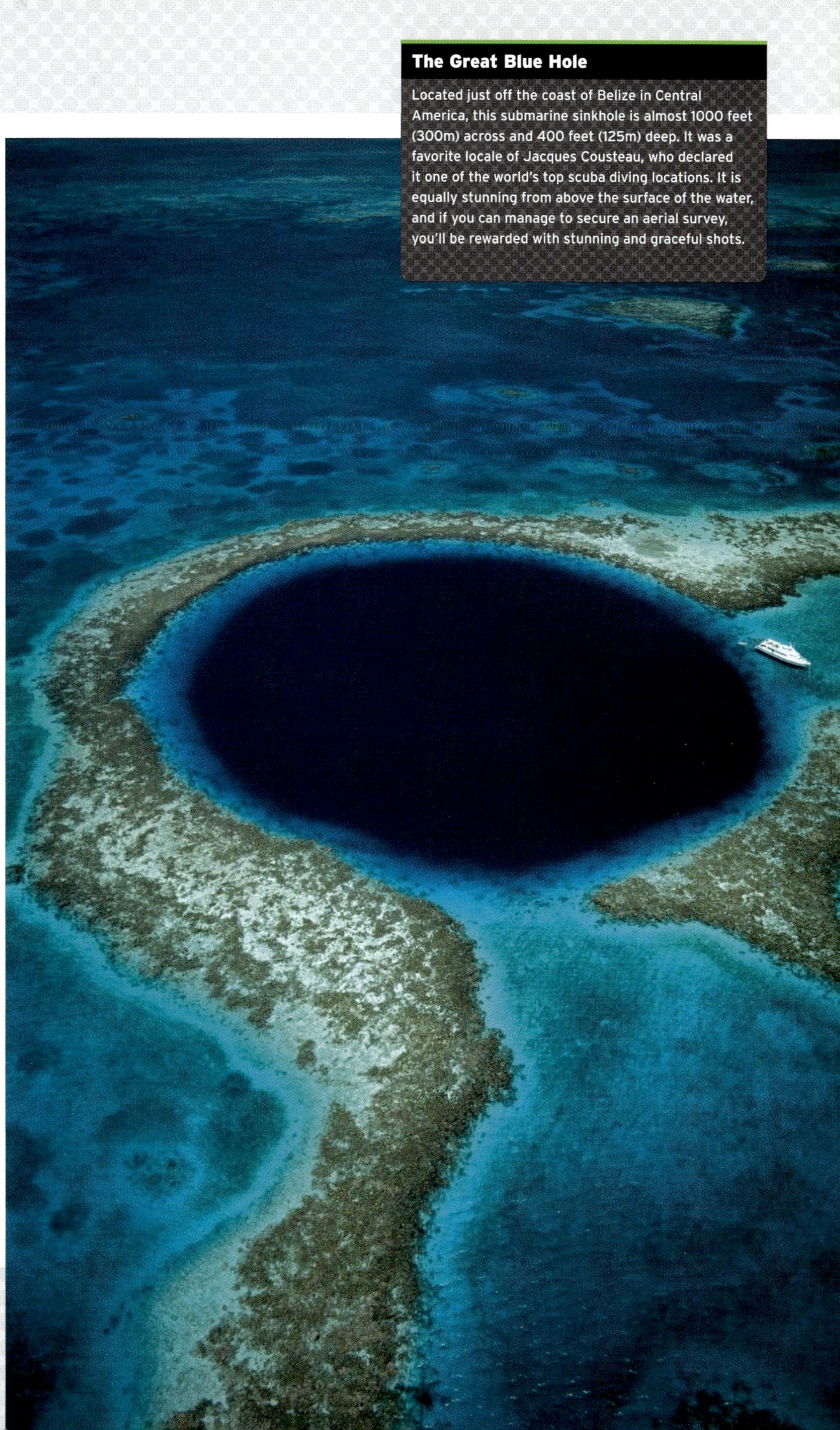

The Great Blue Hole

Located just off the coast of Belize in Central America, this submarine sinkhole is almost 1000 feet (300m) across and 400 feet (125m) deep. It was a favorite locale of Jacques Cousteau, who declared it one of the world's top scuba diving locations. It is equally stunning from above the surface of the water, and if you can manage to secure an aerial survey, you'll be rewarded with stunning and graceful shots.

!

Shooting Tips:

> If you're on the ground, a wide angle is going to be the best way to include a sense of the surrounding environment, which tends to add useful context.

> If at all possible, try getting in the air above a sinkhole, or down below them—either underwater or in a subterranean chamber. These shots are invariably more exciting.

Photographing in Extremely Hot Environments

Many areas of the world experience temperatures high enough to be considered quite uncomfortable, if not dangerous. People who live in high-temperature environments have learned how to deal with such extremes. Visiting photographers need to take precautions for themselves and their equipment. Accordingly, here are a number of equipment dos and don'ts that are worth taking into consideration when working in very hot environments.

(1) Avoid having the camera exposed to direct sunlight during the hottest portions of the day for any length of time, as when mounted on a tripod. Most cameras and lenses are heat-absorbing black. If the equipment gets hot to the touch the absorbed heat may be exceeding the working temperature of the camera. Furthermore, digital sensors tend to generate higher levels of noise as their operating temperature rises (thermal noise). The easiest way to protect the camera is to drape light-colored or reflective materials over it when tripod-mounted in the sun. Even a light-colored spare hat placed on the camera will help. A more elaborate approach is to use an umbrella arrangement such the Omega Portable Protective Umbrella. It is designed to clamp on a tripod and sit above the camera and will also afford some sun protection to the photographer.

(2) Never leave photo gear in a closed car parked in direct sun and especially in the glove compartment or trunk. For example, on a typical 90-degree Fahrenheit (32-degree

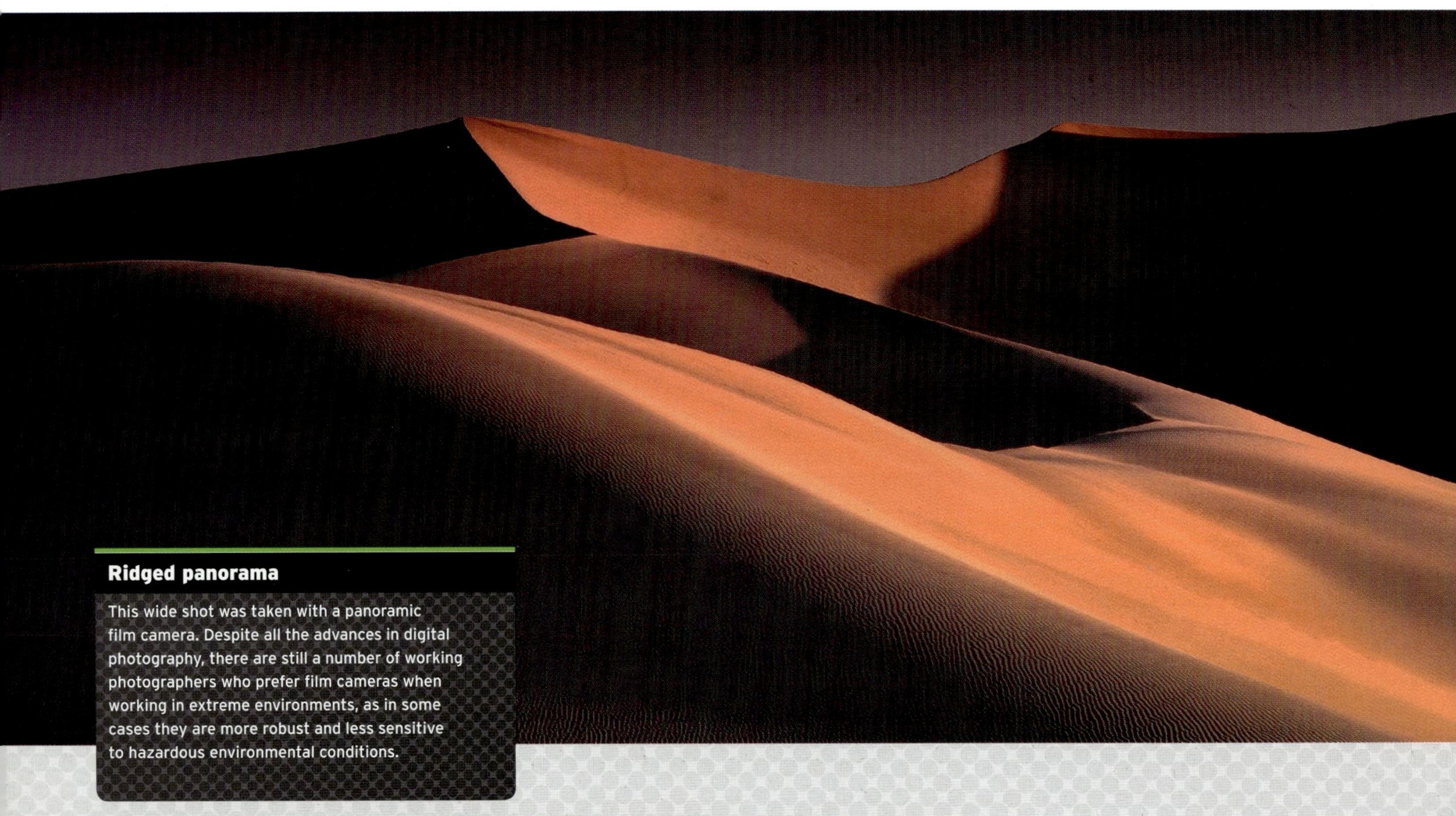

Ridged panorama

This wide shot was taken with a panoramic film camera. Despite all the advances in digital photography, there are still a number of working photographers who prefer film cameras when working in extreme environments, as in some cases they are more robust and less sensitive to hazardous environmental conditions.

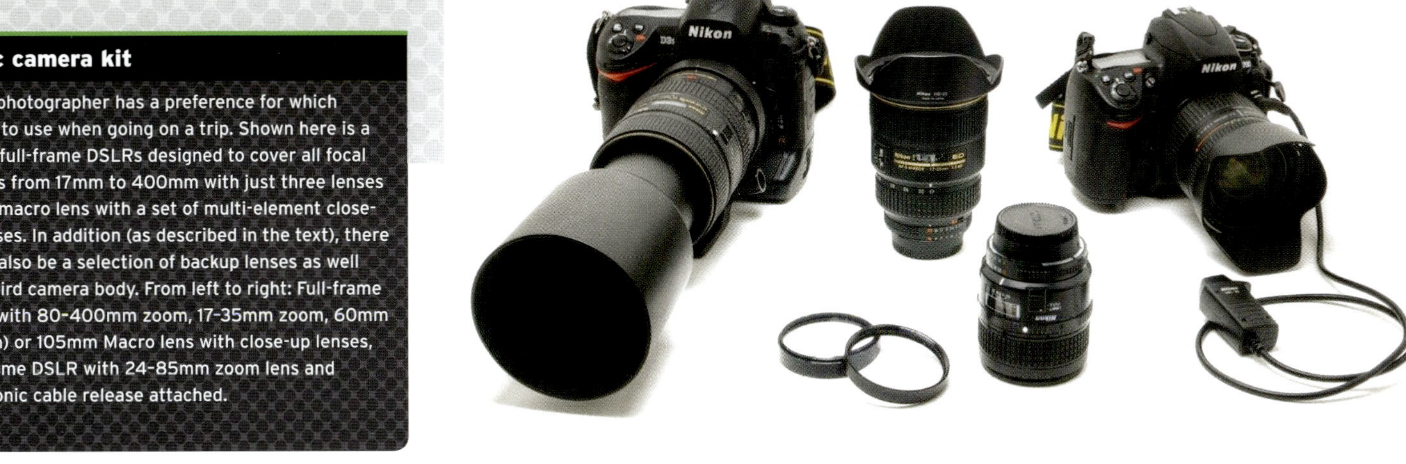

Basic camera kit

Every photographer has a preference for which lenses to use when going on a trip. Shown here is a kit for full-frame DSLRs designed to cover all focal lengths from 17mm to 400mm with just three lenses plus a macro lens with a set of multi-element close-up lenses. In addition (as described in the text), there would also be a selection of backup lenses as well as a third camera body. From left to right: Full-frame DSLR with 80-400mm zoom, 17-35mm zoom, 60mm (shown) or 105mm Macro lens with close-up lenses, full-frame DSLR with 24-85mm zoom lens and electronic cable release attached.

Celsius) day in the desert, interior temperatures can increase 10-20 degrees Fahrenheit in less than ten minutes and can go up 30 degrees or higher in about a half hour. It is also recommended that cameras and lenses never be packed in checked luggage when traveling by plane as cargo hold temperatures can potentially reach 20-40 degrees Fahrenheit below freezing.

(3) Work as quickly as possible when changing camera data cards or lenses in an atmosphere of wind-blown sand. If the atmosphere is very heavy with fine sand, perform these operations in a protected setting such as under the material used for sun protection. See also "Backing Up Images in the Field" on page 140.

(4) A grinding sound when the legs of a tripod are collapsed indicates sand is in the locking collars and leg sections. These parts should be disassembled and cleaned. Metal tripods become very hot to the touch in direct sun (and very cold in frigid weather) whereas carbon fiber models absorb comparatively less heat and are not as cold to the touch. One solution is to wrap the upper legs of a metal tripod with tennis racket handle wrap. There are also commercially available leg coverings from various tripod manufacturers.

Many locations discussed throughout this book have extreme temperature conditions as well as atmospheres of wind-driven sand or snow. Using photographic equipment under such extreme conditions requires that it be cared for in ways different from photographing in moderate climates. In addition, these extreme environments are in remote, even isolated locations. That means serious thought has to be given to selecting appropriate backup cameras and lenses to deal with possible equipment failures. This is one of the most important aspects of planning a trip to a remote area. Accordingly, the following sections cover suggestions for backup equipment.

In addition to dealing with equipment needs, these two chapters consider the unique photographic opportunities offered by places like the American Southwest and regions of the Arctic. In both locales, there is a need to be prepared for very different types of topography. Indeed, there will be daily challenges for how to compose an interesting photograph from the unusual landscapes that will be encountered. Accordingly, both chapters contain suggestions and illustrations for working with the very different visual elements and extraordinary quality of light in these remote locations.

Most of the illustrations in this chapter were taken in the deserts of the American Southwest during the warmest months of the year (June through August) where temperatures many times reached well over 100-degrees Fahrenheit (37+ degrees

Celsius). All the information concerning planning, equipment care and composition can apply equally to photographing in other arid and hot areas of the world.

Planning the Trip

Taking the time to carefully plan any photographic field trip by researching the location and properly selecting and preparing equipment is critical to having a successful experience. This is especially true if the trip to a remote location will be for several weeks. The first step is to look into how the equipment is rated for operating in the extreme conditions that will be encountered at the location. That means becoming familiar with the camera's "working range" for temperature and humidity as well as fit against dirt, moisture, and general robustness. See "How Tough is Your Equipment?" on page 41 for more information.

Another consideration is the length of time the equipment will be subjected to extreme conditions. This is often an overlooked variable when preparing for a trip. The longer the equipment operates in extreme conditions, the greater the risk that problems will occur. Photographers who routinely work under extreme conditions take Murphy's famous law very seriously: "Anything that can go wrong will go wrong." The best preparation is, therefore, to take along carefully selected backup equipment. In addition, a number of key photographic accessories should also be included. Some of these accessories are as basic as a blower brush, lens cleaning cloth and a flashlight.

Selecting Cameras and Lenses for the Trip

Camera failure is the most disastrous equipment event that can happen while off in a remote location. The only option is to bring two or three extra camera bodies and make sure the batteries for these cameras are in good working order. Backup batteries are also a must (See "Backup Battery Options," page 139). Some might choose a sophisticated point-and-shoot camera as backup to a single DSLR. This is up to the photographer, but consider that trips to remote locations can be very expensive investments and, in some cases, a once-in-a-lifetime experience. The raison d'être for going is to get the best pictures possible and that means taking the equipment that most adequately meets the challenges of the trip.

Deciding on which lenses to take on any photographic trip is dependent on many variables, such as the type of subject (e.g., wildlife vs. landscapes), different lighting conditions (e.g., flash vs. natural light vs. low-light subjects) and how much weight can be carried comfortably. Then there are the variables of individual style, the goals of the photographer for the trip and personal resources. Here are recommendations for the contents of a hypothetical camera bag that will cover a complete range of needs within the four main lens categories. That is, from wide-angle to normal and telephoto, as well as close-up photography. (Note: The focal lengths referred to in each category on the following pages are based on using a full-frame DSLR or a 35mm SLR film camera.)

Zoom Lenses

Zoom lenses have become the most popular choice among professional and amateur photographers. Just two or three zooms can cover every focal length between extreme wide-angle to long telephoto. Consequently, as noted below, the main lens for the wide-angle, normal and telephoto categories in our camera bag will be a zoom. While the zoom design is the most versatile, a failure means the photographer loses all the focal lengths covered by that lens. Needless to say, that can be a very critical loss. Consequently, many photographers will routinely carry smaller, single focal length lenses plus a tele-converter as backup to their main zoom lenses along with a set of high-quality multi-element close-up lenses. While these backup lenses are not a complete replacement for the range provided by zooms, they will allow the photographer to continue working within all four of the lens categories. In addition, these backup choices offer some unique advantages of their own.

Telephoto Range

The main uses of telephoto lenses are to get closer to distant subjects and/or to visually reduce the appearance of distances between the foreground and the background (telephoto compression). In the case of very small wildlife such as birds, specialized "super telephotos" in the 500-800mm range are usually required. Most photographers, however, use telephoto focal lengths in the 200-400mm range. Accordingly, a zoom such as an 80-400mm, a 100-400mm or a 200-400mm will cover most telephoto needs quite well. Telephoto zooms will be the largest and heaviest lenses carried on a trip. Unfortunately, single focal length back-up choices such as a 300mm or 400mm lens also tend be large and heavy—even those models with relatively slow maximum apertures. Another option is using a 1.4x or a 1.7x tele-converter, which, on a slow 300mm lens, would produce a 420mm and a 510mm focal length respectively.

Middle Range

Zoom lenses such as a 28-85mm or a 28-105mm are popular choices for covering moderate wide angle, normal and short telephoto focal lengths. This represents a working range that covers everything from landscapes to portraits as well as close-up subjects. As a backup lens, the fast and small 50mm f/1.4 is an excellent choice. In addition to covering the versatile normal focal length, the wide f/1.4 maximum aperture is superb for low-light work. When used with a 1.7x tele-converter the 50mm becomes an 85mm lens for portrait applications. The 50mm focal length can also provide a moderate wide-angle look when the subject-to-camera distance is increased. One simply needs to backup to take in more of the scene. Finally, normal lenses generally focus quite close and even closer when used with a tele-converter. They can even approach life-size macro magnification when high-quality close-up lenses are attached. In sum, the 50mm focal length has long been considered the most versatile lens, and many photographers are never without one on a trip.

Wide-Angle Range

For the wide-angle category, zooms such as a 17-35mm or a 16-35mm will handle situations where a significantly wide view is desired in addition to more moderate views. Ultra-wide-angle lenses are also effective at exaggerating foregrounds to help bring attention to any subject matter in these areas (often called "foreground dominance"). Backup choices are either a 20mm with a horizontal view of about 80 degrees or 24mm lens with about a 74-degree capture. Used appropriately, these lenses will produce a very wide capture and can certainly exaggerate foreground subject matter. Both are quite small, even models with relatively fast maximum apertures of f/2.8 take up very little room in the camera bag.

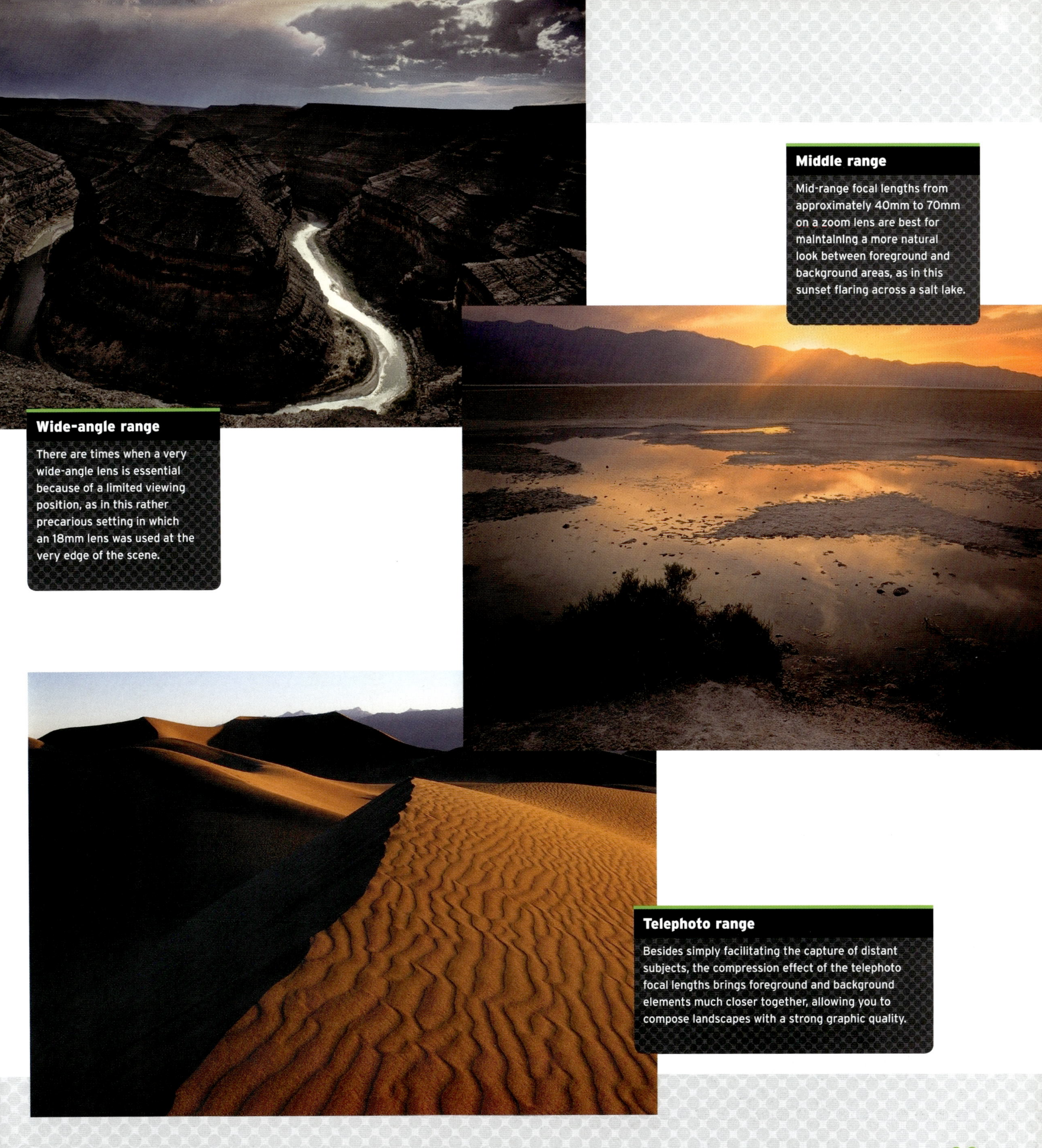

Middle range

Mid-range focal lengths from approximately 40mm to 70mm on a zoom lens are best for maintaining a more natural look between foreground and background areas, as in this sunset flaring across a salt lake.

Wide-angle range

There are times when a very wide-angle lens is essential because of a limited viewing position, as in this rather precarious setting in which an 18mm lens was used at the very edge of the scene.

Telephoto range

Besides simply facilitating the capture of distant subjects, the compression effect of the telephoto focal lengths brings foreground and background elements much closer together, allowing you to compose landscapes with a strong graphic quality.

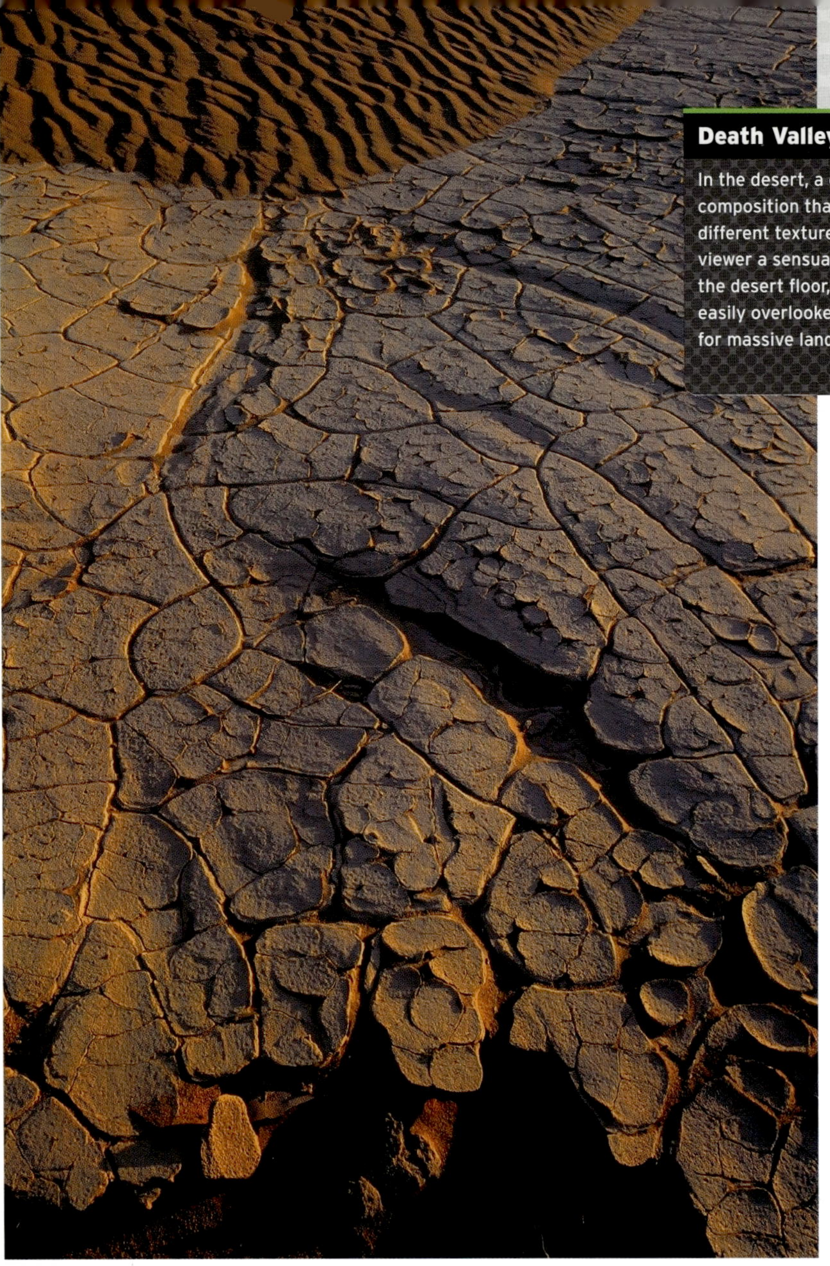

Close-Up Work

Photographers who plan to do extensive close-up and even 1:1 macro captures might consider packing a long focal length macro lens to double as a telephoto backup. For example, a 180mm or 200mm macro lens used with a 1.7x tele-converter produces a 306mm and a 340mm telephoto respectively. The 180mm or 200mm macros have a large working distance (distance between the lens and subject) as compared to a 50mm equipped with a close-up lens. This is a very desirable quality when photographing insects and to avoid casting shadows when coming in close to subjects such as small flowers. Both of these lenses can also be used for portraits.

The All-in-One Lens Option

An alternative to the single focal length backup choices is to take along an all-in-one, wide-angle to telephoto zoom such as a 28–300mm zoom. This will certainly provide a good range of focal length choices but there are drawbacks compared to the single focal length lenses. First of all, the 65-degree view from the 28mm setting is relatively moderate compared to the 80 degrees and 74 degrees for the 20mm and 24mm lens respectively. A focal length of 28mm is simply not wide enough for photographers who want a more dramatic optical rendering of subject matter. Second, all-in-one lenses have maximum apertures considered slow for low-light work, especially when compared to the f/1.4 speed of the 50mm lens. Third, these lenses generally cannot be used with tele-converters or if they can, the results may be disappointing. Finally, while some all-in-one lenses can focus fairly close and can be used with close-up lenses, the results are generally not as good as with a 50mm alone or a 50mm with a multi-element close-up lens, and certainly cannot compare with the excellent results from macro lenses in the 180mm and 200m range.

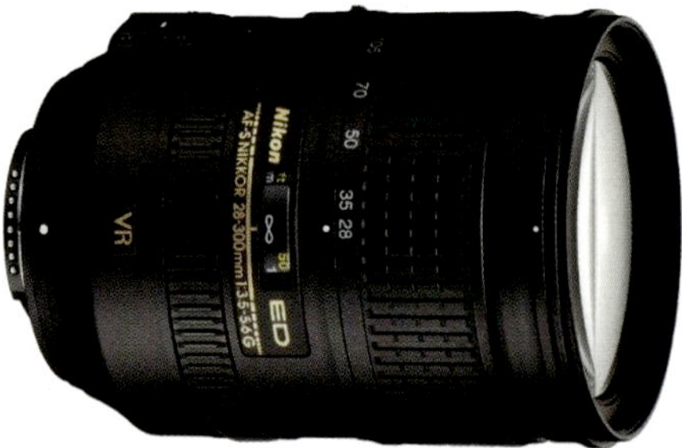

Stitched panorama

This composite of several vertical shots taken with a moderate telephoto can support a composition in which the most important areas are actually isolated and emphasized.

The Panoramic Option

In the film era, a panoramic view of a scene capturing 150-360 degrees horizontally required taking along a specialized (and expensive) rotation panoramic camera. Today, any digital camera can produce comparable results by taking successive overlapping frames of a scene and stitching the results together in specialized software. For more information, see "Producing Stitched Panoramas" on page 148.

In summary, selecting which lenses to take on a trip is determined by many factors, and in the end the final decision comes down to the type of subject matter, location conditions, personal resources, and goals for the trip. Nevertheless, there is a need to seriously consider the consequences of a camera or lens failure while off in a remote location.

How Tough is Your Equipment?

Manuals and websites for camera models will supply information on camera operating temperature and humidity ranges under "specifications." A typical temperature working range for a modern DSLR is between a low of 32-degrees Fahrenheit (0-degrees Celsius) to a high of 104-degrees Fahrenheit (40-degrees Celsius).

In addition, there should be information on fit and resistance to dust and moisture, as well as the materials used to construct the camera. The more extensive camera reviews will usually give some indication of the robustness of the camera. In general, cameras and lenses intended for professional use have a better build quality and therefore can withstand the stresses of long-term exposure to extreme conditions.

When not in use, the front and rear caps on lenses and the body cap on backup cameras should always be in place even when this equipment is stored in a camera bag or backpack. Memory cards should be stored in a dustproof carrier and not left loose in a pocket, camera bag or pack. Very fine airborne dust in desert environments can get into everything and this dust is abrasive. Any outlets on the camera body, such as those for an electronic cable release, should have their covers in place.

Lenses should be used with a lens hood and a UV or skylight front filter for protection. Any sand or dust should be blown off before cleaning the protective filter with a cleaning cloth or lens cleaning fluid and tissue. A good-quality camera bag or backpack is essential for protecting equipment and compartments should always be kept closed.

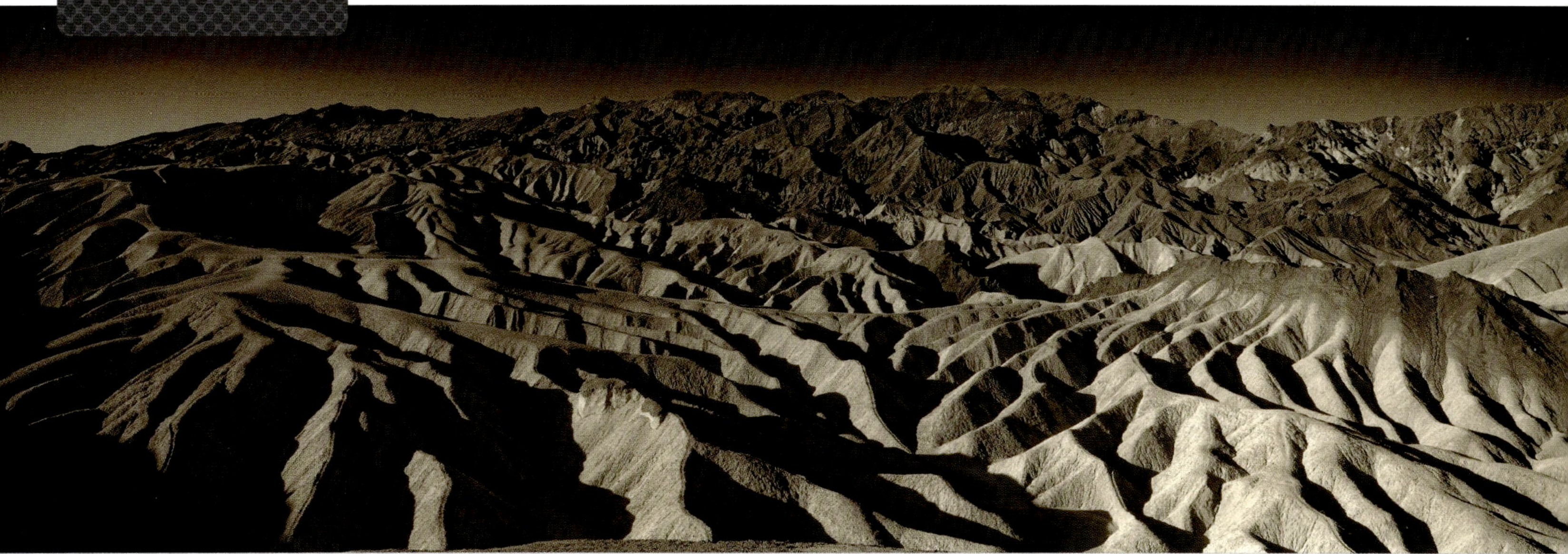

Air

Of all the elements discussed herein, air is of course the most ephemeral, and in many ways the most challenging—as you can't exactly capture this invisible-but-omnipresent subject directly. Rather, you must observe and record its more corporeal effects—its impact as it blows in gales through trees and cities, or the way it shapes and moves the clouds that transform the sky above every landscape. Indeed, learning to understand those cloud formations forms a base of knowledge that will allow you to predict the coming weather conditions, thus giving you the upper hand in visualizing your shots and getting to the right place at the right time. In terms of extreme photography, air also embraces the powerful storms that drive away less adventurous photographers, leaving you (with appropriate weatherproof gear) to capture the one-of-a-kind, elemental shots that reveal the full force of this planet's climate.

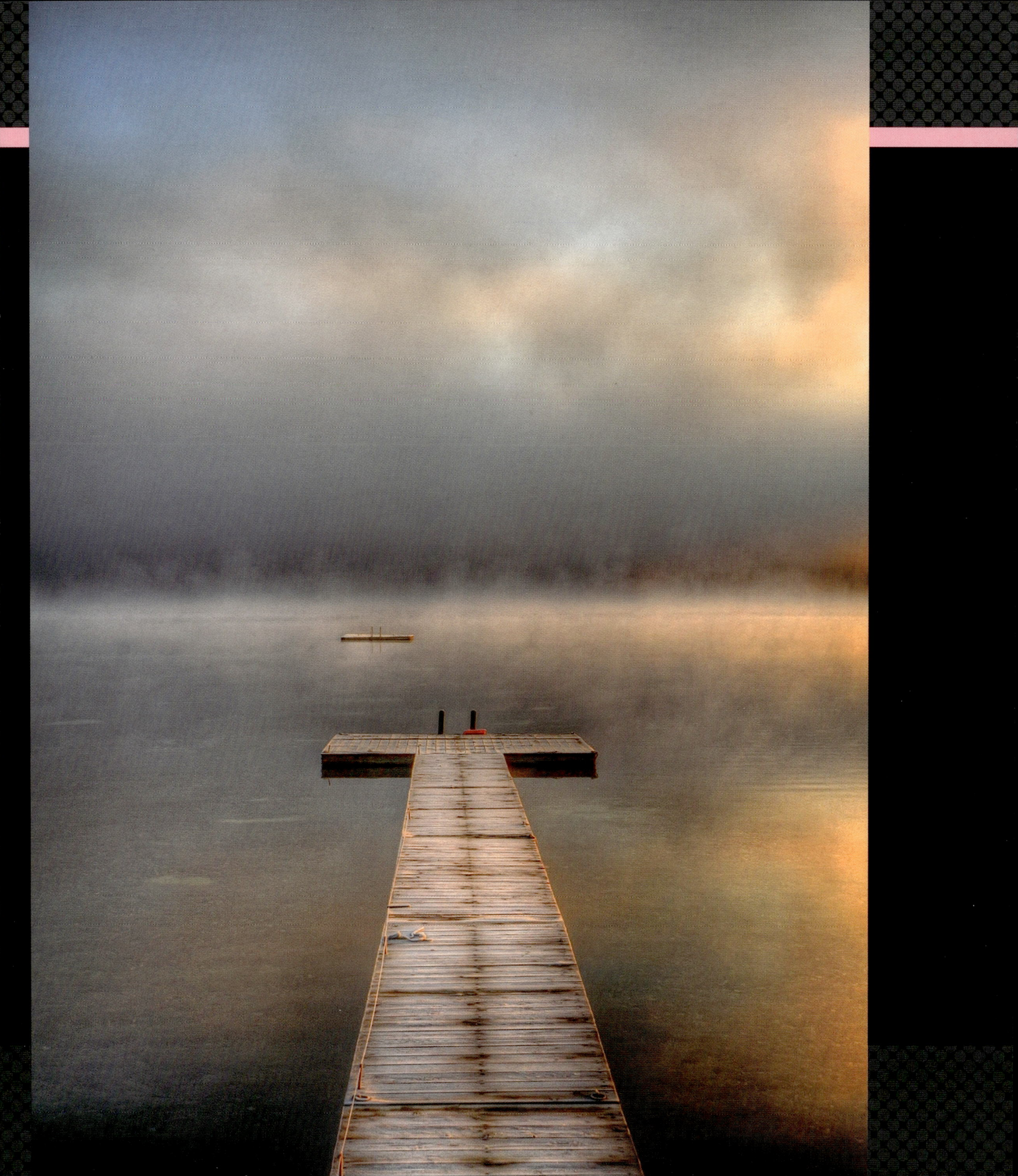

Forecasting Clouds

Arguably, weather is the most important defining factor for landscape and outdoor photography. Different types of weather, cloud cover, and atmospheric conditions have a significant impact on the final images. The weather does not just provide the background setting of an image, it also dictates the type and quality of light that is available to the outdoor photographer and, therefore, the mood, feel and look of the image.

In their constant search for ideal or perfect light, most professional landscape photographers are also obsessed with weather forecasts, and are often amateur meteorologists themselves. But it goes far beyond watching the local forecast for macro events, such as rain, sun, fog, ice or snow. Being able to predict with reasonable accuracy whether, for example, a storm will clear from the west or east, or if it will coincide with a sunset, can make the difference between an average landscape image and one that jumps out from the pack. Renowned landscape photographer Charlie Waite, for example, often looks for the moment that weather fronts arrive or pass, while David Noton admits to being a weather forecast obsessive—his first book *Waiting for the Light* describes his almost daily search for the right weather and light for his landscape photography.

> For the vast majority of these cloud shots, a polarizing filter will help the clouds pop out against a saturated sky.

> Many of these formations are rare and fleeting. It's a cloud hunter's trademark to act quickly as they see a worthy subject forming overhead—even if that means pulling the car over and setting up on the side of the road!

There are a number of tools available to the outdoor photographer for forecasting weather and light, aside from national or local weather services, which can allow the landscape photographer to put themselves in a position for shooting amazing images when the majority may have stayed at home. One of the most natural ways to forecast your own weather is by using the clouds. Different cloud formations, depending on type and height, can hint at the coming weather for up to 30 hours in advance.

Clouds are classified by their size and shape and are divided into three main categories: Cirrus, which comes from the Latin for curl [of hair] or fringe; Cumulus, which means heap or pile (often referred to as puffy clouds); or Nimbus, which means rain-bearing. In addition, the term "Stratus" is used to characterize spread-out clouds or clouds forming a layer. Stratus can be added to the three categories for more specific cloud definitions; for example, nimbostratus defines a thick, gray, damp blanket or layer of cloud. Likewise, the term "alto" describes mid-level clouds, hence altocumulus clouds are mid-level, puffy clouds. Cirrus are always high-altitude clouds.

Clouds are categorized into an in-depth table of families and geni, but for the purposes of this book, the following sections outline the broader forms of cloud types and some interesting geni that photographers are likely to come across.

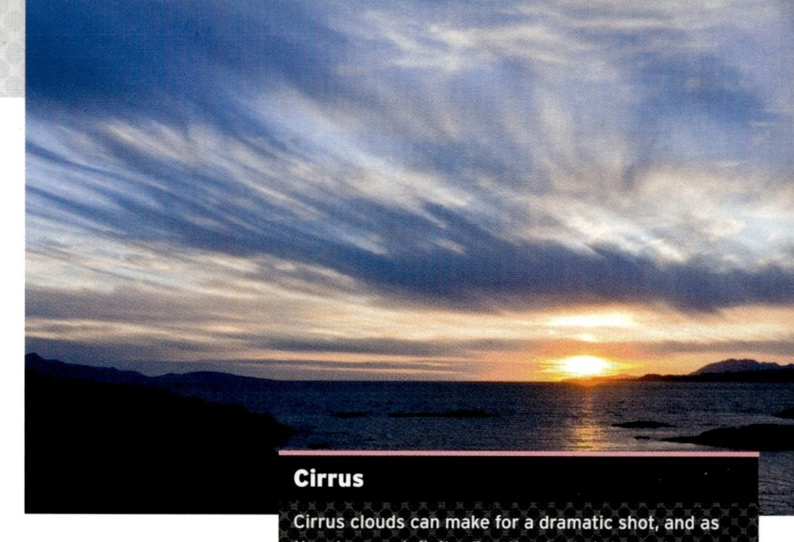

Cirrus

Cirrus clouds can make for a dramatic shot, and as they have a definite direction in their long wisps, you have compositional control in terms of what angle you point your camera. They are not so heavy as to obscure too much sunlight either, so you'll tend to be working in conditions with plenty of light for an adequate exposure.

High Clouds

Cloud bases forming about 3.7 miles (6km) above sea level, which are usually composed of ice crystals only.

Cirrus

Cirrus are abundant high-level clouds which appear as thin, wispy or feathery clouds that are blown into streaks by strong winds at high altitude—hence, they are commonly known as mare's tails. Single or few cirrus clouds can indicate that fair weather is on the way, while gradually increasing levels of cirrus are predictive of an incoming warm front. The direction of the streaks usually indicates the direction from which the weather is coming. Cirrus usually indicate that the weather will change in the next 24 hours.

Cirrocumulus

Cirrocumulus are often rippled or grainy in nature, and can sometimes appear like fish scales, when it is termed a mackerel sky. Mackerel skies at sunrise and sunset are particularly appealing to landscape photographers. Cirrocumulus can predict the arrival of stormy weather (as in the old folk saying "Mackerel sky, storm is nigh") but are usually associated with calm, cold weather.

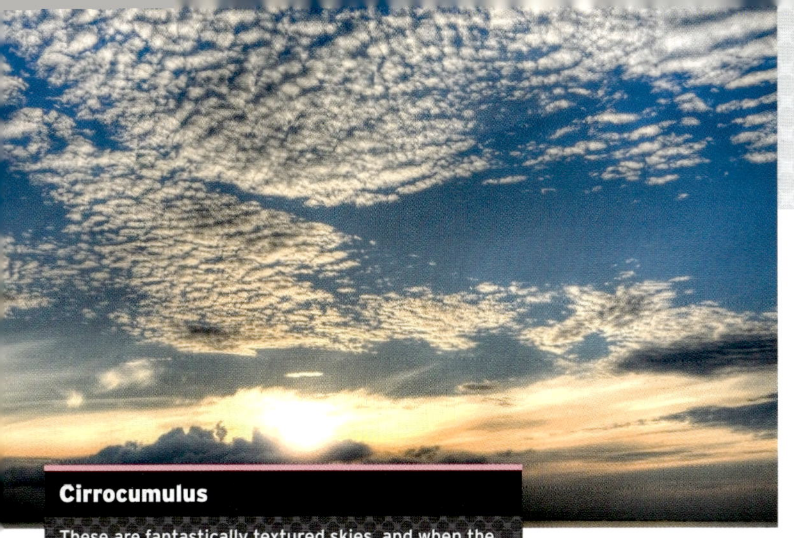

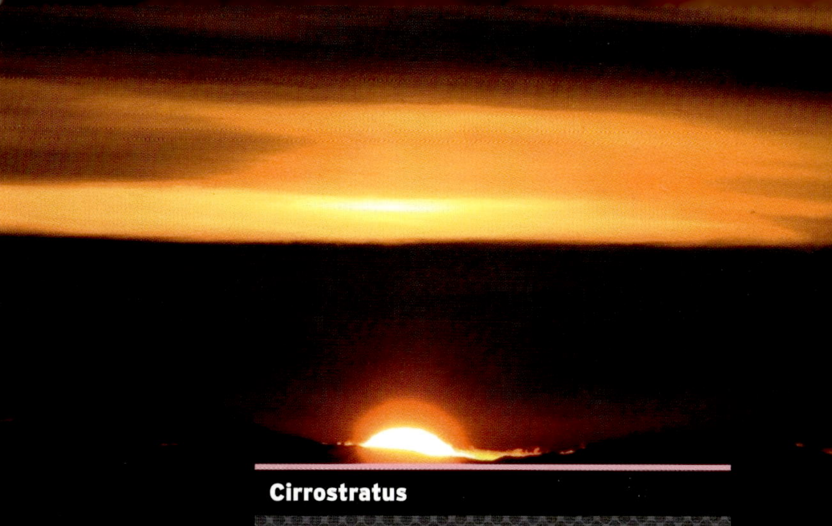

Cirrostratus

Cirrostratus appear as thin sheets of cloud spread across the sky. Not particularly cloud-like in appearance, cirrostratus turn the sky a milky or pale white appearance, with the sun and moon visible through them, often producing halos. Cirrostratus indicates the arrival of rain or snow within 12-24 hours.

Mid-Level Clouds

Cloud bases forming between 1.2-3.7 miles (2-6km) above sea level. Mid-level clouds are usually composed of water droplets but can contain small ice crystals, and are usually gray-blue sheets of cloud covering the entire sky.

Altocumulus

Mid-level clouds composed of water droplets, and are gray, puffy and irregular in appearance. They are organized into a distinct layer of small puffy clouds and so can appear like a mackerel sky. When seen on a warm, humid morning, they usually predict the arrival of a thunderstorm later in the day.

Altostratus

Can become thick enough to obscure the sun, but it will still be visible as a bright area in the sky through the clouds. Altostratus appear a few hours ahead of a warm front carrying precipitation. These can thicken into nimbostratus clouds associated with long-lasting precipitation.

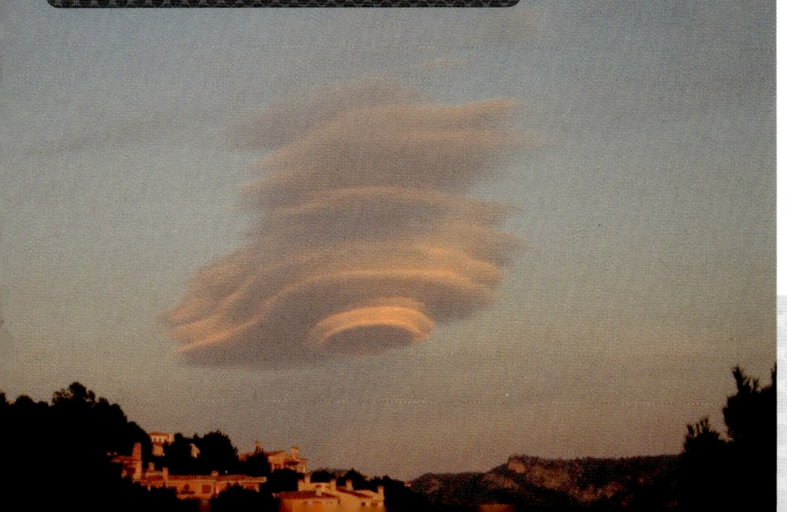

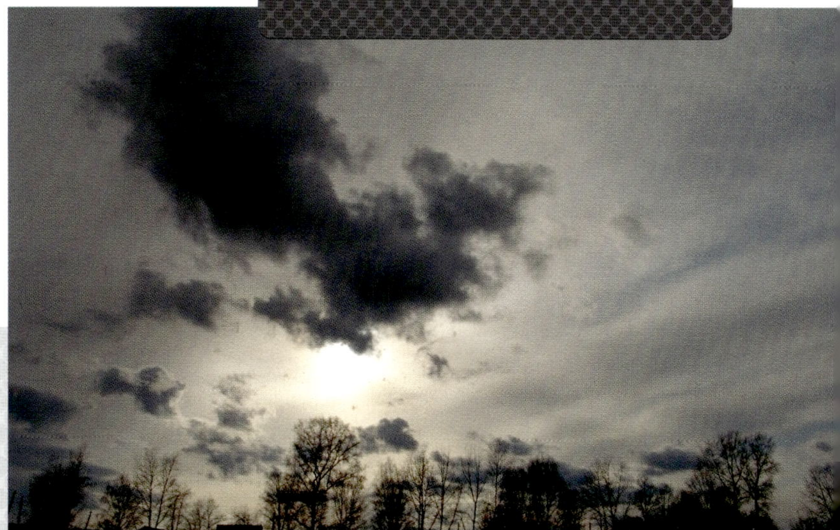

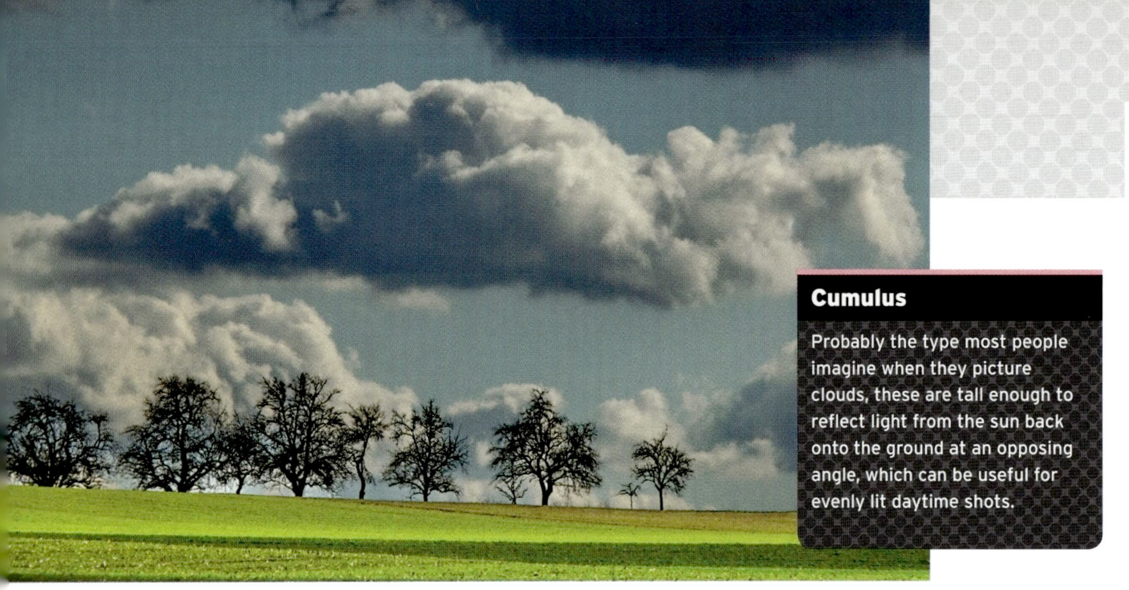

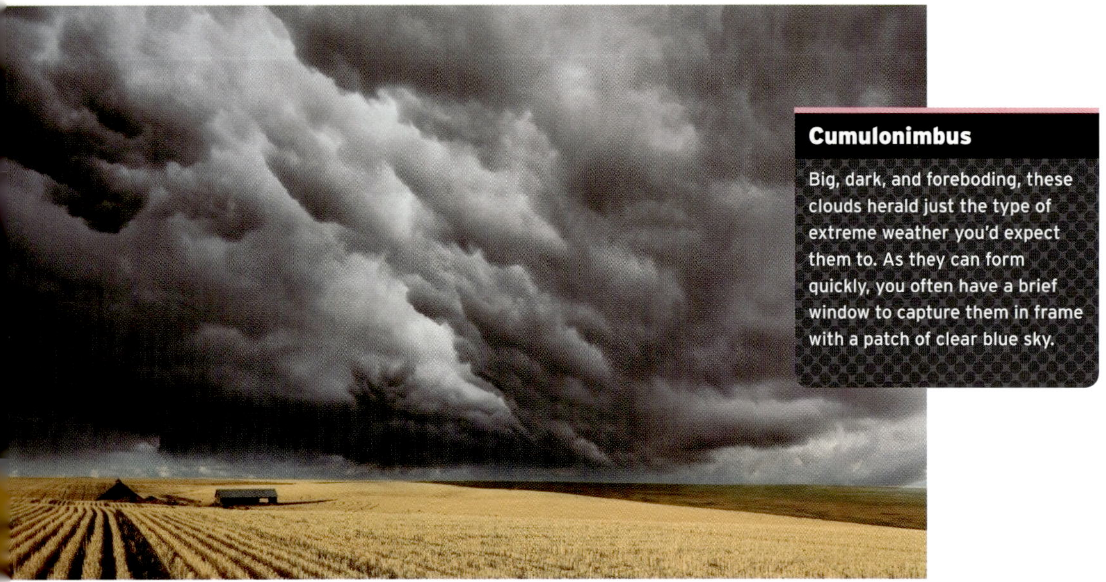

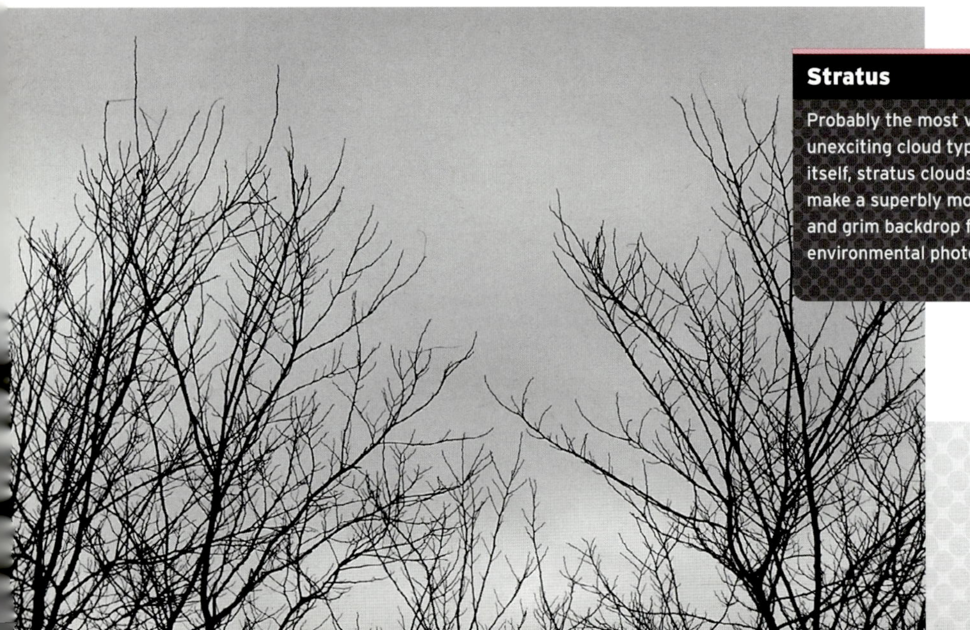

Low-Level Clouds

Clouds forming under 1.25 miles (2,000m) above sea level, and composed of small droplets of water.

Cumulus

Cumulus clouds are known as fair-weather clouds, and are characteristically flat at their base and stacked into puffy towers at the top. Cumulus clouds with a cauliflower- or cotton ball-shaped dome are called cumulus congestus, or "towering cumulus," and can grow vertically in height to higher levels. They are associated with fair, dry conditions, and are often short-lasting. They can be concurrent with light showers or precipitation, however, they may continue to grow upward, forming giant cumulonimbus, or thunderstorm, clouds.

Cumulonimbus

Cumulus clouds that continue to grow upward, perhaps due to rapid or strong heating of the land, can evolve into cumulonimbus clouds—otherwise known as thunder clouds or thunderheads. When the top of the cloud reaches higher levels, strong winds in the atmosphere can form the cloud into an anvil shape, which usually points in the direction that the storm is moving. The base of cumulonimbus is often dark. Cumulonimbus predict more extremes of weather, such as heavy rain, hail or snow, thunderstorms and hurricanes. Cumulonimbus can also form funnel clouds, which indicate an imminent tornado, if the funnel touches the ground.

Stratus

Dull, featureless gray clouds that cover the breadth of the sky in a thick layer. If stratus touches the ground it becomes fog. Rarely associated with anything other than light precipitation such as drizzle or a dusting of fine snow.

Stratocumulus

Low, lumpy, gray clouds that form in rows, sometimes with blue sky visible between them. Precipitation is rarely associated, although there is a risk of light rain.

Rare and Unusual Clouds

Clouds that cannot be classified into the cloud types above, and which represent rare atmospheric conditions.

Mammatus

Mammatus look like undulating bulges hanging down from low-lying cloud. They are formed by saturated, sinking air, and are associated with severe storms. Their appearance, however, suggests that the storm is moving away, rather than toward the observer (see page 60 for more).

Contrails

Thin, feathery clouds made up of condensed water droplets, these elongated formations signify low pressure and temperature.

Green Clouds

Associated with severe weather, including supercell storms and tornados, green clouds are thought to be caused by green light reflected from green vegetation on the ground onto low-lying cloud.

Nacreous

Resemble pale cirrus clouds, but are characterized by brilliant colors after sunset, caused by light diffraction. Nacreous clouds occur at between 12–18 miles (20–30km) altitudes and are thought to consist of spherical ice particles, a deduction from the diffraction patterns they cause.

Noctilucent

Noctilucent, or night, clouds also resemble cirrus clouds, becoming visible in deep twilight—the name is roughly translated as "night shining" in Latin. They are only visible when illuminated by sunlight from below the horizon. They are the highest clouds in the Earth's atmosphere, occurring at altitudes of between 45–55 miles (70–90km). They appear mainly in summer and latitudes of around 50–70 degrees north and south of the Equator. Noctilucent clouds show a blue-silver tint, sometimes orange-red, and are thought to be increasing in frequency as a result of climate change, and reflect unknown changes in the upper atmosphere.

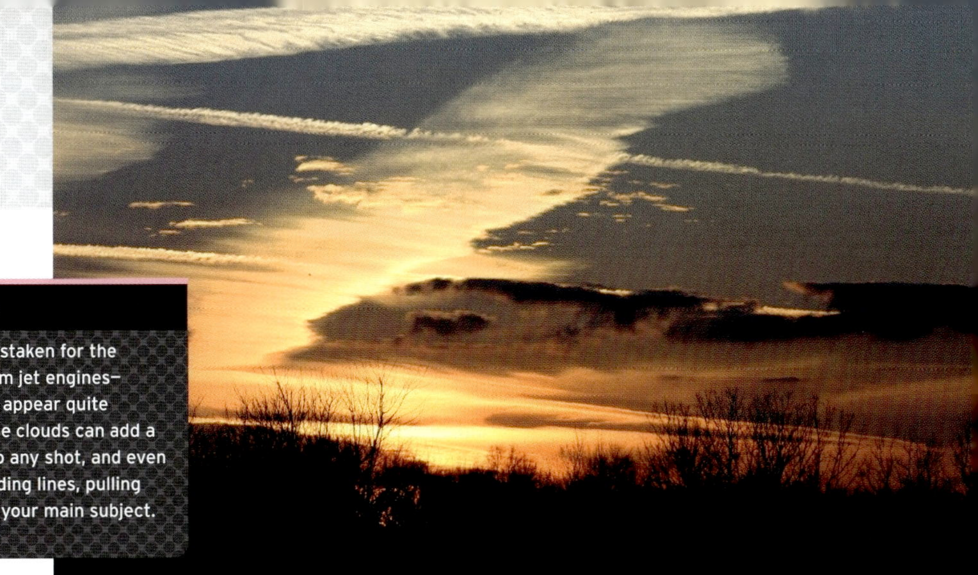

Contrails

Not to be mistaken for the contrails from jet engines—though they appear quite similar—these clouds can add a dynamism to any shot, and even serve as leading lines, pulling attention to your main subject.

Nacreous

Rare and exquisitely beautiful, Nacreous clouds can cover the entire sky or exist as a single tuft of cloud, floating along like a lost rainbow. They're mostly observed only near the north and south poles, where their color stands out strongly against snowy white landscapes.

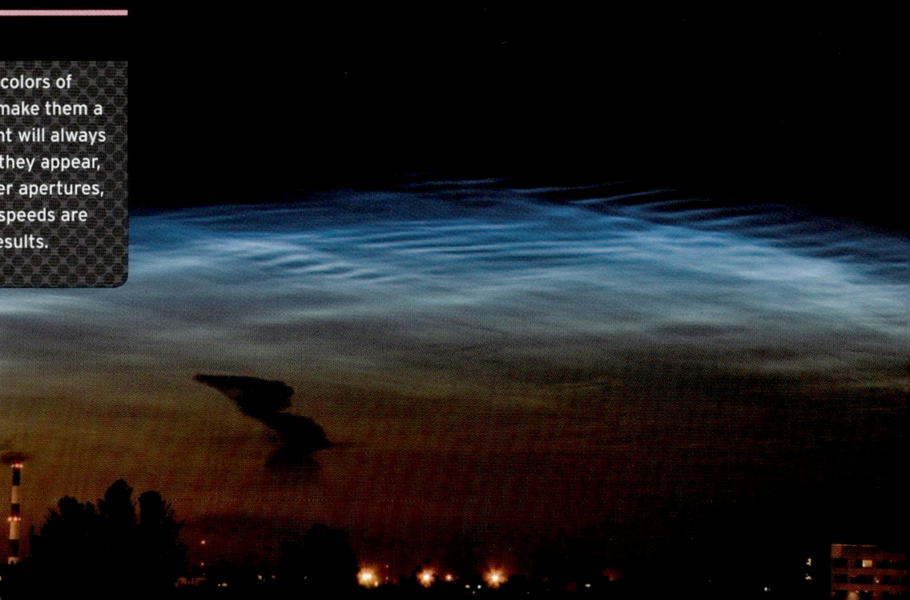

Noctilucent

The rich, saturated colors of noctilucent clouds make them a unique find. The light will always be dim by the time they appear, so higher ISOs, wider apertures, and longer shutter speeds are essential for best results.

Cloud Time Lapse

Time-lapse photography is a classic technique for revealing and manipulating the passage of time, and can provide some stunning results. From rising and ebbing tides, to the movement of people in cities, to decaying matter, time-lapse photography can provide fresh opportunities to get creative. The only equipment required is a DSLR with an interval timer, a tripod, a computer, and a bagful of inspirational ideas.

Time-lapse sequences can reveal the hitherto hidden rhythms and patterns of daily events and movements that are normally concealed from human perception. The results can be equally hypnotic, revealing, and surprising.

Clouds make a particularly appealing subject matter for time-lapse photography. The accelerated version of time that time lapse produces captures the ethereal nature of clouds as they form, disappear, and reform apparently in a random fashion. It will also reveal unseen patterns in a location's microclimate—for example, the movement of clouds around hills and peaks, or the natural patterns of clouds rolling in from the sea onto dry land. Building storms, rising mist, cloud motion around land masses will all make fascinating time-lapse subject matter.

Today's generation of DSLRs make it relatively easy for anyone with a little know-how to create remarkable time-lapse cloudscapes. A video function is not required, as time lapse involves the merging of hundreds of single images to create the perception of movement.

The only camera function necessary is a timer that allows the photographer to set a sequence of images and the length of interval between each shot. Depending on the camera, this timer will either be built-in or, if not, numerous remote controllers and intervalometers are available to provide that function. In some cases, the function may be available by software or firmware download.

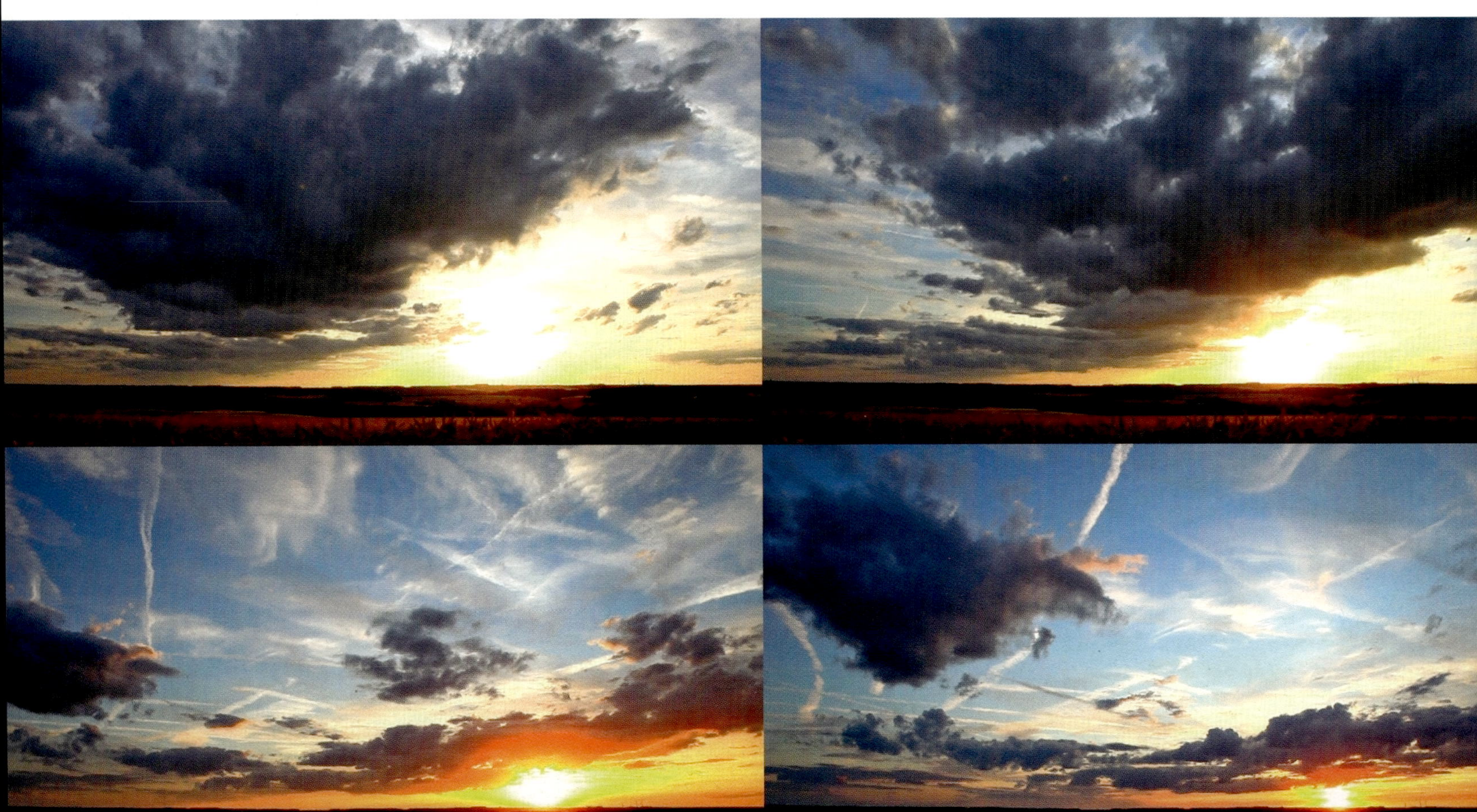

The basic premise of time lapse is to merge numerous single images into a movie sequence, much like a movie or TV recording made up of thousands of individual frames. In normal movie making, the camera captures images, or frames, at 24 frames per second (fps), which are then played back or projected at 24 frames per second, producing normal time that is seen as natural or "filmic."

Speeds of 24-30 frames per second are normally used as they are fast enough for the human eye to subconsciously merge the individual frames into an apparently seamless moving film running at normal speed. That means that at 24 fps, for example, a one-minute film projected at normal speed requires 1,440 individual frames or images (24 frames every second, for 60 seconds).

The main aim of time lapse, however, is to reveal an accelerated passage of time. With the ability to control length of exposure (of each individual image) and, more importantly, the time interval between each image, the photographer has creative control over the final effect. The result is a fascinating and surreal representation of an accelerated version of time.

If, for example, the photographer chooses to take one image every second, and then play it back at 24 frames per second, the result will show the passage of time at 24 times faster than normal speed.

To think about it another way, take the example of a cloudscape at sunset. Let us say that the sunset takes one hour, and the photographer decides to shoot one frame every 10 seconds. This would result in 6 shots per minute (one every 10 seconds) for 60 minutes, with 360 final images. Of course, when played back at 24 fps, the hour would be condensed into 15 seconds (360 divided by 24). It is plain to see that the potential of time lapse opens up new realms of creativity.

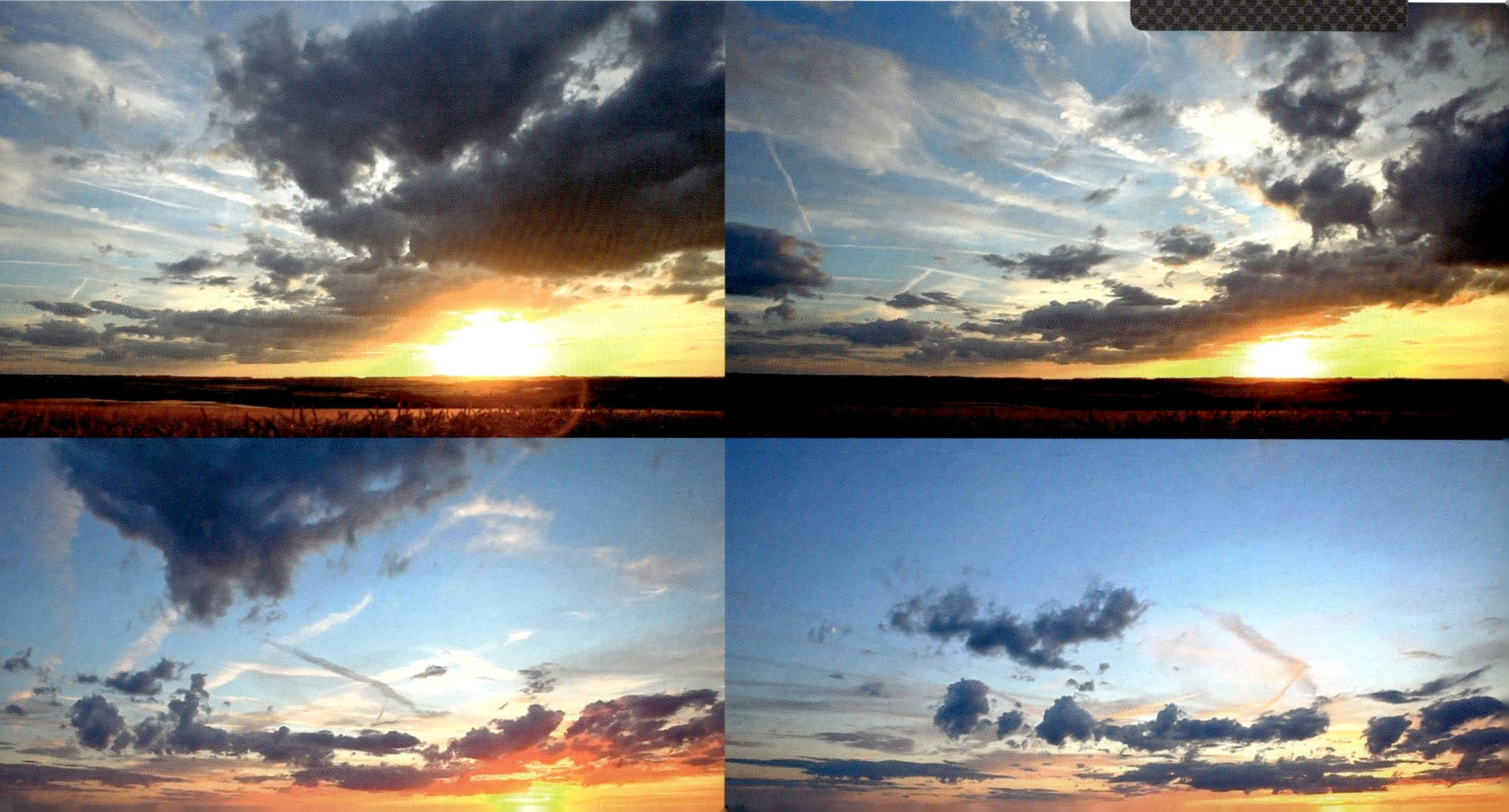

How to Set Up a Time-Lapse Sequence?

Sweeping wide-angle lenses often work well for cloudscapes, catching the majesty of the shifting cloud patterns as they move across the landscape, or a building weather front or storm. Telephoto lenses work well when the aim is to capture the flow of clouds around a single subject, such as a lone mountain peak.

For time lapse, where the camera is left alone for a set period of time, camera settings need to be switched to Manual Focus (to prevent autofocus searching as the cloud formations alter). Infinity focus is fine for sweeping cloudscapes, but when including foreground interest (recommended, as it adds dramatic perspective to the scene) the photographer should focus using an established technique—such as focusing one-third of the way into the scene, or using hyperfocal distances.

To set exposure, the easiest option is to switch the camera to Aperture Priority, as light levels are likely to fluctuate during the length of the time-lapse sequence. However, the advanced or experienced photographer can use Manual Exposure in order to retain fixed aperture and timer settings for creative purposes. However, it's worth noting that this method does require stable light levels, which are impossible for even the most seasoned photographer to predict!

When starting and finishing the exposure bear in mind that, like any movie, the time-lapse sequence will have more impact if there is some kind of beginning and end. Of course, future events cannot be predicted, i.e. the end, but with a little forethought, the photographer can avoid an apparently random cloud-lapse sequence—beautiful as it may be.

One of the most important creative decisions that will impact the final effect is that of choosing exposure length and interval time between each exposure. As discussed, the number of shots, or frames, and the interval will have a direct effect on the length of the final time-lapse material, as well as the apparent acceleration of time.

However, the interval between each exposure also has a significant effect on the final feel of the time lapse movie. Shorter intervals, such as every minute or less, tend to provide a smoother outcome. This is not so much an issue for cloudscapes, as they are relatively fast-moving.

A photographer may want to create a cloud lapse over a full day, shooting at an interval of, say, every 10 minutes. In this case, the final result will be more jerky, like claymation, as the interval between each exposure is longer and the scene has significantly changed. Short intervals equal smooth outcomes; long intervals produce a more blocky feel.

For cloudscapes, the exposure time should generally be just under one half of the interval time. So a one-second exposure every 2.5 seconds would yield good results.

For more advanced photographers, one way to make time-lapse sequences stand out from the crowd is to use some form of dolly or moving camera support to very slowly move the camera between each exposure.

Set the camera up as described to perform the desired time lapse. However, moving the camera in tiny increments between each exposure will create the illusion that the camera is moving or "panning" at normal pace, while the clouds rush overhead at exhilarating speed. This contrast between relative motion speeds can add real wow factor to time-lapse sequences.

Other things to consider include carrying sufficient battery life and memory card storage, and ensuring that the camera is left in a place where it is not going to be knocked between shots, blown over, or rained on.

Post-processing wise, time-lapse photography yields large numbers of images, depending on the length of the sequence. However, numerous time-lapse friendly software packages are available to automate the process. After downloading the images onto a computer, applications such as iMovie will automatically stack the images by batch process into a single movie sequence. This can then be processed, edited, and given special effects.

As always, practice and experimentation will help to hone technique and creative vision, and hopefully produce a mesmerizing time-lapse cloudscape.

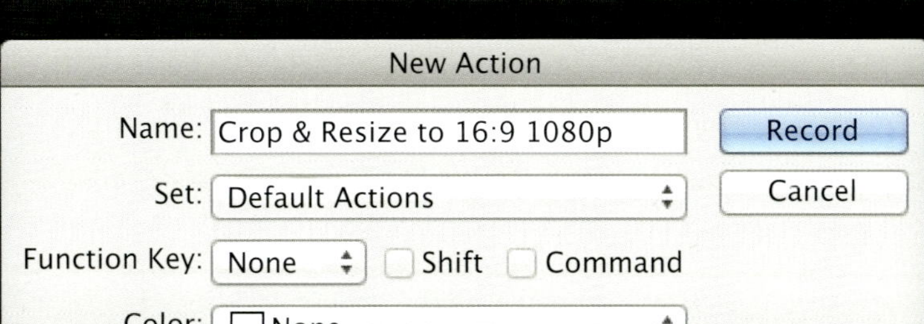

Crop and resize

The first step is to batch process all your time-lapse shots, cropping them to the 16:9 aspect ratio and resizing them to 1080p resolution (1080 x 1920, or about 2 megapixels).

The timeline

Once you import your still images into the video-processing software of your choice, they will appear sequentially along a timeline. To make changes to the entire time lapse, highlight all the still images.

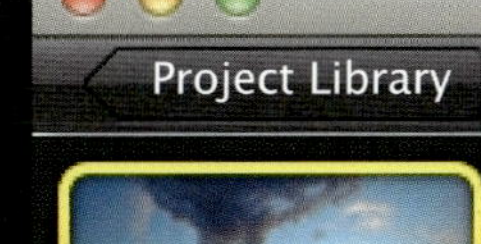

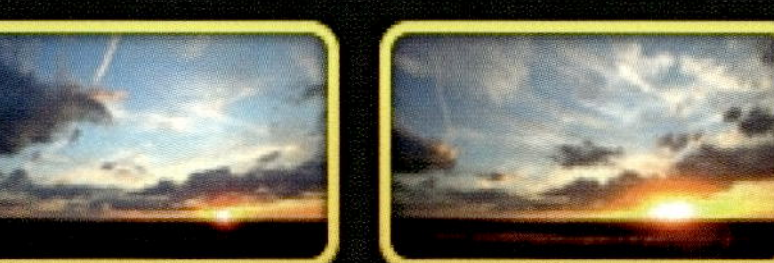
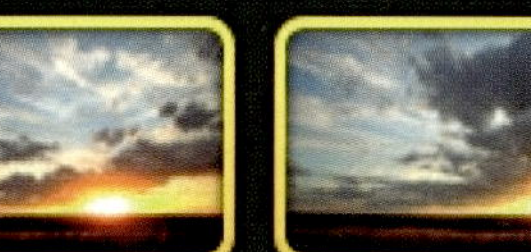
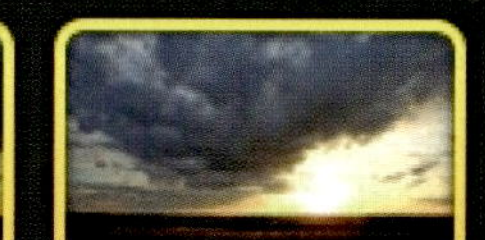

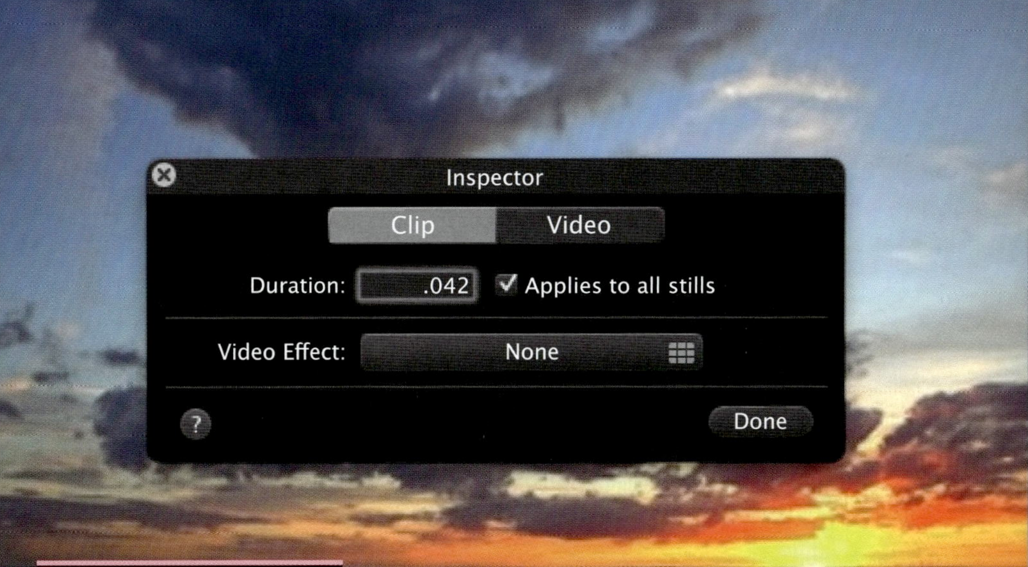

Setting the duration

Setting each slide to play for a duration of .042 seconds will add up to 24 frames per second—the ideal frame speed for the classic "filmic" look. (iMovie is the software used here, but other programs work similarly.)

Fog & Mist

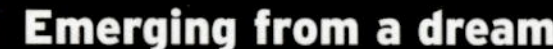

Effect on the Quality of Light

The formation of atmospheric fog and mist can occur when the temperature of moist air reaches its dew point, causing the condensation of tiny water droplets. These droplets scatter light by reflection and refraction to produce a cloud-like, colorless atmosphere with reduced visibility. The difference between fog and mist is based on moisture density, with fog having a significantly higher concentration of water droplets. The American Meteorological Society defines fog as reducing visibility below 1km (0.62 miles). Mist is basically a lesser form that has smaller droplets and tends to appear as a thin layer near the ground. Fog can appear in many forms, providing the photographer with numerous compositions. For example, radiation fog forms during a clear, calm night near the ground while evaporation fog looks like scattered wisps of smoke rising up from the calm surface of a lake or pond. Smog, on the other hand, is a form of air pollution in which particulate matter is suspended in the air and may have a weak coloration produced by these substances. If the moisture content of fog reaches a high enough level, the droplets will combine into larger drops, resulting in drizzle or even a very fine snow on cold days. A search of the Internet using the phrases "fog and mist" and "types of fog" will provide extensive meteorological information on these atmospheric conditions.

The light-scattering effects of fog and mist will alter the four key photographic qualities of light:

(1) the intensity or brightness
(2) the contrast between tones
(3) the direction of the light source, and
(4) the color content

In various ways and to various degrees, fog and mist lower both intensity and contrast levels, and diffuse or even obscure the direction of the light source through a neutral-gray atmosphere that tends to lower the saturation level of all colors in a scene. Some of this loss in contrast and color can be compensated for with HDR exposure techniques using the tone mapping option (see page 149). As the sun warms the atmosphere, the condensation process gives way to the evaporation of the air's moisture that eventually clears the atmosphere.

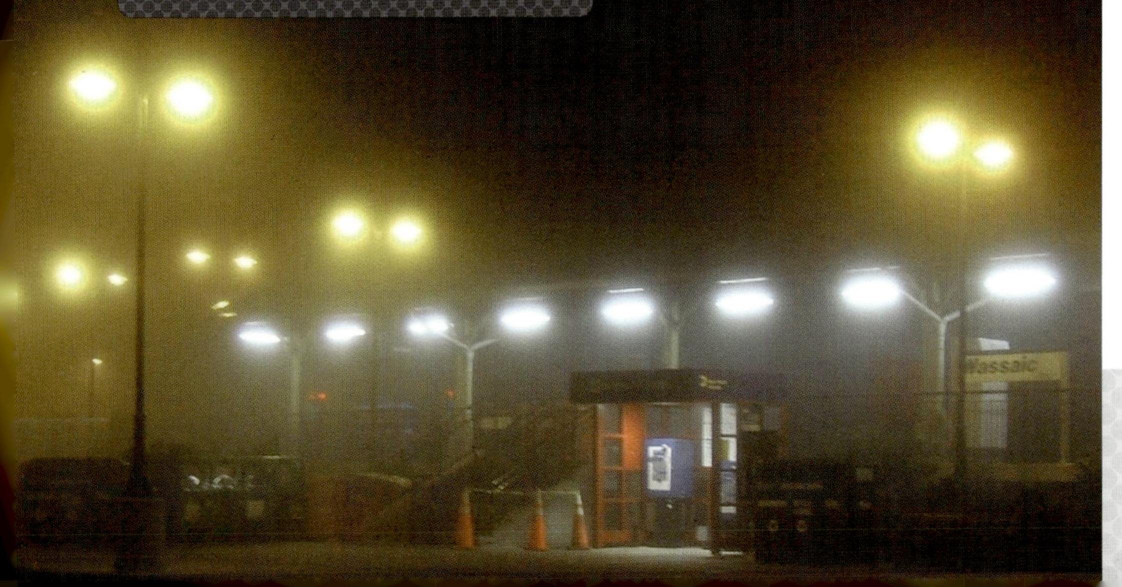

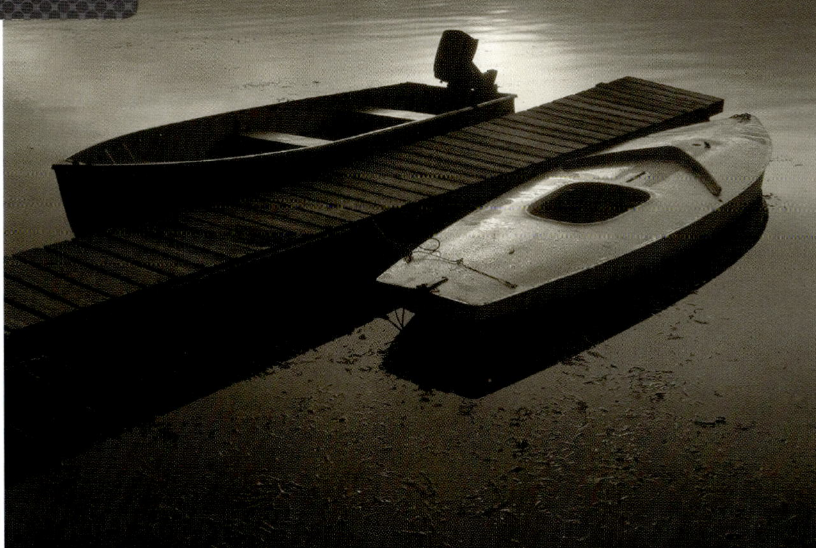

Atmospheric Compositions

Composing a scene with areas of fog or mist means having to work with a quality of light that is portraying the world very differently. Instead of a picture made up of delicate highlights and defined shadows, along with colorful shapes and crisp textures, the photographer must now look for strong visual elements that will survive the reduced visibility and very soft rendering. In addition, fog will exert a kind of depth-of-field control that presents some interesting opportunities when composing. Normally, changes in f/stop settings are used to determine the total depth-of-field area of sharpness from the point of focus in the picture. Instead, fog will reduce sharpness as a function of the build up of more and more density as the distance from the camera increases. Thus, the photographer can control how visually prominent a subject appears and conversely how muted the background will be rendered by varying the camera-to-subject distance. For example, choosing to deal with a location that has an interesting main subject but very distracting backgrounds by photographing it on a foggy day.

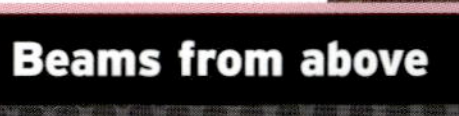

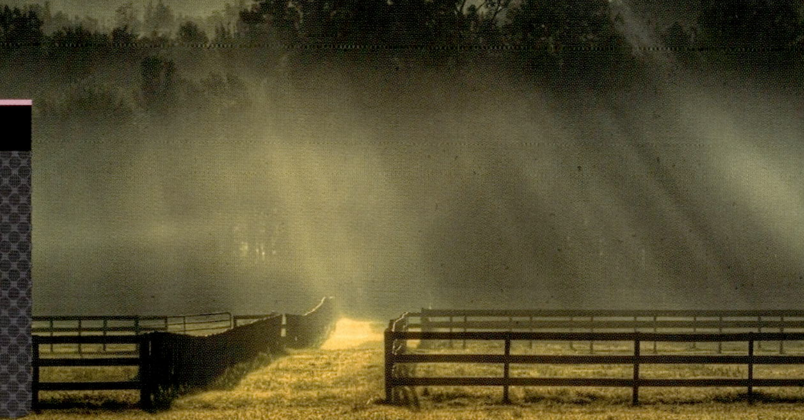

When fog and mist appear only in certain areas of a scene, the effect is to delineate parts of that scene usually without significantly affecting the rest of the scene. A common example is when fog forms low in the valleys between layers of distant mountain ranges separating out each ridgeline. This is a form of radiation fog called Valley Fog. The result is a greater sense of depth than in sunlight where similar ridgelines will tend to blend together. Another unique condition occurs when a low sun with warm coloration backlights a patch of fog, giving this normally neutral mass an orange coloration. This can be very striking when it takes place against a blue sky and white clouds. Still another example of a backlighting effect is the appearance of "light rays" from the sun that radiate through the fog. Such a unique and dramatic situation is created when the angle of the sun is high enough and just before its warmth burns off the moisture. This is on average about 1-2 hours after sunrise and is generally a short-lived phenomenon.

Finally, there is the way mist and fog can cloak a scene with a certain ambience and even an emotional quality—an illusion that writers and poets have called attention to for centuries. For example, a feeling of serenity emulating from the soft and gentle rendering of subject matter, or perhaps a sense of mystery or even fear about what might emerge from the fog. Horror movies have certainly made good use of these atmospheric settings. For the photographer, the emotional effects of fog and mist will be very dependent on the subject, the setting, and the specific composition, as some of the illustrations provided in this section demonstrate. In the end, it will be the viewer who will relate to this aspect of the picture. Still, there is no question that a scene with a diffused atmosphere, muted details and whole sections hidden from view will certainly be perceived as out of the ordinary.

One never really knows exactly what different forms fog will take on a given day and how this will change as the sun burns off the moisture. Furthermore, the transition to a clear atmosphere can range from subtle to dramatic and often occurs in a remarkably short period of time. Consequently, the photographer must be prepared to work fast to recognize and capture every opportunity as the atmospheric veil over the scene disappears. The best way to make the most of the photographic opportunities offered by fog and mist is to spend as much time as practical photographing under these conditions and carefully evaluating the results at home on your computer.

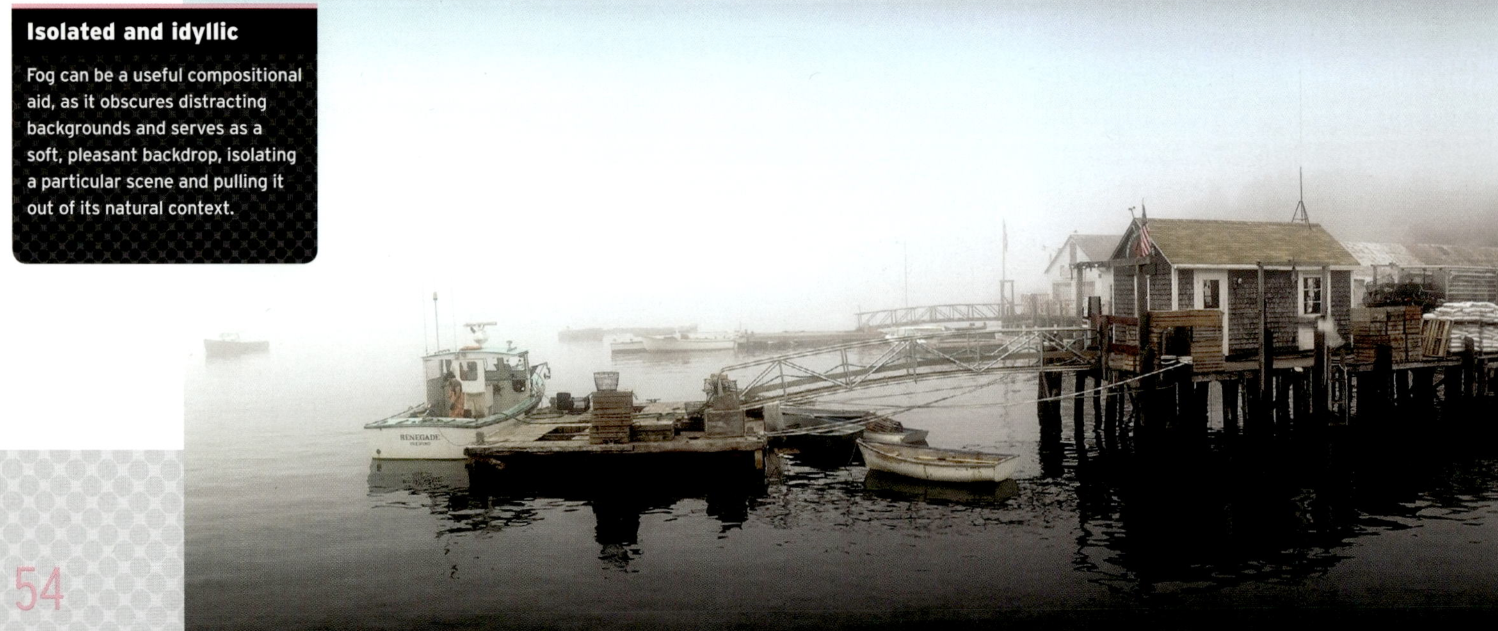

Isolated and idyllic

Fog can be a useful compositional aid, as it obscures distracting backgrounds and serves as a soft, pleasant backdrop, isolating a particular scene and pulling it out of its natural context.

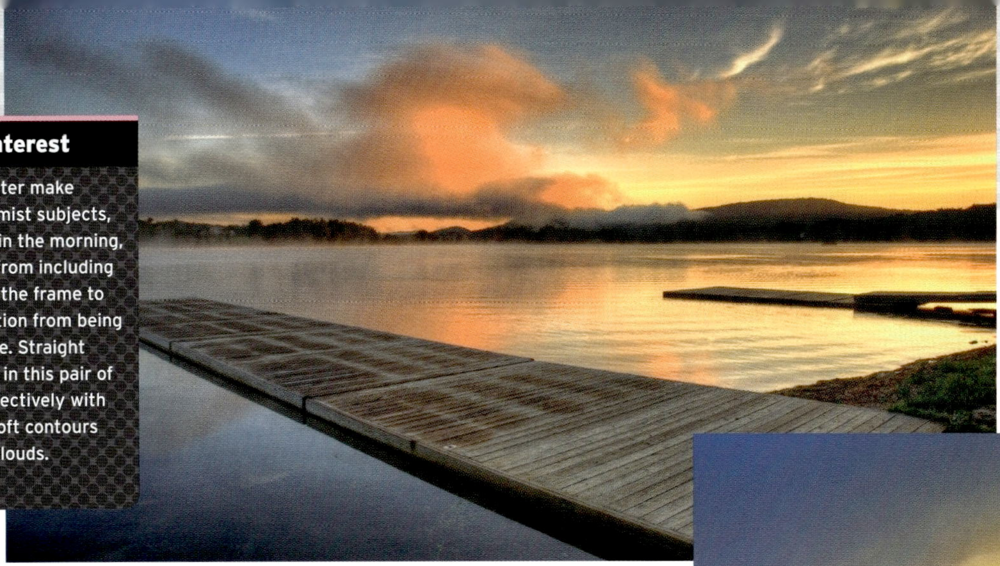

Foreground interest

Open bodies of water make excellent fog and mist subjects, particularly early in the morning, but often benefit from including other elements in the frame to keep the composition from being too still and serene. Straight lines like the ones in this pair of docks contrast effectively with the surrounding soft contours of the water and clouds.

Floating above the water

A lifting fog may seem to get stuck around certain parts of a scene, such as the shrubs, boats, and docks shown here, making for an interesting composition—and one different from a uniformly foggy scene.

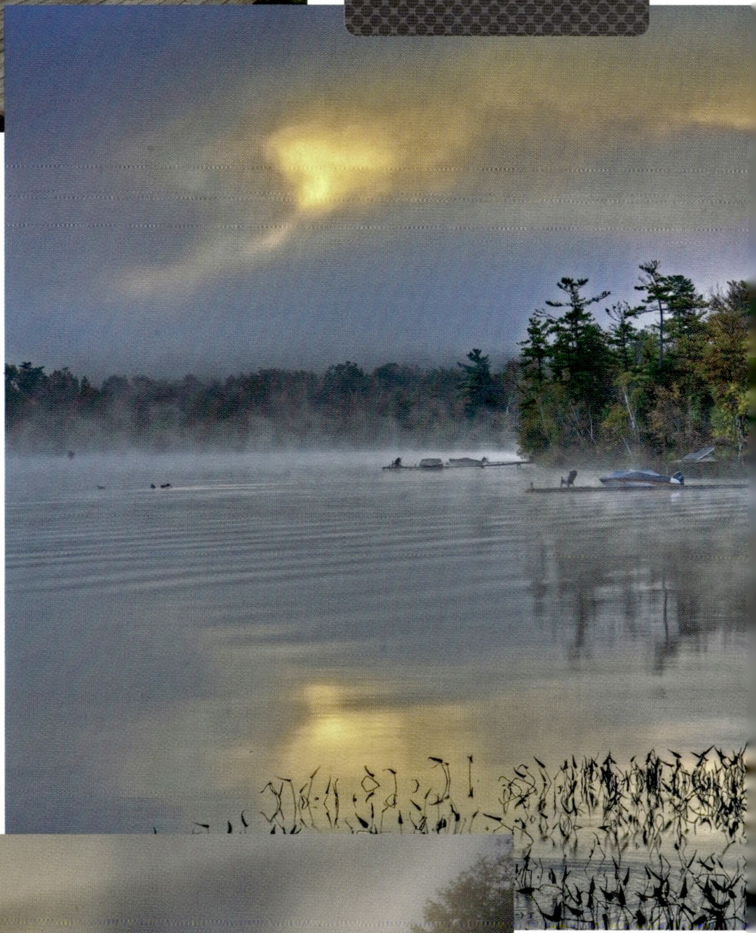

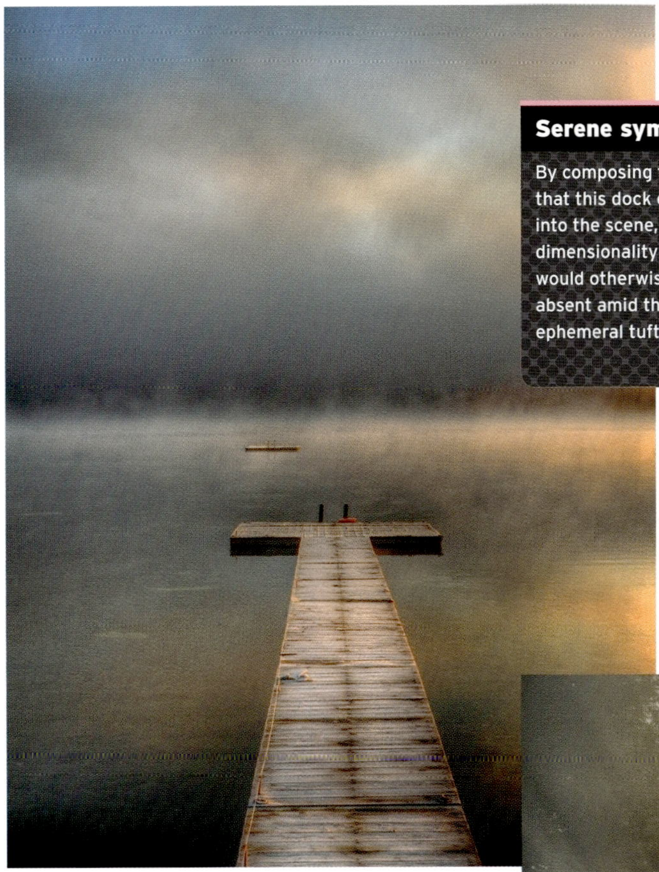

Serene symmetry

By composing the shot such that this dock extends out into the scene, a depth and dimensionality is imparted that would otherwise have been absent amid the ethereal and ephemeral tufts of fog.

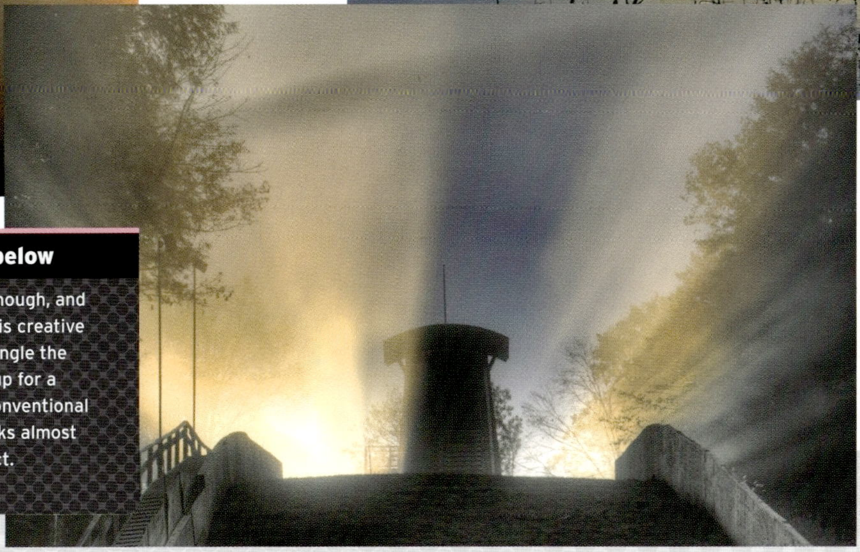

Beams from below

If the sun is low enough, and your composition is creative enough, you can angle the crepuscular rays up for a powerful and unconventional shot—one that looks almost like a special effect.

Storm Clouds

Chasing tornados may represent the exciting end of the wedge, but photographing stormscapes can provide images that are just as dramatic, and arguably with a more brooding atmosphere. A building storm can create immense cloud- and skyscapes, while passing storms are often accompanied by unusual lighting effects and colors. Enter the world of storm photography and prepare to meet strange new cloud formations with exotic names such as anvils, walls, haboobs, and scuds.

A building storm is a wonder to behold. Towering clouds, dramatic light, approaching curtains of rain or hail, and complex cloud formations all offer fantastic opportunities for the intrepid photographer. During a heavy or severe storm, it may be prudent to take cover—if heavy precipitation and wind are present, photographic potential may be limited anyway. However, once the storm begins to pass the photographic feast can begin again, as things to look out for will include clear, vivid light with the atmosphere cleansed by the storm, rainbows if there are breaks in the trailing cloud, biblical rays of light, or a golden glow and up-lit storm clouds if the sun is low in the sky.

A zoom lens will allow the photographer to capture close-up shots of sunbeams and billowing cloud formations, which may be side-lit or silhouetted, as the storm builds and partially blots out the sunlight. However, a wide-angle lens will capture the scale and majesty of a building storm, and allow for the inclusion of foreground interest to add the all-important perspective.

Composition for sweeping, wide-angle shots will benefit from either a high vista that provides a clear and panoramic view of the storm skyscape as it builds, or equally a wide expanse of flat land such as a plain or prairie that can act as a stage on which to set the storm as the lead player, without too many distracting elements. Using wide-angle lenses not only allows the photographer to include foreground subjects, but also lead-in lines. Paths, fences, a line of telegraph poles—all will provide both perspective and a means to draw the viewer into the unfolding drama.

Likewise, urban locations can provide that all-important scale, giving the viewer a sense of the storm's power and presence. Think tall buildings, roads, and junctions with ominous dark clouds dominating the land- or cityscape—a classic midwestern scene in America springs to mind.

Ambient light levels will likely be relatively low during a storm, or will get progressively lower as the storm builds. However, there is still likely to be a large difference in exposure levels between land and sky, so always carry a range of graduated (hard and soft) neutral density filters (up to 3 f-stops should be fine) in order to avoid blowing out the highlights in the brighter parts of the sky and clouds, and bring the foreground exposure out of the shadows. A general rule of thumb is to ensure that the sky is always at least 1 f-stop brighter than the land. So if the difference in exposure between a neutral tone in the sky (gray cloud or blue sky away from the sun) and a neutral tone on the ground (rock, a light-gray road, grass) is, say, 4 f-stops, use a 3 f-stop graduated ND filter to make the difference 1 f-stop.

Of course, the photographer may wish to silhouette darker clouds or foreground elements against, for example, a lone sunbeam peeping through the billowing storm clouds, in which case they should expose for the sunbeam and add a few f-stops of exposure compensation (i.e., overexposure to compensate for the camera's metering system, which tries to meter for 18% gray), while checking the histogram for blown-out highlights.

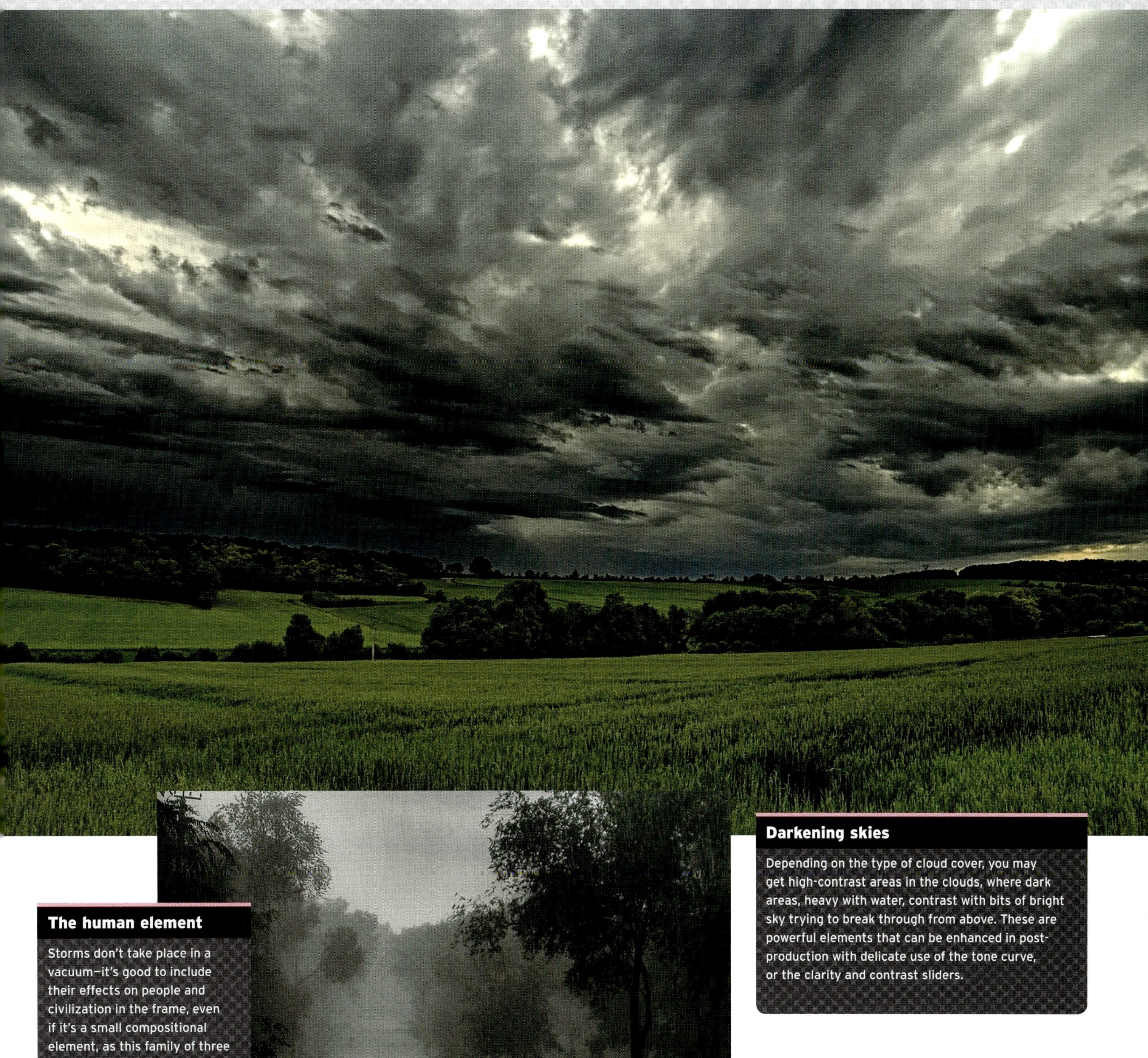

The human element

Storms don't take place in a vacuum—it's good to include their effects on people and civilization in the frame, even if it's a small compositional element, as this family of three taking cover from the rain.

Darkening skies

Depending on the type of cloud cover, you may get high-contrast areas in the clouds, where dark areas, heavy with water, contrast with bits of bright sky trying to break through from above. These are powerful elements that can be enhanced in post-production with delicate use of the tone curve, or the clarity and contrast sliders.

A polarizing filter is a very useful piece of equipment for any kind of photography involving the sky. Polarizers are used to cut down glare or polarize ambient light, which has the effect of making clouds pop out from a blue sky, adding a measure of depth to skyscapes. As a storm builds, a polarizer can add a punch to both zoomed-in shots and wider angle compositions. A common mistake, however, is to overuse the polarizer–that is to use too much strength–which can create an unrealistic look to the sky, as the blue is overly darkened. With circular polarizers try not to use the full amount of polarization available by only turning it halfway, for example.

Likewise, polarizers are strongest when used at a 90-degree angle to the direction of sun or light source, so be careful when using a wide-angle lens. A wide lens incorporates a wide angle of view, so when used with a polarizer it can result in a thin strip of dark blue sky in the center of the image (which is at 90 degrees to the sun and so is strongly polarized), while the effect is not present at the edges of the composition. This unwanted effect may be reparable in post-processing, however, if there are many elements in the scene it could be very time consuming. If in doubt, and particularly when using a wide-angle lens, leave the polarizer off.

Setting exposure will depend largely on your composition–whether a close-up of dramatic storm clouds or a wide-angle view. In general, stick to a low ISO setting to avoid noise, shoot in Raw mode (which offers more latitude in post-processing for altering exposure, Levels, Curves and so on), and think about the balance between aperture (for maximizing depth of field for focus) and shutter speed. For wider-angle views, higher aperture numbers (smaller aperture) are normally used, particularly when using foreground elements and lead-in lines in the composition. Bear in mind that apertures smaller than f/16 (such as f/22, f/32, and so on) can cause the unwanted effect of chromatic aberration, an artifact of optical physics that creates halos and ghosting around edges.

Smaller apertures (higher numbers) will also increase the shutter speed, which could create motion blur in the clouds as strong or severe storms will be moving or building quickly. A shutter speed of 1/125th of a second should freeze the motion, but that may require a higher ISO setting (try to stay under ISO 400, if possible) and a wider aperture, such as f/11, f/8 or even lower. The use of hyperfocal distances can maximize depth of field at wider apertures. The use of a tripod is always recommended for landscape photography–the ratio of useable to lost shots will be significantly improved.

Look out for specific storm characteristics and cloud formations and take a wide variety of shots. Storms change and evolve rapidly so work quickly but methodically, checking exposure on the histogram regularly, as

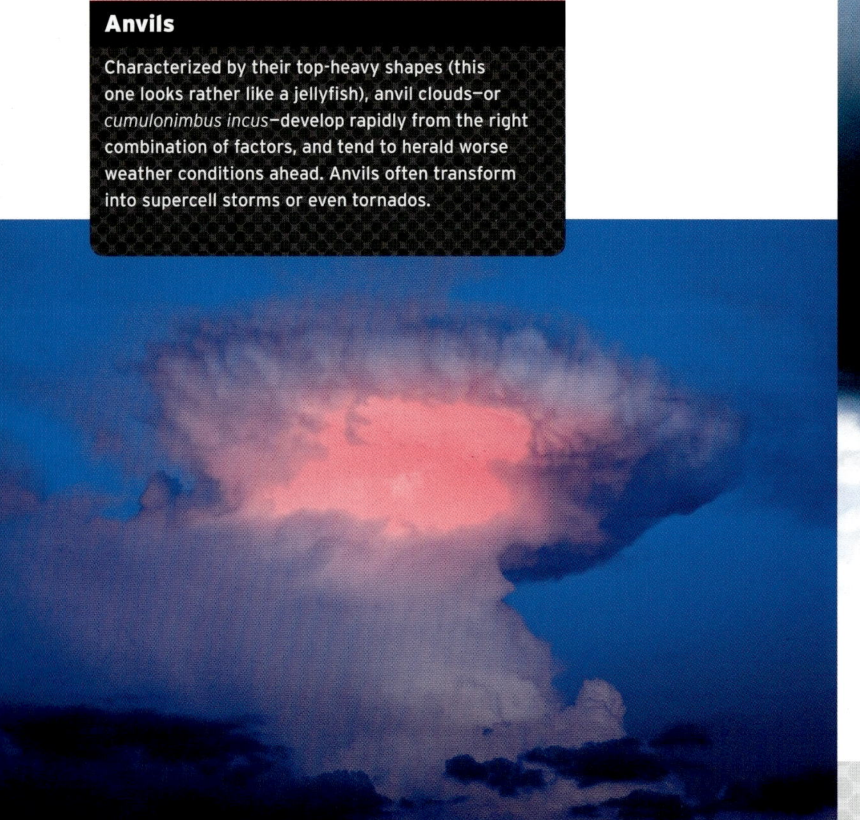

Anvils

Characterized by their top-heavy shapes (this one looks rather like a jellyfish), anvil clouds–or *cumulonimbus incus*–develop rapidly from the right combination of factors, and tend to herald worse weather conditions ahead. Anvils often transform into supercell storms or even tornados.

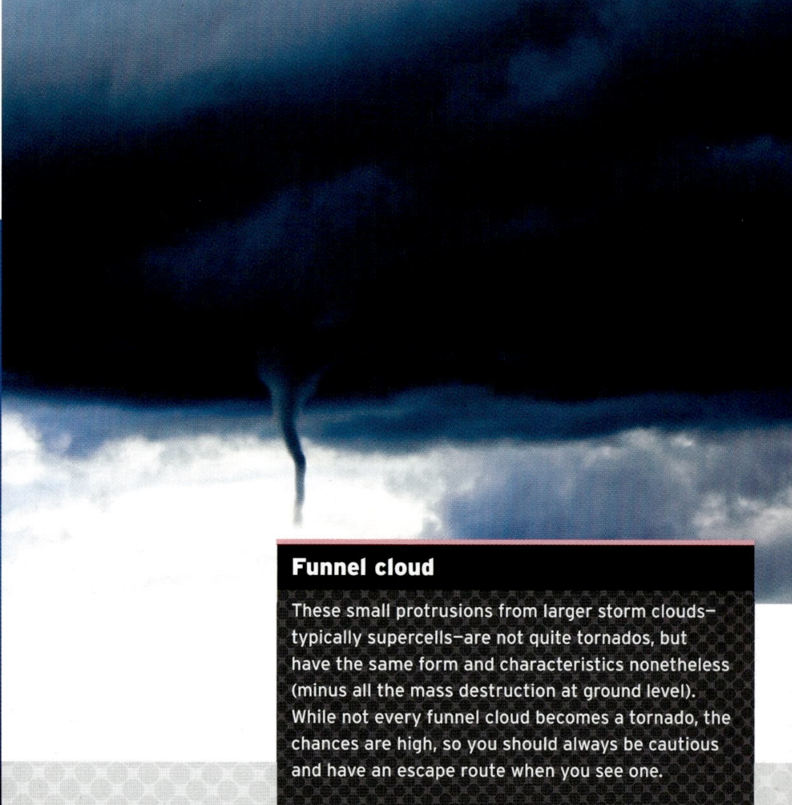

Funnel cloud

These small protrusions from larger storm clouds–typically supercells–are not quite tornados, but have the same form and characteristics nonetheless (minus all the mass destruction at ground level). While not every funnel cloud becomes a tornado, the chances are high, so you should always be cautious and have an escape route when you see one.

ambient light levels are likely to fluctuate significantly throughout the storm's journey.

It may also be prudent to retire to a sheltered location when the storm is directly overhead, as it is probably going to be very wet and windy, and the danger of a lightning strike is very real. On the upside, the best shots are likely to be achieved before and after the storm anyway, particularly when they occur as the sun is low in the sky. A final word of advice is to check the weather forecast beforehand—successful storm chasers are usually advanced amateur meteorologists.

Storm Cloud Characteristics

Anvils

When land is heated rapidly, warm updrafts of air known as thermals carry large volumes of moisture high into the atmosphere. As the water vapor rises, it cools and condenses into liquid—this process gives off latent heat, which warms the surrounding air further. When the rising air reaches the troposphere, it can rise no further. Instead it spreads out sideways, creating the characteristic anvil shape of a developing thunderstorm.

Funnel Clouds

A funnel cloud is the visible portion of a tornado, which is produced from condensation in a rotating column of cloud. Only when the funnel reaches the ground is the rotating mass called a tornado.

Gust Fronts

Gust fronts are formed by a leading downdraft of cold air and precipitation (rain or hail) as a thunderstorm builds. This cold front of air creates sudden changes in wind direction and speed and can appear in many forms, including a curtain of rain or a dust cloud. Its form can change unpredictably.

Haboobs

A haboob is the nickname given to a sandstorm or duststorm created by a gust front—from the outflow of cool air from the bottom of a forming thunderstorm. Haboobs often form in late evening, when the temperature difference between land (which has been heated up by the sun all day) and cooling air is at its greatest.

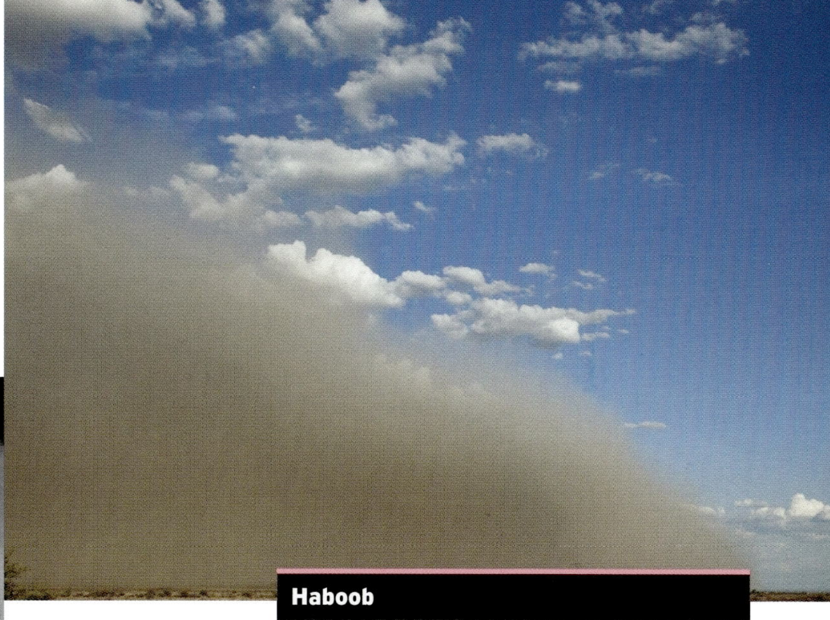

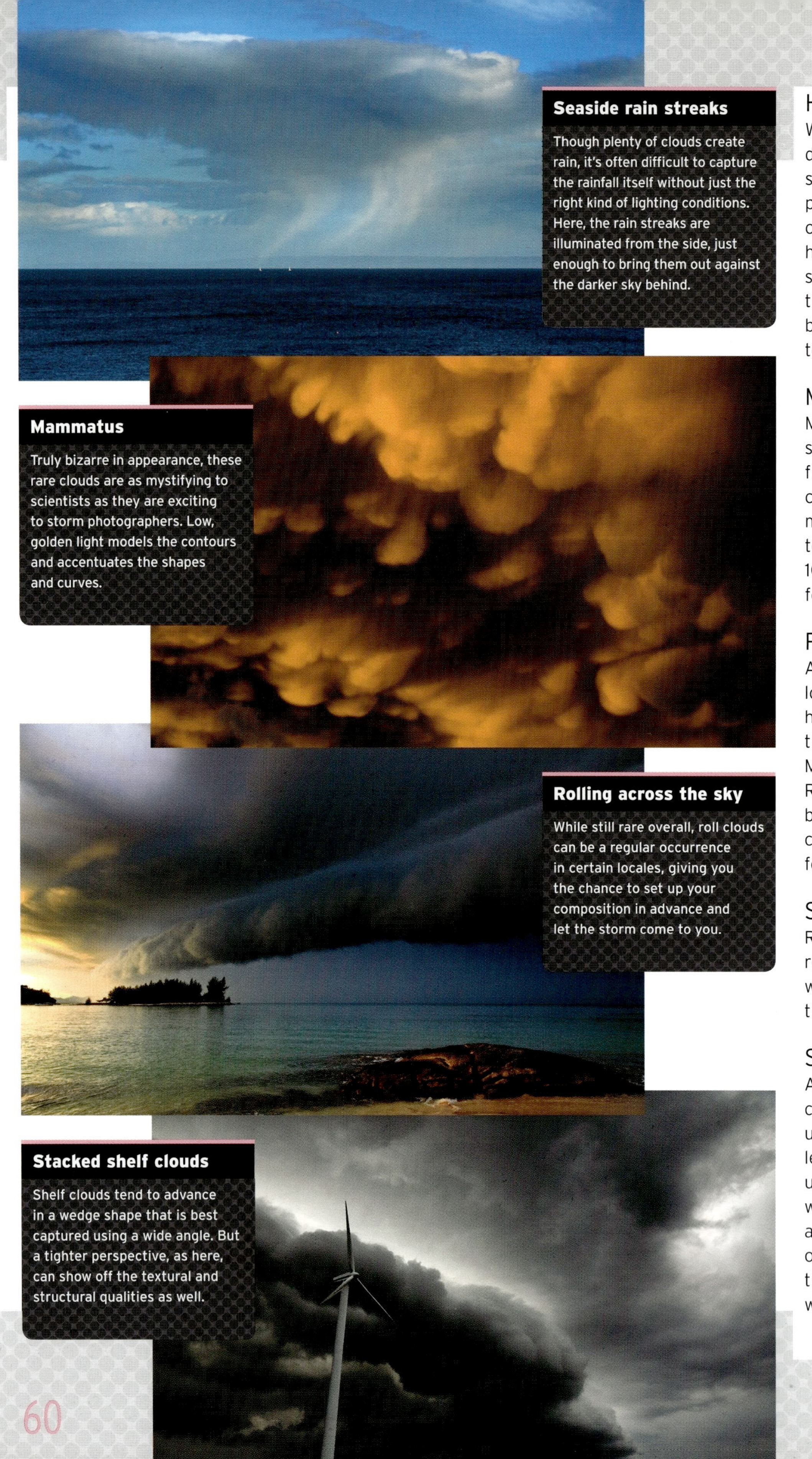

Hail or Rain Streaks

When a large storm forms, updrafts and downdrafts of air currents can be particularly strong. In such cases, streaks or lines of precipitation can be seen as they are carried on the strong vents of air. Where large hailstones have formed, these will appear as strong white lines running up and down the thunderstorm wall. In strong storms, hail will be caught in the updraft with rain falling next to it in the downdraft.

Mammatus

Mammatus clouds are undulating, pouch-shaped clouds that appear to hang down from the bottom of a thunderstorm's anvil cloud head. They form as a result of heavy moisture-laden air, which causes the cloud to sink–once relative humidity falls below 100% they disappear. Mammatus tend to form during severe storms.

Roll Clouds

A rare form of arcus cloud appearing as a low, tube-shaped mass stretching across the horizon. Appears to roll at high speed. One of the most famous frequent occurrences is the Morning Glory cloud in Queensland, Australia. Roll clouds are caused by a downdraft of air, but differ from shelf clouds in that they are completely detached from other cloud features. Equally fascinating and menacing.

Scud Clouds

Ragged clouds at the base of a storm, representing the region of precipitation as water vapor condenses in the cool air below the cloud base.

Shelf Clouds

A low shelf of cloud similar to a roll cloud but characterized by its attachment to the underside of a thunderstorm cloud. The leading edge shows clouds rising, while the underside often appears turbulent, a result of wind shear between the gust front and warm air closer to the ground, which creates a shelf of turbulence. Shelf clouds always appear at the leading edge of a thunderstorm, while wall clouds occur at the trailing edge.

Single-Cell Thunderstorm

Occurs when there is little wind shear at higher altitudes, which has the effect of slowing down the cycle of updraft and downdraft that feeds a strong storm. As a result, single-cell storms are poorly organized and defined, and generally last less than an hour. Multi-cell storms are made up of numerous short-lived single-cell thunderstorms running simultaneously or one after the other.

Supercell Thunderstorm

The severest of all thunderstorms, super-cells are formed from multi-cell storms when wind shear separates the downdraft and the updraft portions of a storm (which normally run next to each other). This separation can create a vortex of spinning air between the two. Supercells can create their own weather fronts and spawn tornados. Tend to last several hours.

Tail Clouds

Tail clouds appear as half-formed tornados, visible as a tail of cloud being dragged behind the area of downdraft in the cell of a storm. Tail clouds are in fact associated with precipitation, not tornados.

Updraft Cumulus

In strong storms, large masses of cumulus cloud can be clearly seen rising rapidly toward the anvil of the storm as a result of strong updrafts. Updraft cumulus clouds are often accompanied by hail streaks.

Updraft Turrets

Caused by strong updrafts near the ceiling of a mature thunderstorm, which force the cumulus clouds into turret shapes.

Wall Clouds

A wall or pedestal cloud is a large, towering, and rotating mass found at the base of a cumulonimbus cloud and indicates the point at which the updraft portion of the storm is strongest. Wall clouds can appear as a straight wall of cloud, but more commonly appear as a triangular-shaped plug at the base of the cumulonimbus.

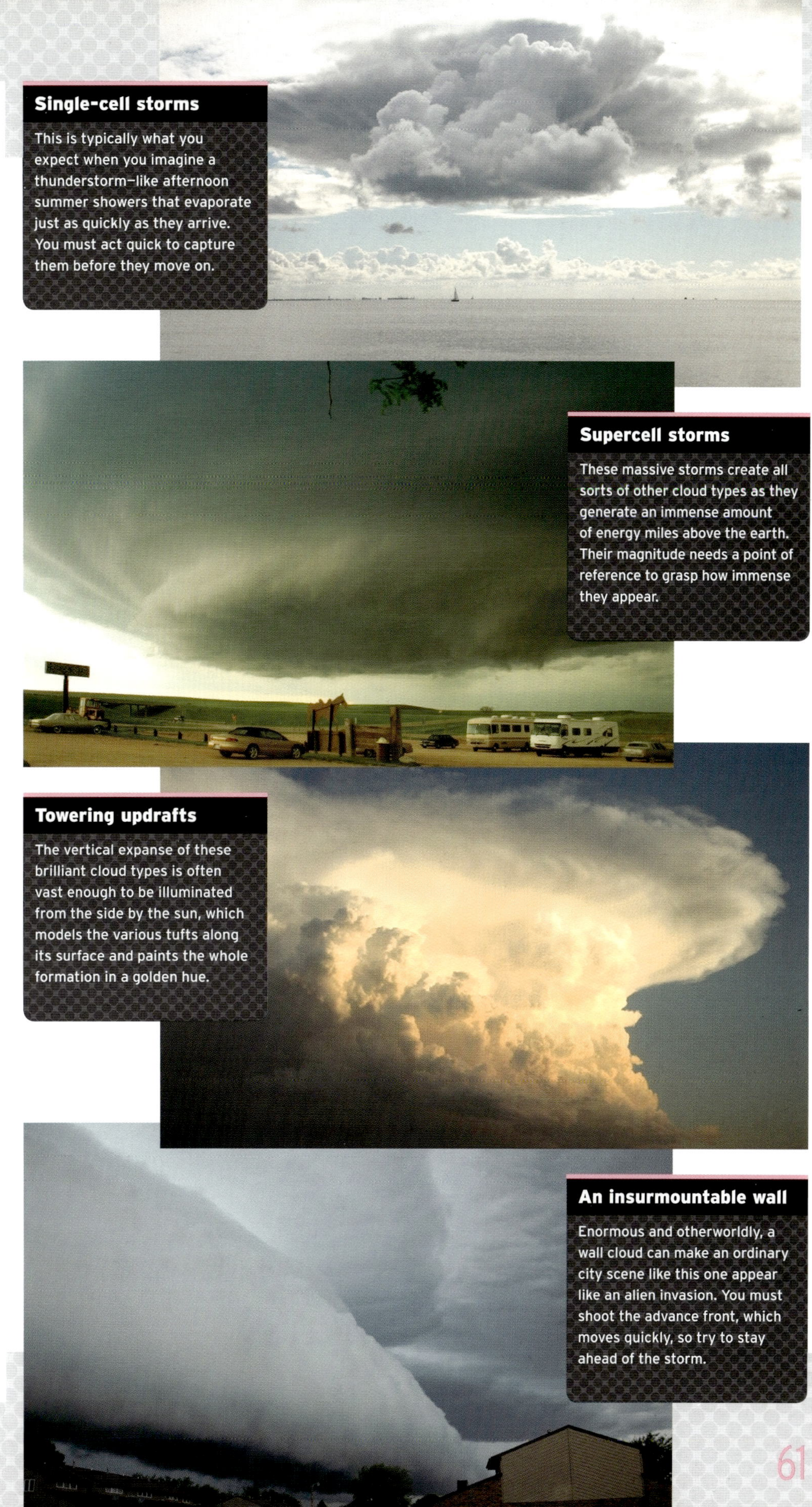

Single-cell storms

This is typically what you expect when you imagine a thunderstorm—like afternoon summer showers that evaporate just as quickly as they arrive. You must act quick to capture them before they move on.

Supercell storms

These massive storms create all sorts of other cloud types as they generate an immense amount of energy miles above the earth. Their magnitude needs a point of reference to grasp how immense they appear.

Towering updrafts

The vertical expanse of these brilliant cloud types is often vast enough to be illuminated from the side by the sun, which models the various tufts along its surface and paints the whole formation in a golden hue.

An insurmountable wall

Enormous and otherworldly, a wall cloud can make an ordinary city scene like this one appear like an alien invasion. You must shoot the advance front, which moves quickly, so try to stay ahead of the storm.

Tornados

One of the most coveted shots of the dedicated storm photographer is that of a fully formed tornado backlit by a low sun. While that may be the pinnacle of storm photography, capturing any tornado on camera is rare and provides breathtaking imagery regardless of the lighting conditions.

Tornados are one of the most awe-inspiring and powerful forces of nature, often leaving a path of devastation and destruction in their wake. They are associated with large or severe thunderstorms (often known as supercells—see page 61), which form as strong updrafts of warm, humid air rise rapidly into the sky reaching heights of 40,000 feet. While the precise reason is not known, these columns of warm air sometimes start to rotate. One suggestion is that different wind flows at different heights create wind shear and start to twist the column, creating a horizontal column of spinning air. If the column is caught up in the supercell updraft, its spin can tighten and it starts to rotate more rapidly (much like an ice skater spinning faster when their arms are pulled in closer to their body).

This horizontal spinning column of air underneath the storm base is known as a funnel cloud, and is a strong indicator that a tornado is about to form. If the funnel cloud then touches the ground, having been forced into a more vertical orientation by the downward force of rain or hail, it becomes a fully fledged tornado. Potential tornados can also be identified by warning signs such as a dark green sky, large hailstones, and a powerful, train-like roar. Waterspouts are tornados that form over a body of water.

Around 1,000 tornados occur every year, 75 percent of which happen in the US. Tornado Alley, comprising South Dakota, Nebraska, Kansas, Oklahoma, northern Texas, and eastern Colorado, is home to the most powerful and frequent tornados. A tornado can happen at any time of the day and in any season, but most tend to occur in spring and summer between 3pm and 9pm as the ground is heated rapidly throughout the day, or as a result of the rapid build-up of powerful thunderstorms.

Tornado winds are the strongest on Earth, reaching up to 250mph (400kph), and can cut a path 1 mile (1.6km) wide for over 31 miles (50km). They are, however, quite short-lived for the most part. Tornados themselves travel at speeds of around 18mph (30kph), but can top 68mph (110kph). Tornados are categorized as F1–F5 severity, with F5 the strongest but accounting for less than 1 percent of all tornados. Twisters can easily lift people, trains, vehicles, and entire houses into the air, and flatten wide swathes of land. They cause around 80 deaths and 1,500 injuries every year.

Funnel touchdown

As a funnel cloud makes touchdown and becomes a tornado, the debris it stirs up from the ground makes an excellent compositional counterpart to the tip of the funnel, and can create a powerful shot showing off impeccable timing. It's usually possible to predict where the touchdown will occur, as the funnel swells and reaches steadily closer to the ground.

The most obvious and difficult task in tornado photography is that of locating a tornado, which are unpredictable and difficult to forecast accurately. However, weather forecasts, Internet discussion groups for fellow storm chasers, meeting up with a storm-chasing crew, or joining a paid-for tour can yield a better success rate.

Local and national weather services also issue severe weather warnings. In the US, for example, the National Oceanographic and Atmospheric Administration (NOAA) provides a public radio service—the National Weather Service (NWS)—which broadcasts severe weather warnings, watches, and hazard information 24 hours a day. In the UK, meanwhile, the Met Office website issues ongoing weather alerts and warnings.

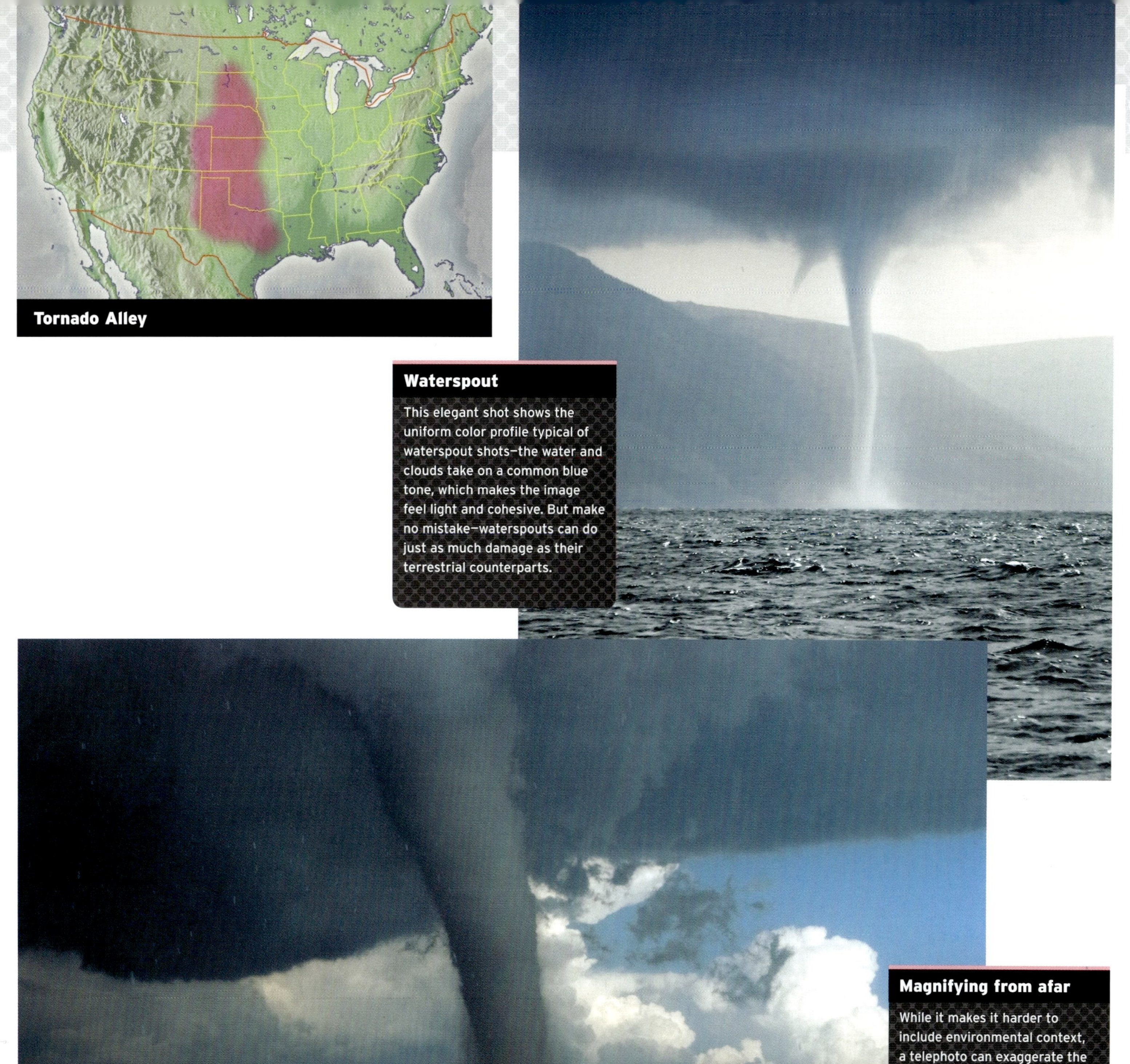

Waterspout

This elegant shot shows the uniform color profile typical of waterspout shots—the water and clouds take on a common blue tone, which makes the image feel light and cohesive. But make no mistake—waterspouts can do just as much damage as their terrestrial counterparts.

Magnifying from afar

While it makes it harder to include environmental context, a telephoto can exaggerate the proportions of a distant tornado. These trucks along the highway do a good job of giving scale to this massive twister as well.

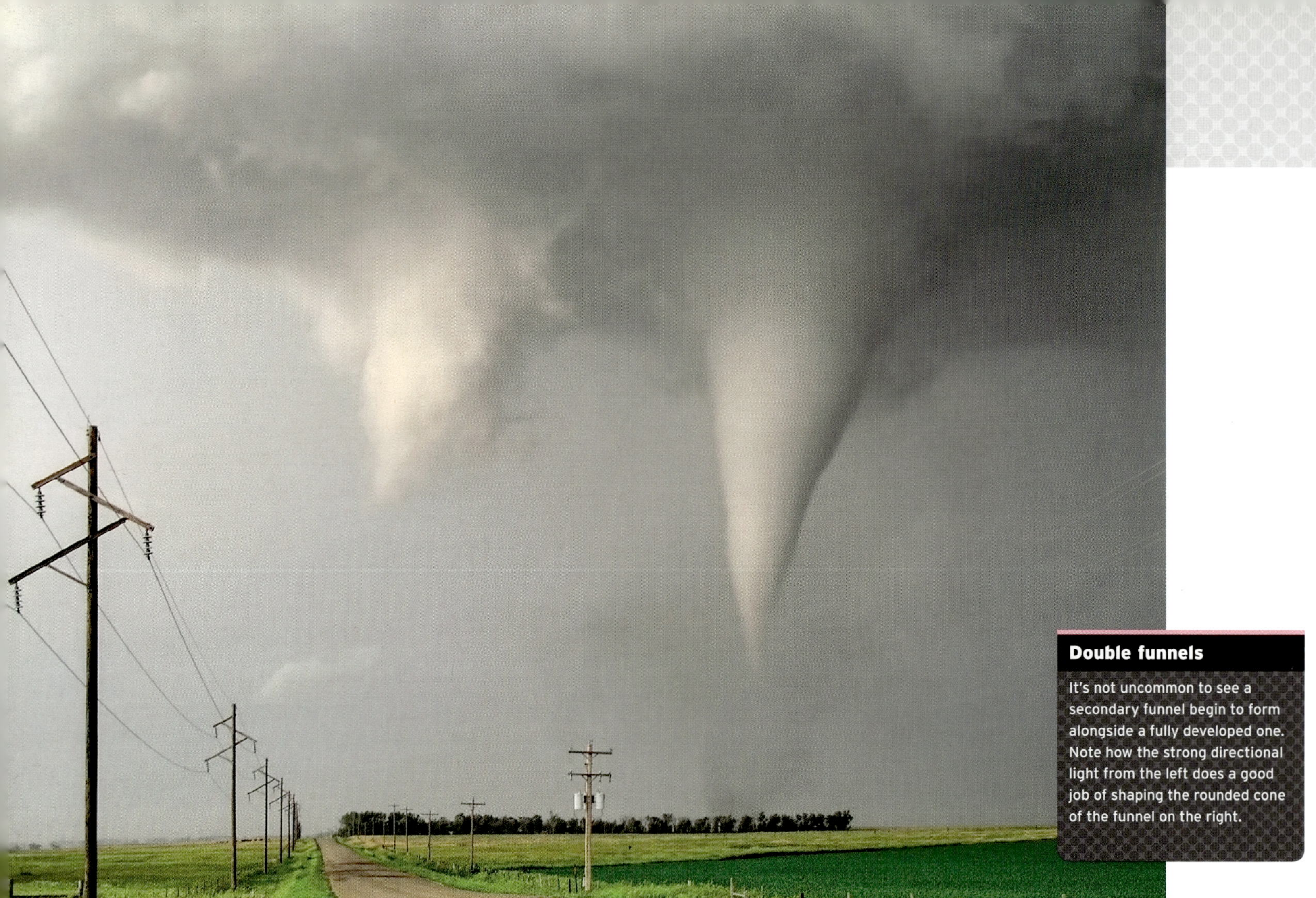

While weatherproofing of camera and lenses is advisable, the best tornado images will be captured when out of the rain or hail curtain. Heavy precipitation does nothing for outdoor images, not to mention camera equipment. Luckily, tornados and supercell storms do have a predictable structure, with precipitation usually associated with, and confined to, the area at the base of the storm underneath the updraft. This means that it is usually possible to locate oneself with a clear view of the tornado, without the photographer getting wet and without the tornado being obscured by rain or hail.

As a rule, tornadic storms move in a west to east direction (in the US and UK at least), which means that a location south and east of the storm will usually provide a clear view of the storm structure and, therefore, any tornados that form under the base of the storm. A distance of around 1 mile (1.6km) is the generally accepted safe distance from which to photograph a potential tornado. This also provides the opportunity to capture the entirety of the storm, including foreground interest (to provide perspective and scale) and the supercell cloud structure. The use of a tripod is advisable, as light levels will be low. As usual, ISO should be kept to a minimum to decrease image noise and improve image quality.

A wide-angle lens is ideally suited to this type of shot, although farther distances may require a standard or telephoto lens. Of course, if a tornado is well formed and relatively near, the use of a telephoto lens could capture a frame-filling shot of the spiraling mass of air, dust, and debris. Where possible, use ambient side-lighting or backlighting—from a low sun that has managed to punch through the underneath of the storm base—which will provide dramatic images and make the tornado funnel stand out better from the background.

Front-lighting will often make the tornado funnel appear white (as it is illuminated from the photographer's perspective), while backlighting and side-lighting will generally make it appear dark gray or black—although such lighting will also provide rim-lighting of the tornados edges, making it pop out from the background with greater dimensionality.

If the photographer is with a team of experts, a guide or a certified tour, it may also be possible to move under the wall cloud and nearer to the heart of the storm (while avoiding the dangerous tornado), which will provide a different view of the power of the storm. Light levels will be low, so again a tripod may be necessary in order to maximize depth of field (if using small apertures). In this scenario, try including buildings, streets, or people with the ominous supercell directly above, or tilting the camera slightly upward to magnify the apparent size of the storm in relation to the surrounding environment.

Composition will depend on distance, view, focal length, and other factors, but look for shapes and lead-in lines. If in doubt, stick to

the rule of thirds for composing wider landscape images. Ensure enough memory storage to allow you to continue shooting, and let the creative juices run free. The last thing the photographer wants is to run out of storage space—or battery power—in the midst of a rare and powerful experience.

Once the tornado has passed, it may be possible to visit the path of the storm. Here, a more photojournalistic approach might be adopted to capture the trail of devastation and damage that the tornado has caused. In extreme cases, entire villages may be razed to the ground, and there may well be people requiring help. In less severe storms, capture upended cars, uprooted fences, and fallen telephone poles.

Even if a tornado fails to materialize, supercell storms are awesome sights in their own right. There will often be stunning sunsets or glorious post-storm lighting. So keep shooting!

Supercell scenery

The massive storm clouds from which tornados emerge can be difficult to fit into frame, but they do provide an excellent backdrop—particularly when compared to a relatively tiny sliver of land along the bottom.

Hurricanes

Hurricanes represent one of the most violent and ferocious natural forces on Earth. Also known as cyclones or typhoons, hurricanes occur in the Atlantic, Pacific and Indian Oceans, and the Caribbean Sea, and can wreak widespread havoc, devastation and loss of life. As well as extremely strong winds, hurricanes can cause large tidal surges, which add to the damage.

Hurricane Katrina, which flooded and destroyed New Orleans, was one of the costliest and deadliest hurricanes in history, while the 1970 Bhola Cyclone in Bangladesh is ultimately blamed for causing the deaths of up to 500,000 in the months after its impact. Hurricanes are to be respected, and for the photographer safety is of paramount importance at all times, above and beyond the need to get the image. For this reason, shooting the build-up and the aftermath of a hurricane is the safest approach.

Hurricanes are formed from two essential ingredients: warm water and moist warm air, which is why they tend to originate in specific regions of the world. When water surface temperatures exceed 27 degrees Celsius and they meet warm, humid winds, water vapor evaporates rapidly from the ocean surface, and rises high into the air. As it rises, it encounters cooler air, causing it to cool and condense. This condensation process releases latent heat, which in turn heats the surrounding cooler air causing it to rise. This makes room for more warm air to evaporate from the water surface.

This cycle feeds the growing storm, drawing in more warm, moist air and transferring more heat from ocean to atmosphere. If the rising air was taken away by the action of

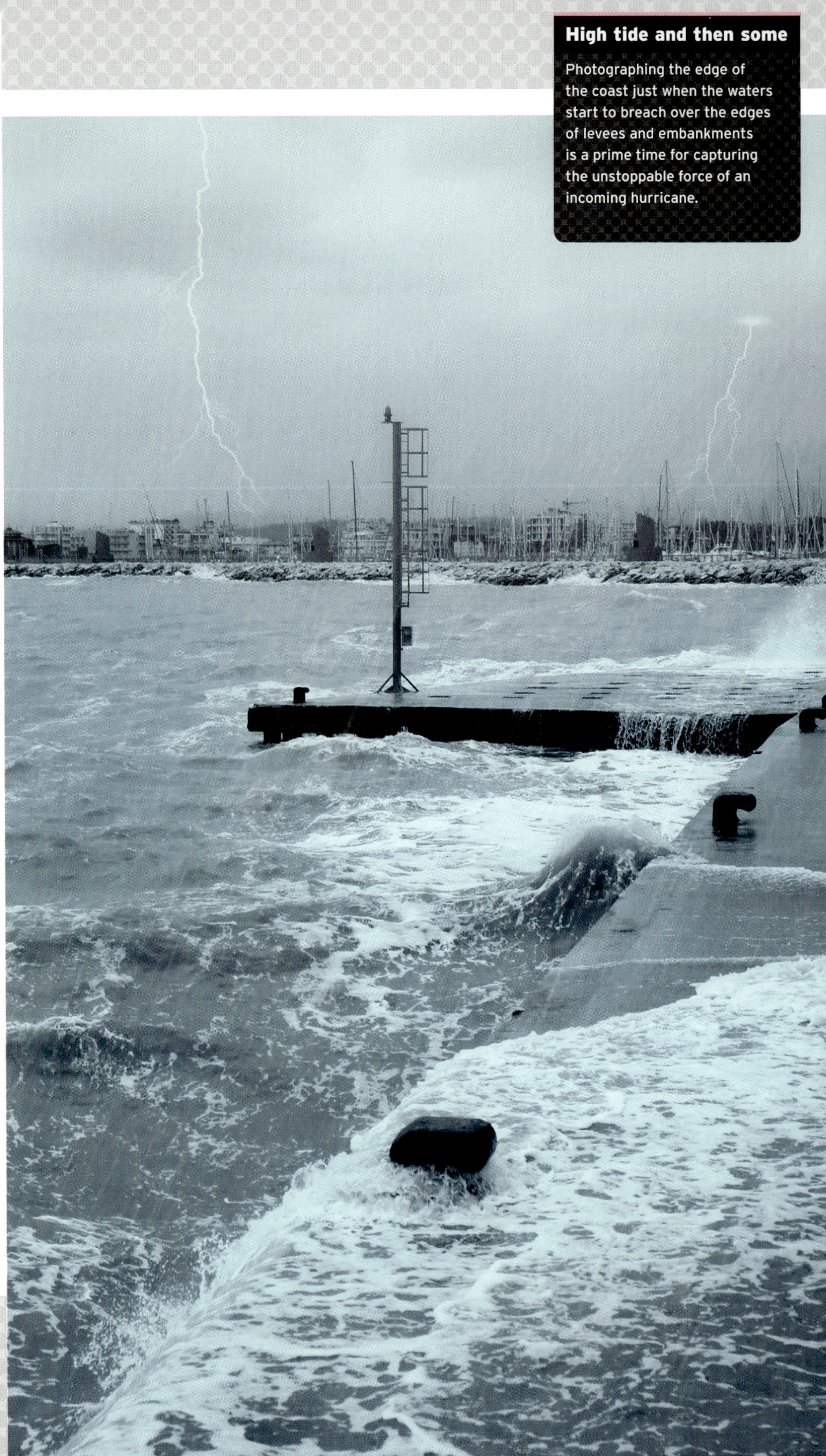

High tide and then some

Photographing the edge of the coast just when the waters start to breach over the edges of levees and embankments is a prime time for capturing the unstoppable force of an incoming hurricane.

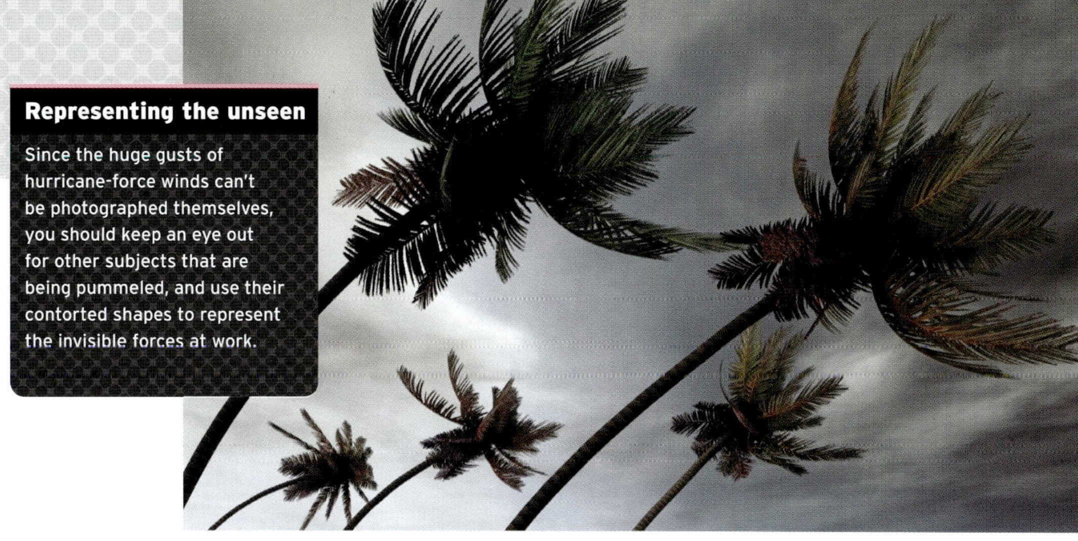

wind shear at higher altitudes it would create a thunderstorm, and the heat may be dissipated, but when there is no wind high up, the cycle continues.

Converging winds near the ocean's surface increase the circulation of warm air and combined with high-altitude winds that draw warm air away from the storm's center start to create a wind pattern that spirals around a relatively calm and cloud-free center, known as the eye, with increasing strength—the classic cyclone effect. The effect is an intense area of low pressure at the center.

The hurricane passes through three distinct stages as it grows: tropical depression, with wind speeds less than 38mph (62kph); tropical storm, with wind speeds between 39-73mph (62.8-117.4kph); and hurricane, with wind speeds above 74mph (119.1kph).

Hurricanes are categorized in intensity by the Saffir-Simpson Hurricane Wind Scale, ranging from categories 1 to 5, measured as the sustained wind speed over 1 minute. Category 1 storms consist of wind speeds between 74-95mph (119-153kph) and will cause some damage to buildings, while Category 5 storms exhibit wind speeds over 155mph (249kph) and can cause catastrophic damage.

For the photographer, traveling light is important in this situation as there will be little time, or shelter, for changing lenses mid-storm. Carrying a standard zoom lens or even a fast prime lens is a slight compromise in terms of ideal focal length range coverage, however, time will be limited and conditions will be anything but ideal. So traveling light, without having to consider changing lenses, will focus the photographer on the job in hand. Fix a clear or UV filter to the lens to protect it from loose, flying objects.

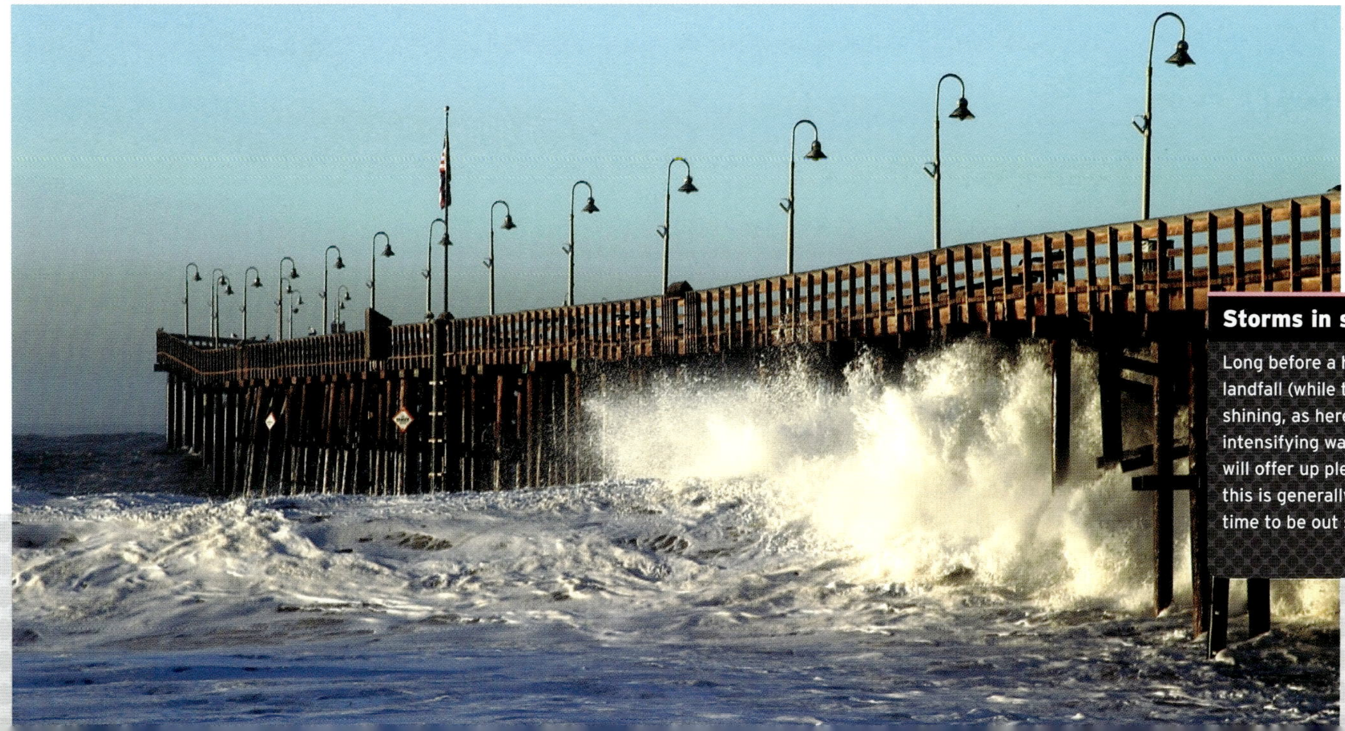

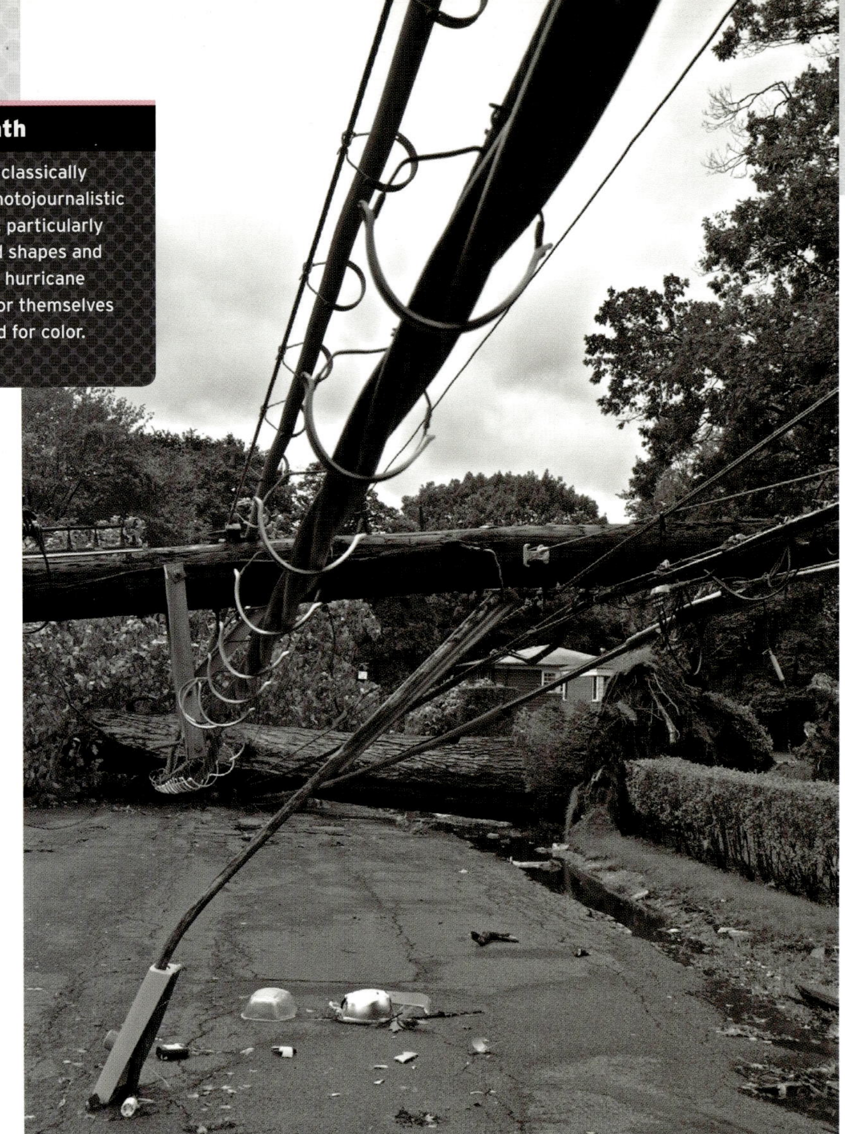

The aftermath

Black and white classically lends itself to photojournalistic representations, particularly as the contorted shapes and twisted metal of hurricane damage speak for themselves without the need for color.

Hurricanes will be well forecast in advance, allowing for appropriate travel and planning. Wind speeds onshore will steadily build in intensity up to 24 hours before landfall, which is a good opportunity to shoot the building storm. For any kind of violent or severe weather, there will be a lot of movement involved—flying debris, windblown trees, sheets of rain, high waves and tides—so sequences of shots of the same scene tend to work well in telling the story.

Sea fronts and coasts provide dramatic locations for capturing the growing impact of the storm as it heads toward land, with waves crashing over sea walls, a high tidal surge that swamps normally dry land, and so on. Try to include foreground interest that captures the storm status of the scene—for example, palm trees being bent over by the strong winds, people having to push against the wind to walk around, cars being swamped by large waves on the sea front, blowing debris and normal objects.

The ambient light is likely to be relatively low, and unfortunately a tripod is typically of limited usefulness—it will vibrate in strong winds, rendering it useless, and adding unnecessary weight and bulk to the photographer. Again, not ideal, but handheld photography will allow much more flexibility and maneuverability, as events move quickly.

The faster the lens, the better, bearing in mind that wide apertures will reduce depth of field. Wide apertures allow for faster shutter speeds, which should largely avoid the issue of camera shake at slow shutter speeds.

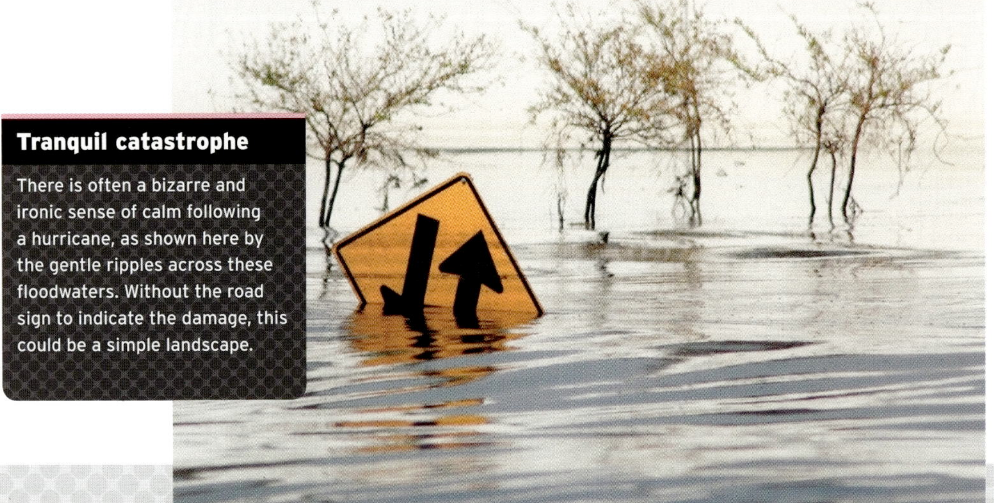

Tranquil catastrophe

There is often a bizarre and ironic sense of calm following a hurricane, as shown here by the gentle ripples across these floodwaters. Without the road sign to indicate the damage, this could be a simple landscape.

Shooting Tips:

> As one of the most serious and powerful elemental forces discussed in this book, extreme care and caution should be exercised at all time—and under no circumstances should you interfere with rescue or recovery efforts after the storm has passed.

> The need for fast shutter speeds in low-light conditions means wide apertures and high ISOs are essential.

Setting the camera to Aperture Priority and autofocus is probably the best option, allowing the photographer to concentrate on shooting. Try using bracketing of exposures too, whereby the camera takes three shots at a setting under and over the normal set exposure (e.g. one f-stop below; set exposure; one f-stop above).

In severe hurricanes and tropical storms, structural damage will be occurring, with roofs blown off houses, lampposts and trees uprooted, and large-scale debris, such as trashcans and signs, flying through the air. So the photographer should have a pre-organized safe shelter to which they will retreat as the storm intensity reaches its height. This is of paramount importance. Proper plans should be in place—including where the shelter is, and how the photographer is going to reach it before the full force of the storm hits. A contingency plan is also a good idea, for example, if the route to the shelter becomes blocked.

Take shelter during the landfall of the storm, but if the eye of the storm is passing through the close vicinity, it is possible to go back outside and enjoy the eerie calm and clearness of the storm's eye. Depending on the storm, its speed, severity, and tightness, the eye can last anywhere between 5-35 minutes. The sun or moon is likely to be visible, as well as the inner wall of the following half of the storm. Take shots of the damage caused so far—however, be aware that the following part of the storm is often stronger than the first section, so work quickly and ensure that the shelter is within easy reach. After a quick shoot, the best thing to do is to sit out the severest part of the remainder of the storm. Remember that shots of people taking shelter during the storm will also add to the story.

Once the storm has eased sufficiently that it is safe to venture outdoors, the photographic approach will naturally lean toward photojournalism. There is likely to be a lot of structural damage to buildings, collapsed buildings, debris, smashed street furniture, displaced vehicles, and possibly flooding.

The most striking imagery is often taken after a severe storm, telling the story of the effects of the storm and its aftermath. Strong cloud formations and clear light occur after storms and will add to the atmosphere. Dramatic sunrises and sunsets also follow powerful storms, so try juxtaposing the ugly effects—the devastation, damage, and debris—against a glorious and beautiful sunrise or sunset to create bittersweet images or images that hint at emotive concepts, such as survival and hope.

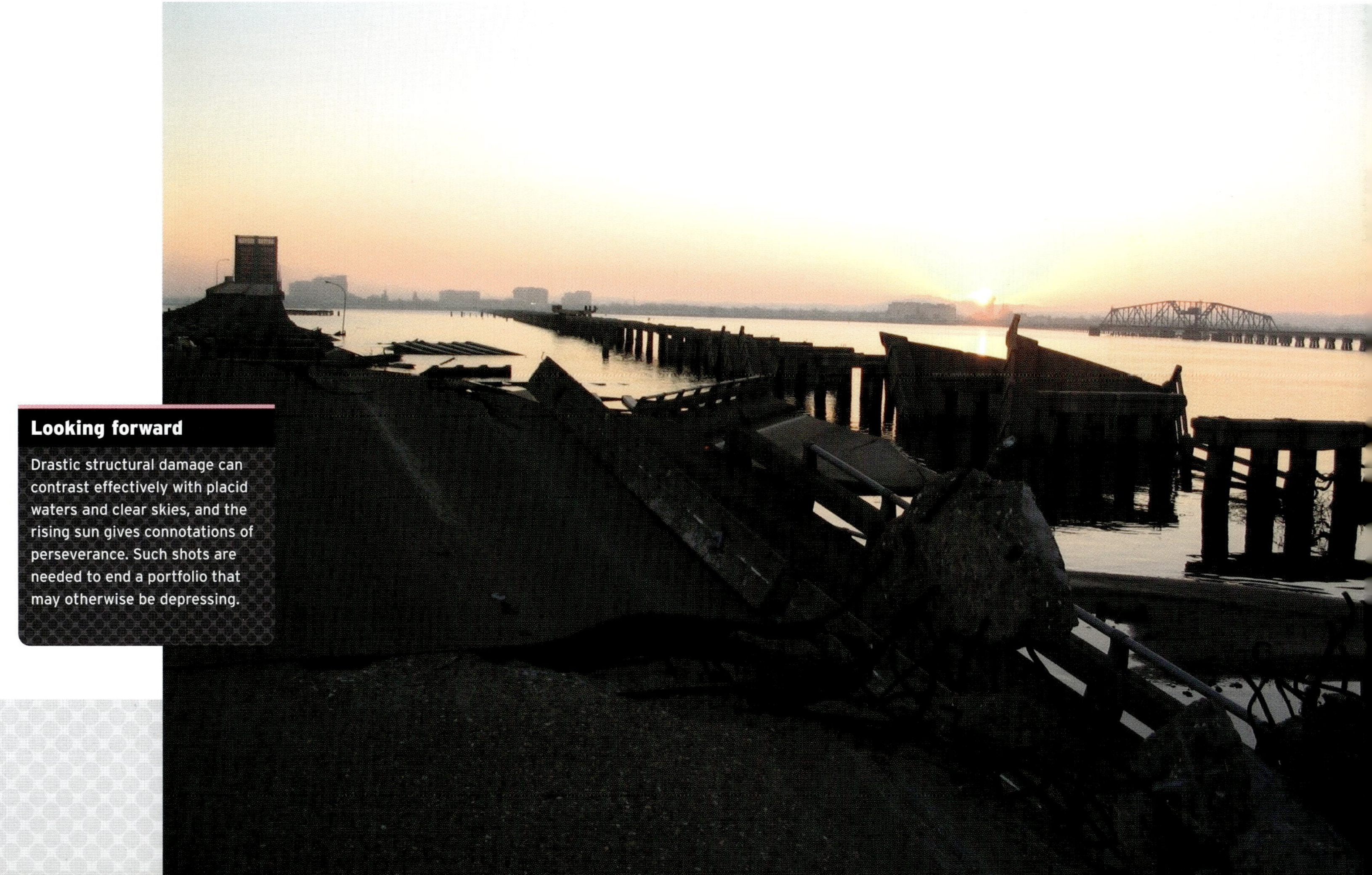

Looking forward

Drastic structural damage can contrast effectively with placid waters and clear skies, and the rising sun gives connotations of perseverance. Such shots are needed to end a portfolio that may otherwise be depressing.

Sandstorms

The sight of a mile-high wall of sand and dust racing across the landscape at rapid speed is an awesome and frightening spectacle. While sand or dust storms—also referred to as haboobs or simooms in different parts of the world—look terrifying, they are relatively harmless, which allows photographers to capture some amazing and surreal images, either from a distance or from within the heart of the storm itself.

Of course, vision in the heart of some sandstorms will be limited to a matter of meters but, equally, a fading or mild sandstorm can pervade the atmosphere with an eerie red or orange glow, making for fantastic photo opportunities.

Sandstorms usually occur in arid or semi-arid regions of the world, and are caused by the combination of drought and wind. A sandstorm can be associated with a gust front from a large thunderstorm, strong winds caused by local weather patterns and microclimate, or a large temperature differential between two regions. These winds pick up large amounts of dry soil, dust, and sand particles and transport them, by suspension, across the land.

Sandstorms can be colossal, reaching a few miles in height and carrying large volumes of suspended particles at speeds of up to 80mph (130kph)—although this will depend on the prevailing wind speed. Larger sandstorms appear as a towering wall or bank of dust rolling across the landscape.

The term sandstorm is usually applied when the phenomenon occurs in deserts, such as the Sahara and the drylands around the

Arabian peninsula (where they are known as simooms). The United States, Iran, Pakistan, India, and China are other regions of relatively frequent sandstorms. Storms in urban areas are often referred to as dust storms. Some theorists suggest that sandstorms are becoming more frequent as a result of climate change, poor irrigation, and intensive farming techniques, which loosens topsoil even further.

While sandstorms remain relatively unpredictable, some of the more technologically advanced countries, such as the US and China, are able to predict and forecast sandstorms to a fairly accurate degree using forecaster's experience combined with satellite imagery to monitor air and dust movements. Some sandstorms can be forecast up to three days in advance, giving the photographer ample warning to prepare for a trip and scout out potential locations and shots.

Before shooting any sandstorm, the photographer should take steps to protect their equipment from the damaging grains of dust and sand, which will not only obscure the sensor but also cause expensive damage to electrical (and mechanical) parts. Use a clear plastic bag, or even a rain cover, that completely encloses the camera and lens—apart from a hole at the front through which the lens glass can protrude—but also allows enough flexibility to easily change camera settings, control function menus, and view the LCD screen. This should prevent sand clogging up the camera's sensitive electronics. Even for weather-sealed cameras, it is better to play it safe and use protective covering.

Crossing the street

Not all sandstorms are so dense that they completely obscure the sky—often they can simply serve as an interesting element to push the composition to the next level.

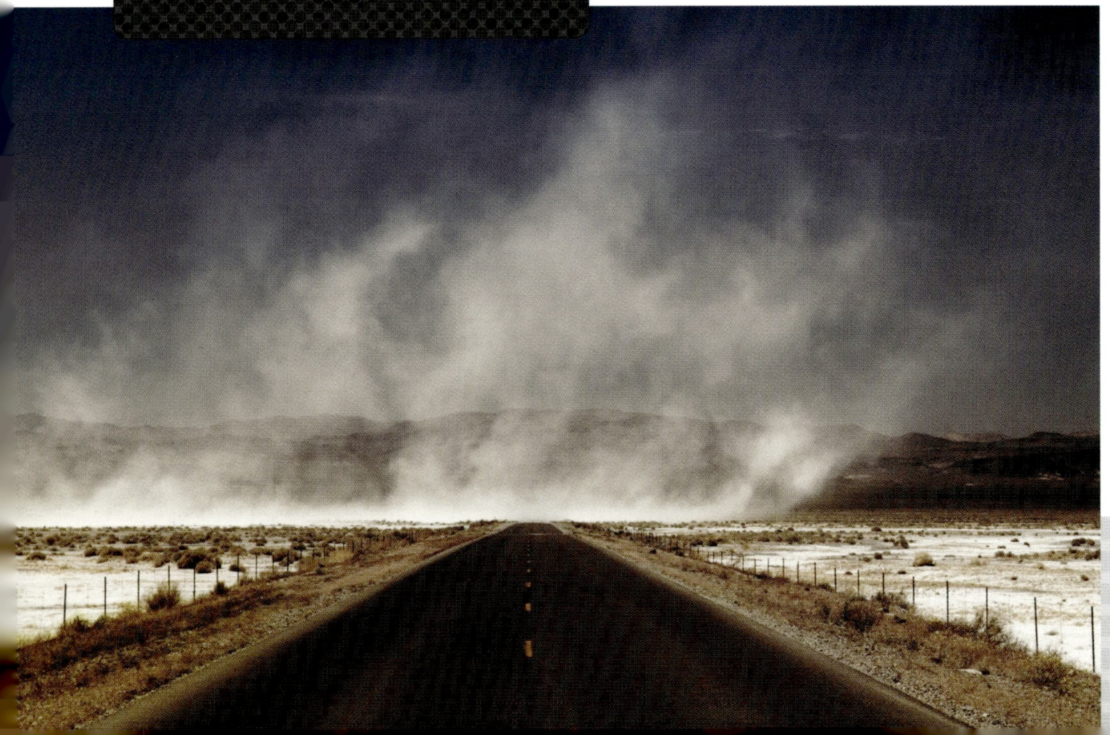

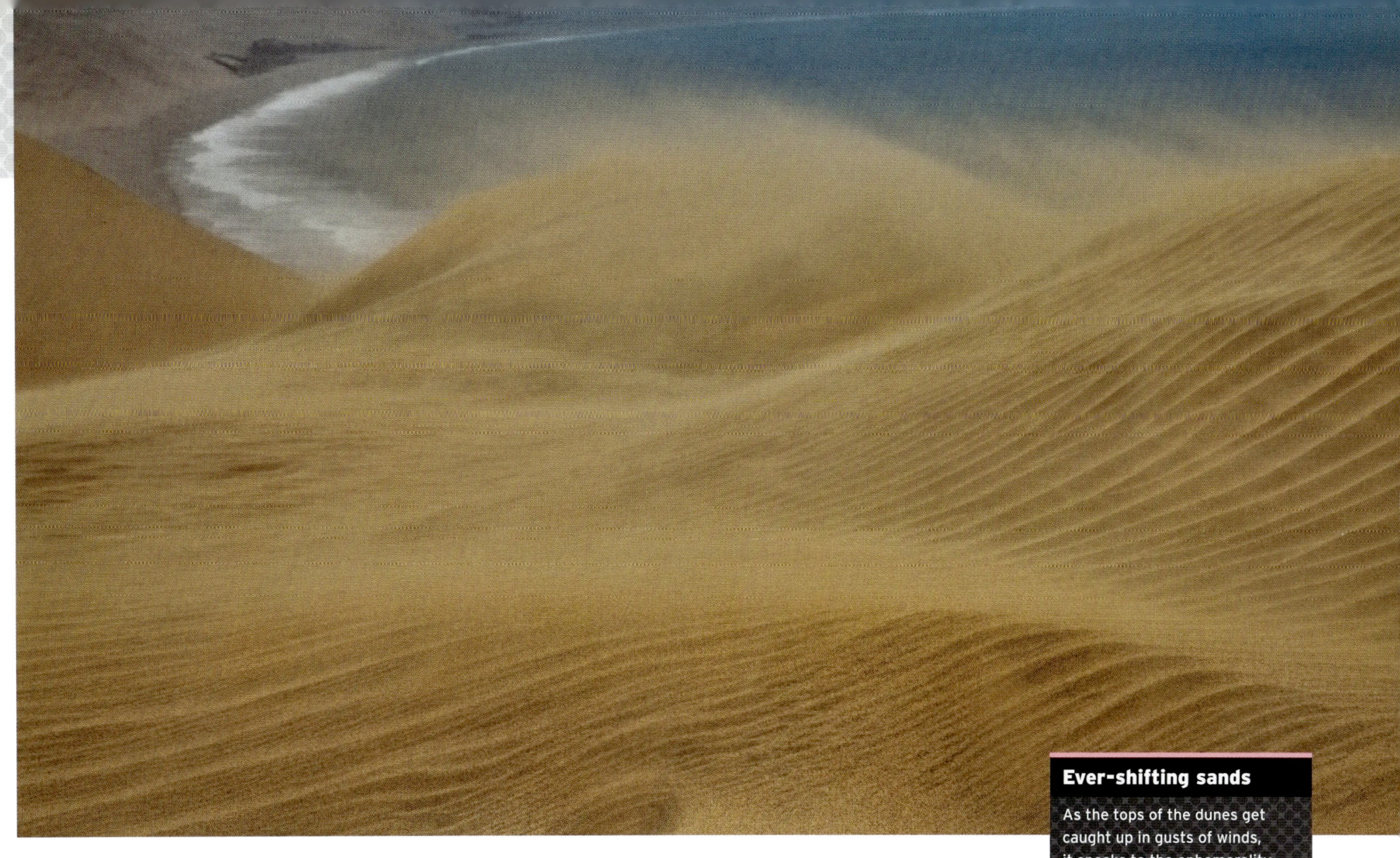

Shooting the leading wall of a large sandstorm can provide dramatic images, particularly if it can be composed in context with man-made or natural landmarks to provide perspective and scale. Where possible, seek a high vantage point, but anywhere in front of the storm is also fine. If possible, a view slightly to the side of the advancing storm, that is looking along the leading edge of the sand cloud, will provide nice lead-in lines looking along the front wall of the storm into the distance.

Depending on the speed that the sandstorm is moving, the photographer should have ample time to capture a sequence of shots showing the advancing wall of sand. If there is an interesting focal point or landmark, before, during, and after shots can provide an engaging and compelling image sequence. Using a tripod will allow lower ISO settings and smaller apertures for maximizing depth of field (start at around ISO 100–200 and f/11, check the histogram and adjust as necessary) and will help to remove camera shake from the resulting slower shutter speeds. Using a standard-to-telephoto zoom lens (around 70–200mm or 50–135mm) allows the photographer to shoot the advancing storm from a reasonable distance, highlighting its size, as well as offering a wide range of focal lengths to track the advancing storm as it bears down on the photographer without the need to change lenses.

Remember that the point of focus will change as the sandstorm gets closer. Furthermore, there may be large amounts of auxiliary dust and debris as the storm approaches, so switch the camera to manual focus as the autofocus may not be able to lock on to the swirling sand (for lack of contrast), and remember to refocus at intervals as the storm advances.

You will need:

> A weather-sealed DSLR

> A wide-angle to standard zoom lens OR standard prime lens

> A telephoto zoom (if shooting from a distance)

> A tripod

> Plastic zip-locked bags for camera with elastic hole for lens

> A lens cloth

> Lens cleaning liquid (to remove dust from lens)

> Appropriate clothing (including a scarf for mouth and face protection, and protective glasses for the eyes)

A Time-Lapse Approach

Another technique for providing dramatic footage of an advancing sandstorm is to use time-lapse photography. In summary, time-lapse photography involves taking numerous still images, which are set to expose automatically by the camera or third-party accessories at regular intervals for a set period of time. The interval between each image will depend on artistic intent, the speed of movement of the storm, and the length of final footage required. Remember that in general, for a smoother-looking final video output, exposure length should be half the interval time—for example, a one-second exposure taken every two seconds.

Exposure settings will depend on the ambient light levels, weather, height of the storm and the time of day. If the photographer is shooting an advancing wall of sand from a reasonable distance, it may be possible to use a graduated neutral density (ND) filter to balance the exposure between ground and sky. However, this may not always be practical, so expose for the important section of the image—the leading wall of the sandstorm, which will be fairly neutral in tone—then check the LCD screen and take it from there.

Shooting in a Raw format might allow the photographer to salvage any moderately blown highlights in the sky, but if the dynamic range is too high for the sensor, try a few well-known techniques (presuming there is enough time as the sandstorm approaches) such as using a graduated ND filter, taking two exposures rapidly (one for the ground, one for the sky—but bear in mind that the storm will be moving), or recomposing to avoid bright areas of the sky.

Remember that as the storm approaches, if the bank of sand is high then it is likely to blot out the sun, and, likewise, reduce ambient light levels, so keep checking the exposure histogram on the camera's LCD. If shooting time-lapse footage, switch the exposure setting to Aperture Priority, which will take care of the falling ambient light levels, without the photographer having to constantly change the exposure.

If the sandstorm occurs at dusk or night, higher ISO settings such as 800 and wider apertures such as f/2.8 or lower will be required; but slow shutter speeds may make motion blur of the sandstorm unavoidable, depending on its speed. This can be mitigated to by staying at a reasonable distance from the storm—motion will appear faster the nearer to the storm the photographer is. Imagine a high vantage point shooting a sandstorm as it approaches and engulfs a streetlight-illuminated town at dusk.

Whether the photographer decides to stay as the sandstorm front actually hits is a personal choice, although video footage is likely to capture the drama of the moment of impact better than still images. In this case, the photographer should ensure that their face and eyes (and other parts of the body) are not exposed to the sandblasting that can occur! It may be prudent to retire to a vehicle or building before the leading wall hits.

In the midst of the storm, it is likely that conditions are too uncomfortable for walking around—again, it will depend on the severity and speed of the storm, the type of particles it is carrying, and personal choice.

However, be ready for the beautiful tail-end of the sandstorm and its slow-settling aftermath, which often provides stunning quality of light with a Martian-like red, yellow, or orange atmosphere. Streets are likely to be relatively empty, providing the opportunity for eerie and surreal images.

Ambient light levels will be low, so set a relatively high ISO setting (start at ISO 800), a wide aperture (again, something like f/4, if light levels allow), which will allow handheld shutter speeds if necessary. Use the tripod as much as possible, but the opportunities need to be taken quickly before the sandstorm settles and clears, so handheld shooting may be preferable.

However, a tripod will allow longer shutter speeds, which can sometimes let the camera to see through the haze better than the human eye, providing edges, such as buildings, with real clarity in juxtaposition with the hazy atmosphere.

Look for silhouettes of structures, such as bridges and piers disappearing into the haze, or shoot famous landmarks literally in a different light. Or capture tall buildings from ground level, looking directly upward—as they would in low-lying mist, skyscrapers will fade and disappear into the sandy haze. Figures of people huddled together and walking in silhouette within the glowing cloud of sand and dust also work well.

Lights of all kinds—streetlights, house lights, car headlamps, and so on—will be dimmed and can look beautiful in the red/orange haze. The thick atmosphere may also allow for shooting directly into the sun (if it is visible at all) creating unusual and dramatic lighting and compositions.

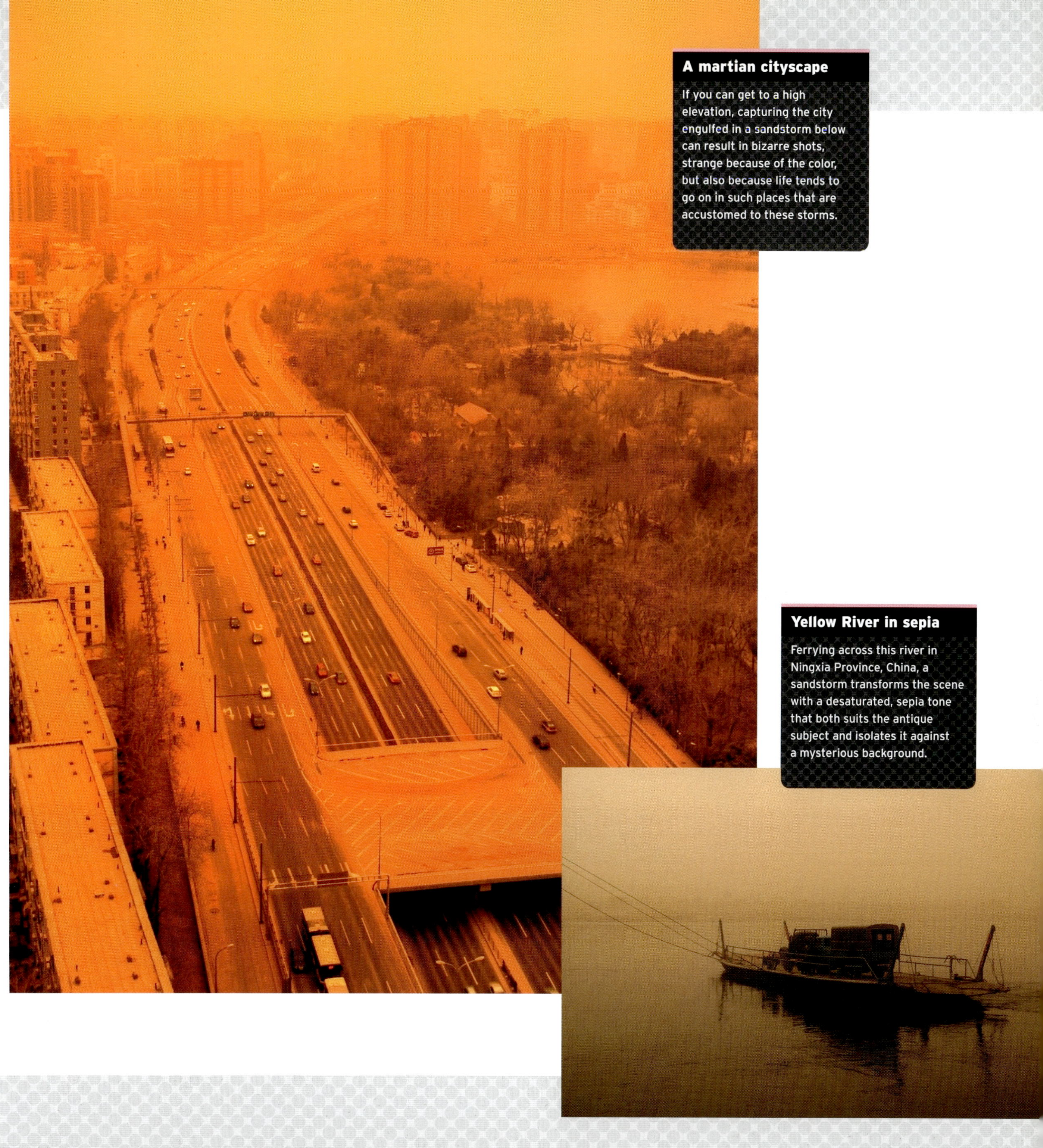

A martian cityscape

If you can get to a high elevation, capturing the city engulfed in a sandstorm below can result in bizarre shots, strange because of the color, but also because life tends to go on in such places that are accustomed to these storms.

Yellow River in sepia

Ferrying across this river in Ningxia Province, China, a sandstorm transforms the scene with a desaturated, sepia tone that both suits the antique subject and isolates it against a mysterious background.

Fire

More than any other elements, fire presents an imminent danger. It is by its nature wild, uncontrolled, and erratic. And as a result, it appears in photography as an exotic, exhilarating, and stunning subject. Even in its more metaphorical incarnations—the Aurora Borealis, for instance, or lightning—it embraces an unpredictable dynamic that brings images to life, showcasing an inevitably fleeting moment that could have been captured only at that very instant. This, of course, places much greater demands on the photographer, who must compose scenes rapidly as they appear, all the while ensuring their own safety and security. Fortunately, there are a number of tricks and tips, contained herein, to aid in your infernal quest—and we even end this chapter with a discussion of the post-production techniques unique to fire and other incandescent lighting conditions.

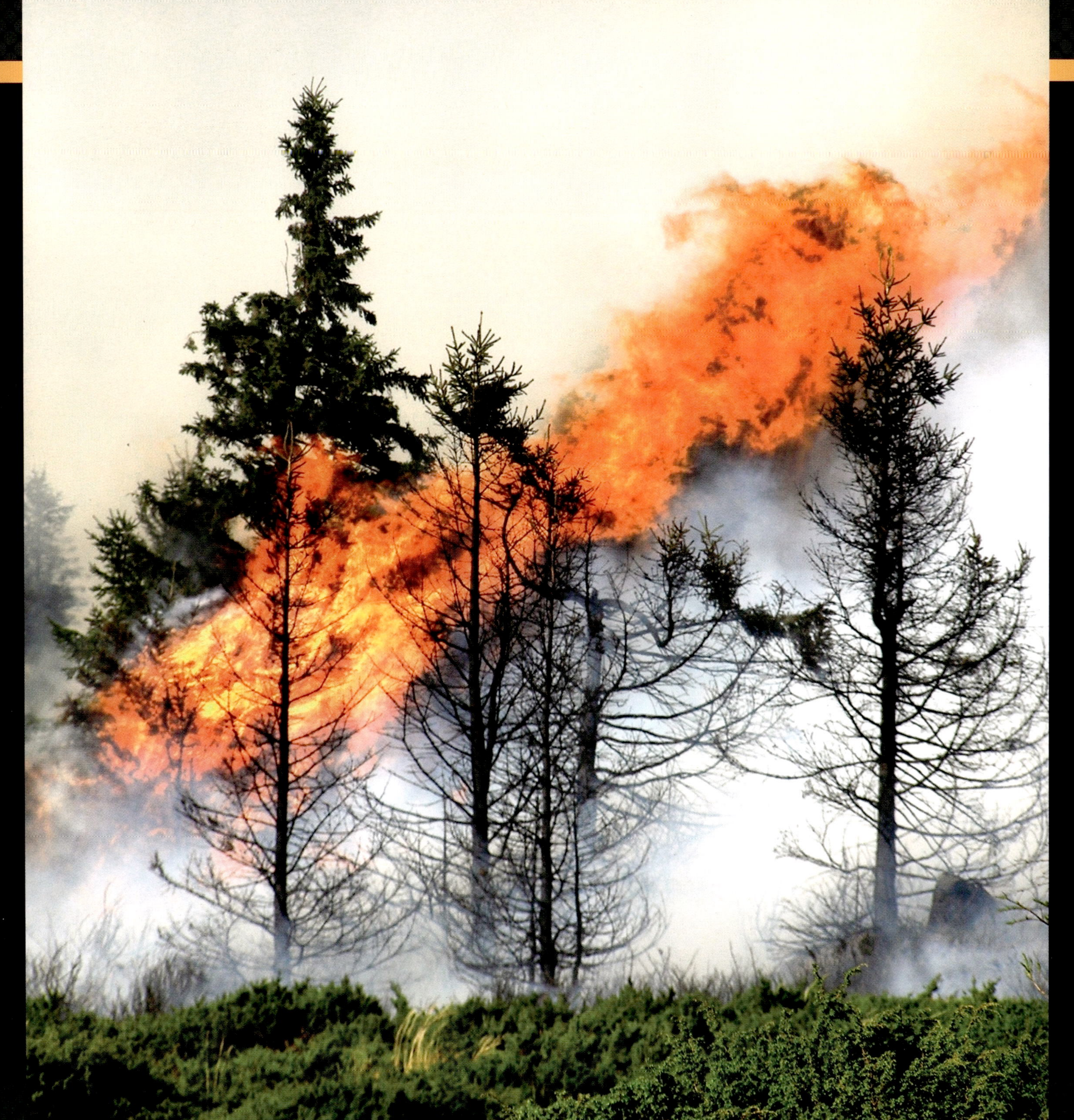

Aurora Borealis

The Aurora Borealis, or Northern Lights, are as magical as their name suggests. Around once a month, the night skies of the most northerly regions on the planet are illuminated by an ethereal, dancing light show of vivid colors and patterns as nature puts on one of its most dazzling spectacles high up in the Earth's atmosphere.

Named after the Roman goddess of dawn, Aurora, and the Greek name for north wind, Boreas, the Aurora Borealis are created when solar radiation from the sun (known as the solar wind) hits the Earth's magnetic field. The shape of the magnetic field means that these energized solar particles are channeled toward the Earth's poles, where they collide with atoms high in the Earth's atmosphere (the thermosphere).

These high-energy collisions ionize the oxygen and nitrogen atoms in the Earth's atmosphere, emitting photons in the process. These emissions are visible as vivid reds, greens, and blues. The southern hemisphere's counterpart is known as the Aurora Australis, or Southern Lights.

The appearance of the Northern Lights can vary from a soft greenish glow low on the horizon (the nearer to the poles, the higher the position of the lights) to pinwheels of vivid light and on to rippling curtains of different colors, such as reds, blues, and purples that stretch across the entire sky.

Unfortunately for most photographers, the Northern Lights tend only to appear in the most northerly latitudes—between 65 and 72 degrees North (and South)—such as Alaska, Canada, Iceland, and northern Scandinavia. Although, they are occasionally seen as far south as Scotland in the UK and have even been reported in Georgia in the US. The lights mainly appear between October and May, and can only be seen at night as they are relatively dim compared to daylight.

For those lucky enough to travel to see them, careful planning and preparation are required in order to maximize the opportunity. Consider working with a local guide, or contacting a fellow photographer who knows the region and is happy for you to tag along. The Northern Lights are notoriously elusive so expect long periods of waiting—but stay alert as they can appear at any moment.

Shooting in the Dark

As a nocturnal subject, a tripod is again the essential requirement—alongside the DSLR, of course. At times the Northern Lights can span the entire horizon or sky, so a wide-angle lens is ideal for capturing a 180-degree field of view—a fisheye lens is ideally suited to the wide vistas demanded by the subject.

Carry a range of focal lengths in order to capture a variety of compositions and perspectives. A mid-range zoom, such as a 24-105mm, enables a good mix of compositions in a compact size and weight. The settings on the camera will need to be set to full Manual.

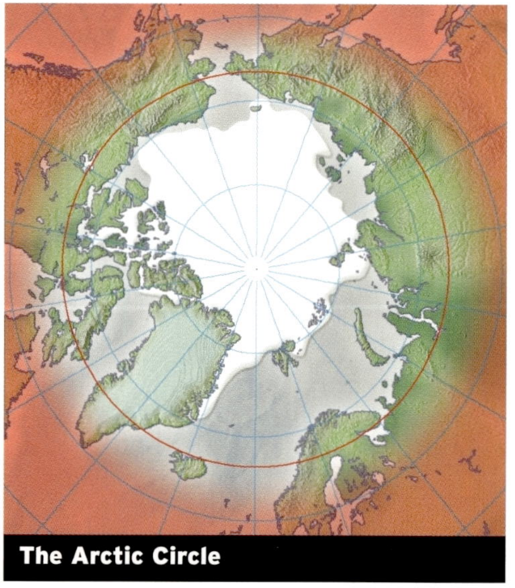

You will need:

> An accurate weather forecast (clear skies are essential)

> A DSLR with decent manual controls that can be operated with gloves on

> A sturdy tripod

> Remote shutter release

> Plenty of extra batteries—kept warm inside a coat pocket

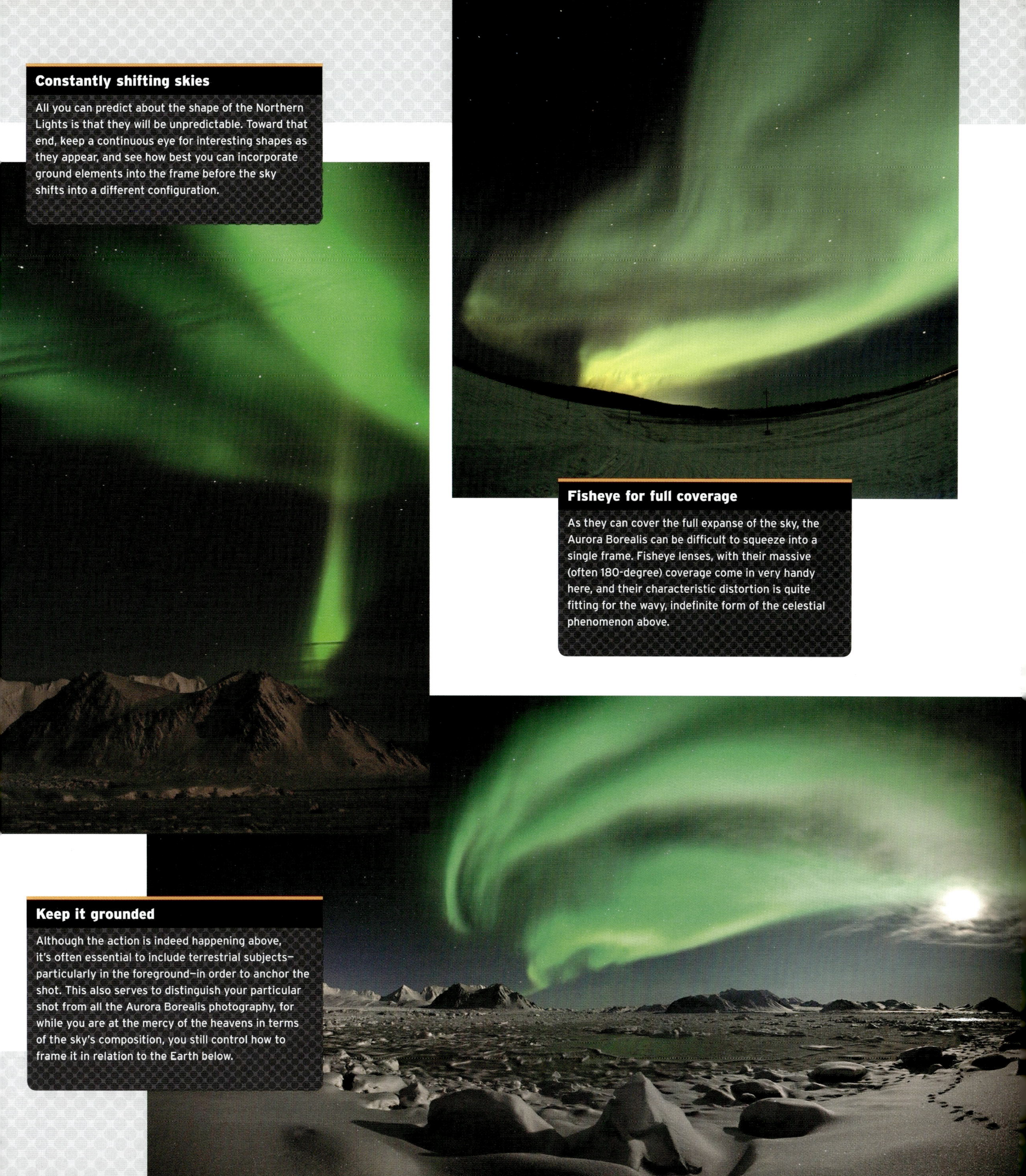

Constantly shifting skies

All you can predict about the shape of the Northern Lights is that they will be unpredictable. Toward that end, keep a continuous eye for interesting shapes as they appear, and see how best you can incorporate ground elements into the frame before the sky shifts into a different configuration.

Fisheye for full coverage

As they can cover the full expanse of the sky, the Aurora Borealis can be difficult to squeeze into a single frame. Fisheye lenses, with their massive (often 180-degree) coverage come in very handy here, and their characteristic distortion is quite fitting for the wavy, indefinite form of the celestial phenomenon above.

Keep it grounded

Although the action is indeed happening above, it's often essential to include terrestrial subjects—particularly in the foreground—in order to anchor the shot. This also serves to distinguish your particular shot from all the Aurora Borealis photography, for while you are at the mercy of the heavens in terms of the sky's composition, you still control how to frame it in relation to the Earth below.

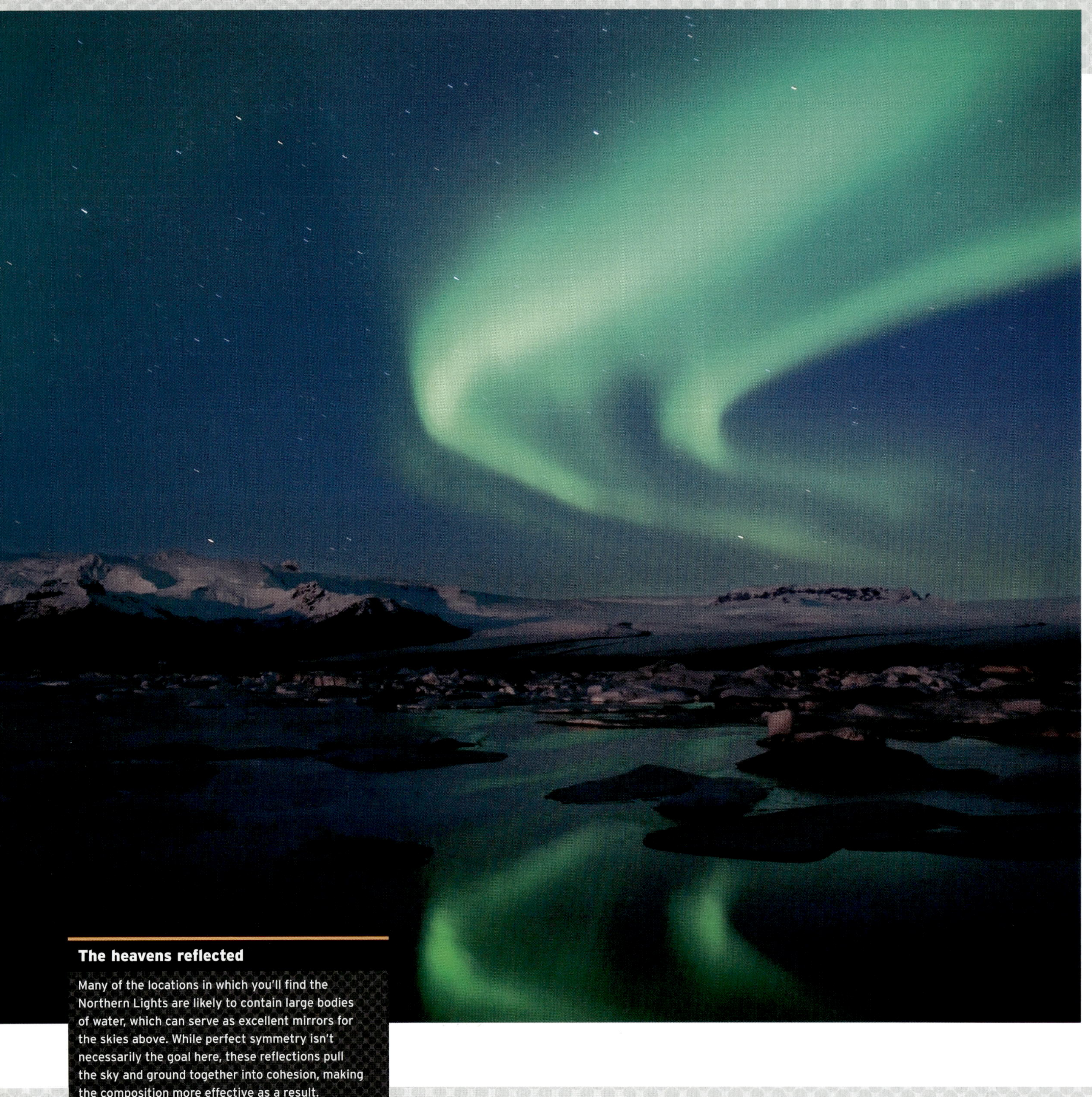

The heavens reflected

Many of the locations in which you'll find the Northern Lights are likely to contain large bodies of water, which can serve as excellent mirrors for the skies above. While perfect symmetry isn't necessarily the goal here, these reflections pull the sky and ground together into cohesion, making the composition more effective as a result.

Long exposures will be required to allow the sensor to gather enough light. For that reason, use wide apertures (low numbers, such as f/4.0) to minimize light to the sensor.

Long exposures also tend to generate noisy images. Shoot at as low an ISO as possible to reduce noise, balancing ISO against length of exposure time. Most cameras will have a noise reduction function, which will automatically reduce noise and produce a clearer image. Be aware that in-camera noise processing results in double the exposure time (time taken for the exposure and the same time again for noise processing).

Shooting in Raw mode can avoid the need for in-camera noise reduction (use noise reduction software applications or functions during post-processing), and offers much more flexibility for fixing under- or overexposed images post-shoot.

Use an illuminated foreground subject, where available, to aid focusing. Otherwise, focusing at infinity is a safe option bearing in mind the shallow depth of field at wide apertures. If in doubt, take some test shots and check focus by zooming in on the images on the LCD screen on the back of the camera.

Conversely, ensure that light pollution levels are at a minimum—this is normally the case in northerly latitudes—as with long exposure times, stray light sources can wreak havoc with the final exposure.

Getting correct exposure can be tricky, as the aurora may not be present when setting up. A good starting point is f/4, ISO 400 and an exposure time of around 15 seconds. But as soon as the aurora start, always remember to check the first exposure. No doubt the excitement will kick in, so fight the desire to just start shooting away. Check the first exposure, and adjust as necessary (perhaps in increments of 5 seconds up or down).

There is no replacement for taking test shots, studying them on the back of the camera, and altering exposure settings as required. Always re-check the histogram periodically as the Northern Lights vary significantly in their intensity, sending exposure levels soaring up and down. With a little experience, setting the right exposure will become more intuitive.

Northerly latitudes often mean cold temperatures so pack warm clothing and photographers need to ensure that they are carrying enough battery power (camera battery life is shorter in cold temperatures). Wrapping a towel or blanket can provide enough warmth to prolong battery life.

Foreground subjects, such as a building, trees, mountain ranges and lakes, can complement the majesty occurring overhead and provide perspective for the viewer. So move around and try out different compositions before the aurorae appear.

Most of all, be respectful of the extreme conditions that will be encountered. Dress appropriately and fully research the challenges of the local environment.

Lightning

Lightning is a spectacular force of nature. Few can fail to be stirred by the awesome power of a towering thunderstorm in full flow. Whether striking a building, forking dramatically to the Earth or illuminating dark, billowing clouds from within, lightning is on the wish list of many photographers.

Lightning strikes occur around three million times every day around the world—or around 30 flashes per second on average. At any one time, it is estimated that there are 1,500 thunderstorms occurring on the planet.

Unfortunately, lightning is also one of the most unpredictable forces of nature. It is impossible to forecast with any accuracy exactly when and where lightning will strike, posing a real challenge for photographers. But following a few simple rules can significantly improve the chances of success.

Lightning is a result of electrical discharge around thunderstorm clouds—these discharges may be between clouds, within clouds, or between clouds and the Earth. It can be caused by a variety of atmospheric conditions, including thunderstorms, volcanic eruptions, and dust storms.

The formation of lightning is still not fully understood by scientists, but in simple terms,

it is thought to be caused by charged water molecules, which separate into negative and positive poles within a cumulonimbus cloud. This causes the cloud itself to become charged, and when the charge is large enough it releases electrical energy as lightning. The lightning bolt also momentarily heats the surrounding air to around 40,000 degrees Fahrenheit (22,200 degrees C), which creates thunder.

The most common form of lightning is cloud-to-cloud (CC), with about twice as many CC thunderstorms occurring in mid-latitudes as cloud-to-ground (CG) strikes. Cloud-to-cloud strikes are also commonly known as sheet or heat lightning

While spectacular itself, sheet lightning is usually of less interest to photographers than cloud-to-ground lightning, which is commonly described as forked lightning—or more formally as bead, staccato, or ribbon lightning, each with a different appearance depending on the prevailing conditions.

There are two main challenges for photographers: first, the unpredictable nature of cloud-to-ground lightning; and second, its brief duration, lasting less than a second. This means that even if the photographer is lucky enough to be pointing the camera in the right direction, very few will have sufficiently fast reflexes to capture a lightning strike using the camera's shutter button or a remote release. The result is often an empty image! Having said that, some photographers claim with experience to be able to hit a reasonable success rate by just relying on their reflexes.

A more tried and tested technique is to photograph storms at night—which tends to give more spectacular results anyway—using either a 30-second exposure or, even better, Bulb (B) mode. The Bulb mode allows the photographer to keep the shutter open for as long as the shutter release is being pressed (most remote shutter releases have a lock function making this even easier).

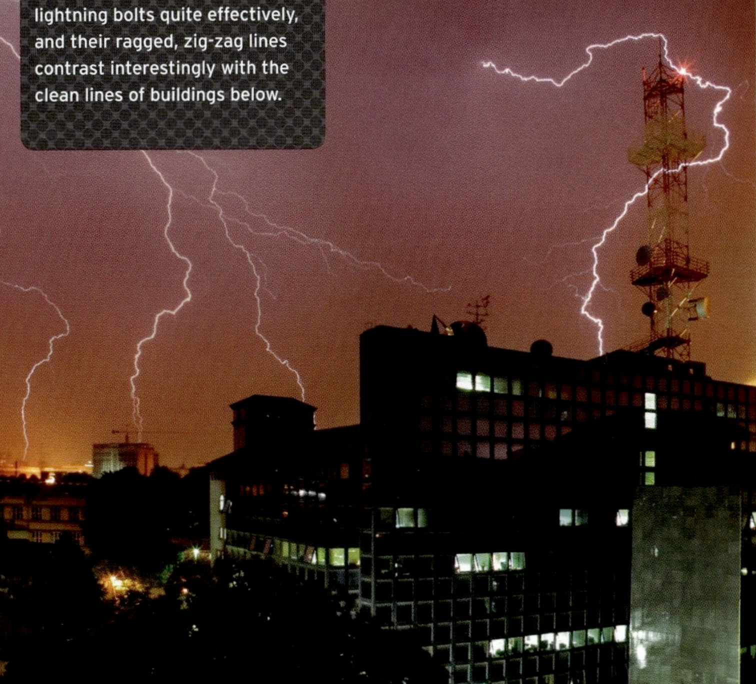

City strikes

The artificial light sources of urban environments complement the blue-white discharge of lightning bolts quite effectively, and their ragged, zig-zag lines contrast interestingly with the clean lines of buildings below.

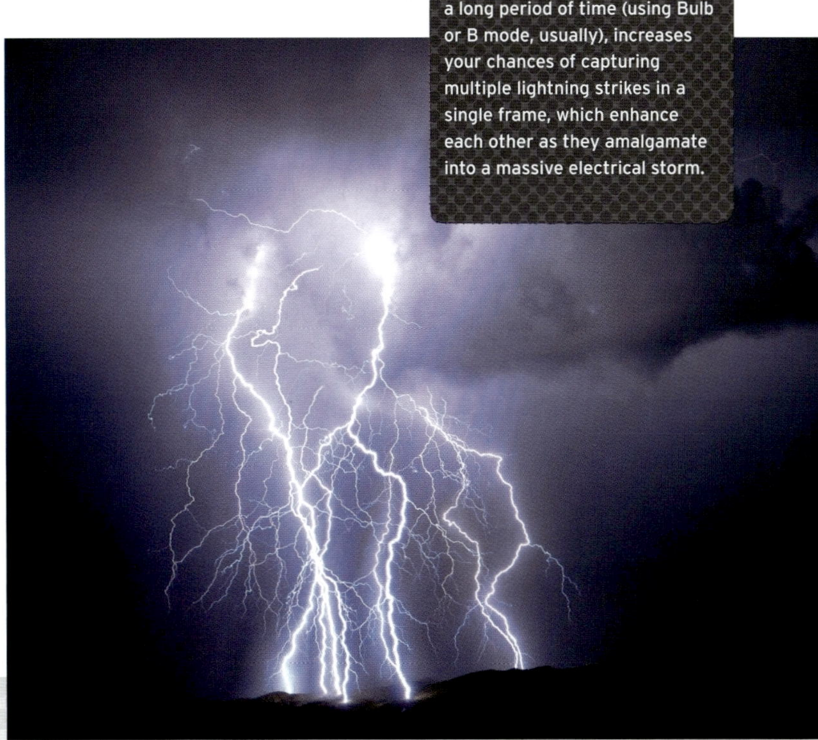

Multiple-strike capture

Leaving your shutter open for a long period of time (using Bulb or B mode, usually), increases your chances of capturing multiple lightning strikes in a single frame, which enhance each other as they amalgamate into a massive electrical storm.

Exposing for Lightning Strikes

So how to expose for lightning? A bolt of lightning is, obviously, extremely bright, particularly if it is close and particularly compared to nighttime ambient light levels. So setting the correct exposure for the night sky or surroundings and waiting for a lightning strike will result in a very overexposed image, due to the relative brightness of the lightning compared to the surrounding scenery.

The trick is to underexpose ambient light levels (i.e. without lightning) over a long exposure. So, for example, typical camera settings might be ISO 100–200, a high aperture number of around f/16 to f/22, and a 30-second exposure. The exposure should be set so that if no lightning occurs, the image is slightly underexposed.

In Bulb mode, use a similarly underexposed setting, but release the shutter as soon as lightning strikes.

This may at first appear counter-intuitive, but it means that when a lightning strike does occur, it appears for such a relatively small proportion of the exposure time (for example, one second out of 30) that it will not be overexposed. At the same time, the lightning will briefly illuminate the surrounding landscape, preventing ambient levels from being underexposed.

Essentially, a long exposure evens out the brief, massive dynamic range between the very bright lightning bolt and low ambient light levels. Importantly, of course, it also increases the likelihood of capturing some lightning! Think of it as casting a wide net. Instead of trying to react to a sub-second burst of lightning, a long exposure allows the photographer to keep the shutter open for at least 30 seconds, which both avoids the need for lightning-fast reactions and increases the likelihood that lightning will strike during the exposure time.

Depending on the frequency and intensity of the lightning, the camera settings may need to be tweaked, but the technique remains the same. Use the histogram to assess a test exposure, and alter as necessary.

Another option for shooting is a lightning trigger, available from third-party providers. Lightning triggers usually attach to the camera flash hotshoe, and are connected to the remote shutter input on the camera body. Whenever the electronic sensor in the trigger detects a lightning flash, it will automatically shoot a frame at the set exposure. The reaction time is much faster than the human brain, and they are reportedly very reliable.

Composition in thunderstorms should generally be weighted toward the sky (that's where all the action is!), with some foreground or landscape interest to provide perspective for the size of the thunderstorm. But go with your instinct, too—a variety of wide and telephoto shots will provide a more dynamic portfolio.

Knowing your location beforehand will also provide better results. A high vantage point over numerous directions is ideal, allowing the photographer to keep track of the storm throughout its journey, and from an adequately safe distance.

Urban lightning photography can also produce stunning results. Exposure technique is slightly different because long shutter speeds will overexpose city lights. Here, balance is the key. Set the exposure for as long a time as possible, without blowing out the highlight details of the city lights, and

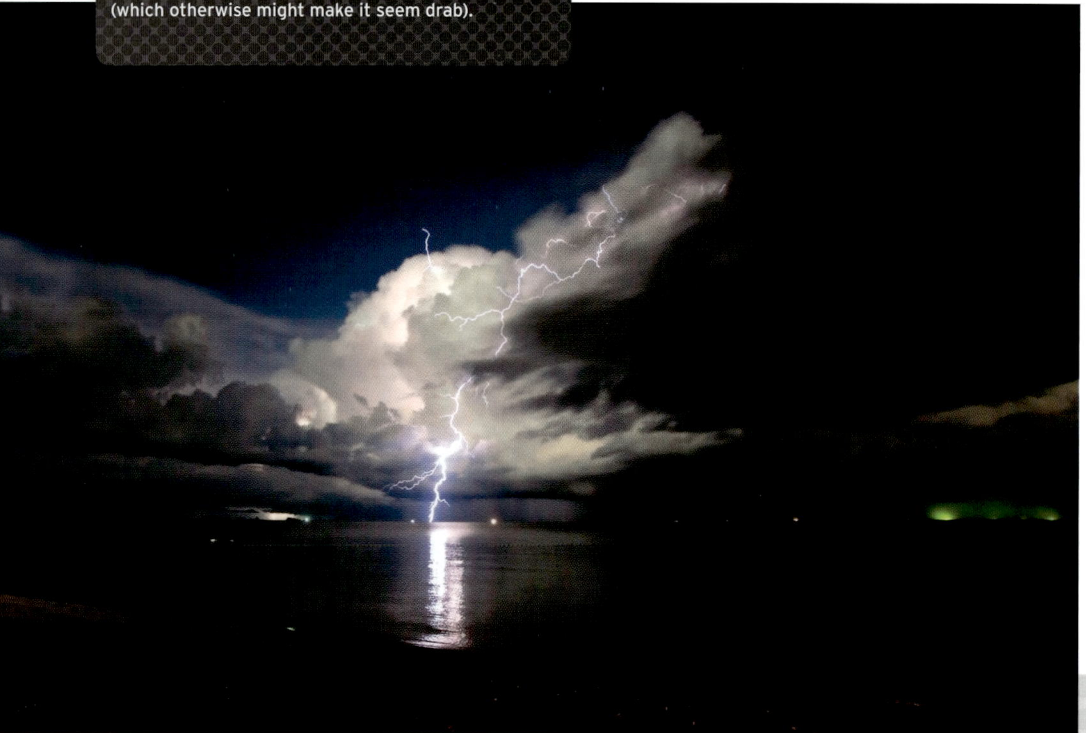

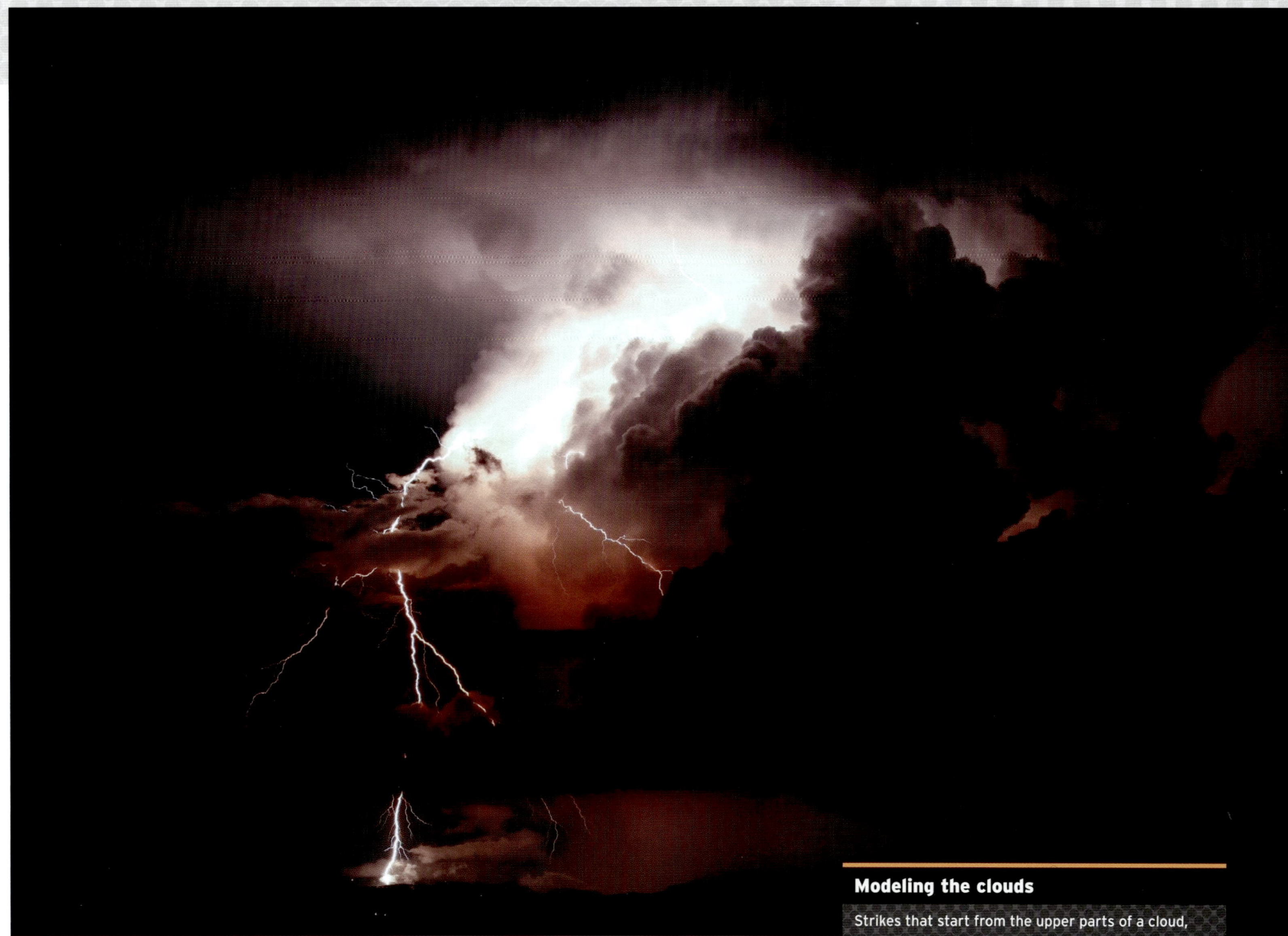

possibly slightly underexposed—for example, 10 seconds.

The disadvantage of shooting in the city is a shorter exposure time—and possibly less chance of catching some lightning in a single exposure. But the advantage is that the difference in light levels between city lights and lightning is smaller, so exposure should in fact be easier, as the bright lights will balance more with the brightness of the lightning. Of course, there is also the chance of capturing a memorable building strike in the city.

One final, but very important, note is that of equipment and photographer safety. Of course, being outdoors in the middle of a thunderstorm, particularly high up or out in the open, can be dangerous. The risk of lightning strike is relatively high. The safest technique is to ensure that the camera and tripod are out of the rain, and then set a long exposure and retire to a safe spot, such as inside a car or a house/building.

If this is impractical, be sensible. Shoot only relatively distant storms, retiring to a safe spot if it is overhead or nearby. If in doubt, don't risk it; just wait for it to pass. At the least, a brewing or clearing thunderstorm often provides the potential for dramatic shots and beautiful light. The lightning can always wait for the next time!

Volcanoes

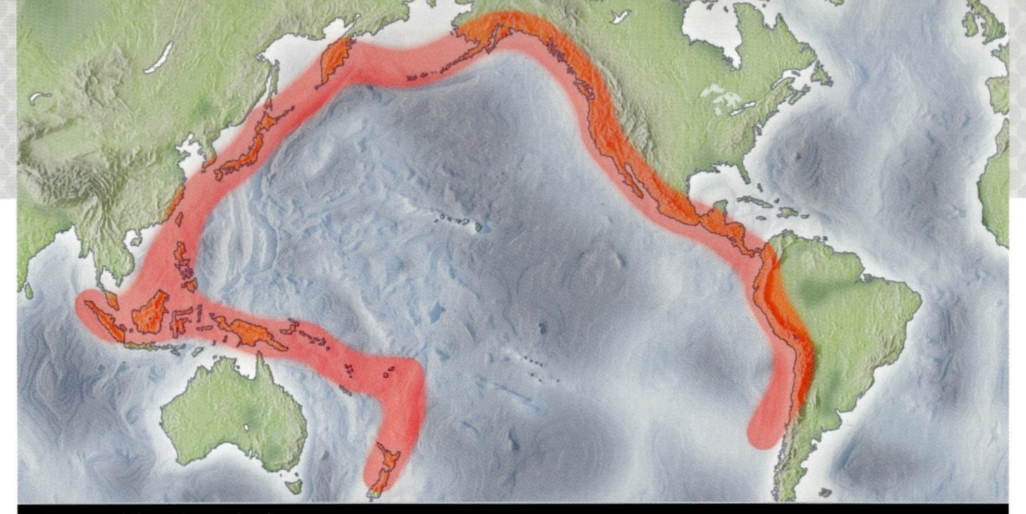

The Pacific Ring of Fire

Volcanoes are one of the most beautiful and destructive forces of nature, and have shaped the face of the planet on which we live since the birth of time. Whether spewing red-hot magma thousands of feet into the air, belching smoke into the atmosphere, dripping hissing lava trails into the sea, or even laying dormant and fertile, volcanoes and volcanic eruptions offer some of the most stunning photographic potential of all of nature's events, whether from far away or up close.

A volcano represents a fissure or weak spot in the Earth's rocky crust. This fissure allows the escape of molten rock, known as magma, as well as other materials and toxic gases, which can be ejected high into the atmosphere or flow down the side of the volcano, depending on the ferocity and type of eruption.

There are three different types of volcano: Active volcanoes erupt continuously; dormant volcanoes lie inactive for centuries but erupt abruptly; and extinct volcanoes are considered not likely to erupt. There are also different types of eruption, often named after the region in which they characteristically occur. Hawaiian eruptions, for example, are characterized by effusive eruptions of very fluid lava, while Strombolian eruptions (named after the Italian volcano Stromboli) are driven by bursting gas bubbles within the magma (see page 91 for a full explanation of eruption types).

More broadly, volcanic eruptions can be split into two types: red and gray. As one might imagine, red eruptions are characterized by the presence of lava (the term used for magma once it has reached the surface), while gray eruptions contain ash, dust, rock, and other non-magmatic material. Each can be equally explosive, photography-wise, but the beauty and elemental nature of red eruptions hold special appeal.

The type and intensity of eruption will of course affect the final photographic effect,

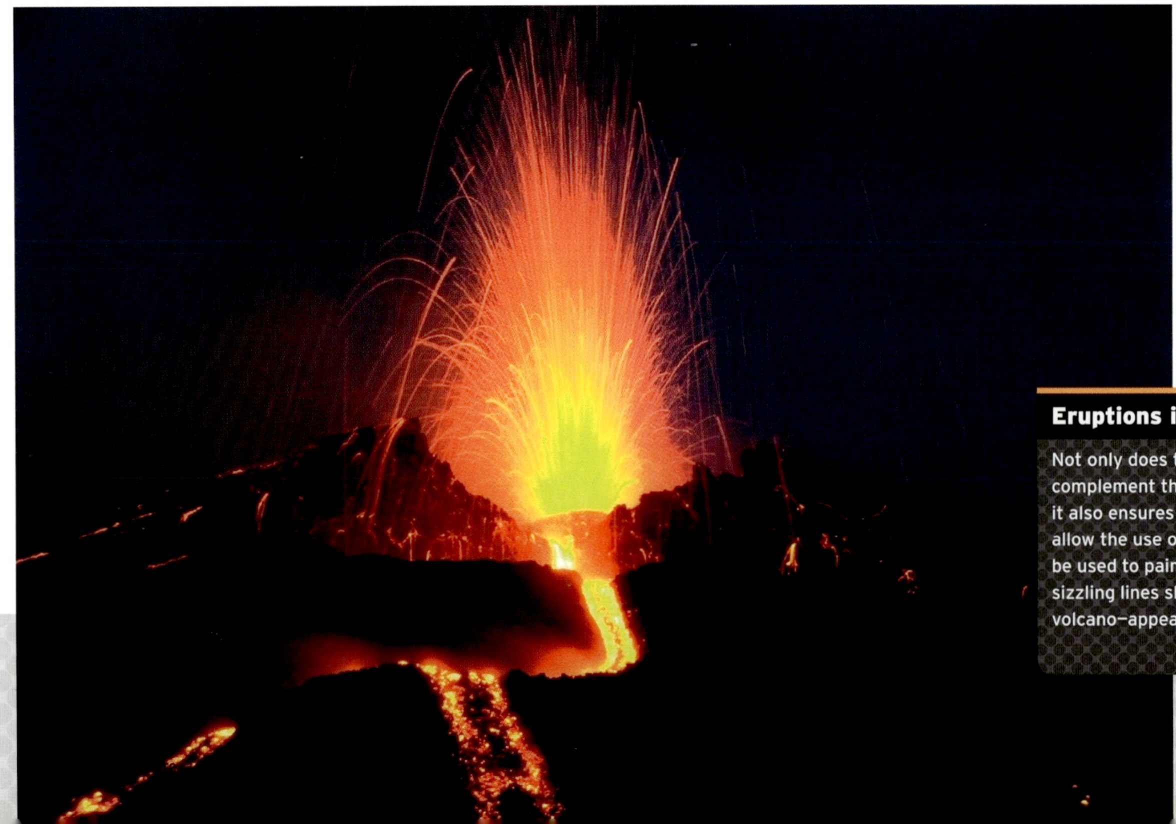

Eruptions in the night

Not only does the dark blue of a night sky effectively complement the vivid reds and oranges of eruptions, it also ensures sufficient low-light conditions to allow the use of long shutter speeds. These can then be used to paint the eruptions in graceful arcs and sizzling lines shooting forth from the tops of the volcano—appearing rather like fireworks.

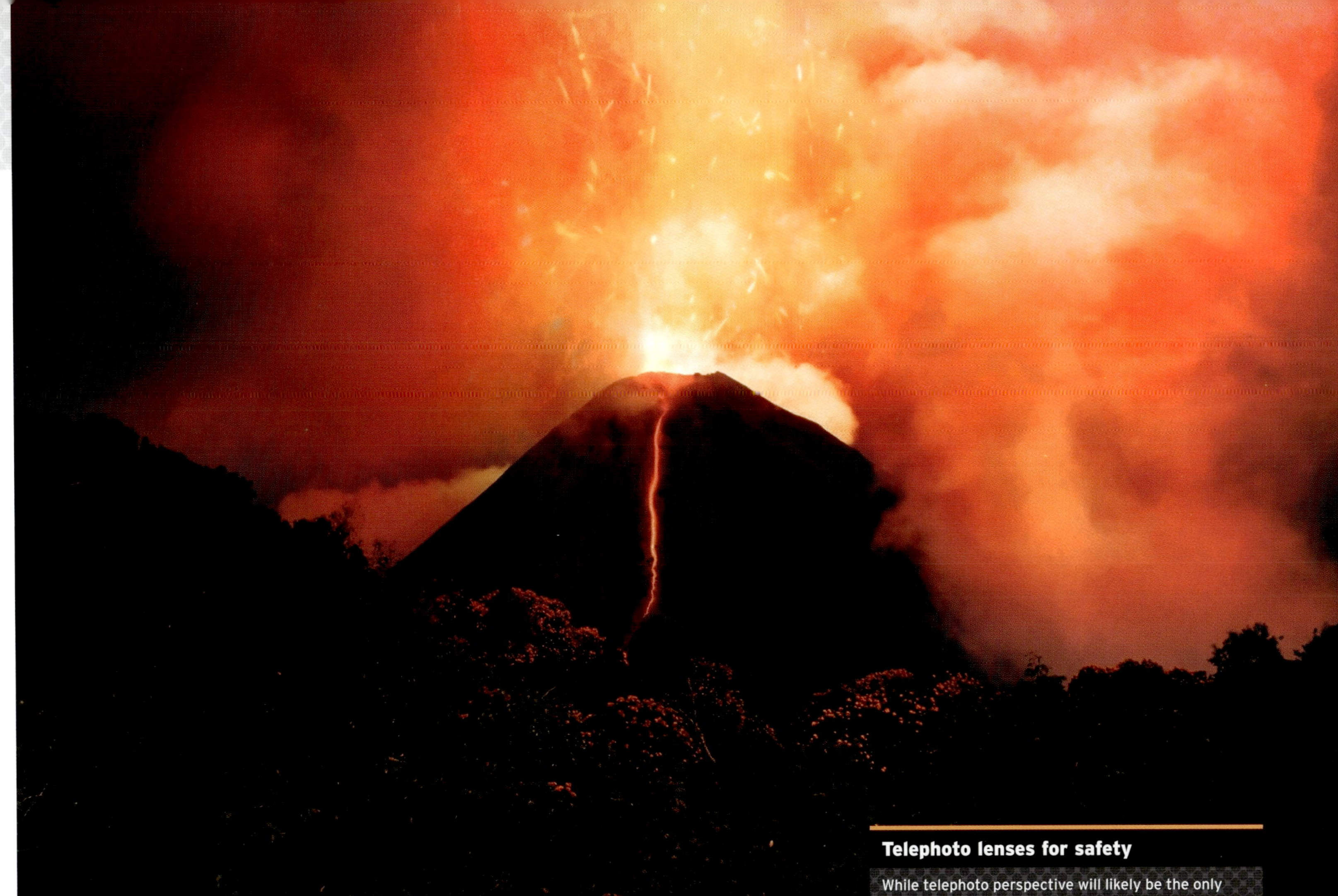

however, it is essential from the outset to point out that photographing volcanoes is extremely dangerous and can be potentially life-threatening. Intra-crater earthquakes, molten projectiles, explosions, unstable ground, and extreme temperatures are just some of the threats.

A more insidious threat is the silent menace of toxic gases that belch out from around even the most benign eruptions. Volcanic gases include sulphur dioxide, hydrogen sulphide, methane, carbon dioxide and carbon monoxide, while other materials found in the vicinity are likely to include silica dust (harmful to lung tissue) and arsenic. Thus, thorough research is essential before approaching a volcanic area.

As a result, close-up volcano photography is only possible in a few regions of the world, with most photography likely to be limited to distant landscapes. The trick is to make the most of the opportunity presented—volcano photography is still a rare event for most, and any shot will be of some value.

Before making any trip, it is essential to perform copious research and to liaise with local organizations and professional bodies about the unique dangers of each individual eruption or region. Be aware that access to the region may even be refused. If the visit does go ahead, working with a local guide or regional expert, or joining up with an experienced photographer, is strongly recommended. Not only is this likely to keep

the photographer safe, it is also much more likely to yield better results through the benefit of local knowledge and expertise.

Presuming that all safety concerns have been met, the type of images that can be achieved from volcano photography will depend heavily on the type of eruption, its ferocity, the region in which it is occurring, and other local and unique factors. To a certain extent, it is simply a case of being prepared for numerous outcomes.

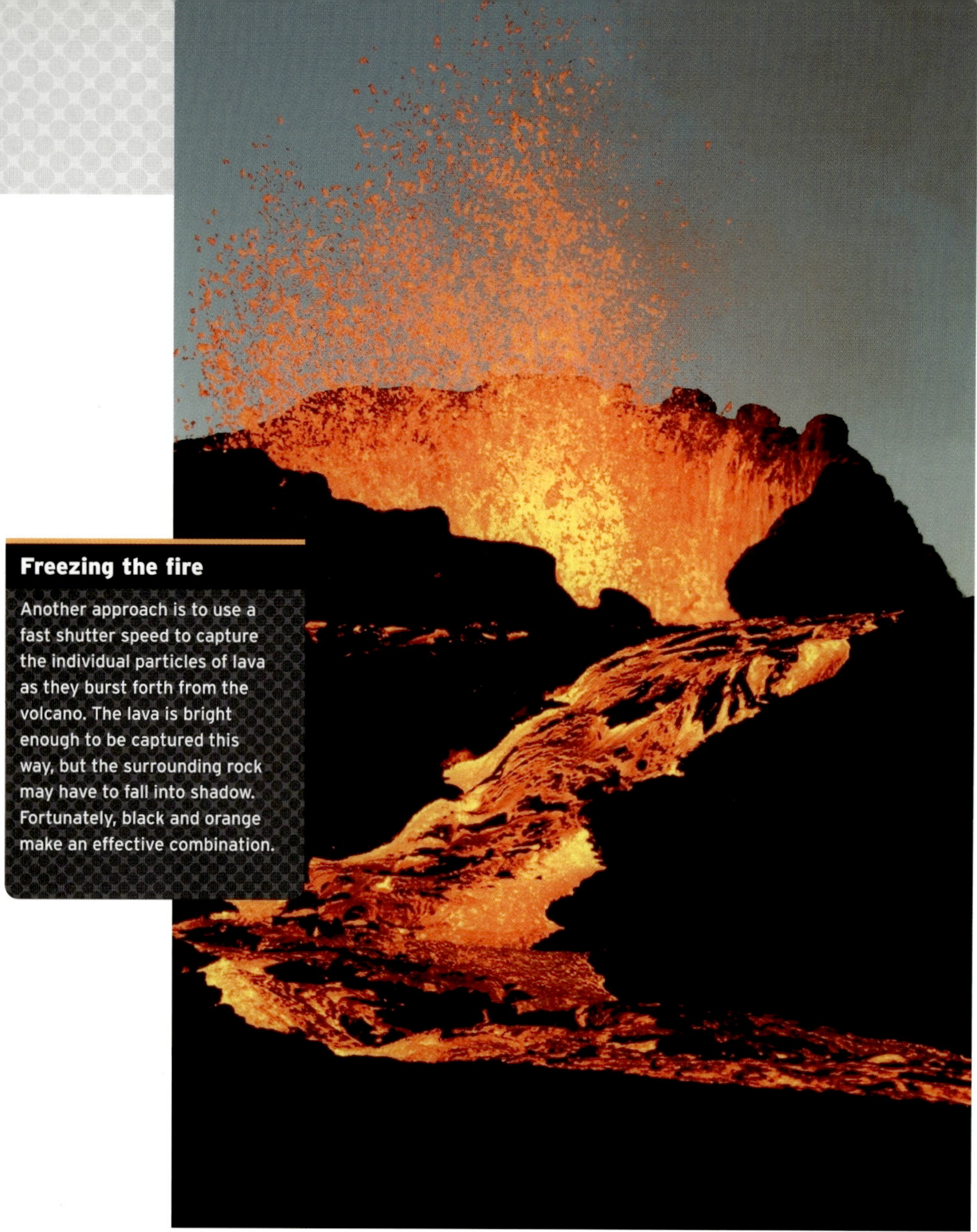

depends on personal preference and shooting style, but as much variety as possible is advisable in order to maximize—or rather, not miss—the opportunities presented.

As mentioned, photographic style and equipment required is likely to be dictated by the unique circumstance of each eruption. If there is an exclusion zone around an eruption, or if the eruption has created a particularly impressive dust and smoke plume (for example, a gray eruption), then a landscape from afar may be the best option.

Photographing ash clouds and plumes is covered in the next section of this book, but briefly: Photographers should follow the more general rules of landscape photography, as outlined earlier in this book. Sunrise or sunset may provide stunning light or background colors against which to place the plume or smoke cloud.

If magmatic eruptions or lava flows are visible, these will be more prominent in darker conditions, such as dawn or twilight—the so-called golden hours. Likewise, shooting at night can also provide stunning shots by enhancing the effect of lava flows.

Always use a tripod for camera stability, but be aware that as light levels drop, slower shutter speeds (as a result of low ISO values and high aperture numbers) will add motion blur to erupting lava or lava flows—how much depends on the distance away, and the speed and intensity of the volcanic display. Whether the photographer wants motion blur present or not is a creative decision, but appropriate balancing of shutter speed with ISO and aperture is key during intense eruptions.

Choice of lens will depend on the distance and the surrounding interest—and the desired outcome. For example, shooting from low down will emphasize the dominance of the volcano over its environment, while a longer focal length will tend to compress perspective and isolate the particular form of the volcano itself, to the exclusion of its surroundings.

Prior Preparation

Prior and intimate knowledge of camera equipment is essential—there will be no time for fiddling around trying to set aperture, worry about ISO, set self timers, or access other menu functions. If in doubt: Practice, practice, practice before even considering heading off to a hot zone.

Of course, a range of lenses with different focal length is essential, particularly when journeying into the unknown. Lenses covering wide, medium and telephoto ranges will ensure that the photographer is armed to tackle most situations they encounter. High-quality zoom lenses will cover a wide focal length range, without the need to either constantly change lenses or to carry numerous fixed-focal-dlength lenses. Bear in mind that volcano photography is likely to involve long-distance treks.

A range of potential lenses might include a 16-35mm, a 24-70mm, and a 70-200mm zoom, which would cover most potential requirements. As always, choice of lens

Unusual cloud formations, plumes and other atmospheric conditions around the volcano are also likely to form, so be sure to incorporate them. The atmospheric disruption caused by volcanic eruptions can often create lightning too, adding to the mesmerizing and humbling show of Mother Nature's power.

If incorporating foreground interest when shooting from distance, try to make sure it adds to the story of the eruption—perhaps a cooling lava flow, or a town on the side of the volcano dwarfed by the magnitude of such a powerful natural event.

Alternatively, head to a populated area in order to capture the tension between the power of nature, and everyday human life. For example, a modestly active volcano may be a normal part of daily life for the local population. Shots of people going about their daily tasks, with a fuming volcano in the background, not only make powerful images, but can also create human-interest, photojournalistic images.

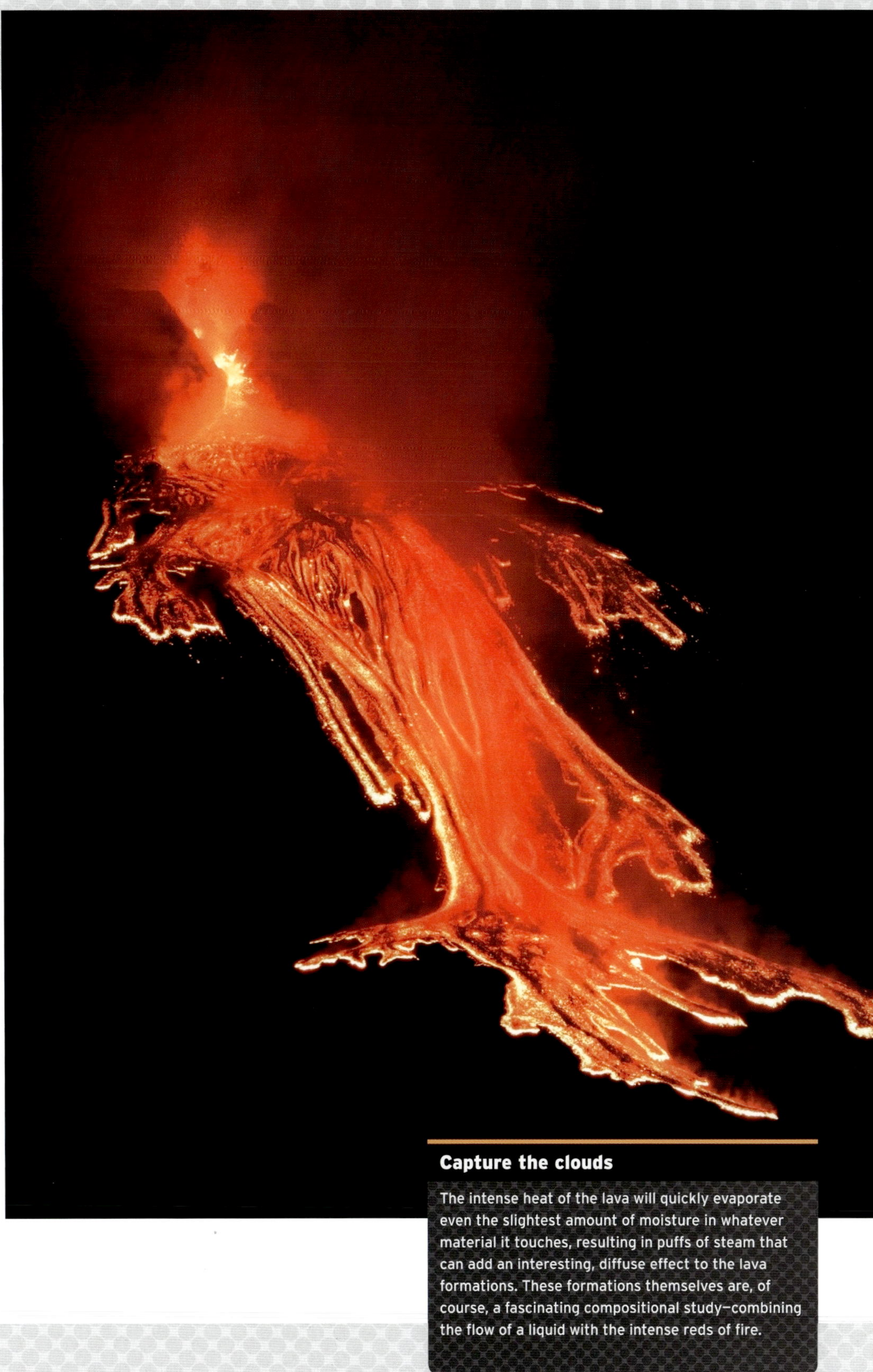

Capture the clouds

The intense heat of the lava will quickly evaporate even the slightest amount of moisture in whatever material it touches, resulting in puffs of steam that can add an interesting, diffuse effect to the lava formations. These formations themselves are, of course, a fascinating compositional study—combining the flow of a liquid with the intense reds of fire.

For those lucky enough to gain close-up access to a volcanic eruption, it is essential to react quickly and unemotionally to what are likely to be amazing and out-of-this-world scenes and vistas—including glowing rivers of intense red, bubbling molten lakes, fireworks of lava, otherworldly rock formations, barren valleys of contorted structures, and hissing vents. Close-up volcano photography can provide an veritable embarrassment of riches for the photographer.

Darker ambient light levels will make lava displays more prominent, pitting the cool blues of a darkening sky against rich, warm reds and oranges. Likewise, any minor lava explosions will stand out like firework displays against the dark blue of a night sky.

If shooting at night and lava is present, expose for the lava (rather than the ambient light), as it is likely to glow much more brightly in comparison. Exposing for the lava avoids overexposing the main subject matter. Its bright glow is also likely to illuminate the surrounding area, thus avoiding black holes in the shadows. Take a meter reading from the lava, and then tweak exposure based on the results of the image histogram.

Indeed, lava explosions can be treated similarly to firework displays, the look and feel of which is significantly affected by shutter speed. A slower shutter speed will blur motion, while a fast shutter speed will freeze the action. Choose shutter speed according to creative intent.

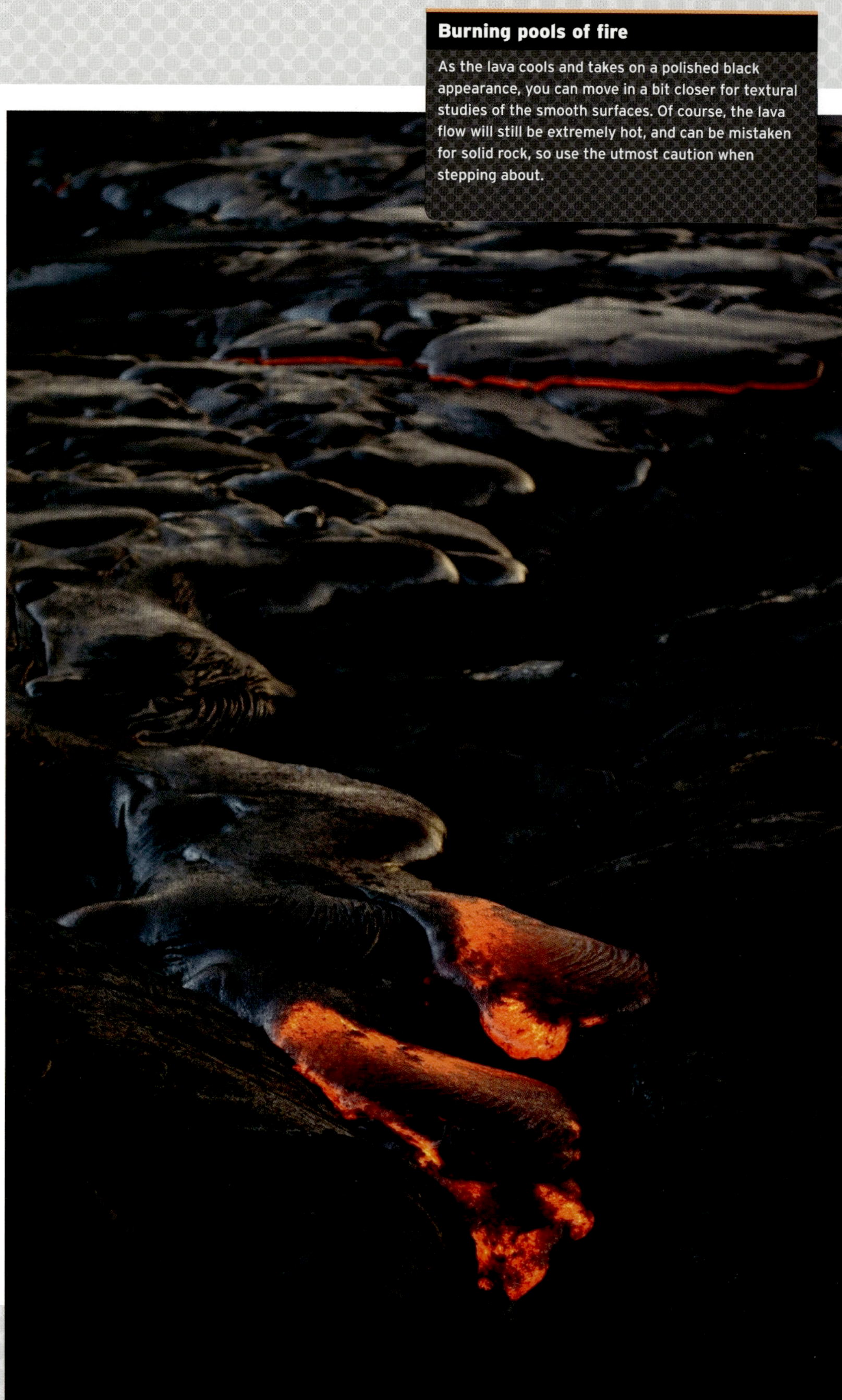

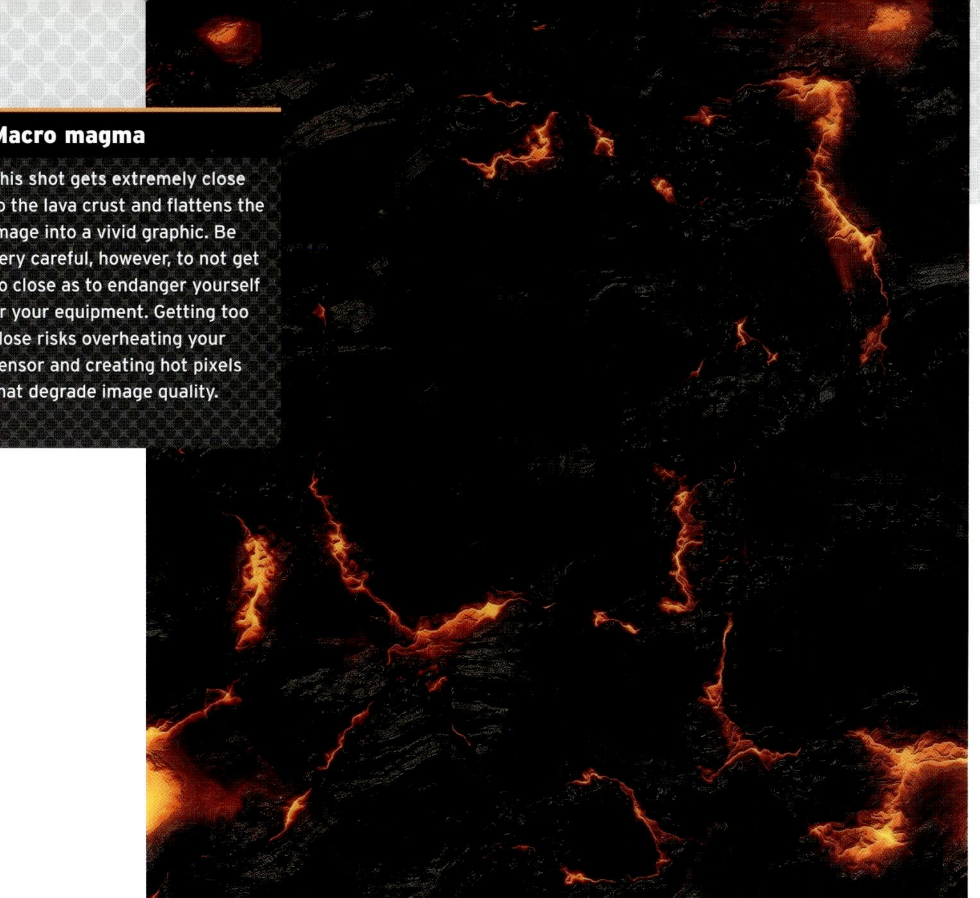

that it creates bubbling pools of boiling water and hissing steam. Essentially, the photographer is witnessing the process by which the Earth's crust was created—eventually the lava is cooled by the sea into solid rock.

One final technique for volcano photography is the tried and tested, and relatively safe, use of a helicopter or light plane to create stunning aerial shots. As long as the pilot is experienced and vetted, airborne photography can provide a way to get close to volcanic activity in a safe manner, at the same time providing dramatic and unusual imagery of a volcano in action. While this may at first appear to be an expensive option, if the photographer can find the right route to market for the sale of the resulting images, their rare and unusual nature could repay the initial outlay many times over across a number of years.

Go for the Graphics

Another tip is to pick out stream-like lava flows and frame them to create graphic or surreal patterns of glowing red lava against dark rock. Again, shutter speed can be tweaked to freeze lava flows or create movement using motion blur—the value will depend on the speed of the flow and the ISO and aperture settings. As a general rule, try to stick to as low an ISO value as possible (which means less image noise), while maximizing depth of field (using high aperture numbers). But these settings should be utilized for creative intent, and will be dictated by ambient light levels—just ensure that the photographer, not the camera, makes the creative decisions!

Another particularly stunning effect of lava flows occurs when they meet water, such as the sea or ocean. Hawaii is noted for its mix of volcanic activity and coastline. When the glowing red lava reaches the sea, its high temperature heats the water so ferociously

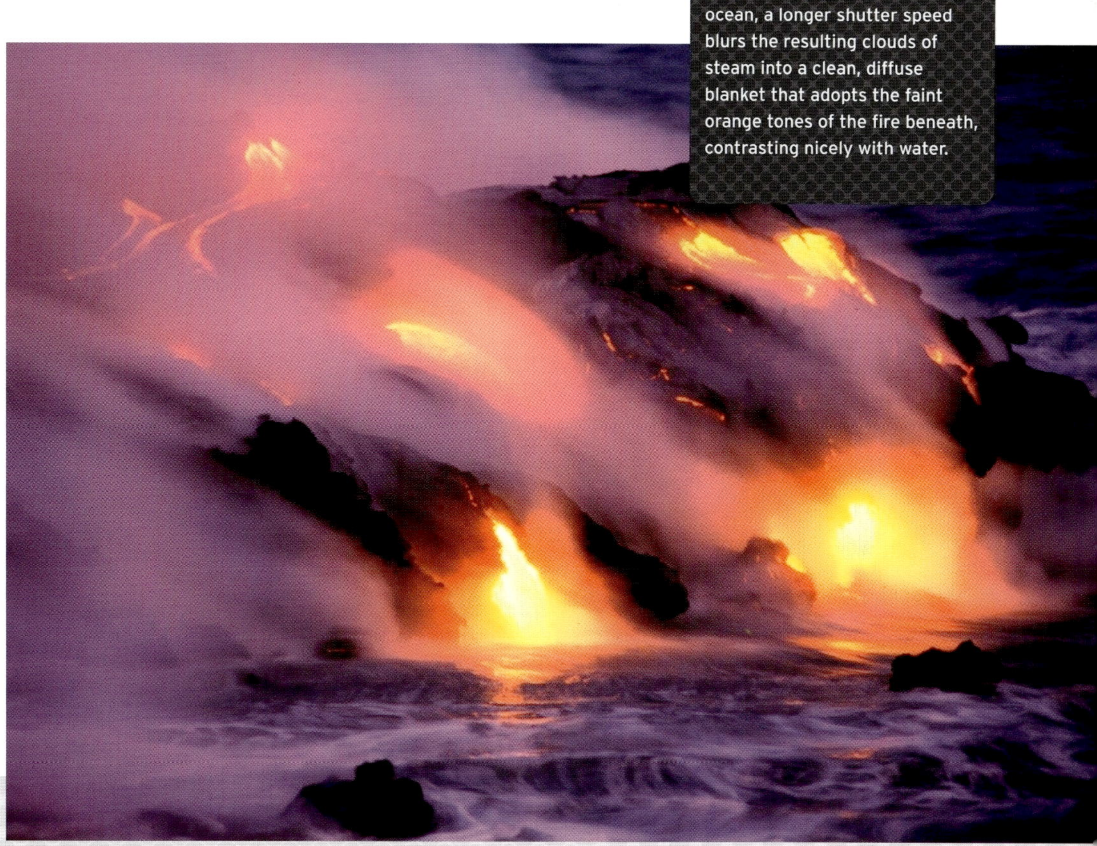

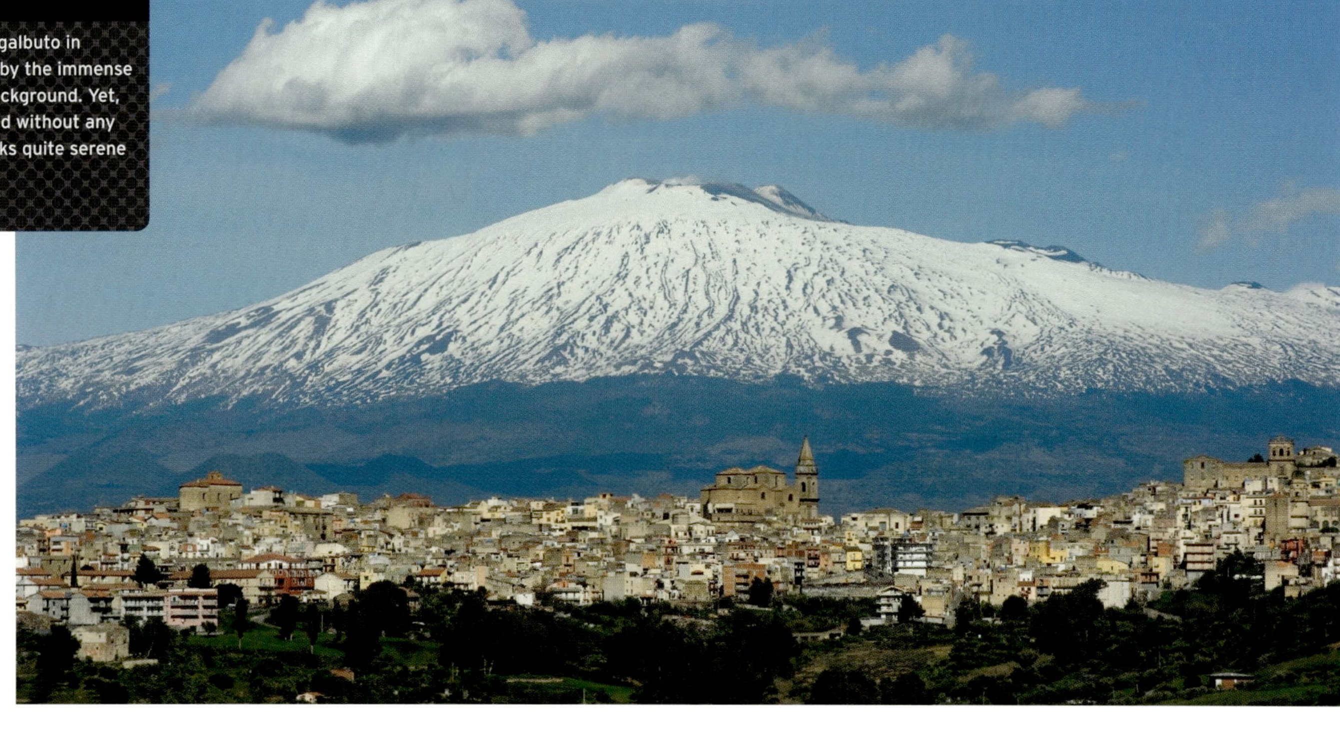

Mount Etna

The village of Regalbuto in Sicily is dwarfed by the immense volcano in the background. Yet, on a clear day and without any ash clouds, it looks quite serene and picturesque.

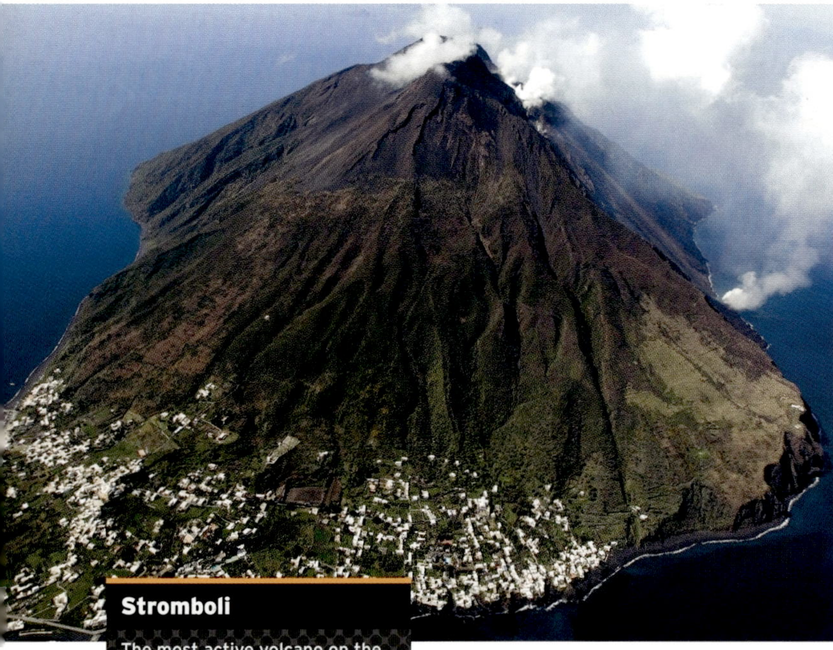

Stromboli

The most active volcano on the small string of volcanic Aeolian islands in the Mediterranean just off the northeast coast of Sicily. From the air you can see the settlements encroach onto the very side of the volcano itself.

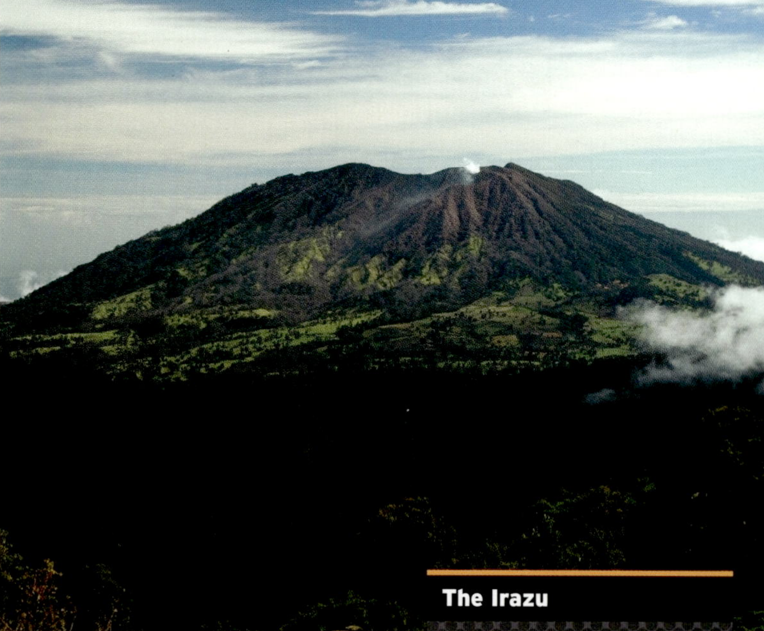

The Irazu

This Costa Rican volcano is quite active with explosive eruptions that always threaten nearby settlements. However, it also enjoys equally long periods of inactivity, and is quite idyllic in its natural surroundings.

Different Types of Magmatic Volcanic Eruptions

Hawaiian

Named after the Hawaiian islands, these are the calmest types of eruptions characterized by the effusive, relatively slow eruption of very fluid lava. Hawaiian eruptions often occur from a ring of vents around the summit, known as a "curtain of fire." Examples include: Pu'u O', Hawaii; Mount Etna, Italy; and Mount Mihara, Japan (1986 eruption).

Strombolian

Named after the Italian volcano Stromboli, which has been erupting for centuries. Characterized by short-lived and explosive eruptions of viscous lava, often high into the air, which form parabolic paths before landing back around the source vent. Examples include: Mount Etna, Italy (eruptions in 1999, 2002-03, and 2009); Mount Erebus, Antarctica; and Stromboli, Italy.

Vulcanian

Named after Vulcano, a volcanic island about 25 miles north of Sicily, and which lends its name to all volcanoes. Highly viscous magma within the volcano makes it difficult for gases to escape, leading to a build up of pressure. Eventually, the pressure pops the cap holding down the magma, resulting in an explosive eruption. More explosive than Strombolian eruptions, these often reach 3-6 miles (5-10km) into the air. Examples include: Sakurajima, Japan; Tavurvur, Papa New Guinea; and Irazú, Costa Rica.

Peléan

Named after Mount Pelée in Martinique, Peléan eruptions are characterized by the appearance of a lava spine—a bulge in the volcano's summit—that preempts the imminent collapse of the central crater. The collapse creates an explosive eruption and a pyroclastic flow of lava moving at tremendous speeds—up to 90mph (150kph).

These fast-moving, molten landslides make Peléan the most dangerous type of volcanic eruption. Examples include: Mount Pelée, Martinique; Mayon, The Philippines; and Mount Lamington, Papua New Guinea (1951 eruption).

Plinian (or Vesuvian)

Named after the AD79 eruption of Mount Vesuvius, which infamously buried the Roman towns of Pompeii and Herculaneum. Plinian eruptions are driven by the rising of volatile gases through the magma, which when forced through the narrow summit explode in a plume, reaching between 1-28 miles (2-45km) into the atmosphere. Surroundings are also showered in suffocating pumice dust, and subject to very fast-moving lava flows consistent with wet cement. Significant examples include: Mount Vesuvius, Italy (AD79 eruption); Mount St. Helens, USA (1980 eruption); and Hekla, Iceland (1947-48 eruption).

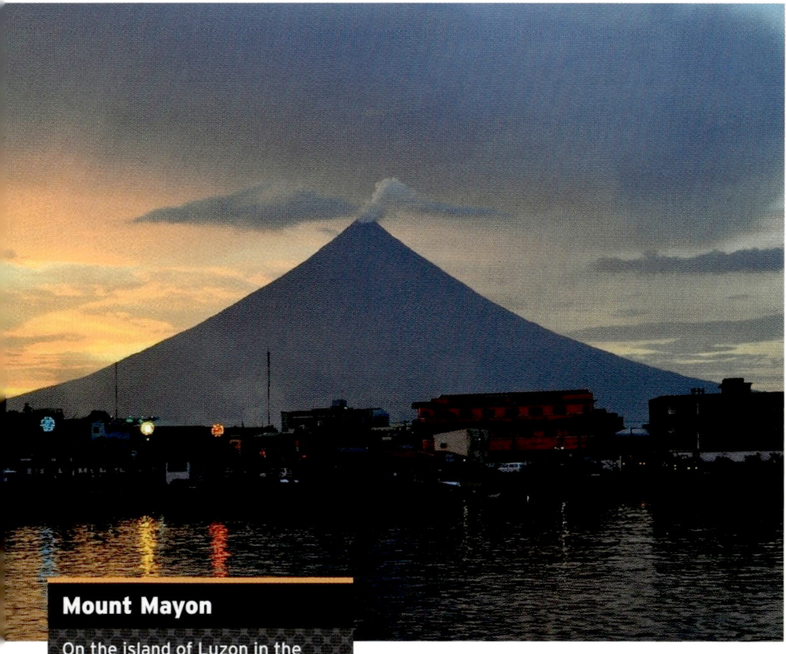

Mount Mayon

On the island of Luzon in the Phillippines, the graceful arch of Mount Mayon is stunningly perfect in its symmetry and shape. Here, it is captured mostly in silhouette, which accentuates its form.

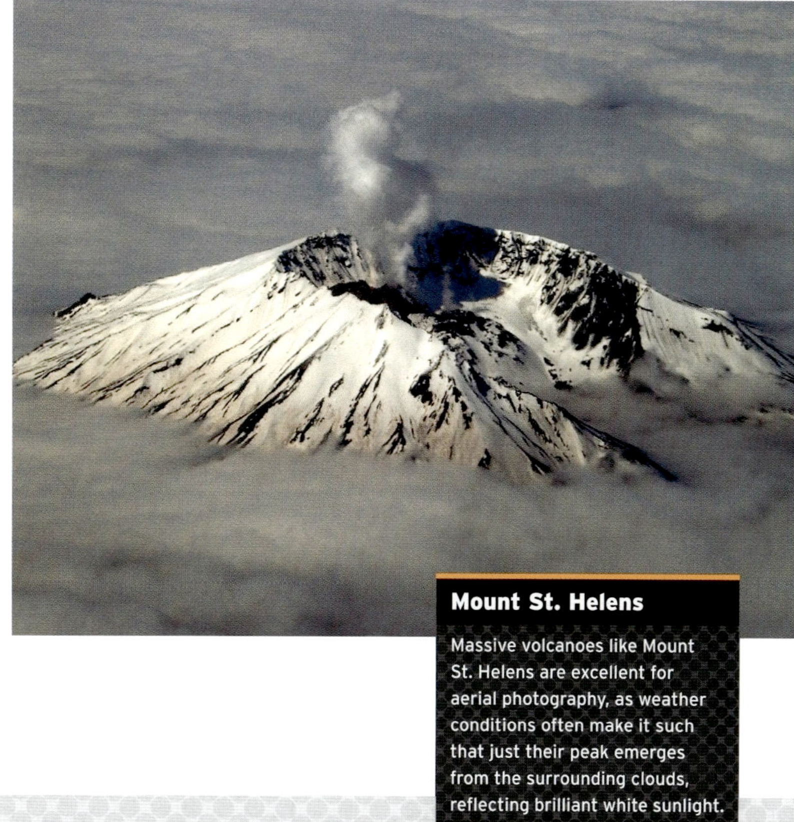

Mount St. Helens

Massive volcanoes like Mount St. Helens are excellent for aerial photography, as weather conditions often make it such that just their peak emerges from the surrounding clouds, reflecting brilliant white sunlight.

Ash Clouds

Between March and May 2010, a volcanic eruption beneath Iceland's Eyjafjallajökull glacier brought European airspace to an unprecedented standstill for weeks as dense plumes of ash spewed high into the atmosphere and scattered over a wide area on unfavorable winds. A year later in May 2011, Iceland's most active volcano, Grimsvötn caused the same level of disruption. For many it was a reminder of the power that nature can still exert over human society, despite our belief to the contrary. Both eruptions drew thousands of photographers from across the globe, each eager to take home a record of this magnificent natural display.

Indeed, many theories state that it is the ash clouds, rather than volcanic eruptions, that have caused ice ages and even mass extinctions over the history of life on Earth. During Earth's history, massive and prolonged eruptions are believed to have created such dense ash clouds in the atmosphere that the sun's light and heat was reflected back into space, causing prolonged ice ages on the surface.

Generally, a moderate ash cloud eruption will turn the sky—even on the brightest day—hazy and pale yellow, while severe ash clouds can turn day to night completely, and create a suffocating no-go area across hundreds of miles. Ash clouds may often be accompanied by rain, and lightning and a sulfurous smell, and will coat every surface with thick, cloying ash or cause slurries of mud on the ground. The ash can also cause ill effects on humans, including (but not limited to) breathing, respiratory, and eye problems.

The point here is that visiting an ash cloud should not be undertaken lightly, or at least without proper planning and safety precautions. Most likely, as occurred in Iceland and similar eruptions around the world, human access to the area will be heavily restricted, limiting the photographer to shots from a distance. Hence, a telephoto zoom lens is the most likely requirement for ash cloud photography. (As discussed later in this section, however, ash clouds can also have far-reaching, and much milder, effects on landscape photography undertaken hundreds of miles away, creating beautiful muted, pastel sunrises and sunsets.)

One of the main challenges of ash cloud photography is that of dust and ash entering and damaging camera equipment, so any form of camera cover or zippable bags are essential to protect the interior of the camera from becoming clogged with the ash. Protect the sensor as well from dust particles; while these can be removed in post-processing, it is far wiser to prevent this at source, whenever possible. There will be ash in the air even if it's not visible, so use a zippable camera cover in which to change lenses with the bag's zips fully closed.

As mentioned, access may be restricted in the region surrounding an eruption, so find the best vantage point from which to view the eruption and resulting ash cloud. Incorporate a wide range of compositions, including foreground interest in wide-angle shots (with the ash cloud and eruption placed appealingly in the frame in the distance), as well as zooming in with a telephoto lens.

With wider shots try to place the volcano or ash cloud in context with its landscape, for example, use a foreground river or valley to guide the viewer's gaze toward the main subject. Including people, other photographers and onlookers is fine, as it is all part of "the story" and provides perspective to the landscape. Such images could also be sold for commercial or journalistic purposes to help pay for the trip—although they would need to be dispatched immediately to the appropriate sources and agencies.

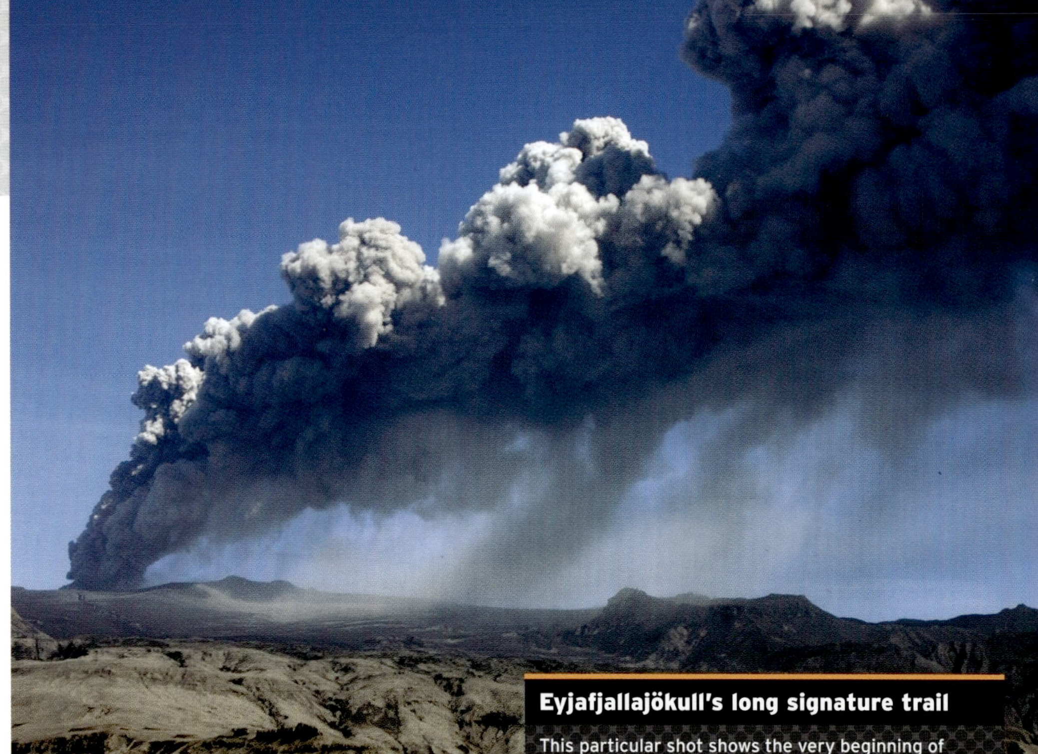

Eyjafjallajökull's long signature trail

This particular shot shows the very beginning of the enormous ash cloud that stretched halfway across the Atlantic and consumed much of the air over Europe. A wide view gives perspective to the immensity of the formation, and the distance it travels can be inferred from the detail seen in the upper right compared to the distant lower left.

You will need:

> A weather-sealed DSLR

> A range of lenses (usually telephoto, and preferably zoom)

> Tele-converters or extenders for extra reach

> A lightweight and sturdy tripod

> Remote shutter release

> A range of neutral density filters (graduated and non-graduated)

> A circular polarizing filter

> Suitable clothing and footwear (possibly a face mask—check with local authorities and experts)

> A camera cover/protector to guard against dust and ash

> A lens cloth with liquid cleaner for removing ash and dust from the lens surface

> Plenty of memory card storage and battery power

> A flask of hot tea or coffee!

Reaching up

Lacking any winds, an ash cloud will reach straight up, lending itself well to a vertical orientation in which the sky will consume the vast majority of the frame, with the earth just anchoring it at the bottom.

Modeling sunlight

The angle of the sun (typical for Iceland throughout much of the year) brings out every nook and cranny in the billowing ash cloud, getting gradually less defined as the cloud disperses to the right of the frame.

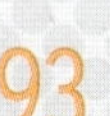

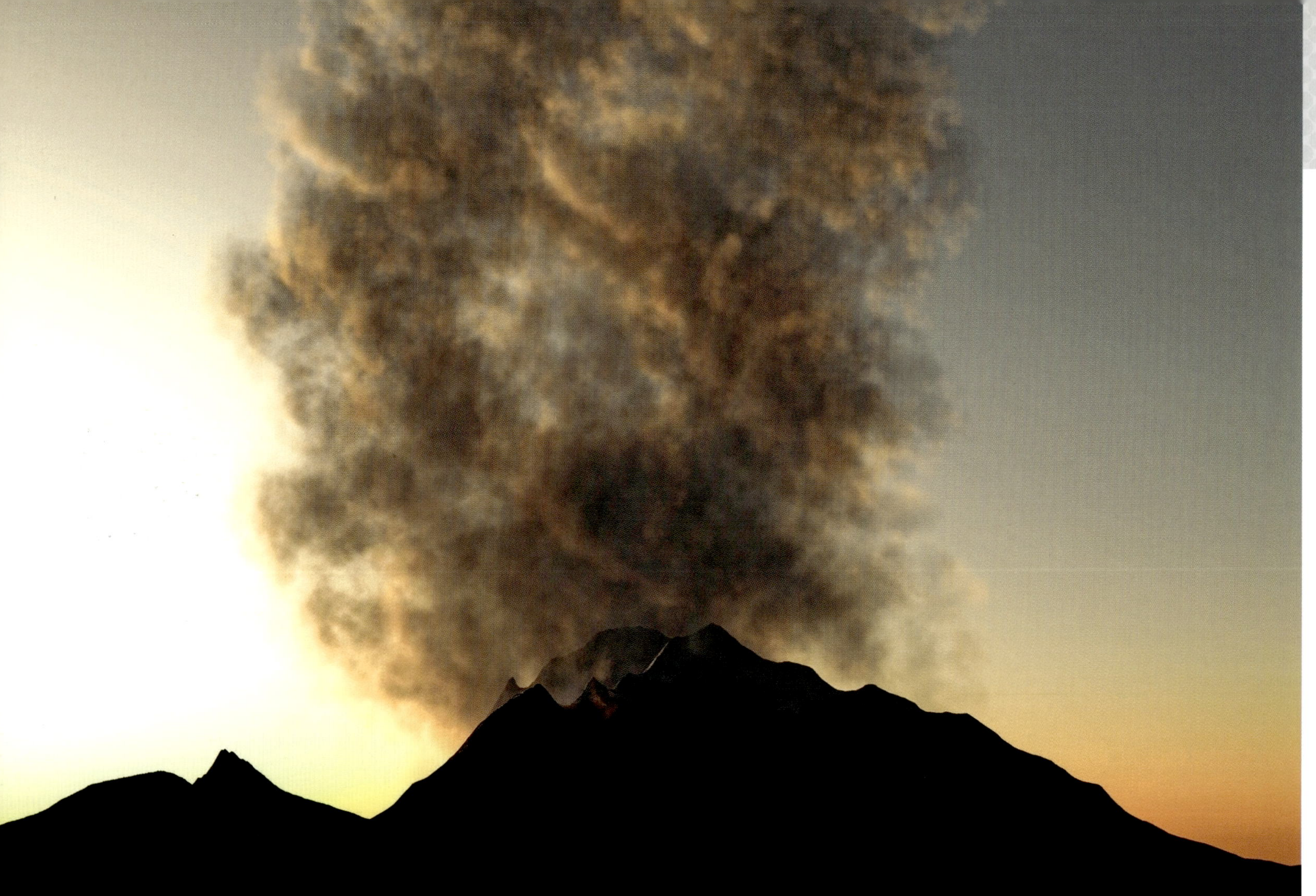

As with most landscape photography, the use of a tripod and shutter release is recommended to eliminate camera shake and blurring resulting from slow shutter speeds—remember the presence of the ash cloud is likely to reduce ambient light levels.

An ash cloud will also linger in the sky above the eruption, often blotting out the sun, which can make for flat lighting. If ambient light levels are low, or even at night, use them to your advantage, and try to capture the brooding mood of the eruption. Even better, if lava is also present, either as a flow or from within the volcano's crater, it will illuminate the ash cloud with a glowing red or orange light if light levels are low or at night. This

illumination will also make the ash cloud stand out from a dark or night sky, with the warm, red glow contrasted against the cool, blue night sky. Experimenting with white balance, either in-camera or in post-processing, can enhance the reds of the lava reflection, or make the night sky even cooler. Shooting in low light levels or at night can therefore create atmospheric shots and add depth to the image.

If there are breaks in the cloud, particularly around sunrise and sunset, try to compose the image so that the ash cloud is either side-lit or backlit by the low sunlight, which will have the combined effect of making the ash plume stand out from the backdrop, and will reveal detail within the cloud as the low-angle light acts as a modeling light, picking out the highlight and shadow detail.

Also look out for lightning associated with ash clouds, as the atmosphere is charged with millions of particles of dust, rock, ice and ash. Ash cloud-associated lightning will be particularly impressive when shot at night.

In terms of exposure setting, apply the same rules as more general landscape photography. A low ISO will reduce noise in the image and give a smoother feel to the final image. Depending on the creative intention, balance the aperture and shutter speed settings to get the desired effect. Of course, low ISO settings require wider apertures and/or slower shutter speeds. If foreground interest is included, aperture settings will need to be small (high numbers, such as f/16). In turn, this will require slower shutter speeds, so make sure that the tripod is stable and to use a remote shutter release to avoid touching the camera and adding unwanted vibrations. Balance this against the effect of motion blur.

If the photographer wants the ash cloud to show motion blur, then a low ISO and small aperture setting is fine. However, in low light or at night, this could be too distracting. In this case, try raising the ISO to a maximum of 400. If the image is still underexposed, reduce the aperture. If only wide apertures of, say, f/4.0 are acceptable, then consider recomposing the image, so that foreground interest is not included, and the focus is trained on the ash cloud or volcano. When using a telephoto lens—if, for example, access is restricted—the use of wider apertures is more forgiving at longer distances.

If the budget allows, hitching a ride with a local helicopter or light-plane operator can set the images apart from the crowd. Circling the ash plume on the upwind side may be possible, offering the opportunity for dramatic aerial shots. In this case, use a standard to telephoto lens (70-200mm, for example) with a faster shutter speed and

wider aperture (smaller number) in order to eliminate camera shake during exposure and vibrations from the flight itself. If the lens or camera has them, turn on image stabilization functions.

As mentioned earlier, if the photographer is not lucky enough to visit an eruption, the effects of ash clouds can be seen from hundreds of miles away. The same effect that grounded UK flights in 2010 and 2011—that is, a layer of ash in the atmosphere carried long distances on northerly winds—also created glowing, pastel-colored sunrises and sunsets across most parts of the UK. Sunrises and sunsets are associated with reds, oranges

and pinks because the low sunlight has to travel farther through the atmosphere, which effectively filters out blue light. The presence of ash in the atmosphere enhances this effect further, offering the landscape photographer some beautiful opportunities, despite being hundreds of miles away from the ash plume or eruption.

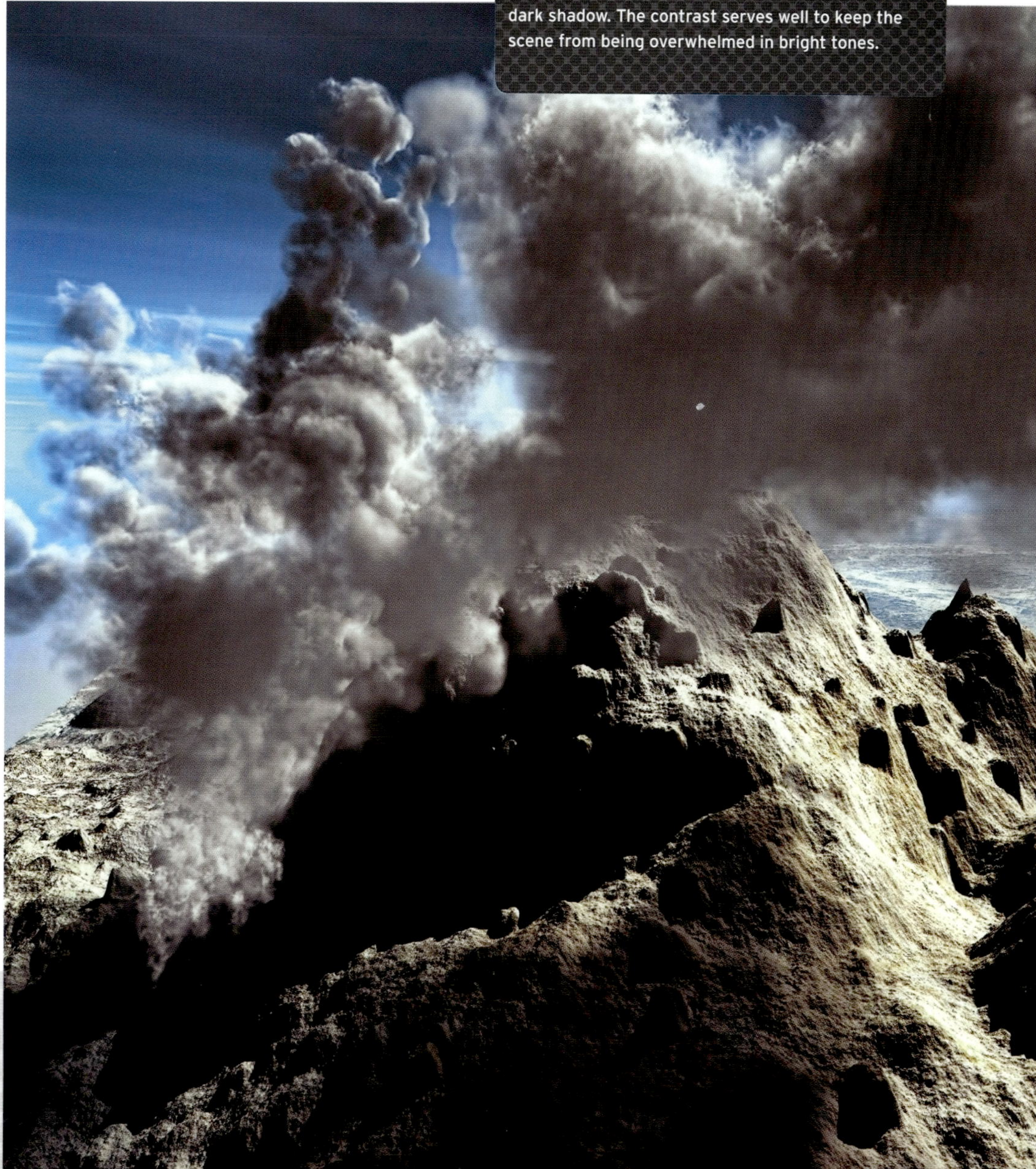

A high-contrast aerial approach

From a sufficient height (as granted by a helicopter ride), ash clouds reveal even more detail as they interact and drift across the craggy rocks of their volcanoes. Here, the direct sunlight fully illuminates the sides of the volcano, while the interior falls into dark shadow. The contrast serves well to keep the scene from being overwhelmed in bright tones.

Firestorms

Photographing firestorms is a particularly hazardous and dangerous job to undertake. Firestorms are intense, extremely fast-moving and unpredictable. Naturally occurring firestorms are usually a result of intense bushfires, forest fires, and wildfires, and create such intense heat that they generate their own wind systems.

A firestorm creates enough heat to pull in surrounding oxygen and air, which in turn sustains the burning air. Due to the strong turbulence created by the intense and violent processes, burning mini-tornados known as fire whirls can also form. These dart around erratically, thus spreading the reach of the firestorm even wider. As well as the intense heat, firestorms can be fatal due to the amount of oxygen they suck out of the surrounding atmosphere, suffocating nearby animals and people.

Conditions that favor the creation of bushfires, and hence firestorms, are periods of drought and high temperatures, such as those experienced in southern Australia in the first decade of this century. This creates the tinderbox of materials that acts as a catalyst for the fire. Thunderstorms, electricity pylons, and human carelessness can provide the spark, but strong fanning winds are usually also required to feed the fire into the scale that can start firestorms.

The biggest challenge for the photographer is gaining access—and staying out of the way of the fire. During a firestorm, access to the area is likely to be banned with evacuation orders in place, so aerial photography, shots from distance, and post-firestorm photography are the most likely option. If access is granted, specialist fireproof clothing and, potentially, breathing apparatus will be the order of the day. One option is to travel as part of a fire-fighting team—however, without specialist training or experience this is also likely to be a fruitless path.

Depending on the topography of the region, it may be possible for the photographer to record this hellish event from afar. A large valley or bowl with high sides might provide just enough distance to offer sufficient protection from the intense, radiated heat of the fire, as well as the lack of oxygen in its midst. Shooting from above can provide for dramatic wide-angle shots, as well as zoomed-in images of specific subjects.

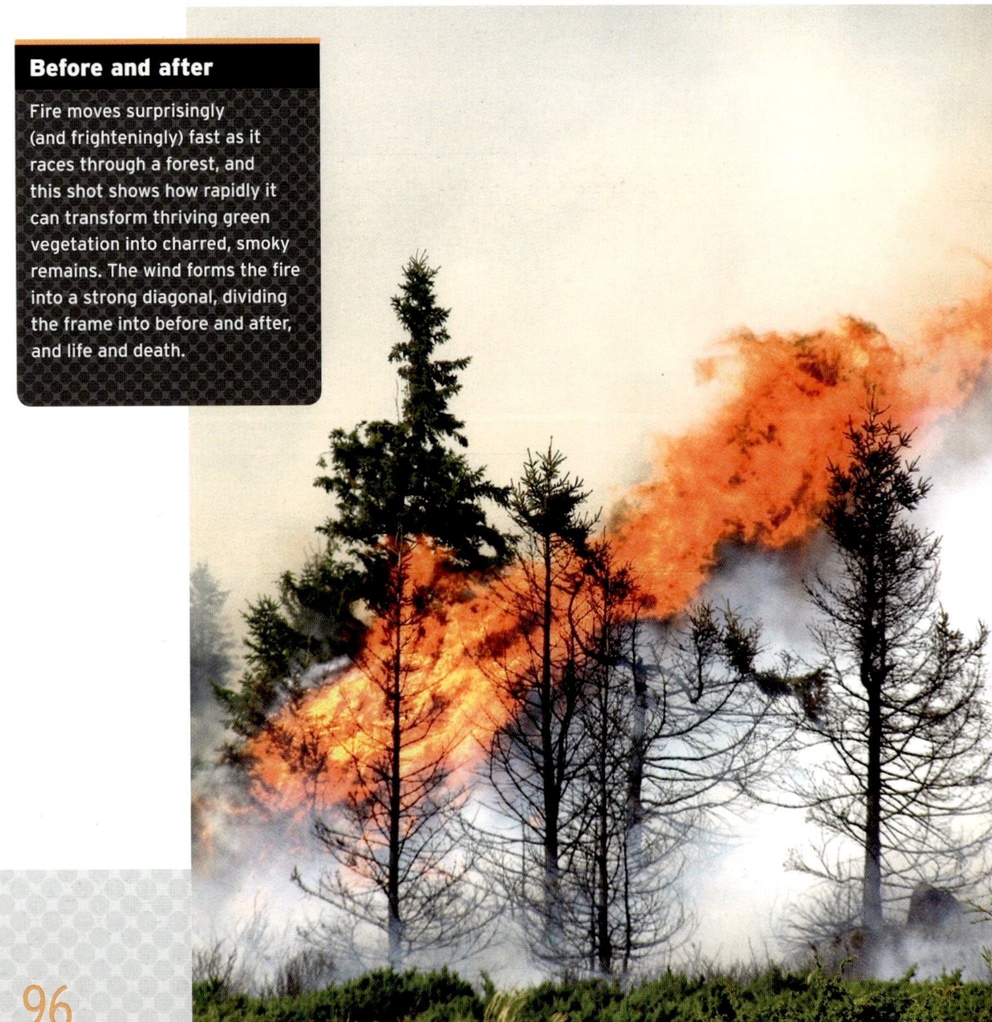

Before and after

Fire moves surprisingly (and frighteningly) fast as it races through a forest, and this shot shows how rapidly it can transform thriving green vegetation into charred, smoky remains. The wind forms the fire into a strong diagonal, dividing the frame into before and after, and life and death.

Fire Preparedness

In most firestorms, the action will unfold quickly and it is likely that the photographer will be unable to remain stationary for long periods of time. So setting the camera to Aperture Priority can reduce the need to be constantly checking and setting exposure settings. If shooting in Raw (which is advisable), slight overexposure will provide the best results.

Fire is inherently bright, so dialing in an extra f-stop, maybe slightly more, of positive exposure compensation will render the fire natural-looking, while boosting the shadow regions, which may be underexposed if the camera is allowed to expose for the fire without exposure compensation. Any slight overexposure or clipping will be retrievable in Raw. However, check the first few shots to determine the right exposure and to avoid completely blown highlights. Light levels should remain fairly stable as the fire will be the main light source.

If the photographer can gain a vantage point during the firestorm, the most dramatic shots will be when ambient light levels are lower—for example, at dawn and dusk, or even at night. The effusive glow of the fire will be particularly spectacular in the dark, and its reach should mean that not much of the surrounding area will be left in shadows.

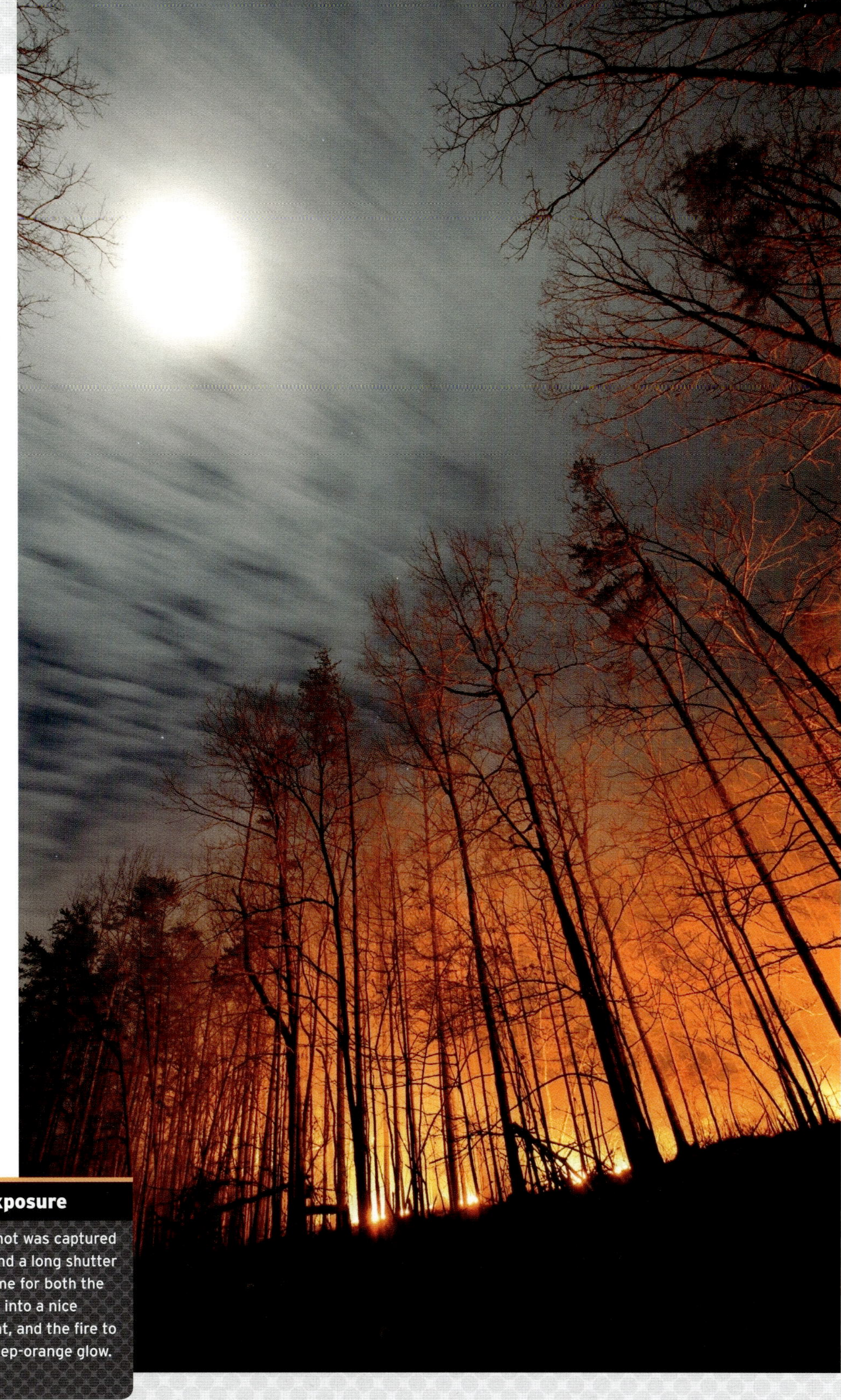

Extended exposure

This dramatic shot was captured using a tripod and a long shutter speed, giving time for both the clouds to streak into a nice diagonal element, and the fire to diffuse into a deep-orange glow.

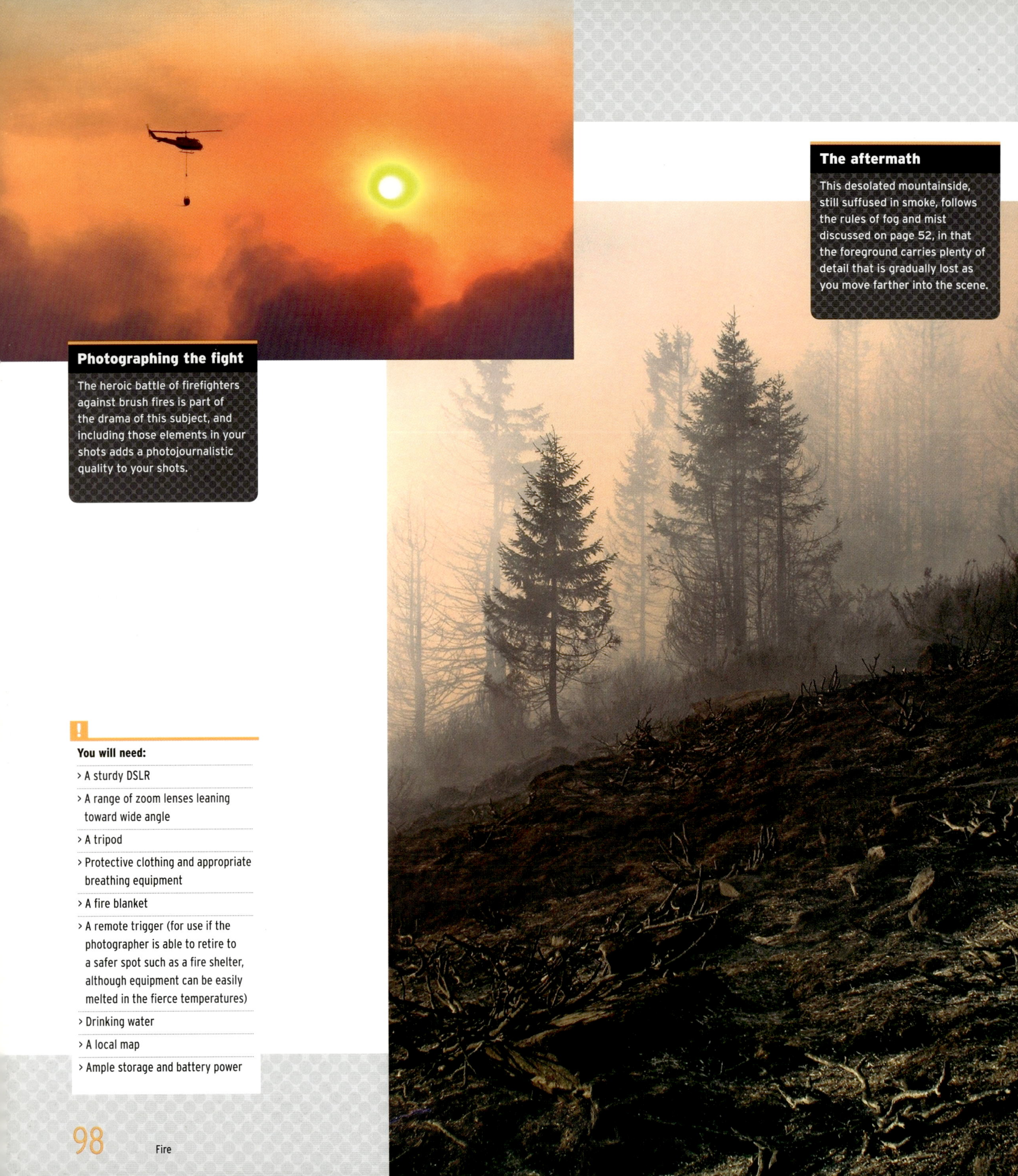

You will need:

> A sturdy DSLR

> A range of zoom lenses leaning toward wide angle

> A tripod

> Protective clothing and appropriate breathing equipment

> A fire blanket

> A remote trigger (for use if the photographer is able to retire to a safer spot such as a fire shelter, although equipment can be easily melted in the fierce temperatures)

> Drinking water

> A local map

> Ample storage and battery power

Fires in the Sky

Firestorms occur on such a large scale that they will likely illuminate the underside of clouds and can be seen for miles around. But the amount of smoke and ash that pours into the sky is likely to drop ambient light levels significantly. So, again, expose for the fire, with extra exposure compensation applied so that the histogram (when shooting Raw) is as far to right as possible. The glow for the fire should illuminate most of the shadows out of complete darkness, and where it does not, the contrast between the fire and shadows will create silhouettes of tree trunks and figures, where present, which make for atmospheric images.

One challenge with shooting any form of fire is focus. Flames are not static objects and are capricious in nature, so focus (manually, if necessary) on a static object, such as a tree, rock, hill or other landmark, which is at the same distance as the fire.

Shutter speed will also have an impact on the appearance of the flames. Slower shutter speeds, for example, will add slight motion blur to the flames, as they will be constantly dancing and moving. Use a faster shutter speed, above 1/100 second at minimum, to freeze them.

There will also be a lot of smoke and ash, which can obscure the view. Alternatively, make creative use of the smoke, for example, to shoot people and figures in the murky atmosphere. A wider, landscape shot taken from a vantage point will also highlight the amount of smoke billowing from the fire. At night, the smoke will be effused with an orange glow from the fire, so look for distinct patterns and shapes in the glowing smoke.

If caught unaware by a firestorm, a large, wide clearing or stretch of water can provide a natural shelter from the radiated heat and lack of oxygen, as well as a relatively safe location from which to shoot. Including companions and other people doing the same thing will add drama to the shot. In such an event use a wide-angle lens, or even a fisheye, to capture the encroaching or surrounding fire, with the clearing or water included in the foreground.

Aerial photography can also provide a safe way to shoot firestorms. Again, lower ambient light levels, such as dusk or night-time will provide dramatic shots, highlighting the intensity and scale of the firestorm within the wider local environment.

If access to the area is not possible, the only other option is to return once the firestorm has abated. Expect to see charred and gnarled tree trunks, melted man-made objects (including metal!), and animal carcasses. Use the unusual, twisted shapes of burned trees to create abstract landscapes, in tune with the otherworldly scene that will be presented before the photographer.

If shooting in Raw, consider converting such images to black and white in post-processing, which will stay true to the colorless aftermath of the firestorm. Keep an eye out for unusual items that escaped the firestorm—for example, in some firestorms in Australia recently it was noticed that eucalyptus trees were spared, while all other surrounding vegetation had been razed to the ground.

Keep returning to the region over the coming months, too, as this could provide a fascinating record of how the countryside or forest regenerates itself, surprisingly quickly. New shoots on the forest floor juxtaposed against the blackened remains can stir emotions and conjure concepts such as survival and rebirth.

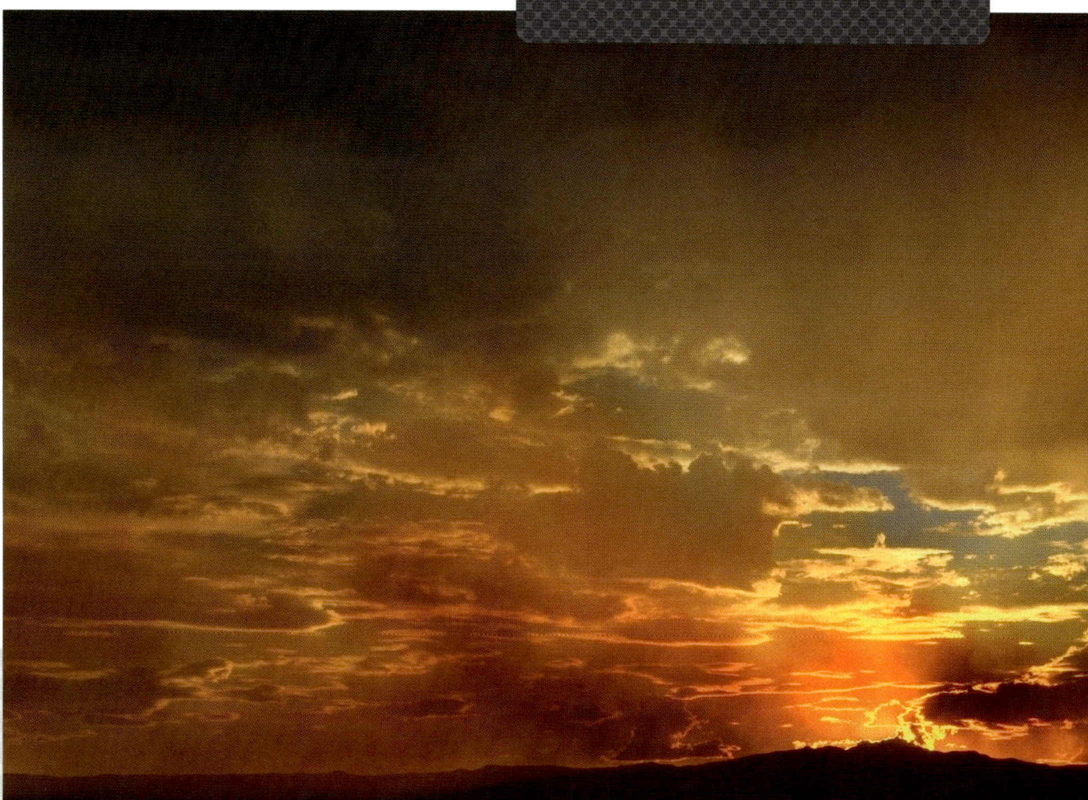

Sunsets

Sunset marks the boundary between day and night, light and dark. This day-night cycle is hardwired into the human brain and has influenced the evolution of almost every species on the planet. So it is no wonder that few photographers can ignore the lure of a slow-burning sunset.

Photographing sunsets is, on the one hand, relatively easy–it is accessible to anyone with a camera and the willingness to spend an hour or two outdoors. On the other hand, it is all too easy to get it wrong. Photography stock libraries are flooded with sunset imagery and almost everyone with a camera has numerous stored on their hard drive. So elevating sunset photography to another level requires planning, dedication, and exemplary photographic technique.

The red, orange, and magenta colors normally associated with sunsets are caused by a phenomenon known as Rayleigh scattering, which describes the scattering or diffusion of light as it hits atoms and molecules in the Earth's atmosphere. During the day, light from overhead is scattered equally in all directions, resulting in a blue color.

At sunset, and sunrise, the sun is low on the horizon so its light has farther to travel through the atmosphere. During this journey, blue light is scattered out of the light spectrum, leaving only reds and magentas, giving sunsets their characteristic colors. Atmospheric conditions, such as an approaching or receding storm front, rough seas, mist or volcanic ash can all add to the impact of this effect and create stunning

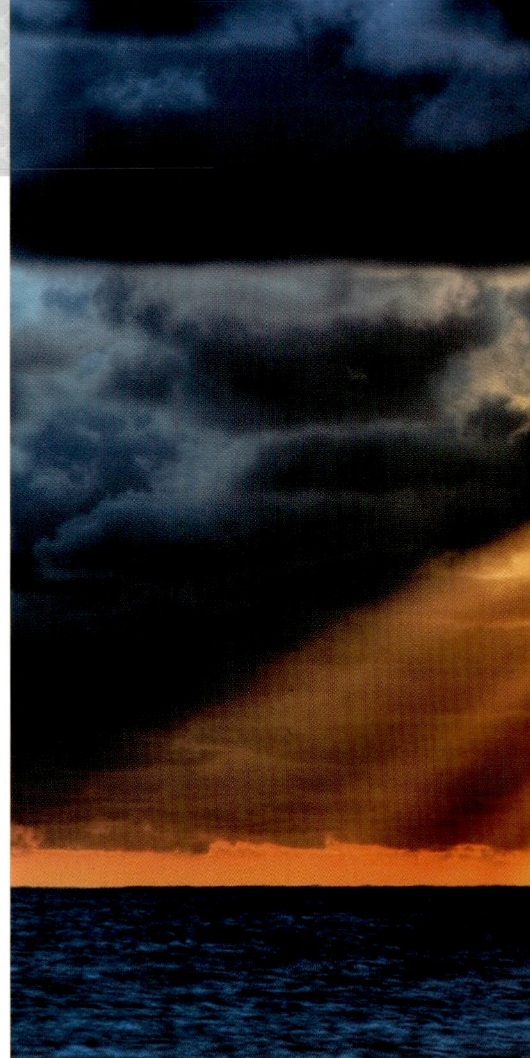

sunsets–conversely, clear conditions can often provide disappointing results.

In photography parlance, this effect is often referred to as the golden hour, which describes the hour around sunrise or sunset (half an hour on either side) when the light is at its most attractive and appealing to landscape photographers.

One of the most common mistakes made by inexperienced photographers seeking a strong sunset image is to pack up and go home once the sun has dipped beyond the horizon. As described by the golden hour, the best light and colors often develop up to an hour after the sun has set.

The classic reflection composition

As the sun follows a predictable path across the sky, you'll be well rewarded if you take the time to scout out an excellent composition ahead of time and wait for the sun to come into position. Here, not only is the sun reflected in a glistening line across the water, but it is also framed by the silhouette of overhanging trees and marshes.

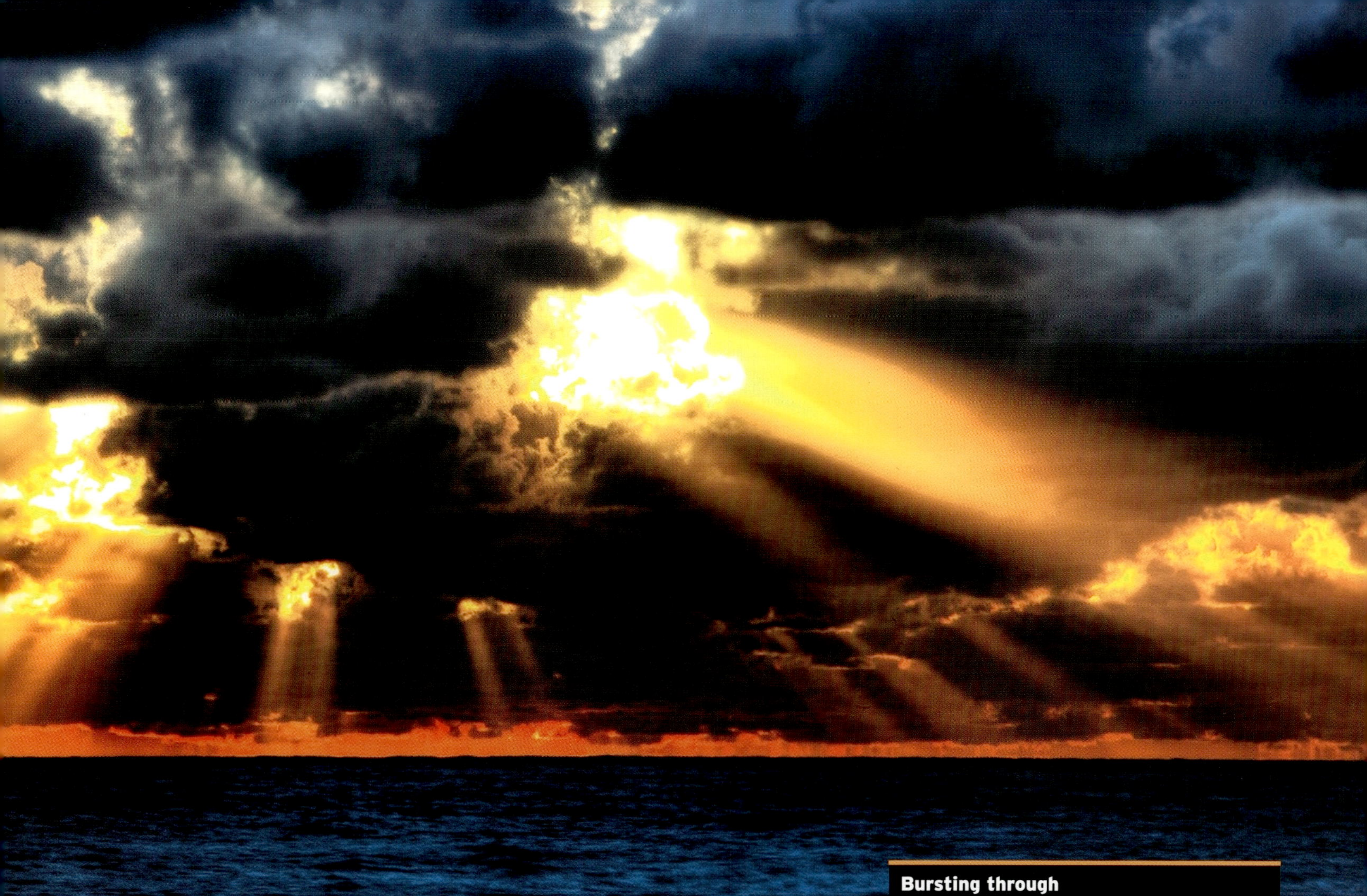

Even when the sun has dropped out of sight for an earthbound viewer, it will still be lighting clouds higher in the sky from beneath with reds, salmon pinks, and magentas. Later still, twilight brings encroaching blue and cyan light, which can create a strong contrast with the orange afterglow from beyond the horizon. Blue and yellow, and red and cyan represent complementary colors on the RGB color chart, and can be used to create drama and impact in the final image. City lights and other light sources add further impact to this day-night boundary.

Even before the sun has set, cloud of any kind can produce more dramatic sunsets than wide, clear skies. A low sun breaking through a gap in the clouds, or even better illuminating a blanket of clouds from underneath can create dramatic lighting, which will serve to give more punch to any sunset shot.

Professional landscape photographers are often studious amateur meteorologists, following weather forecasts meticulously to try to predict the potential for unusual and dramatic sunset conditions.

Planning the location of the shoot is also vital. While a close-up of the setting sun is appealing, it is often the wider-angle shots, including sky, clouds, and foreground interest, that work best. Water reflections, a crashing wave, rocks, trees, gates, pathways. Strong lead-in lines and well-placed foreground objects can add real impact to sunset shots, giving the viewer a sense of being there.

Visiting a favorite location numerous times will also reap dividends, allowing the photographer to work out a variety of compositions, angles, and foreground subjects in order to maximize the photographic opportunities in a single shoot, useful when the conditions are right.

Bursting through

As you know from our previous discussion of cloud types, even large clouds have a hard time completely blocking out sunlight. Particularly when the sun is setting and its light is at a strong angle with a golden hue, it can break through the gaps and appear as clear beams shining down from above. This particular shot contrasts its rich, warm tones with a saturated blue sea to great effect.

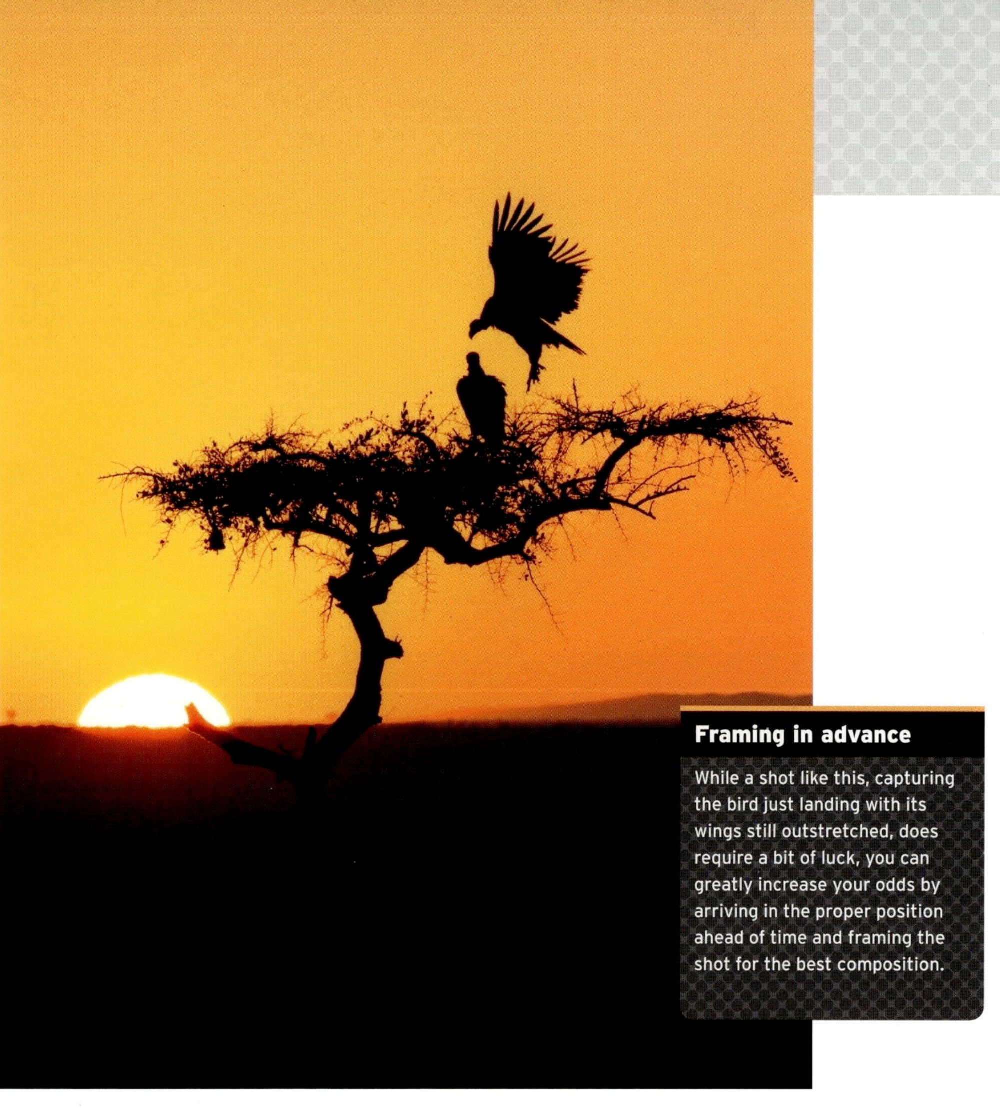

foreground subjects or other points of focus, such as boats, rocks, trees, or the like—and whether the photographer is shooting into the sun, or using the low setting sun to model or side-light foreground subject matter.

Also bear in mind that, particularly when shooting into the sun, using autoexposure modes, such as Program, Shutter Priority or Aperture Priority, is likely to result in foreground subjects appearing as silhouettes. Of course, a silhouette may be the desired outcome, but learning to control the camera manually is no bad thing. Auto settings leave the camera, not the photographer, in control of the creative decision-making process. Shooting into the sun can also cause lens flare, and more importantly, can be harmful to the eyes when viewed directly through the viewfinder.

Set the camera's focus to Manual and use a standard technique—either one-third into the scene or using published hyperfocal distances for the focal length used. Most commonly, a small aperture (high number, such as f/11 or f/16) will be required to maximize depth of field, particularly if foreground subject is being included. A shorter focal length (such as 24mm) will offer greater depth of field. Bear in mind that stopping the aperture down (using a narrower lens aperture and higher f-stop, e.g. f/22) reduces edge sharpness as a result of diffraction, even in expensive lenses.

For the greatest level of control, shoot in Manual exposure mode. Use a neutral tone, such as a gray cloud or light rock, to gain an initial exposure, and then view the results on the histogram at the back of the camera. Evaluative or matrix metering will provide a good starting point, but for fine-level exposure control, advanced landscape photographers will often use spot metering.

Neutral density filters can also help to balance the contrast in exposure between the sun or sky—which will be bright compared to the foreground at this time of day—and the foreground. Even if the image is composed with the sun out of frame, the contrast between ground and sky can still be too high for the camera's sensor to record shadow and highlight details.

ND filters come in a range of strengths, and act to reduce exposure by a set amount in only the top part of the image (or bottom part, if the filter is reversed). Filters are held in front of the lens by a holder and can be moved and placed along the line of the horizon to reduce the exposure in the sky, leaving the foreground untouched.

As a general rule, ND filters should be used to bring the difference between the sky and earth down to around 1-stop. If, for example, your camera's metering shows that a neutral tone in the sky is 4-stops brighter than a neutral tone on the ground in the same scene, then use a 3-stop ND filter to balance the two.

Use hard ND filters—which have a distinct, clear graduation—if the horizon is flat and free of other subject matter. Soft ND filters provide a wider gradation between light and dark areas of the frame and, as a result, they can be used for uneven horizons or in the presence of subjects such as trees.

Focus and exposure settings will depend on the composition—whether including

Embrace the backlight

As you'll naturally be shooting into the sun, you can use that backlighting situation to illuminate fine textures in foreground elements, as with the delicate strands of vegetation at the bottom of the frame.

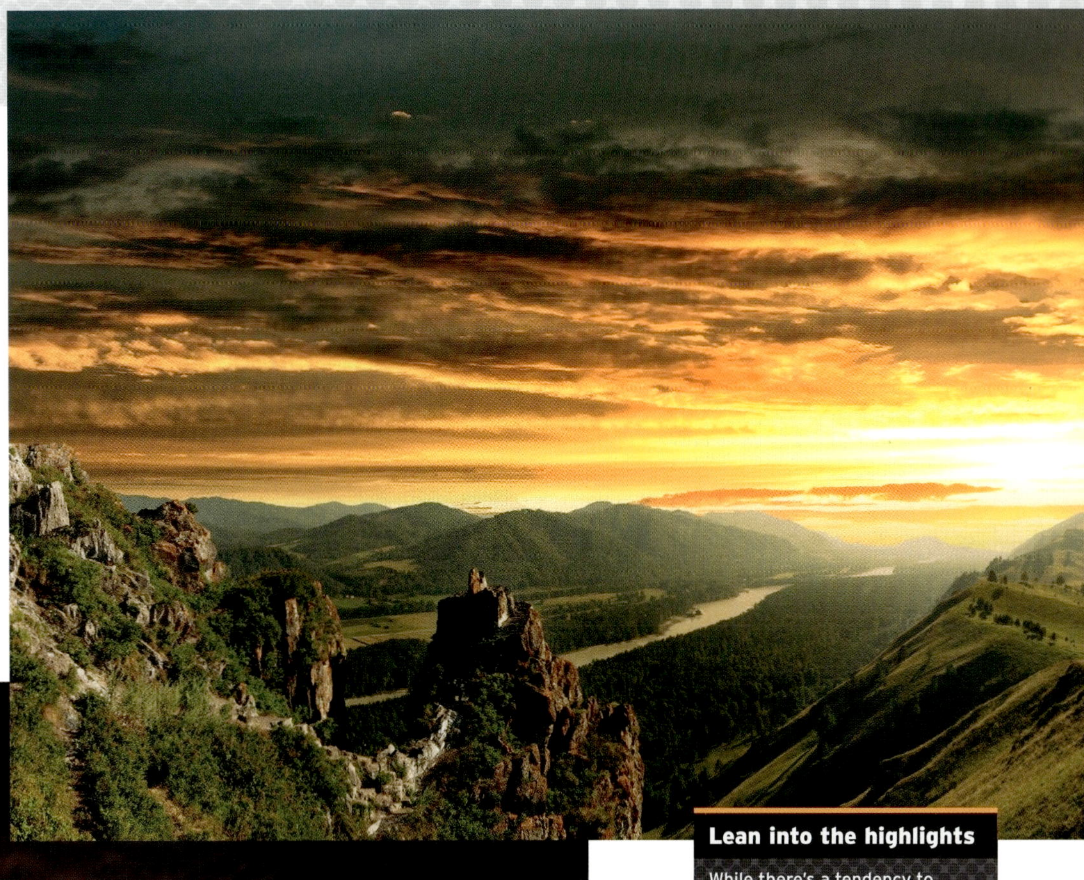

Lean into the highlights

While there's a tendency to underexpose a sunset in order to saturate the skies, there is enough exposure leeway to go the other direction—slightly overexposing the sky in favor of properly exposing the full extent of the rest of the landscape. Of course, this is best suited for compositions that include plenty of ground elements.

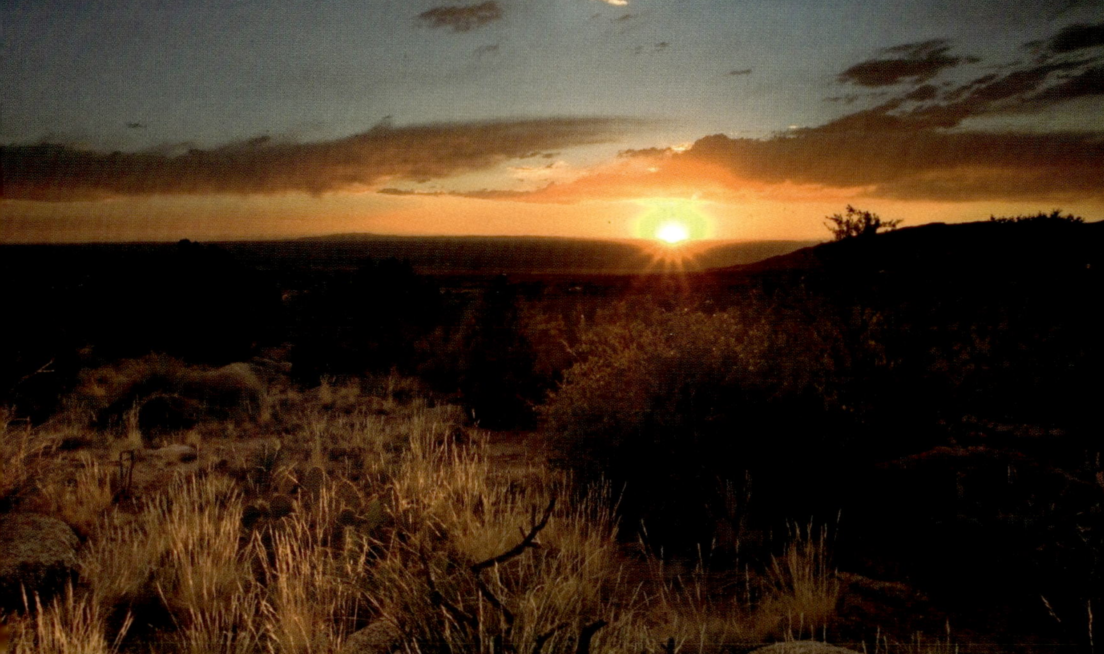

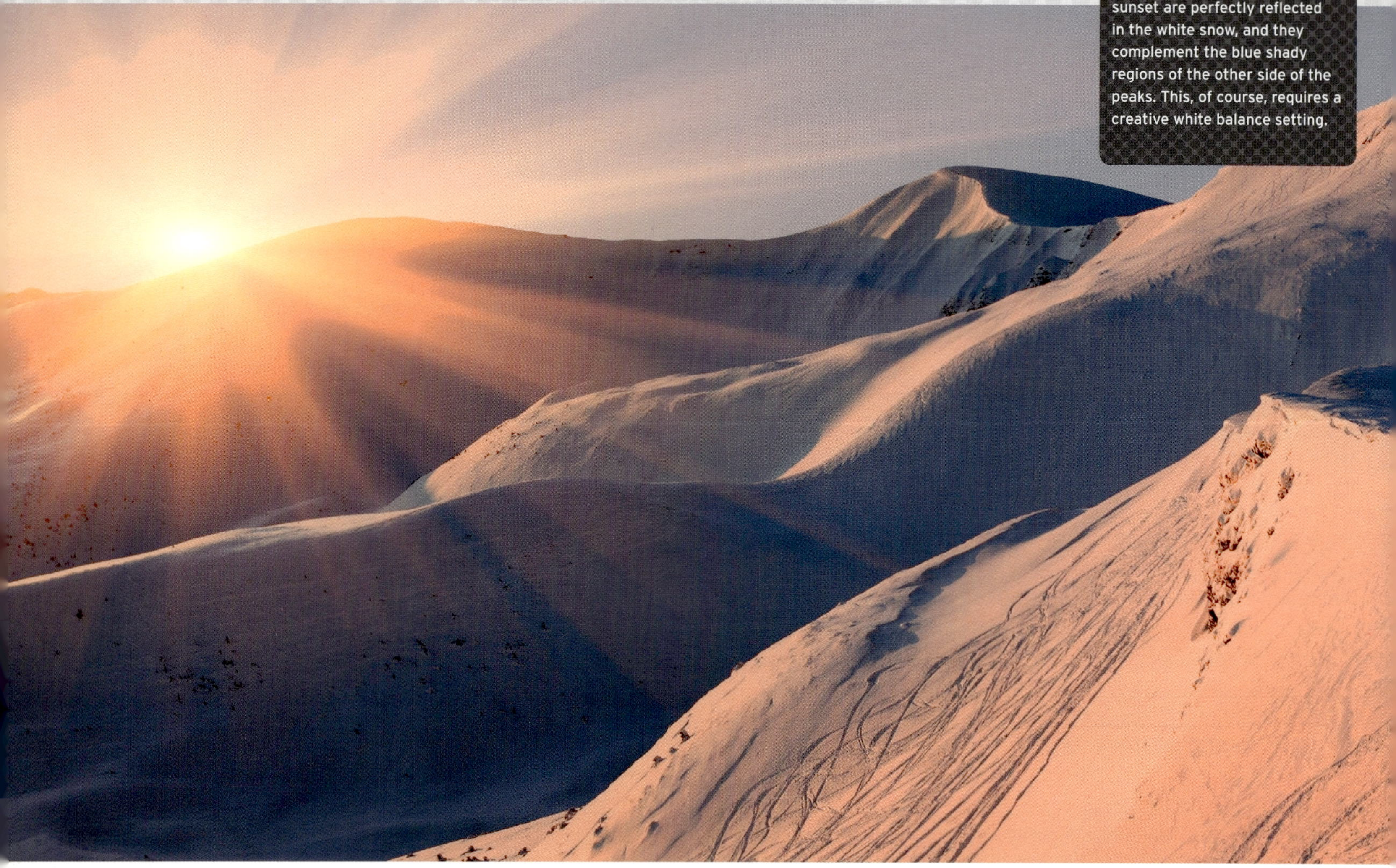

Snowy sunsets

Here, the orange tones of the
sunset are perfectly reflected
in the white snow, and they
complement the blue shady
regions of the other side of the
peaks. This, of course, requires a
creative white balance setting.

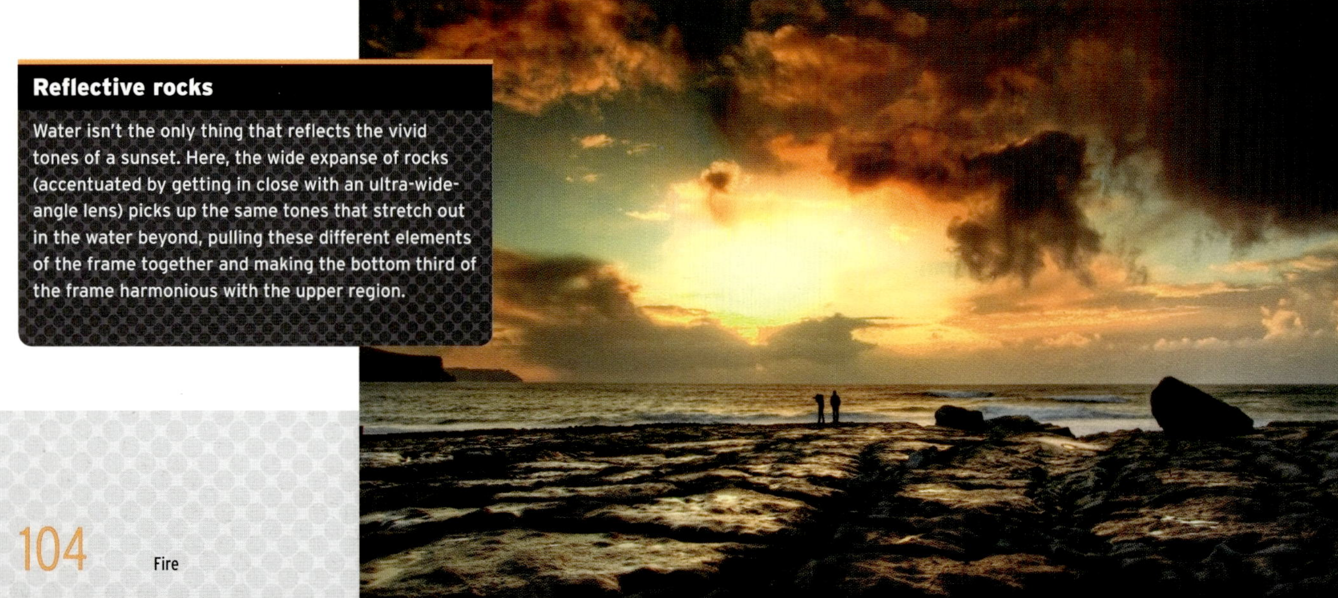

Reflective rocks

Water isn't the only thing that reflects the vivid
tones of a sunset. Here, the wide expanse of rocks
(accentuated by getting in close with an ultra-wide-
angle lens) picks up the same tones that stretch out
in the water beyond, pulling these different elements
of the frame together and making the bottom third of
the frame harmonious with the upper region.

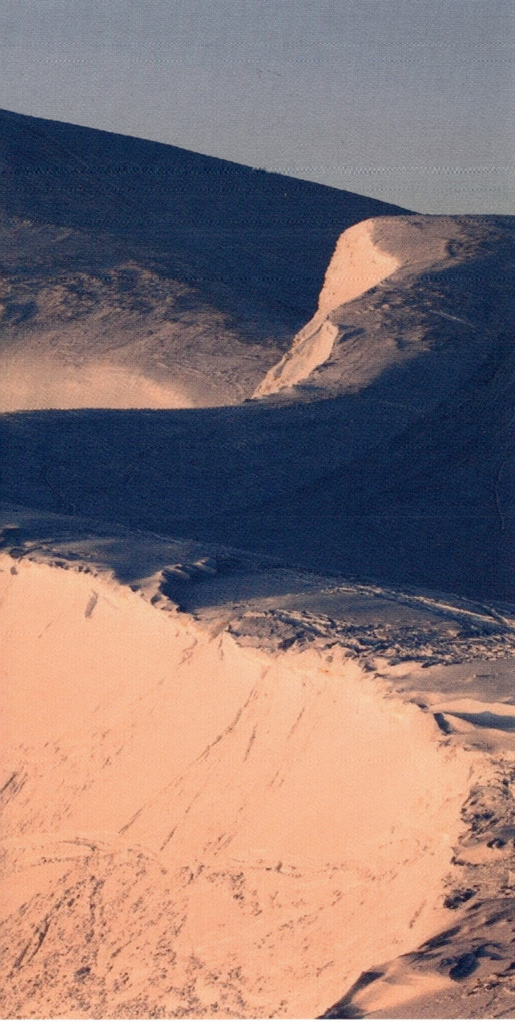

Optimal Sunset Exposures

During exposure, take care not to blow the highlight details—most cameras have a highlight-alert function, which will show blown-out areas as a flashing area on the image. Dial down exposure as necessary.

ISO should be as low as possible to reduce noise in the shadows, and to optimize image quality, while shutter speed is dictated by the creative intention. For example, streaked waves receding on an empty beach are captured using slow shutter speeds of around 2 seconds or more—of course, this will also result in streaked or blurred clouds, which may not be the photographer's intention.

It may not be possible to capture all the shadow and highlight detail in the scene at any exposure—that is, the dynamic range of the scene is too high for the camera's sensor. In this case, there are a number of options available. First, use ND filters as previously described. Second, take two exposures (for example, one for the sky and one for the foreground) and merge them in post-processing. Third, use bracketing and choose the best fit post-shoot. As always, shooting in Raw gives much more flexibility in post-processing for pulling back lost details.

Another option is high dynamic range (HDR) imagery, which can be used on either a single image (presuming the shadow and highlight details are not lost) or better still to take a wide range of exposures, from dark to bright, which can then be merged post-processing into an image that includes shadow and highlight detail.

Special effects, such as colored filters, can enhance the colors of a sunset, but a cheaper option is to experiment with white balance, either in-camera or during processing. Many landscape photographers leave their white balance setting on Daylight, the argument being: Why mess around with nature's colors?

However, shifting the white balance temperature can significantly alter the feel of an image. Shifting color temperature upward (higher) will make the white balance more yellow, while shifting downward will enhance the blues in an image. Alternatively, moving from Daylight setting to Shade will add warmth (i.e. make more yellow), while the Tungsten setting will make the image more blue, removing any of the sunset's original color. As always, practice and experiment.

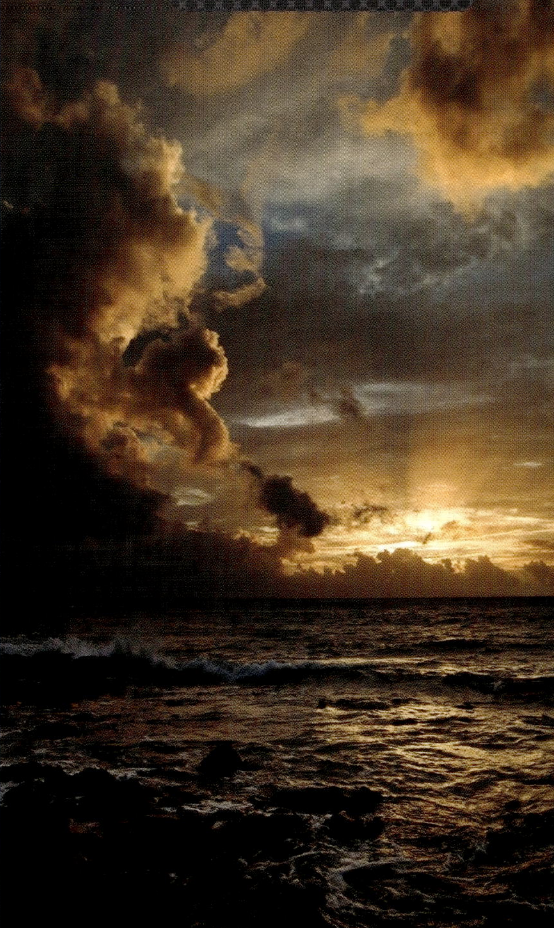

Avoiding oversaturation

As most sunset shots embrace the rich tones and tend toward strong saturation, you can distinguish your shots by desaturating them just a touch in post—though the shot must stand strong in its composition.

Processing for Fire

The first rule of processing for fire is to shoot in Raw. This not only provides some latitude in exposure errors, but also allows much more flexibility for altering Levels and Curves, Hue and Saturation, and White Balance, among other things.

The first step, of course, is to capture the correct exposure in-camera. This usually requires dialing in exposure compensation of around 1 to 2 f-stops of overexposure at the time of shooting. As described elsewhere in the book, the camera's exposure metering system is based on an algorithm that presumes that the average exposure tone is 18% gray. Therefore, white subjects are underexposed by the exposure meter to appear gray, while black subjects are overexposed as they are pushed toward

18% gray. To compensate, white or bright subjects need to be overexposed, and black and dark subjects should be underexposed. While shooting in Raw goes some way to negating this effect, given the latitude it offers in terms of post-processing, it is still best to ensure that the exposure is set in-camera in order to gain the best possible image quality and to avoid image noise in the shadow areas of the shot.

In the case of fire and flames, they are naturally bright, so the photographer will need to manually overexpose (via positive exposure compensation) in order to override the camera's metering. Push the histogram on a test shot as far as possible to the right of the LCD screen on the back of the camera, without clipping the highlights.

Once the file has been downloaded and opened in the photographer's Raw processing application of choice, first tweak exposure, contrast and color saturation in order to

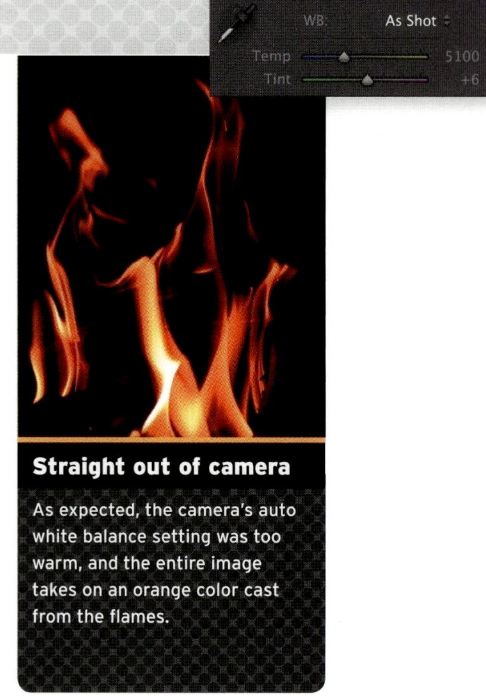

Straight out of camera

As expected, the camera's auto white balance setting was too warm, and the entire image takes on an orange color cast from the flames.

provide a good foundation for further processing in Photoshop—Raw processing applications, such as Lightroom or Aperture, do not allow the use of Layers and Masks, which can really enhance images.

Possibly the most important control at this stage, however, is White Balance (WB). The color temperature of fire and flames is, counter-intuitively, low. Low color temperatures are red, orange, and yellow and give a warm feel to an image. For example, the color temperature of a candle (which gives off a very warm deep-orange light) is around 1700K, while standard midday daylight temperature (which is said to be cool and blue in tone) is around 5600K.

By playing around with the color temperature it is possible to enhance the warm, fiery colors of fire and flames—however, try not to overdo it, as the WB changes will also affect other parts of the image. Red and cyan, for

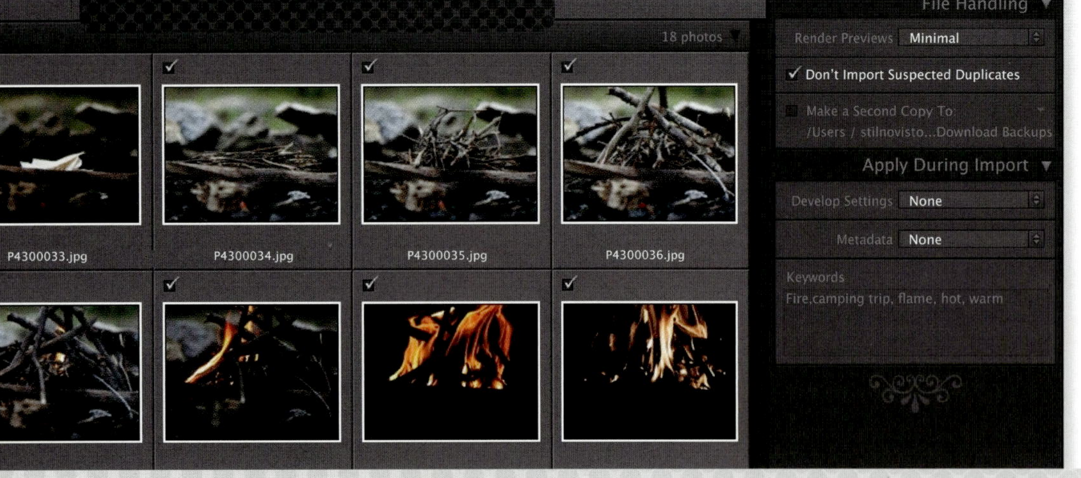

Proper import protocol

Workflow-oriented programs like Adobe Lightroom make image-library management a breeze, so long as you get into the habit of importing your images into a well-maintained catalog, including keywords.

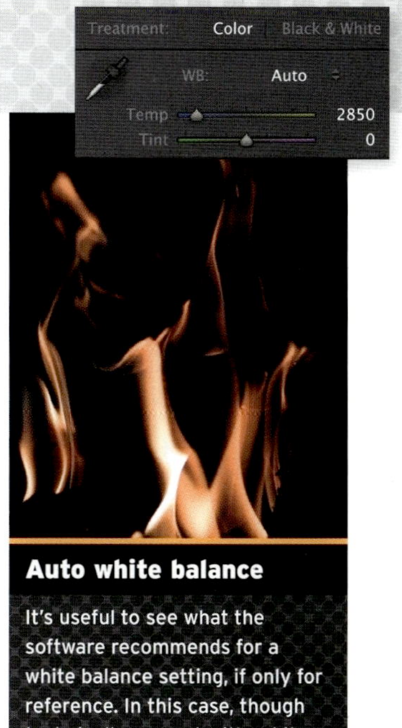

Auto white balance

It's useful to see what the software recommends for a white balance setting, if only for reference. In this case, though technically accurate, it's a bit too cool for the subject.

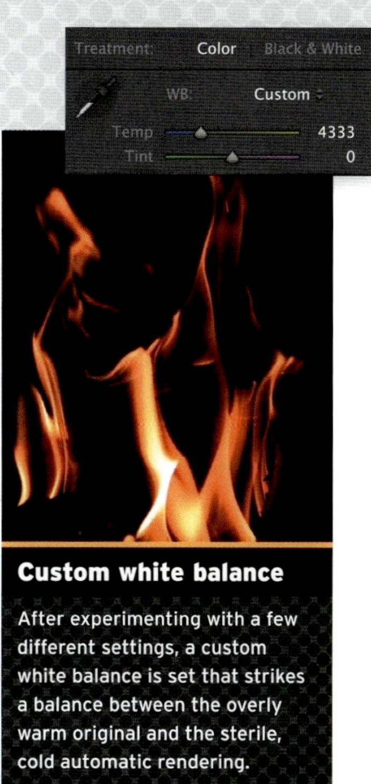

Custom white balance

After experimenting with a few different settings, a custom white balance is set that strikes a balance between the overly warm original and the sterile, cold automatic rendering.

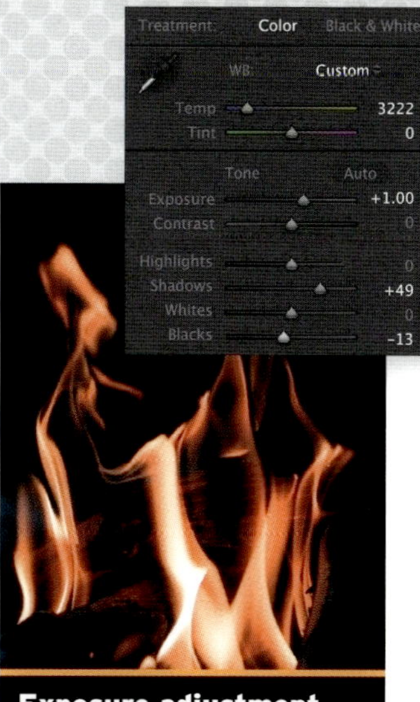

Exposure adjustment

To regain detail in the burning wood, exposure is boosted, along with the shadows. Of course, a positive exposure compensation at the time of shooting would have been a better choice.

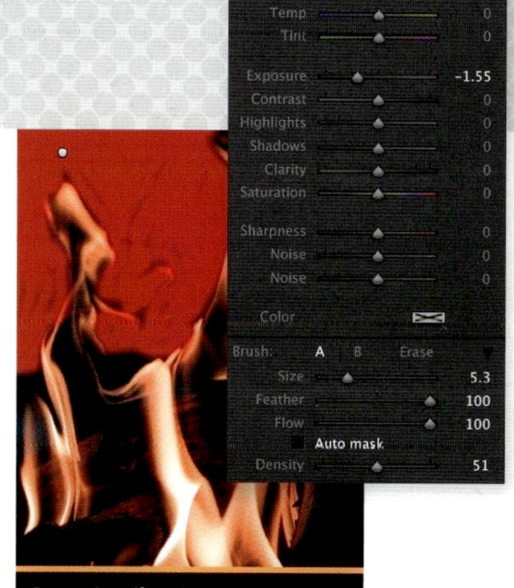

Local adjustment brush

But now the background is too bright. To make it fall back off into shadow, the adjustment brush is set to negative exposure, and painted over the top of the frame (shown in red).

example, are complementary colors—that is, they are opposite on the color chart—which means that when used together in a single image can create drama and tension. So if a blue sky or a night sky is present in the same shot as fire and flames, altering the WB at this stage will minimize this effect. Color hue and saturation can always be added using Layers and Masks in Photoshop so use some moderation when altering WB in the Raw file.

Once the overriding settings have been altered in the Raw file, export it as a 16-bit TIFF file—using 16-bit (the image will later become an 8-bit JPEG file) retains more color information at this stage.

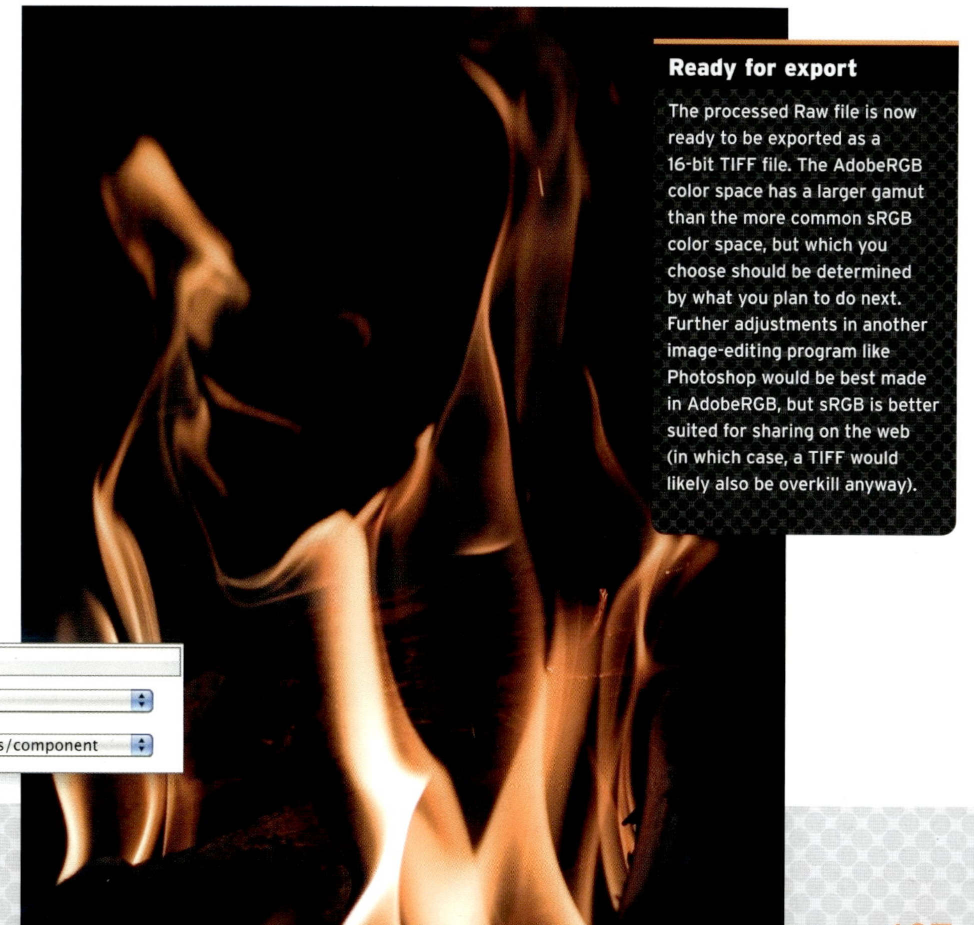

Ready for export

The processed Raw file is now ready to be exported as a 16-bit TIFF file. The AdobeRGB color space has a larger gamut than the more common sRGB color space, but which you choose should be determined by what you plan to do next. Further adjustments in another image-editing program like Photoshop would be best made in AdobeRGB, but sRGB is better suited for sharing on the web (in which case, a TIFF would likely also be overkill anyway).

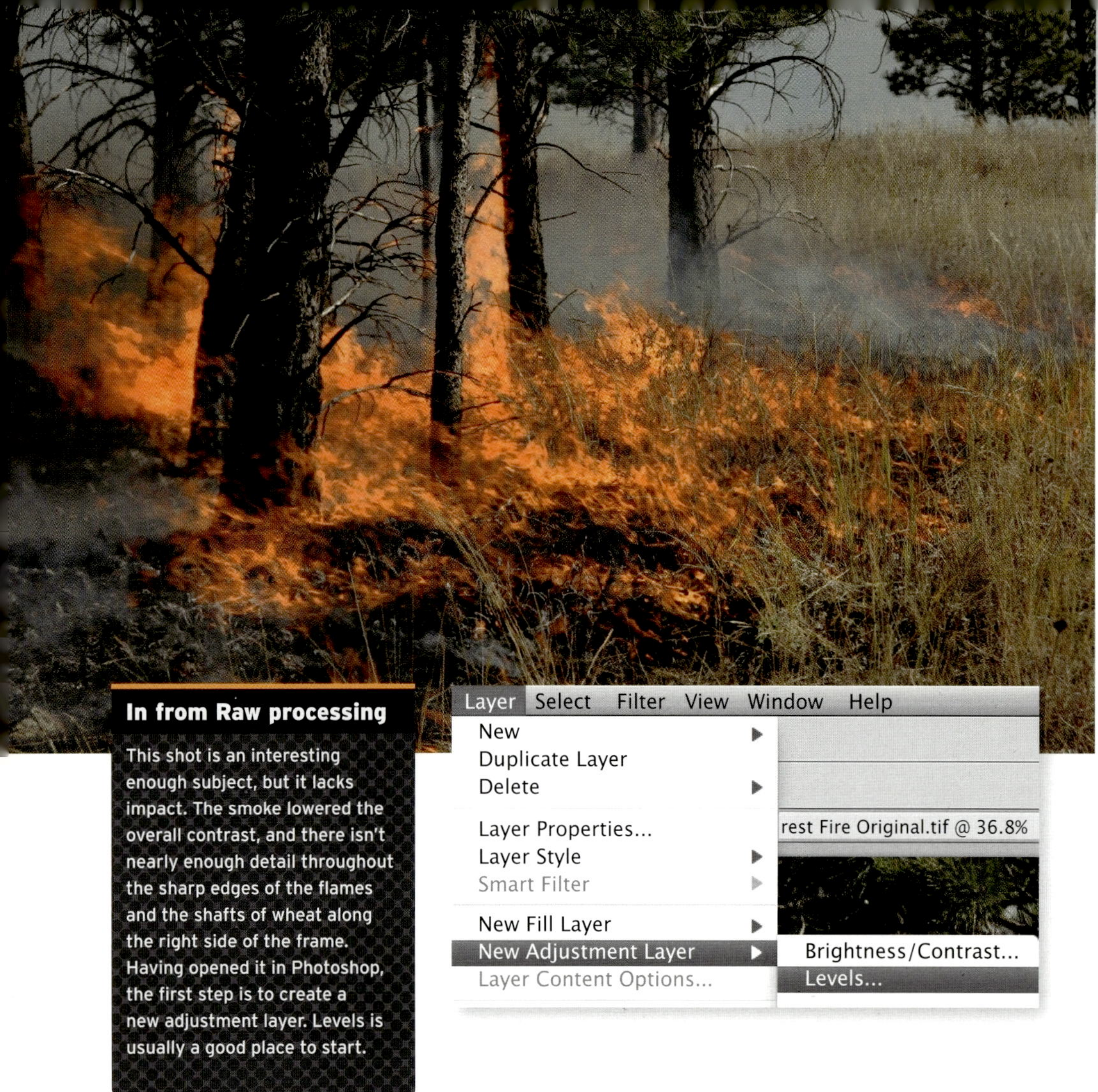

start to give real depth and dimension to the flames. To prevent the effect over parts of the image that do not contain flames, add a mask to the layer adjustment, which allows the photographer to paint in where the effect should be applied using the Brush tool.

This mask can then be reused to alter, for example, the hue and saturation of the flames, with any changes applied to the same parts of the image as the Curves layer adjustment mask. For finer control, create a set of new masks altogether to alter the hue and saturation of, say, oranges, reds, yellows and blues individually. The blue could be applied to the night sky, for example.

A final alteration might be to use Dodge and Burn tools to further boost local contrast between the darker and lighter components of the flames. Again, this should be performed on a layer rather than the background image, that is the original file.

More advanced users can try boosting macro contrast of the whole image by duplicating the original TIFF file without layers, and then changing the Blending mode of the top layer to Multiply. The effect will be too strong, but try reducing the Opacity to around 10-30% until the lighter areas of the image look natural, but deeper than the original. Then add a layer mask and, using the Brush tool set to a low setting (around 40%) reduce the darkest areas where the effect is too strong.

Potential Editing Workflows

Open the TIFF in Photoshop, or any preferred post-processing application that allows Masks and Layers (which are used to make changes to an image without actually altering the original image file, as changes are made literally on layers that sit over the top of the original image).

The main settings to concentrate on when processing for fire are Curves, Levels, Color Hue and Saturation, and Dodging and Burning. Curves and Levels are similar in terms of their overall effect, which is to control contrast in the image, or part of the image if using a Mask. Flames naturally have bright and darker areas—lighter areas are often white or yellow in color, while darker

areas are deep orange or red. There may also be blue present, depending on the material that is burning—and smoke can also be blue.

Levels are often used as a macro alteration, while Curves allow more precise control over the parts of the image that are being altered. Whenever making alterations in Photoshop, always use a layer adjustment where possible, as these changes are applied to layers on top of the original image and do not affect the original image in any way.

In general, flames and fire will benefit from localized boosting of contrast, so try pushing the brighter areas lighter, and the darker areas darker by manipulating the Curves at different points along the graph. This should

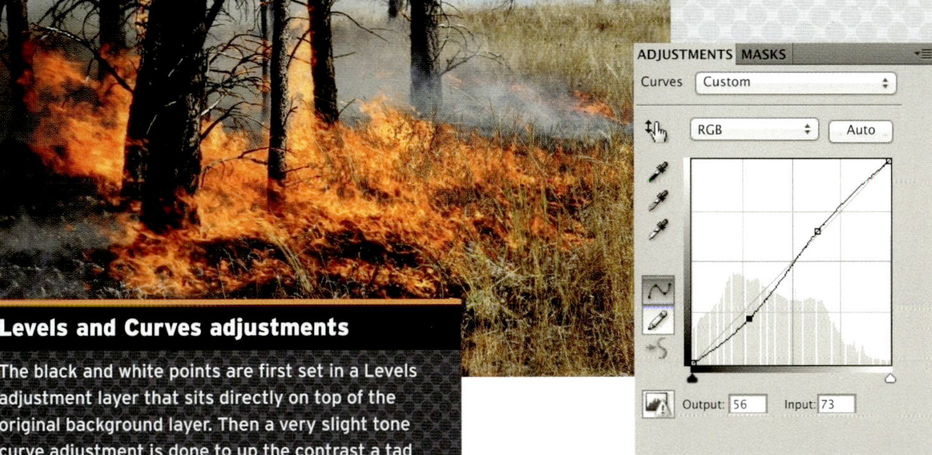
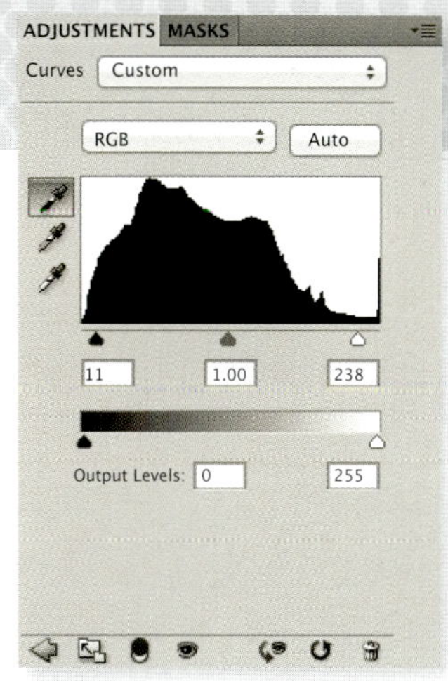

Levels and Curves adjustments

The black and white points are first set in a Levels adjustment layer that sits directly on top of the original background layer. Then a very slight tone curve adjustment is done to up the contrast a tad more. By clicking the eye icon on and off, the effects of each adjustment can be observed independent of each other, and fine-tuned accordingly.

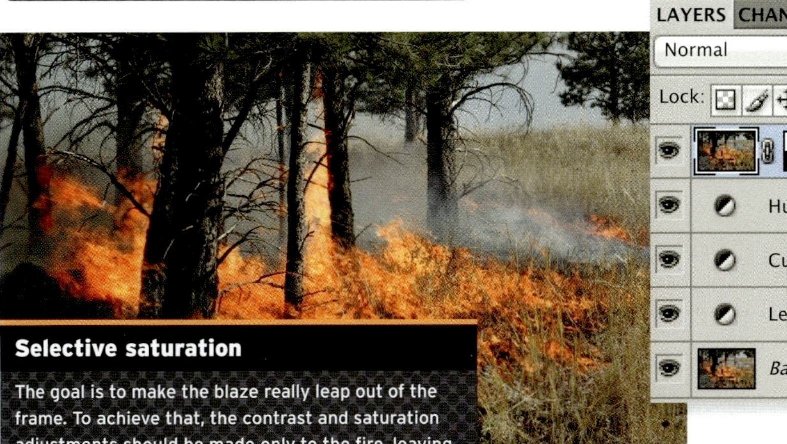

Selective saturation

The goal is to make the blaze really leap out of the frame. To achieve that, the contrast and saturation adjustments should be made only to the fire, leaving the rest of the frame alone. So after upping the saturation in another layer adjustment, a layer mask is applied on top of all the other layers, allowing the effects to pass through only in the fire areas.

Sharpen to finish

With the adjustments limited to only the fiery and smoldering areas of the frame, the last step is to sharpen the entire image for output. First, the layers are merged together, then an alternative sharpening technique is applied via a group of two layers (this technique is fully explained later on in page 181).

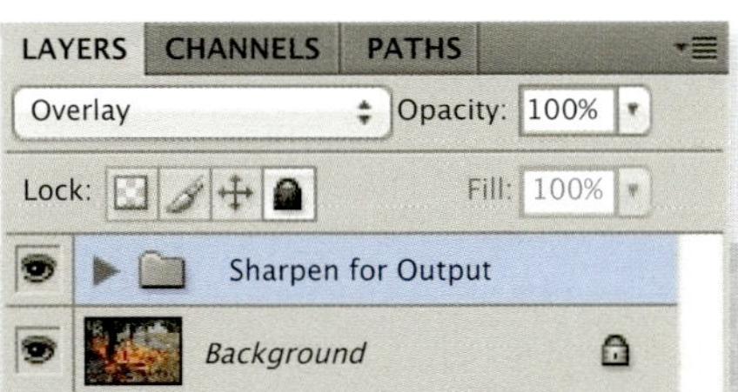

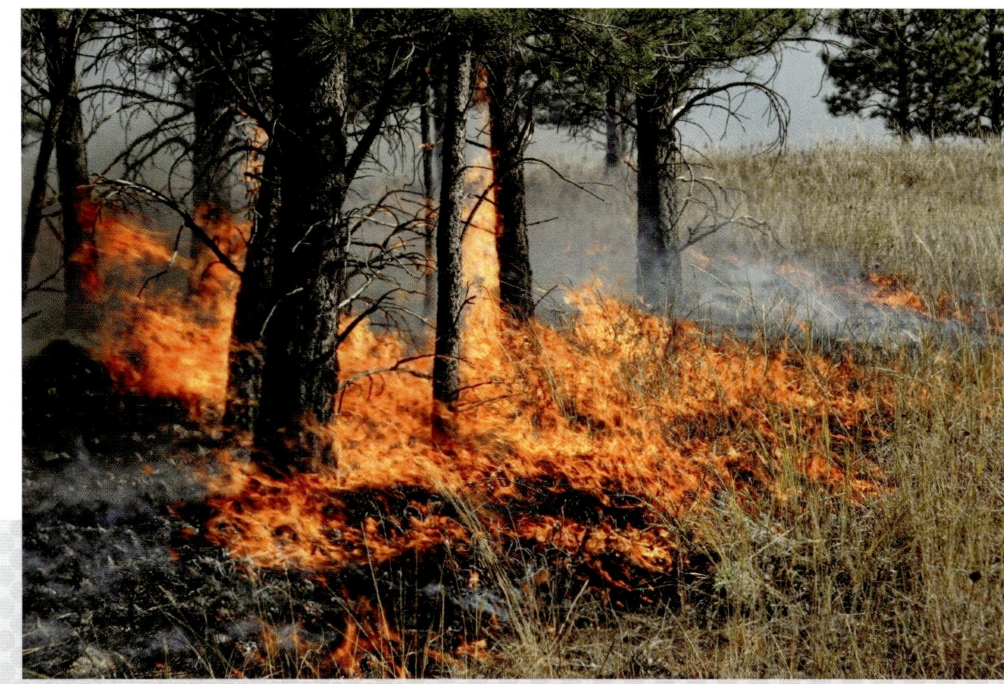

Water

Covering three quarters of the surface of the earth, water is a massive photographic subject, taking on countless forms as it falls, condenses, erupts, freezes, and floods the land both around us and of more exotic locales. While it is a supremely mutable element, there are a handful of tried-and-true techniques that apply rather broadly across its various fluidic representations. Motion, for instance, is frequently a consideration for a water shot, as you can either freeze water in a single instant, or show its graceful curves and torrents spread out over longer shutter speeds. Additionally, water is what makes up so much of the extremely cold environments of this planet, that much of this chapter will be dedicated to not only photographic techniques for capturing those wintry subjects, but also survival techniques for enduring those harsh weather conditions and making it out of the snow and ice with powerful, vivid images.

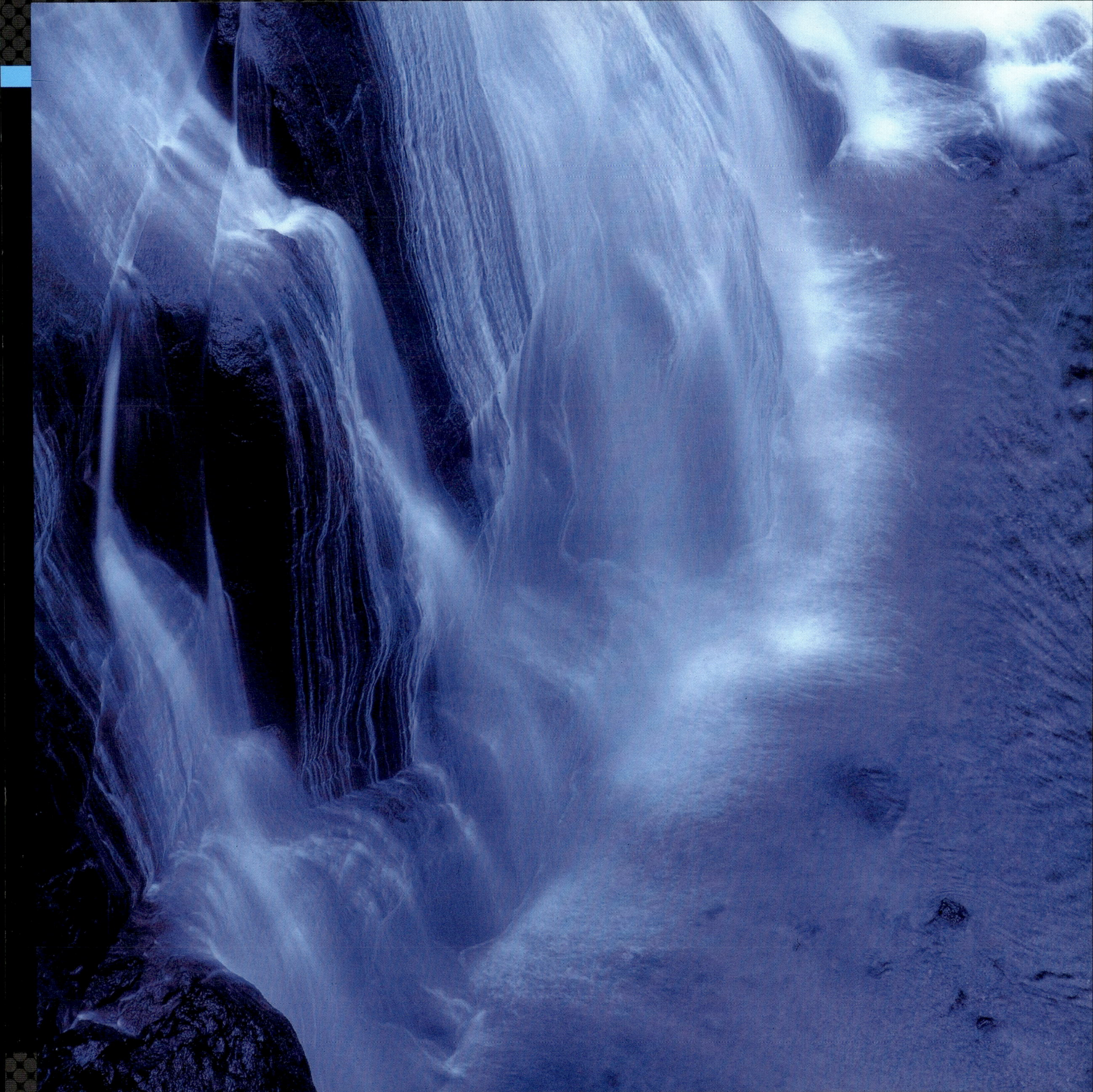

Rain

Far from indicating the end of an outdoor shoot, the onset of rain can open up a treasure trove of creative opportunities for the hardy photographer. As long as photographer and camera are suitably protected, rain in its many forms can offer meditative landscapes, moody cityscapes, beautiful nature close-ups, people and environment action shots, and much more. What is more, by maximizing fine control of the camera's shutter speed, photographers can create a spectrum of creative effects and moods.

It is all too easy to pack and go home at the first hint of the all-too-familiar onset of rain. But the fair-weather photographer is missing a trick by not taking advantage of the myriad opportunities provided by rain. Melancholic seaside resorts, groups of people huddled in doorways, colorful umbrellas, water droplets on leaves and windows, rainbows and rain shafts in the landscape, city reflections, saturated colors, moods and abstracts are just a small collection of the type of creative shot on offer. Rain often triggers memories and feelings, such as melancholia, coziness, damp childhood holidays, romantic walks, or the joy of splashing in puddles. The trick is to embrace the mood and let your imagination run free.

Of course, heavy, prolonged or misty rain will put an end to the day's shooting, but if it is limited to showers, or isolated clouds in the distance, it can in fact increase the variety of shots available to the landscape photographer. For example, it can enhance a landscape image—a distant curtain or shaft of rain can add atmosphere and drama to a wide vista, or create a specific mood or sense of place. Shots of raindrops hitting a body of water, such as the sea or a lake, can also provide atmospheric shots as they create interesting circular patterns or abstracts of ruffled reflections on the water surface. Rain also brings the potential of storms or rainbows to the photographer willing to sit it out.

One of the main requirements for rain photography is some form of raincover. While higher end DSLRs often have weather-sealed bodies, it would still be prudent to purchase a raincover for the camera and lens. A wide range of rain covers is available on the market, from inexpensive transparent covers, which may be discarded after a few uses, to more hardy, expensive covers. A raincover will usually sit over the camera, including the top of the tripod, with a circular opening in the material through which the lens can peer. The opening will fit snugly around the end of the barrel of the lens—by some form of tie-string or elastic—so that only the lens itself is open to the elements. A lens cloth is therefore vital to keep the lens free of unwanted rain droplets and moisture. The cover should also allow for easy access to the camera's buttons, and the better options will allow the photographer to cleanly view the LCD screen. If the rain is heavy, a large umbrella for both photographer and camera will also be a huge benefit—of course, the wind may make this impractical.

A macro lens adds another dimension to rain photography. Close-up shots of an insect on a leaf surrounded by raindrops, dew-speckled flowers, or unusual reflections in a water droplet can all provide striking images. A tripod will be necessary with macro shots, in order to maximize depth of field of focus, which is shorter at closer working distances. An umbrella can also be fitted or rested above the location if the photographer expects to stay in the same spot for some time—but beware of reducing exposure or of color reflections from the umbrella. The use of flash lighting, such as a strobe, a ring flash, or reflectors can all add more impact to macro photography, particularly if they are used off-camera. Remember that ambient light levels may be quite low, so a splash of flash can really pick out close-up subjects.

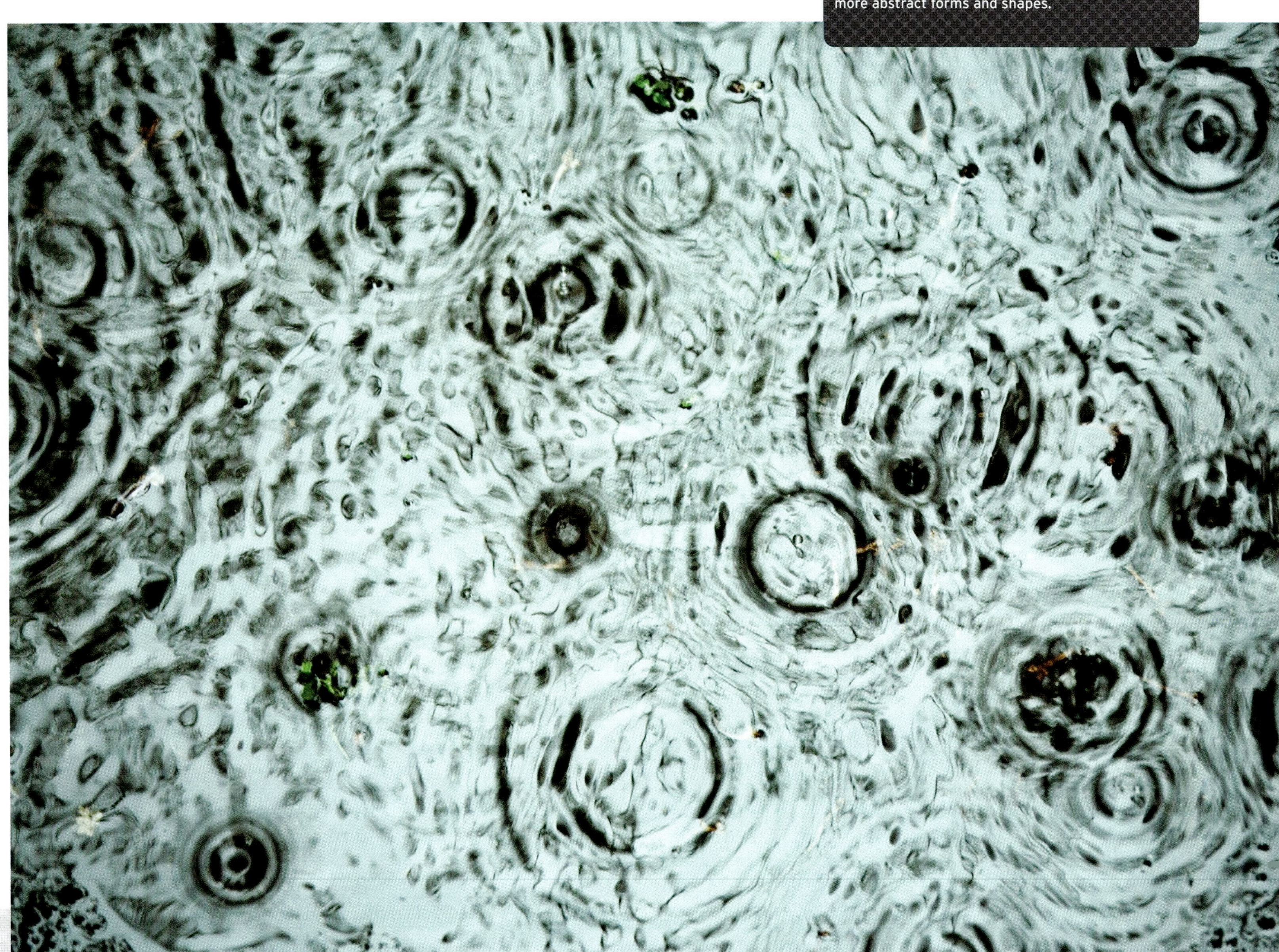

Rippling graphics

The ripples of falling water—particularly when photographed from a perpendicular angle like this—can create images with excellent graphic properties, that rise above their physical subjects and represent more abstract forms and shapes.

Shooting Tips:

> If you're having trouble getting your raindrops to appear in your exposures, try firing your flash—it's somewhat unpredictable and depends a lot on the prevailing lighting conditions, but the drops can often pick up the strobelight.

> For extended use in heavy downpours, even weatherproof camera bodies are not impervious—use a rain jacket.

Exposing for the Rain

The general rules of landscape photography, outlined throughout this book, should be applied—such as maximizing depth of field using aperture, including foreground elements and lead-in lines, using a tripod and employing graduated ND filters to balance exposure between the sky and the land. However, this will depend on the subject matter and intended mood and feel of the final image.

Arguably, the most important exposure setting in the rain is shutter speed, as it can make the biggest difference to the mood and feel of the image. For example, faster shutter speeds will freeze falling rain—very fast speeds, in the 1/1000ths of a second region, may even catch a raindrop exploding as it impacts with surfaces. Conversely, a slow shutter speed will make falling rain appear streaked or blurred, creating a feeling of motion and action, or providing a more interpretive feel to the image.

Using a high aperture and low ISO should allow the photographer to reduce shutter speed to a matter of seconds, particularly if ambient light levels are low. This creative effect will add motion blur to raindrops, making them appear as streaks or lines, rather than droplets, as they fall from the sky. If ambient levels are too high to set a slow shutter speed—even with a low ISO such as 100, and a large aperture number such as f/22—this effect can still be achieved by using a non-graduated ND filter, which has the effect of reducing overall exposure by a set amount. For example, a 3-stop ND filter will add 3 f-stops to the exposure, hence slowing shutter speed and blurring raindrops into longer streaks.

A polarizer, circular or linear, can also be a useful piece of equipment in the rain, as it reduces glare and reflections (which will be strong on wet surfaces) and helps to saturate colors. However, its use is limited to certain subjects, and should be used frugally. For example, if the subject is a reflection on a raindrop-ruffled water surface, a polarizer will tend to completely remove the reflection, rendering the shot useless—in this case, turning a circular polarizer in the opposite direction can actually enhance the strength of the reflection. A polarizer can also be useful for wider landscapes, by saturating colors and reducing glare from wet surfaces.

Arguably, rain has the largest impact on urban photographs—particularly if it is dark. Rain can transform gray city centers into a dizzying blur of reflected shapes, lights and bright colors. Here, experiment with composition, shutter speed and differential focus. The latter effect can be achieved using wide apertures, such as f/4 or lower. Bokeh—the name given to the pleasantly out-of-focus background in an image—can enhance the abstract feel or mood of a wet cityscape. Conversely, a low shutter speed (from using large aperture numbers) will add motion blur, and add to the feeling of motion and action as the city goes about its business at speed. Or, for a more extreme look, try shooting

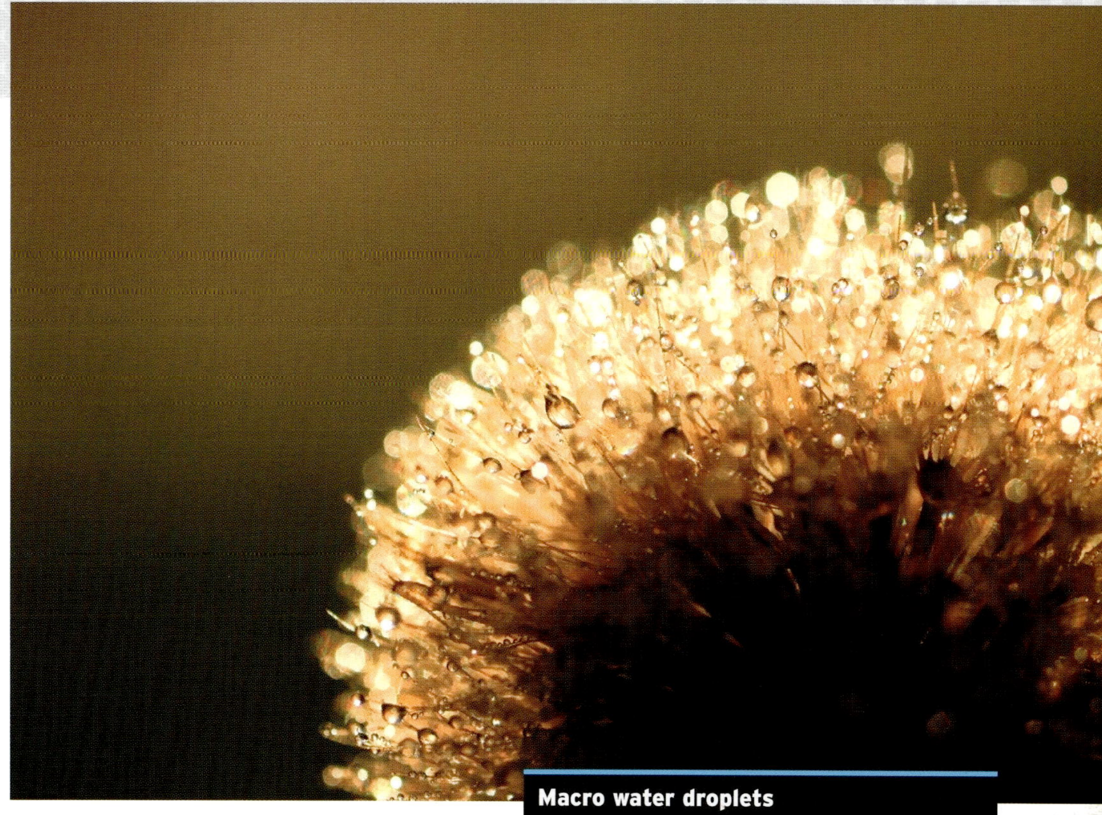

Macro water droplets

Another method of representing rainfall is to capture its effects at the macro level. Here, the bright sun immediately following a brief thunderstorm illuminated the tiny water droplets picked up by this dandelion. Such subjects do an excellent job representing rain without even having to show the rain itself falling.

handheld at shutter speeds of over 10 seconds to create abstract patterns and streaks of colors.

Rain can also allow for very candid, close-up street photography. People are less likely to notice a nearby photographer as they huddle or hunch against the rain, often clenching hoods or umbrellas to their faces while rushing home. This can allow the intrepid street photographer to get closer than normal, without being noticed—but, as with all rain photography, be wary of getting moisture in the camera.

Rainforests

Rainforests provide some of the most spectacular locations on earth, and represent the most diverse ecosystem on the planet. Although they cover a relatively small area of the world (around 7 percent), they act as the planet's lungs and contain 50 percent of the world's total plant and animal species. Rainforests offer the intrepid photographer a wealth of opportunities.

The range and variety of flora and fauna—as well as the atmospheric landscape opportunities around clearings, rivers and waterfalls—is second to none. Expect to see brightly colored and unusually shaped flowers and plants, hummingbirds, insects, amphibians, reptiles, butterflies, vines, dappled clearings, crystal clear pools and waterfalls, not to mention the myriad of animals hidden (but very audible) high above in the forest canopy.

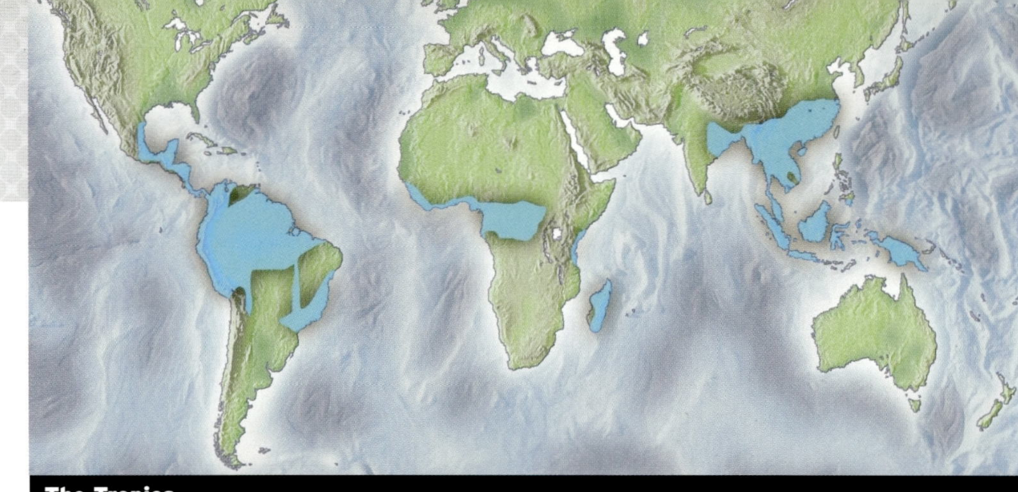

Conversely, rainforests are often remote, difficult to navigate, hot and humid, and dimly lit, at the same time providing some of the most challenging environments for landscape photography. Indeed, the initial factors to consider when planning a rainforest field trip are the technical and logistic challenges that such an extreme environment will present. There are three main problems to overcome: Ambient light levels beneath the forest canopy are likely to be low, making handheld shooting difficult—when the sun does shine through the canopy, contrast levels may be too high for the camera's sensor; the heat and humidity is not only strength-sapping but the high moisture levels can easily damage camera equipment;

and rainforests are often remote and potentially dangerous for the unprepared and uninformed.

Low ambient light levels beneath the forest canopy mean that a tripod is an essential piece of equipment. Using a high ISO setting, such as 800 or 1600, and a wide aperture, such as f/2.8, is advisable and may provide enough exposure for hand-holdable shutter speeds of 1/60 second, and above. However, high ISO levels will introduce noise, particularly in shadowy areas, while a wide aperture significantly limits the depth of field available, particularly for macro and close-up photography. Leaving the tripod at home will significantly limit the photographic opportunities on offer.

If the vegetation is too dense, or a tripod cannot be carried for any other reason, the photographer should seek out clearings in the forest canopy—or areas not covered by canopy such as forest edges, streams, rivers and waterfalls—to optimize the handheld opportunities. Setting the camera against, or on, a solid base such as a branch or rock is not a recommended technique, but could be employed as an emergency measure.

For the same reason, a flash or strobe is necessary. As well as using a flash as a main light source for macro shots, a reasonably powerful strobe can also be used as fill, for example, to pick out animals—such as howler or capuchin monkeys—high up in the canopy

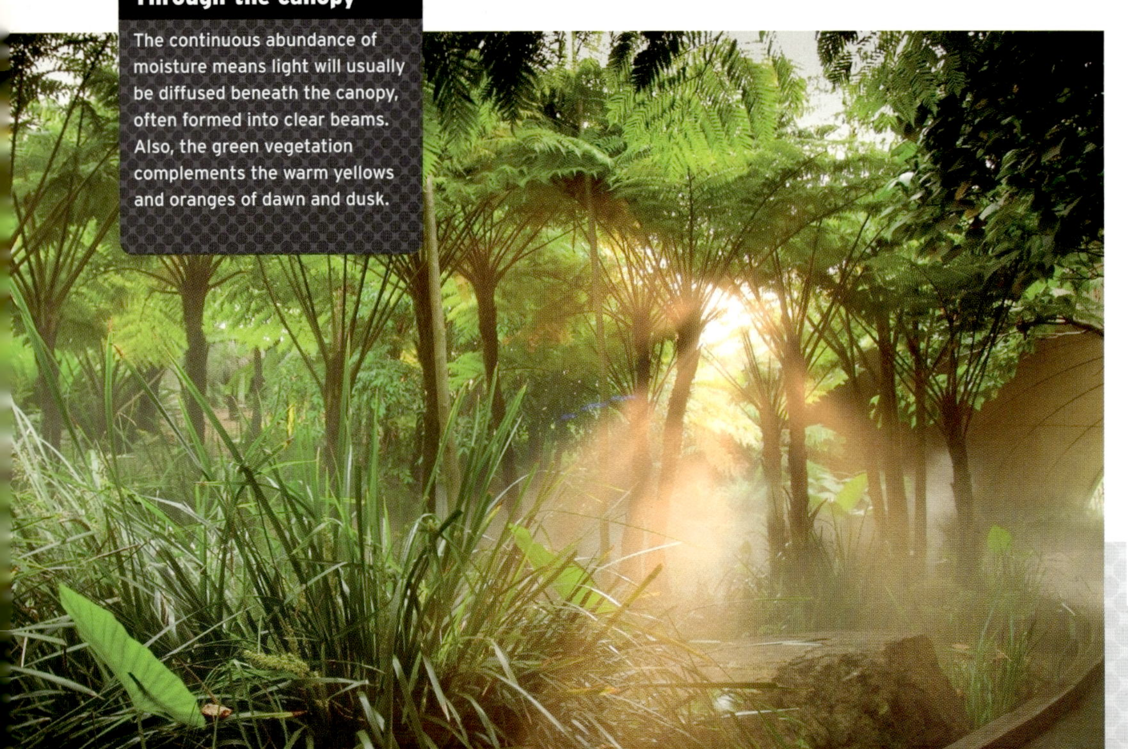

(of course, this will also require a telephoto lens). Fill flash is typically used at one or two f-stops under the aperture set on the camera to provide a dab of light, often in low light levels to pick out a main subject or to prevent silhouetting of a subject against a bright background. Fill flash used in this manner will prevent silhouettes of animals in the canopy, reduce contrast in general, and help to freeze movement at slow shutter speeds.

Fill flash can also reduce contrast when the sun does peek through the lush canopy. While shafts of light piercing the dense and dim forest floor can make dramatic subjects themselves, they can also create high-contrast scenes—for example, a dappled leaf or forest floor—that even the best camera sensor will struggle to deal with. Particularly for close-up photography, fill flash can reduce this wide dynamic range.

Indeed, if the photographer has a tripod the best time to shoot in the rainforest is under a bright but overcast sky, which will provide soft and even lighting under the canopy, or just after it has rained. Look for pools of water or droplets on leaves, and ideally some form of local wildlife, to create stunning macro images. The use of a circular polarizer is recommended in this scenario, as it will reduce glare and reflection from wet surfaces and, in turn, create rich, saturated colors. Of course, it will also reduce shutter times—a further reason for carrying a tripod.

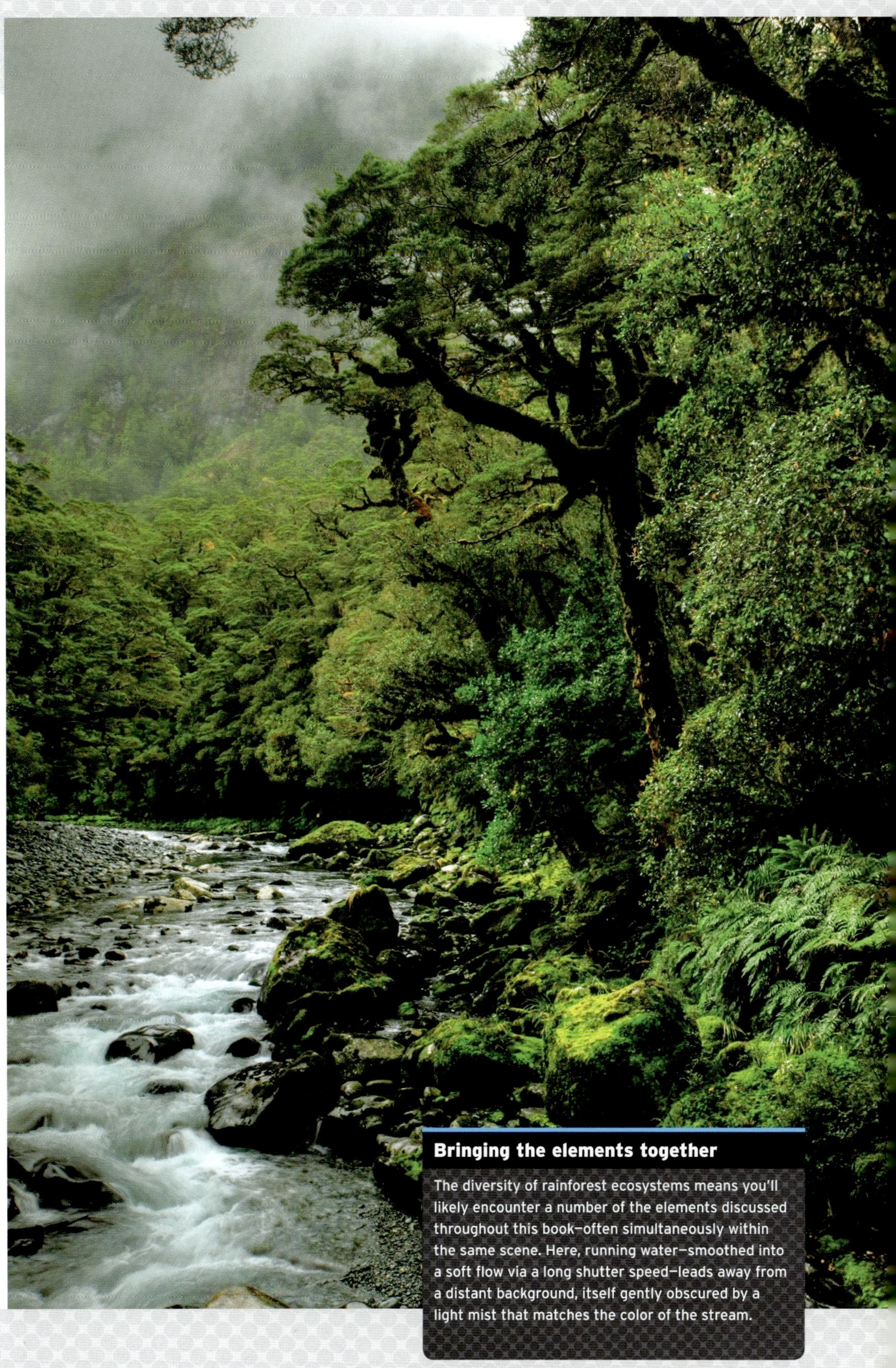

Bringing the elements together

The diversity of rainforest ecosystems means you'll likely encounter a number of the elements discussed throughout this book—often simultaneously within the same scene. Here, running water—smoothed into a soft flow via a long shutter speed—leads away from a distant background, itself gently obscured by a light mist that matches the color of the stream.

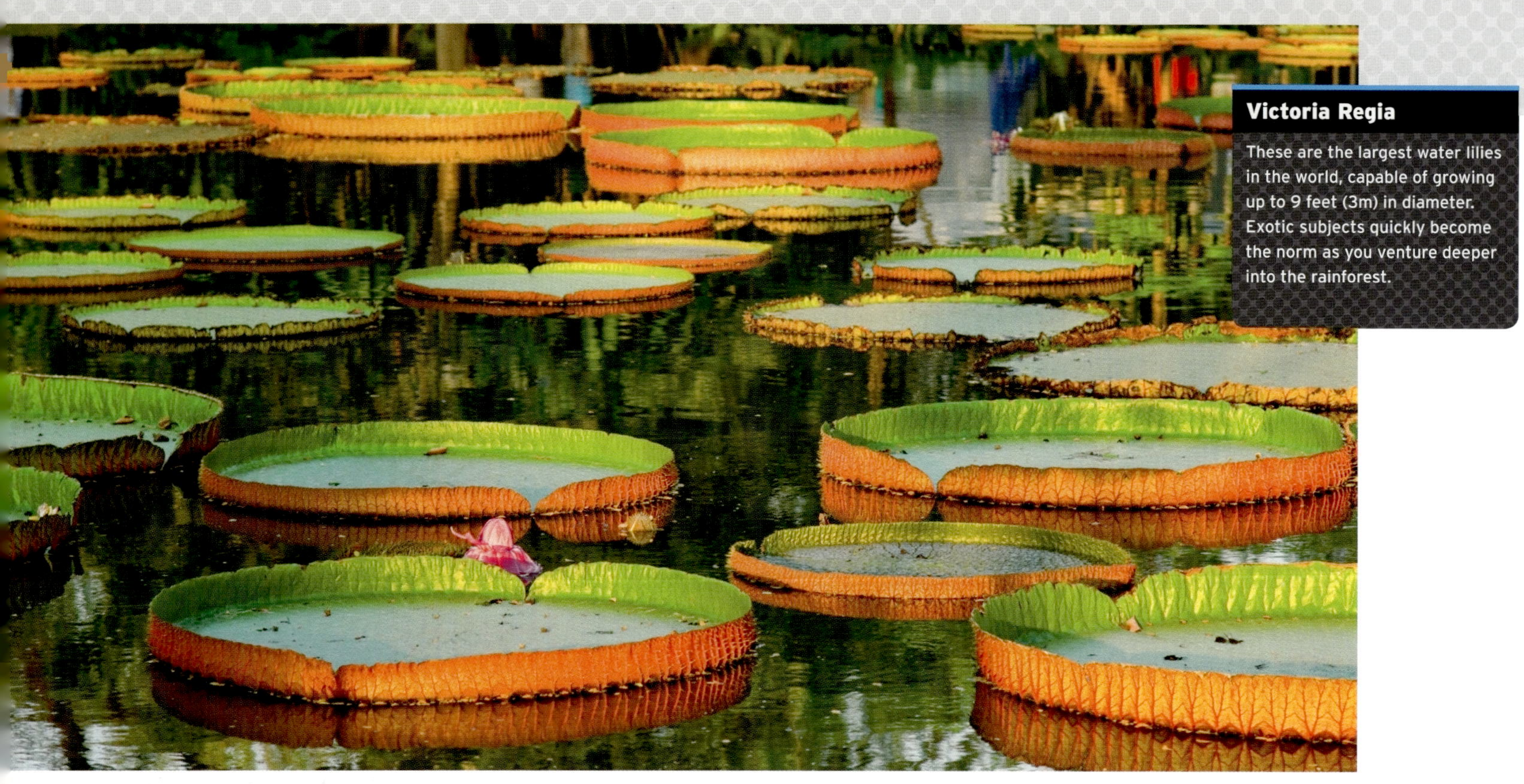

A macro lens is arguably the most important piece of equipment in the rainforest, given the myriad of flora and fauna opportunities. On a general note, when including animals, insects or reptiles in a macro shot, try capturing them in an action or behavioral pose. For example, a reptile in camouflage mode, a spider feeding on an insect, or two animals mating. Behaviors provide narrative to macro shots and so add real drama and tension to what otherwise might be an unexciting record of the local wildlife.

When shooting moving subjects, such as insects, birds or butterflies, set the camera to continuous shooting mode and maximize depth of field as much as possible. But the main exposure control will tend toward faster shutter speeds in order to freeze movement (fill flash can help) and avoid motion blur—be aware that even the slightest movement at macro distances will also be magnified. Another tip is to fix the camera on one spot and wait for the subject to enter or cross the frame. Or, if following an existing subject in the frame, try to focus slightly ahead of the movement and wait for the animal or insect to move across the plane of focus, shooting continuously for the duration.

Make use of complementary colors to create tension, although analogous colors (those of similar tone and hue, e.g. red and orange, or cream and brown) can create more harmonious, almost monochromatic images, which are visibly pleasing.

Aside from macro shooting, a wide or standard zoom lens, such as a 24-70mm or 24-105mm, will allow the photographer to travel light, while covering a decent focal range—in the rainforest, the faster the lens, the better. A telephoto zoom will also help to capture distant or timid creatures in the undergrowth or, more likely, in the canopy. In such dense vegetation, be aware that the photographer will often be able to hear animals, but not see them, so a local guide is of immense help, while from a photographic perspective it is wise to keep the camera exposure set, and equipment to hand, in order to respond quickly to sudden or chance meetings with the indigenous wildlife. Of course, do not forget that chance meetings with local tribespeople may be a distinct possibility, so be prepared for all outcomes!

Staying Dry

Throughout the trip, though, be aware that moisture is the enemy of all electronic equipment—take extra care of equipment in the humid rainforest. If staying in a local hotel, be aware that moving from a cool, air-conditioned hotel room into a hot, wet environment can exacerbate the humidity problem by creating condensation inside and outside the camera. Minimize this threat by storing the equipment in an airtight case when not in use, and transfer it to a Ziplock bag before going outside. Allow the camera to acclimate slowly to the outdoor temperature while it is in the Ziplock for

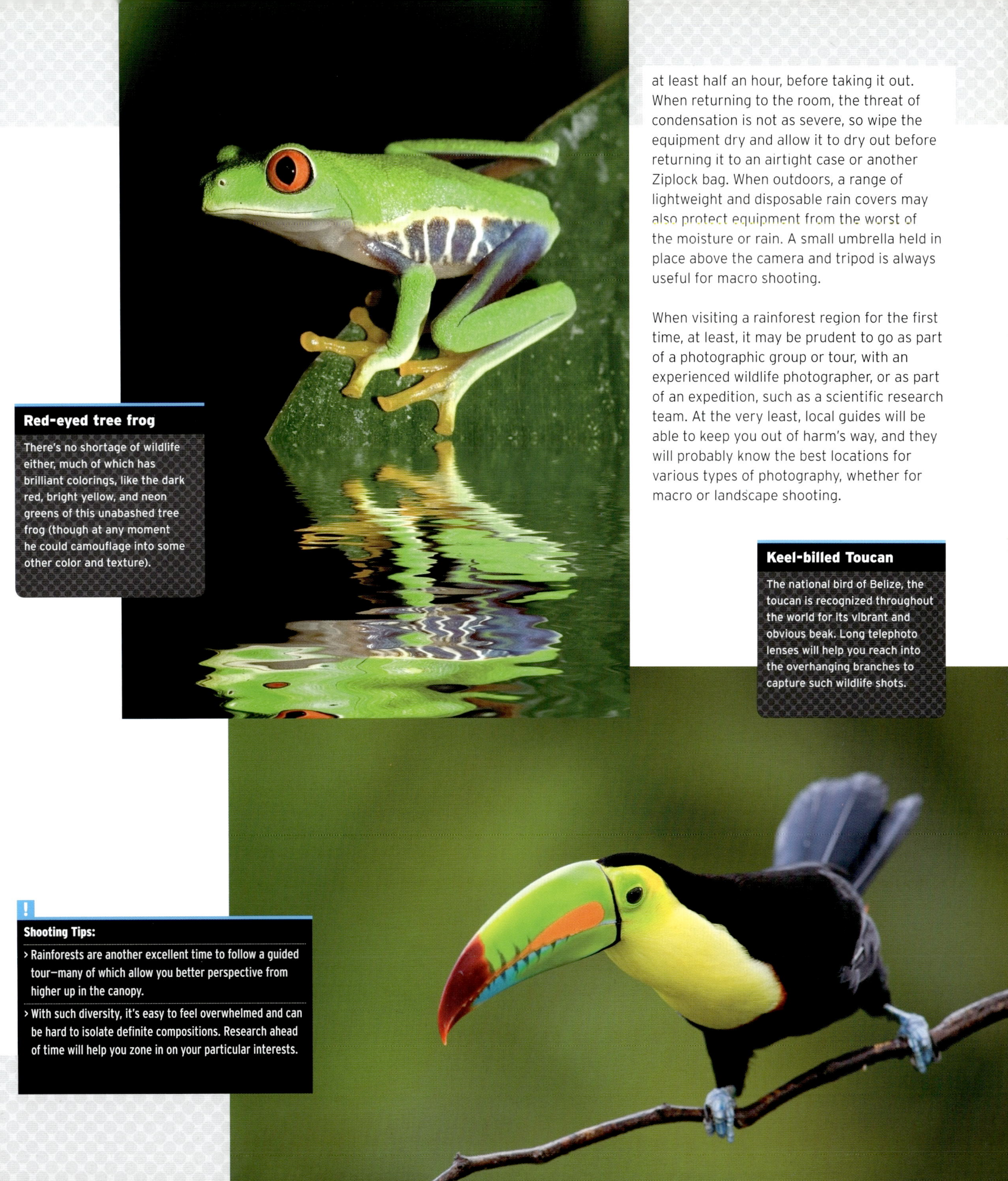

at least half an hour, before taking it out. When returning to the room, the threat of condensation is not as severe, so wipe the equipment dry and allow it to dry out before returning it to an airtight case or another Ziplock bag. When outdoors, a range of lightweight and disposable rain covers may also protect equipment from the worst of the moisture or rain. A small umbrella held in place above the camera and tripod is always useful for macro shooting.

When visiting a rainforest region for the first time, at least, it may be prudent to go as part of a photographic group or tour, with an experienced wildlife photographer, or as part of an expedition, such as a scientific research team. At the very least, local guides will be able to keep you out of harm's way, and they will probably know the best locations for various types of photography, whether for macro or landscape shooting.

Floods

From the monsoon rains in the Far East to sudden flash floods in more temperate climates, floods have the potential to cause widespread destruction and human misery on a biblical scale—washing away belongings, vehicles, trees, crops, people, and even entire towns. While we have all seen the disturbing footage from the flooding caused by the recent tsunamis in the Indian Ocean and Japan, these events are extreme, one-off occurances triggered by mid-ocean earthquakes. Weather-based floods, on the other hand, can occur almost anywhere on earth (barring desert regions).

For the photographer, floods offer something out of the ordinary, and require a broad range of skills to fully tell the story. Shots of semi-submerged towns and infrastructure, flooded valleys and countryside, burst riverbanks, floating vehicles and other belongings, and, of course, people trying to go about their daily lives in unusual fashion.

There are a number of causes of flooding, but they are usually the result of heavy rainfall or thunderstorms, high tides allied to stormy weather, seasonal effects (such as tropical monsoons), or the rapid thawing of snowfall. In themselves, these events may not trigger flooding, but local factors (natural and man-made)—such as low-lying river flood plains, steep valleys, or insufficient drainage systems in urban areas—can combine to create problems. Less prolonged, but just as severe in impact, flash floods are caused by extreme volumes of precipitation in a short space of time.

On a more ominous note, many believe that global warming is contributing to more turbulent weather patterns and increased

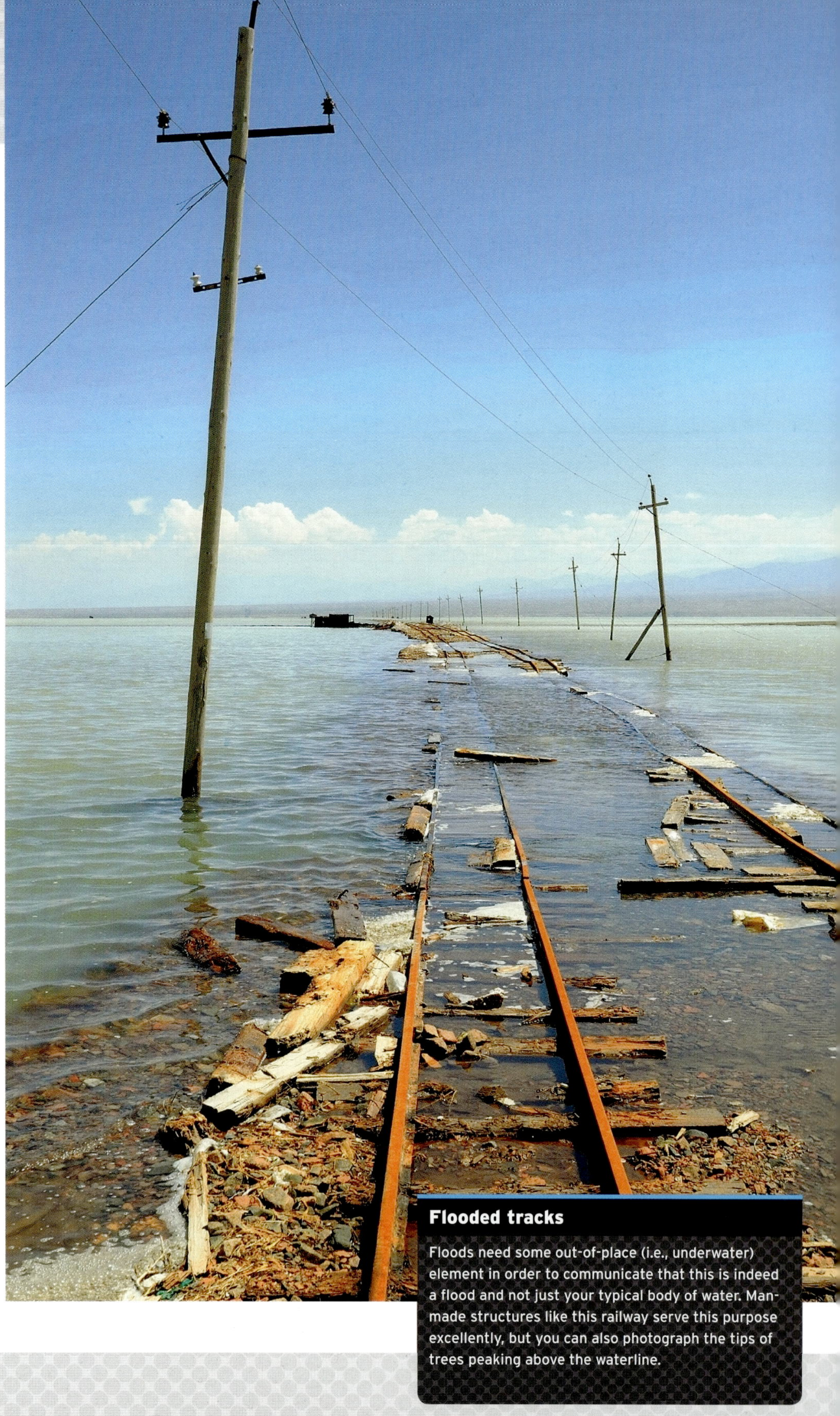

Flooded tracks

Floods need some out-of-place (i.e., underwater) element in order to communicate that this is indeed a flood and not just your typical body of water. Man-made structures like this railway serve this purpose excellently, but you can also photograph the tips of trees peaking above the waterline.

levels of precipitation, while evidence suggests that melting polar ice caps could submerge wide swathes of low-lying land around the world. In addition, deforestation and urbanization (concrete does not allow surface water to drain away) are further contributing to the problem. As a result, flooding as a phenomenon is expected to occur more frequently in future.

There are two approaches to shooting floods: a photojournalistic or documentary approach in order to record the devastation and the impact it has on people's lives; or a more artistic approach, better suited to rural environments. The former is the most common approach.

Similarly, the photographer can consciously try to find a flood, for example, by visiting regions of the world that are known to have cyclical precipitation patterns or rainy seasons, or wait in anticipation for flooding to occur closer to home, in the hope that travel will be possible. A more active approach to the latter is to watch the weather forecast and travel to areas that are prone to flooding—such as flood plains and river basins—in anticipation.

One of the obvious problems of working in a flooded area is that of transport and the ability to move around, depending on the severity and nature of the flood. Having access to a small boat can be invaluable, particularly if someone else is in control, leaving the photographer to shoot away. More likely, only the lower lying parts of a locality will be submerged, with some movement on foot possible.

If the photographer is caught in the midst of a developing flood, the need to reach a safe haven, such as a building or high ground, does not need to be overstated. Indeed, safety aside, a high vantage point can provide one of the best spots for shooting floods, either in an urban or rural environment.

In urban environments, the photographer is likely to be drawn to the eye-catching and obvious scenarios: submerged houses, roads and vehicles; people using unusual means of transport, for example boats in the high street; cars creating wakes as they try to negotiate flooded roads; emergency service operations; household belongings washed up in bizarre places; people clinging together for safety on high points above the water; broken walls, bridges and other structures; large volumes of pouring water; and many other out-of-context shots. Detail shots can also work well: look for items that are out of context relative to normal life, such as a shoe caught high in the branches of a tree, or the tip of a road sign poking out from the surface of the water.

You will need:

> A DSLR (preferably with weather-sealing or rain covers)

> A tripod and/or a monopod

> A range of zoom lenses, covering a broad focal length range (ideally, from at least 17mm at the wide end to at least 200mm at the long end)

> A remote shutter release

> Waterproof and warm clothing, with appropriate footwear

> An umbrella

> Airtight plastic bags for transporting kit

> A circular polarizing filter and graduated ND filters

> A waterproof backpack

> A stash of dry lens cloths or towels

> Adequate memory card storage and battery power

> A mobile phone or means of communication

> A lifejacket or buoyancy aid

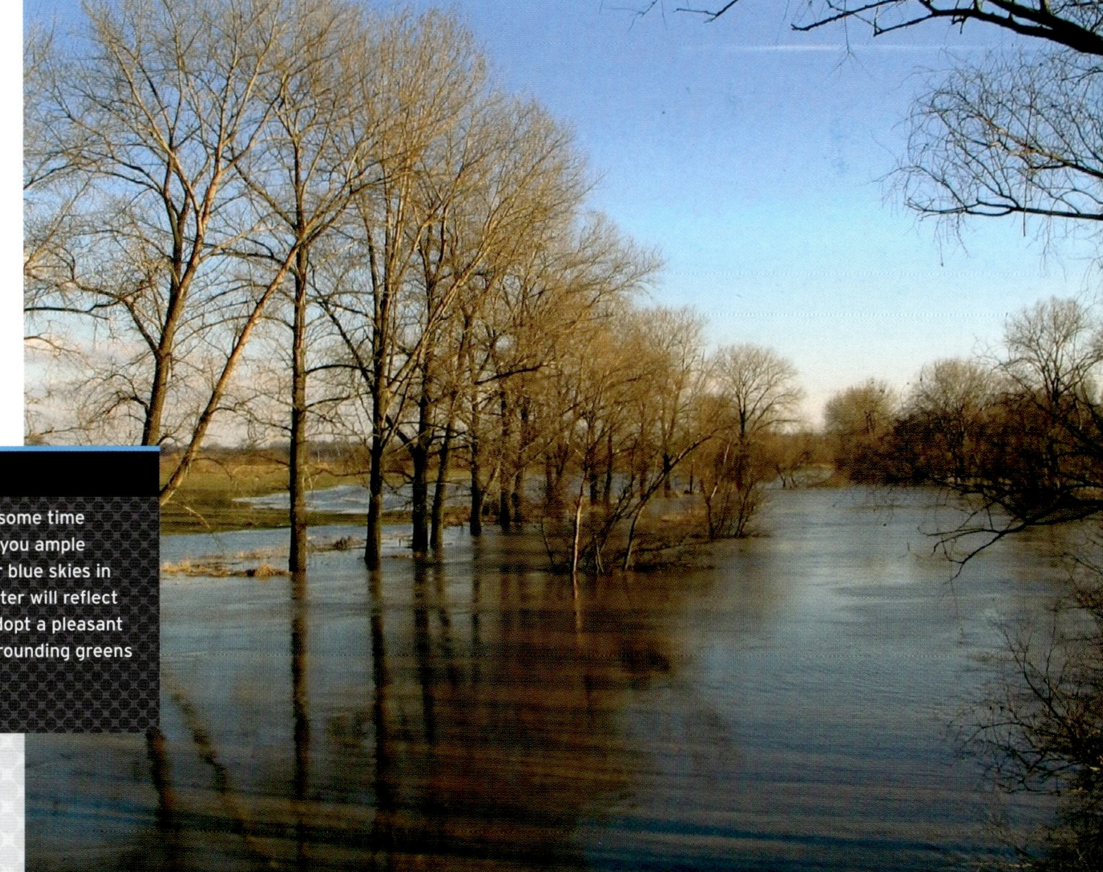

Clear skies from below

Areas can easily remain flooded for some time after the initial storm is over, giving you ample opportunity to include brilliant, clear blue skies in your compositions. Naturally, the water will reflect the sky above, and as in this shot, adopt a pleasant blue tone that complements the surrounding greens and browns effectively.

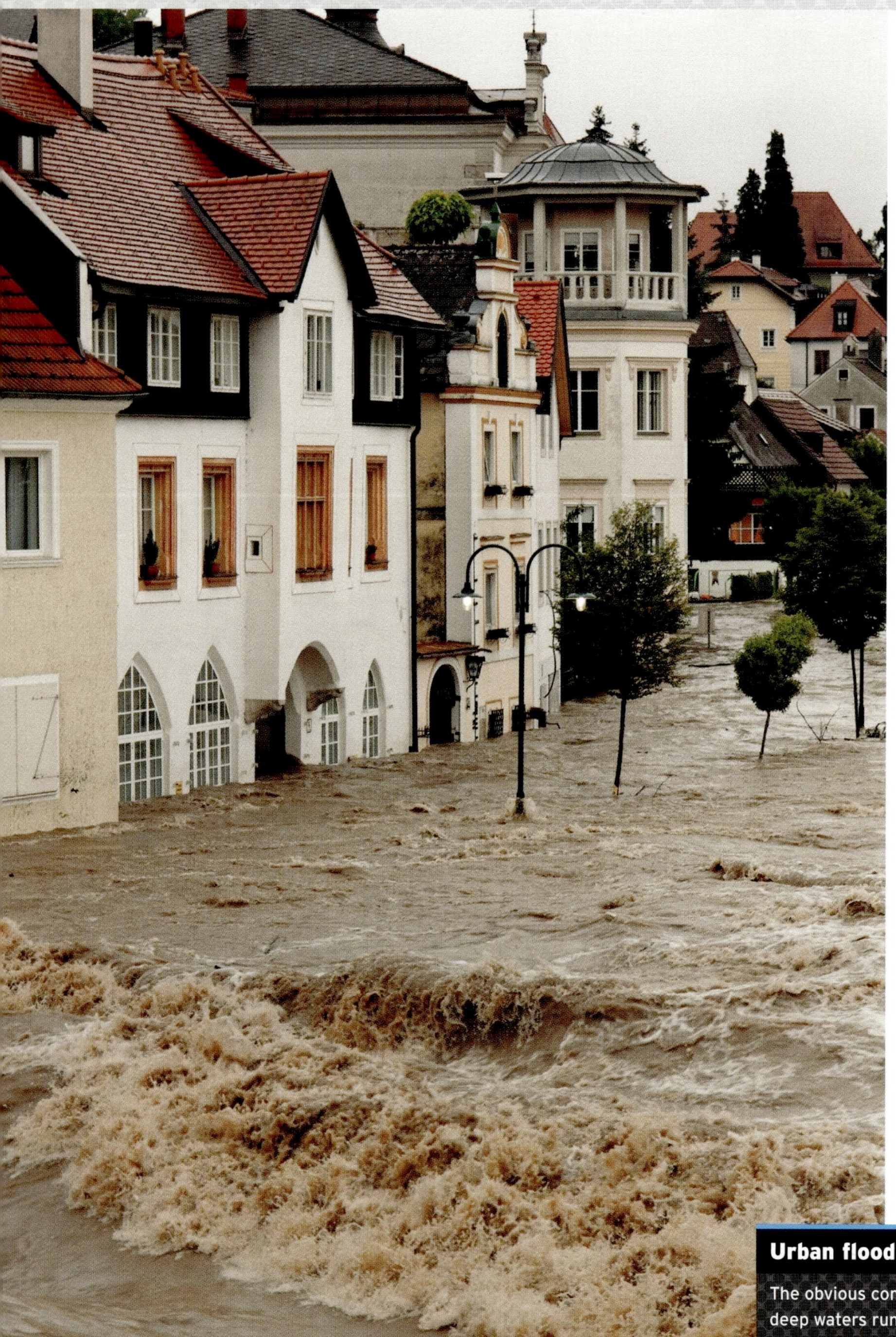

Importantly, look to place partly submerged objects in most images in order to give the viewer an idea of the depth of the water. A shot of a flooded country road, for example, might look just like an ordinary stream or river unless there are indicators that something is not right—such as a submerged traffic light. Without these visual clues about the depth of the water, the images will completely miss their intended purpose. In some instances, it may be obvious that a house is semi-submerged or a car should not be floating! But in most shots it will be essential to provide visual context.

In the midst of a flooded town or region, the photographer does not want to be worrying too much about exposure settings. So setting the camera to Aperture Priority can allow the photographer to concentrate on getting the shots. Try starting at an aperture of around f/8, and dial down to f/5.6—or, if necessary, f/4—if the exposure is too low. Be aware that shutter speed should be above 1/60th of a second in order to avoid camera shake and movement blur of people and objects, and preferably faster than 1/125th of a second. In turn, despite the fact that modern camera sensors can handle high ISOs with minimum image noise, sticking below ISO 800 is recommended to maintain image quality—ISO 1600 is acceptable if the photographer is happy with the IQ of their camera at this setting, based on experience.

The use of a monopod might help here, providing the photographer with some stability and support to allow slower shutter speeds if light is low. The advantage of a monopod over a tripod is ease of portability and speed of setting up—a retractable monopod can remain attached to the camera while the photographer moves around. However, most photographers prefer to be unrestricted in such scenarios. The shutter speed and composition will determine whether shots can be handheld. Remember to check images regularly on the back of the camera—if shutter speed is too low, it is best to fix it sooner rather than later. Dial down the aperture setting (i.e. a wider aperture) or increase ISO to gain shutter speed.

Of course, making use of slow shutter speeds can also add a creative edge to the images. Where there is lots of color, for example, in a bustling Indian or Thai town during monsoon season, a more free-form approach could be taken, making deliberate use of the slower speeds (around 1/15th second) to create abstract-like shots of blurred colors, shapes and people moving around with brightly colored umbrellas, for example.

The use of a circular polarizer (CP) filter will cut glare and reflections from water surfaces, adding depth to colors. However, a CP filter when fully turned will reduce exposure times commonly by 2-1/3rd f-stops. In context, this would reduce shutter speed from 1/125th second to 1/25th of a second.

For photographers not wishing to adopt the photojournalist approach, a rural environment may be suitable to more traditional landscape shots. The bonus is that after a storm or bad weather, the air has often been cleansed and can result in crisp, clear lighting with little or no haze.

A high vantage point over a flooded valley can provide dramatic images, particularly if the skies have cleared and there is appealing light. For landscape-style shots, the use of a tripod will allow slower shutter speeds, and therefore the use of a CP filter (presuming the photographer intends to cut reflections from the water surface), low ISO settings (such as ISO 100), and smaller apertures (such as f/16) to maximize depth of field. Again, shots showing the depth of the water can add drama to the image, such as partly submerged trees.

Another option for flooded regions is aerial photography. Images of flooded towns cut off the rest of the world by flooded approach roads, for example, can capture the essence of the flood and the impact it has on man-made infrastructure.

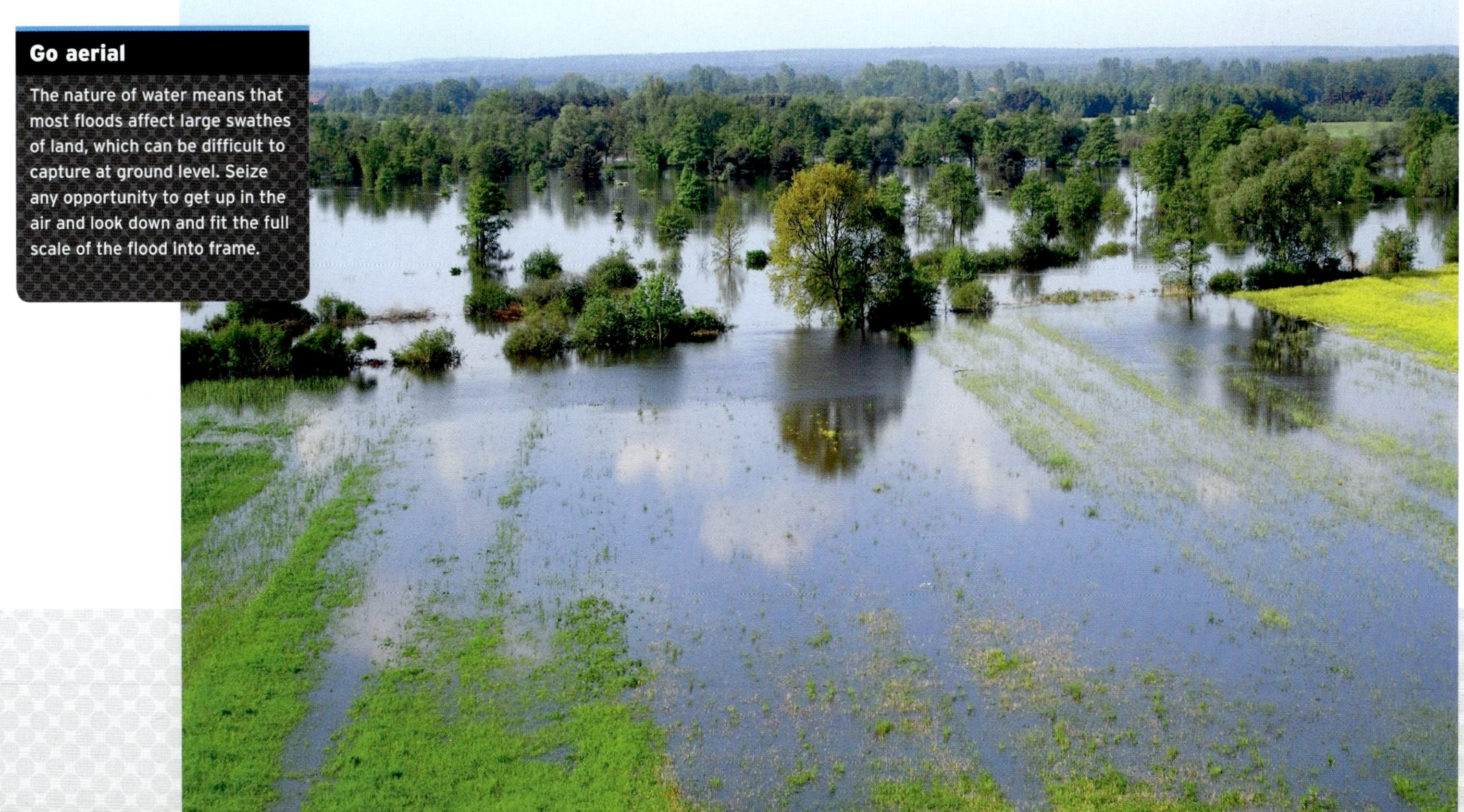

Waterfalls

The flow of water coming over a waterfall is a predictable and consistent event. So the composition comes down to thinking first about the structure and setting of the falls and then how the motion of the water will be recorded. Waterfalls vary in both height and width, as does the makeup of the catch basin below the falls. This is the area where the falling water impacts, usually into a small pool. The catch basin is often overlooked compositionally but it can provide some very interesting content for the photograph. It also gives the viewer a more complete view of the waterfall setting if that is the purpose of the picture. Accordingly, it can be quite useful to think about compositions for waterfalls as having three main components: the falls itself, the catch basin area, and the motion of the water. Here are some options in composition to consider while keeping in mind that each waterfall setting is, to some degree, unique.

Option 1

To place the emphasis on the catch basin with the waterfall in the background, set the camera low to the ground and up close to the basin area using a focal length between 28mm to 17mm. The wider the focal length, the more emphasis on the basin and the smaller the falls will appear, especially if the camera is set in a landscape versus a portrait position. Very often a catch basin will have elements that can add significantly to the setting such as a fallen tree, colorful autumn leaves floating on the water's surface and interesting rock formations. If the water in the basin is calm near the camera, then a polarizing filter can penetrate the surface glare giving a clear representation of the bottom for an extra visual element. Using a polarizer will also reduce the glare from wet surfaces, especially rocks, causing them to appear darker and will give colors a more saturated appearance. On the other hand, a polarizer will reduce or eliminate any rainbow activity present in the spray. Also, be aware that waterfalls with a heavy flow are likely to have a significant volume of spray that could reach the camera position.

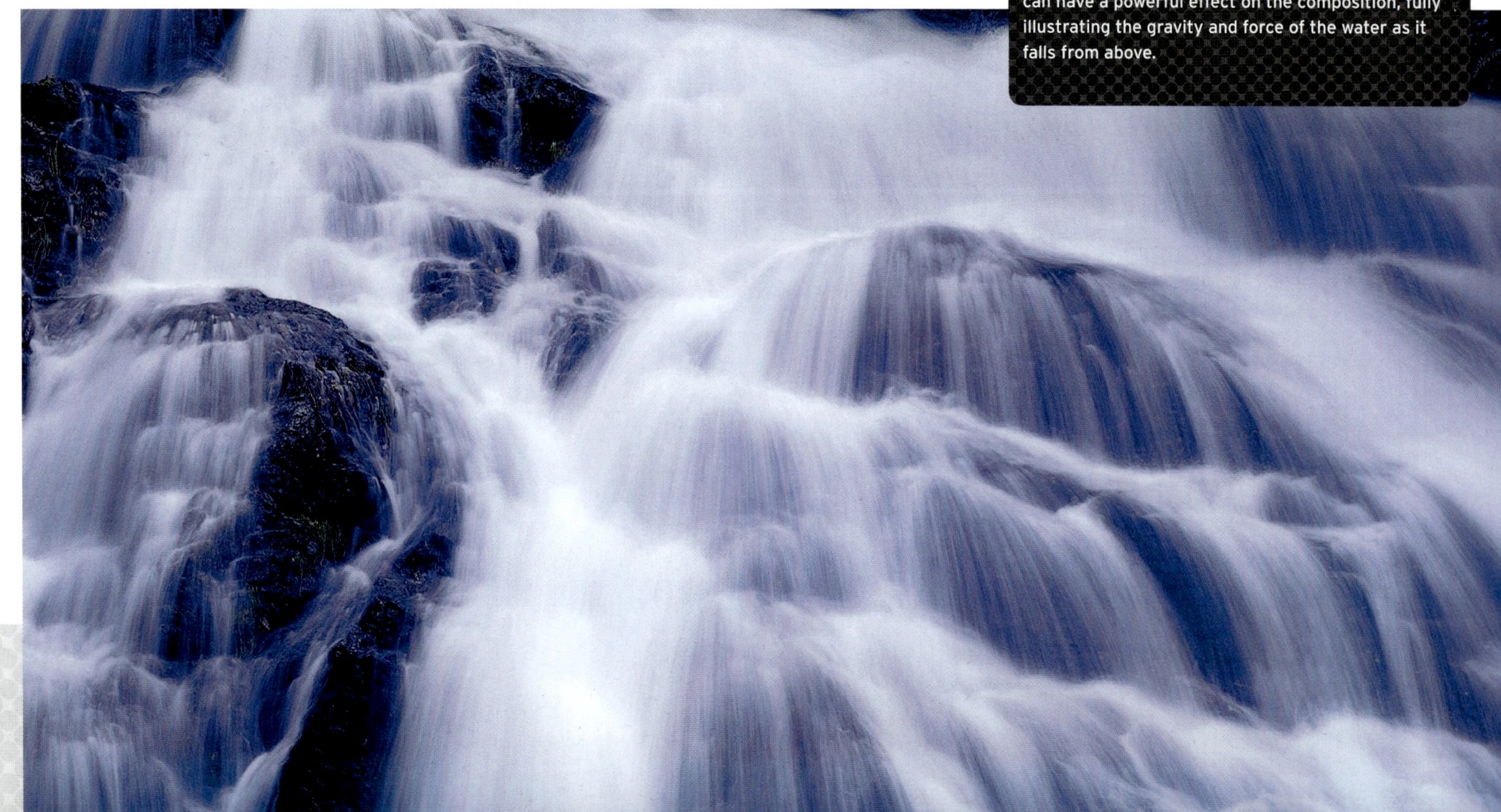

Option 2

Using a camera from a standing position with a normal to moderate telephoto will exclude the catch basin and place more emphasis on the structure of the falls. The question here is how much of the total structure will be included. Having the camera in a landscape position will bring in elements on the sides of the falls such as shrubs, tree limbs, flowering plants and interesting rock formations, all of which might add to the composition. A portrait framing, on the other hand, will cut down on the side areas bringing the length of the falls into greater prominence. If the falls are very tall, then the camera will have to be titled up to take in everything, producing a keystone effect. That is, the falls will appear to be leaning backward with the top appearing proportionally smaller in the frame than the bottom. This can be corrected to a large degree in software. In anticipation of doing this, the photographer should take a slightly wider framing for leeway during the software correction. Alternatively, the use of a PC (perspective control) lens will eliminate or greatly reduce the keystone effect.

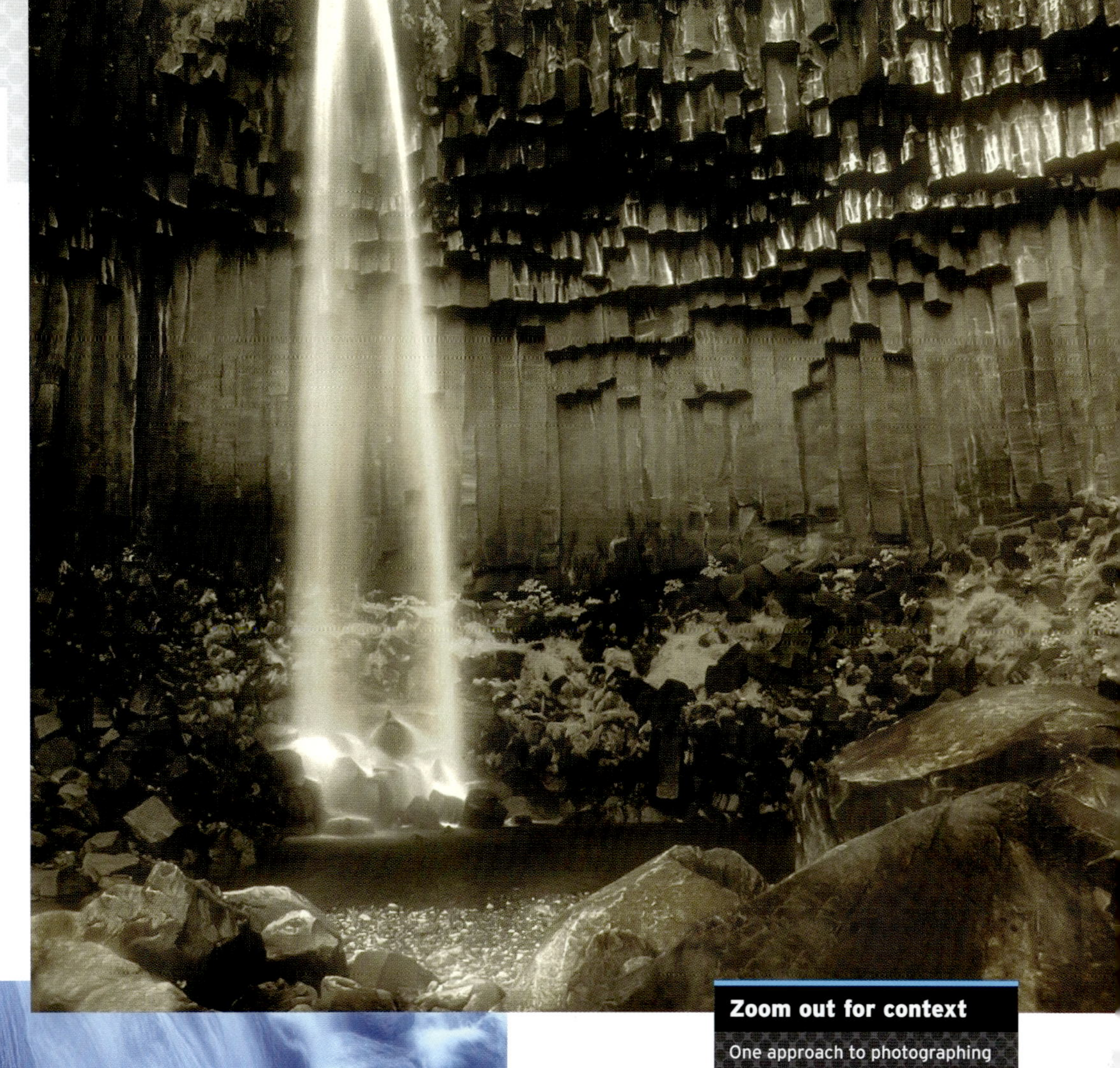

One approach to photographing a waterfall is to include the general physical setting as well as the catch basin area. In this case, a wide-angle lens is key.

Some photographers prefer a tighter composition concentrating on specific details. For example, the thin "fingers of water" that show up in a falls with a moderate flow. Feel free to experiment with various color casts, as the long exposure already opens up the shot to a creative interpretation.

Option 3

In this approach, the idea is to produce a tight capture of details within the falls, such as small pools with water spilling over rocks, plants or flowers growing in parts of the falls. Such smaller details are only visible when a waterfall is flowing with a low volume. Moderate to longer telephoto focal lengths in the 200mm plus range will be required to produce what really amounts to a tight, almost close-up composition.

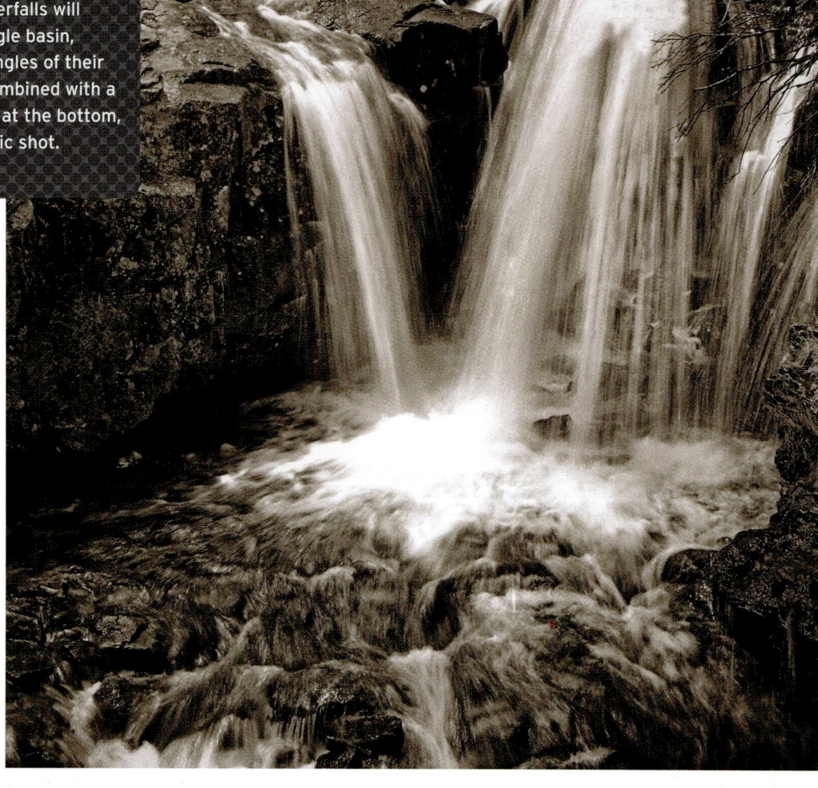

Motion

The final decision has to do with how the
motion of the water will be rendered. The
suggestions concerning shutter speed in the
wave section can serve as a reference for
capturing waterfall motion. To estimate how
long the shutter should remain open to
produce a smooth blur effect, follow a section
of water from the top to the bottom counting
out the seconds. Use this as a beginning
point and then double the length of the
shutter speed time and then double it again.
Ultimately, the best understanding of how
slow shutter speeds render the motion of
water coming over a falls is to take a wide
range of slow shutter speed settings
beginning with 1/60 second up to the
maximum of 30 seconds. The results will

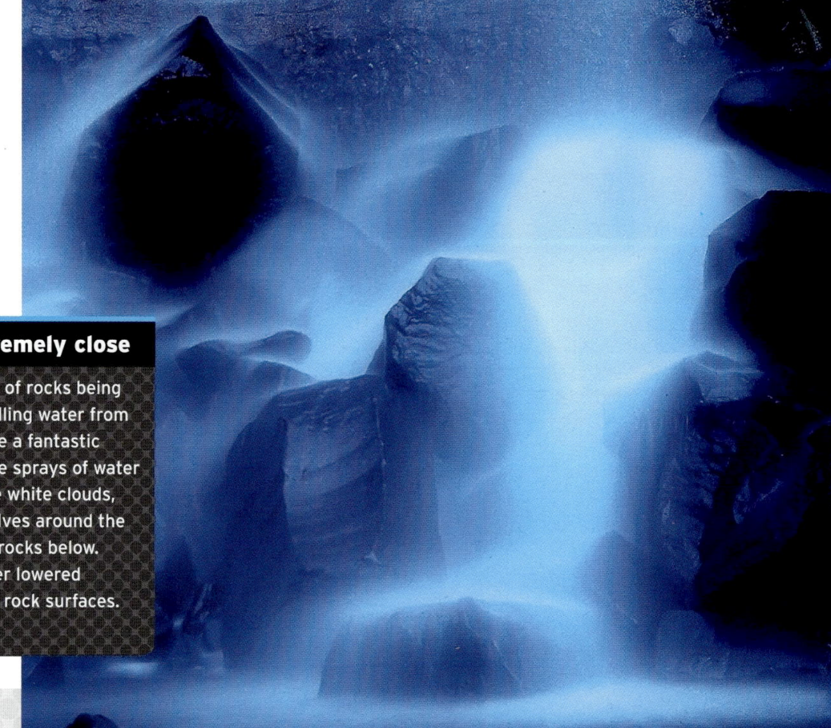

appear quite different depending on the amount and speed of the water flow. This is one of the best ways of gaining insight into exactly how different shutter speed settings will produce different renderings of a waterfall setting.

The best conditions for the slow shutter speed capture are on overcast days, when the sun is behind a cloud or the entire waterfall is in shade. Direct sunlight produces very bright reflections off flowing water and a generally high-contrast rendering with washed-out highlights and shadows that lack details. One final suggestion is to try photographing the falls with the camera's white balance set on tungsten if using a JPEG capture or clicking on the tungsten white

balance option when processing a Raw file. A strong blue coloration seems to be complementary to a shade or overcast setting in which the motion of a waterfall with a low flow rate has been blurred.

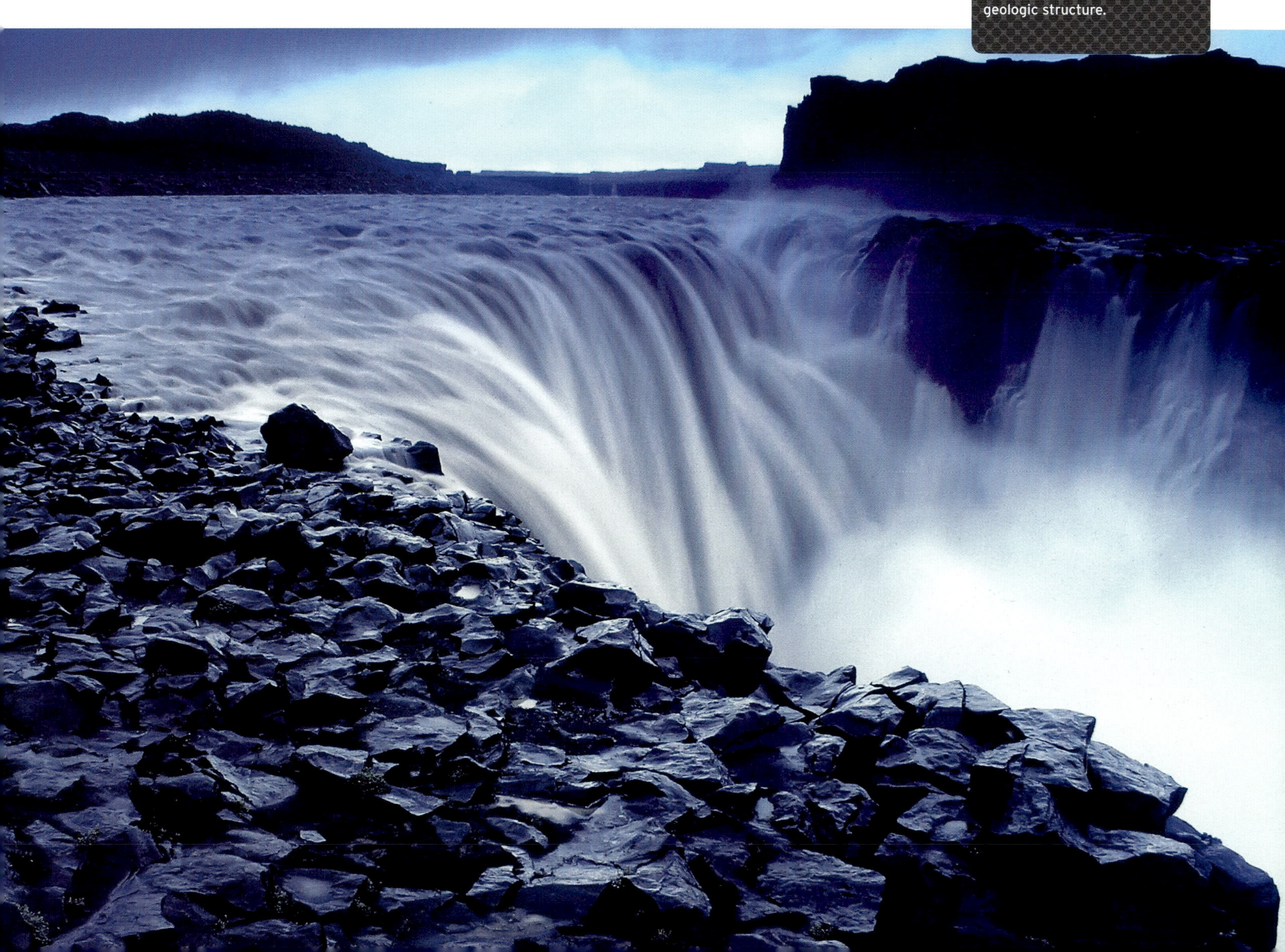

Farther upstream

While the previous shots concentrated on the waterfall itself, this shot also includes the origin of the falls, giving a fuller perspective to the surrounding geologic structure.

Seascapes

The appearance of waves will have a dramatic impact on any seascape picture. Consequently, the information covered in the previous section also applies to any seascape composition. Unlike wave photography that is dominated by a single subject, a typical seascape is generally a wider setting that offers more variety and therefore more planning when composing. A typical seascape might have at least some of these visual considerations: (1) How the quality of light is rendering the beach or any structures such as rocks, piers, breakwaters, etc. (2) How the structure of the clouds and the color of the sky are affecting composition. (3) How much

of the shoreline will make up the final composition. (4) What mood or impression does (or could) the seascape convey?

With more variety to choose from, the first step is to decide on what will serve as the main subject and build the composition around that subject. For example, choosing a focal length that will frame a breakwater or pier to one's preference. A camera equipped with a wide-angle lens placed close to such structures will exaggerate the size and lines of these subjects, leaving the sea and shoreline to play a secondary role. If the sky area is given major space in the composition, the use of a graduated ND filter in the upper section of the framing will keep a bright sky area within the latitude of the camera. Establishing a mood could then come from the dominating colors of the sky. For example, a polarized deep blue sky against shapely

white clouds. Alternatively, on an overcast day a graduated ND filter would give the upper portions of the sky a dark ominous look, coupled with a slow shutter speed to smooth out the waves.

Some of best times to produce dramatic photographs of seascapes are, as with waves, at or about sunrise and sunset. At this time of the day, it seems appropriate to have the sky play more of a role in a seascape composition but there should also be concern about the sky overwhelming a subject such as a low-lying breakwater. It is also tempting to give impressive storm clouds more space in the composition. Usually, the sky will play a supporting role, but there can be times when the sky is so dramatic that the composition is reworked to give it the attention it deserves. This is especially true of brilliantly colored skies that can appear at dusk and dawn with

Day-lit panorama

The panoramic approach often helps encompass the whole scene, from inland mountains to a distant horizon along the sea, which may not otherwise be capable of being captured (you do tend to run out of space to move as you approach the edge of cliffs as high as these).

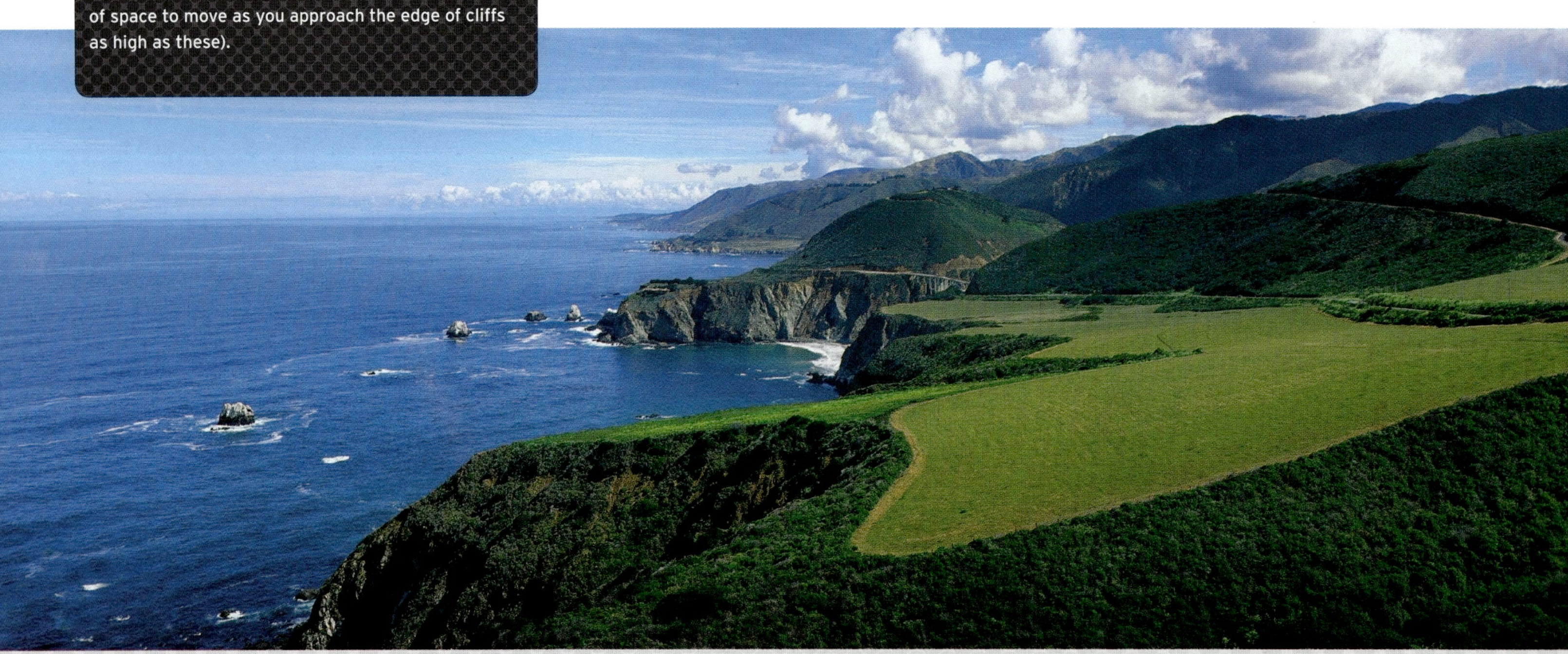

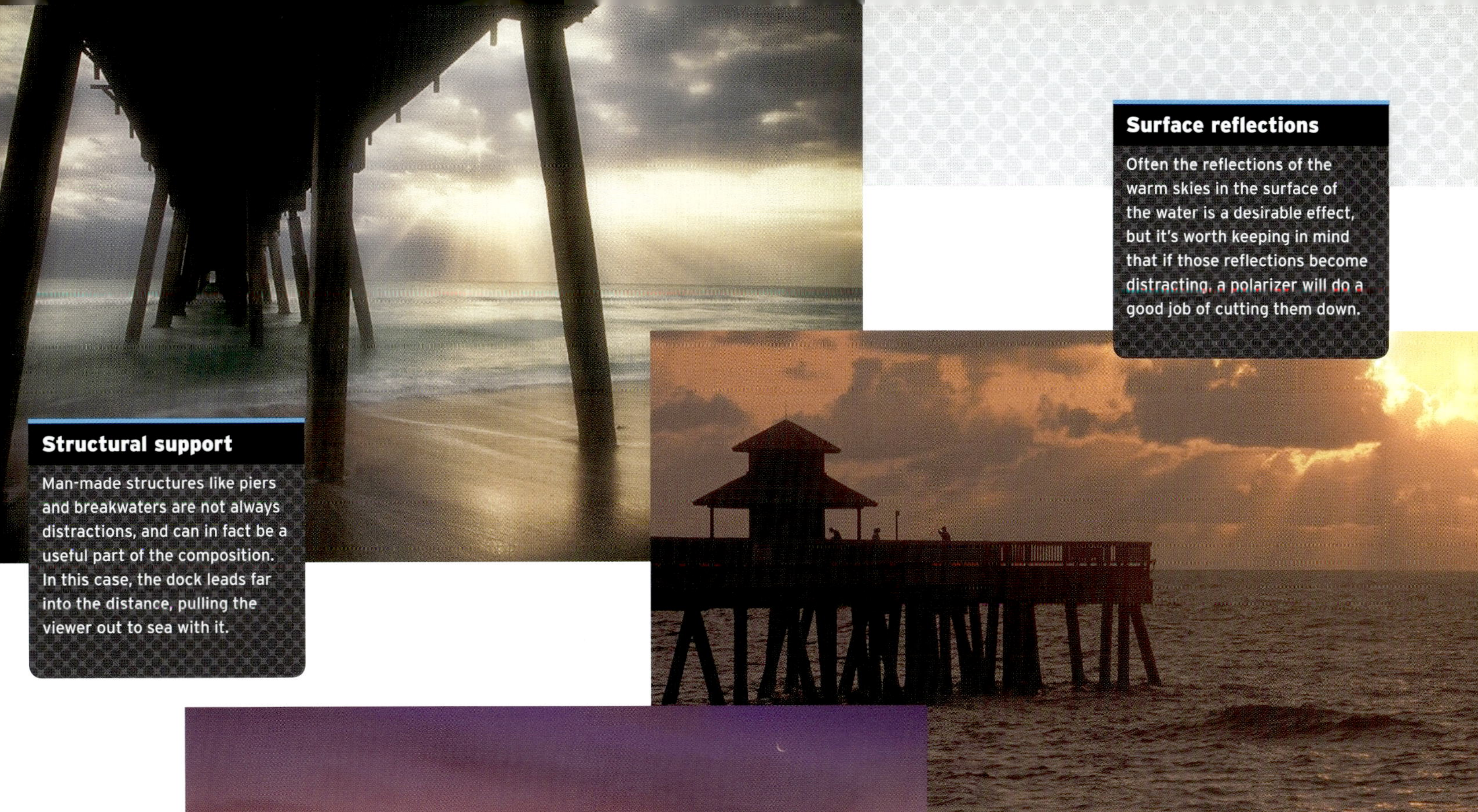

transitions between blues, shades of magenta, as well as yellows and reds. These colors will often be reflected across the ocean's surface and be picked up by any clouds present. This is the so-called afterglow period of dusk or the golden hour before sunrise. Depending on weather conditions, the coloration can be quite striking but the peak colors in these wonderful events will often last as little as 5-15 minutes. To exploit these conditions the photographer should follow the practice of arriving well before sunrise or staying well after the sun drops below the horizon, and be prepared to work quickly. The challenge very often becomes how to seek a balance between the strength of a very colorful sky and the main subject in the lower portion of the picture.

Waves

The force of wind moving across the surface of a body of water is the most common reason for the formation of a wave pattern. The stronger the wind, the more pronounced the effect and the larger the wave. Thus, the mirror-like calm of a lake can be quickly transformed by a gentle breeze into a surface texture of ripples giving off a shimmering mass of reflected direct sunlight. If the breeze develops into a strong wind it can churn up small waves complete with white caps. While smaller bodies of water have interesting surface changes, the larger waves found in the ocean are also affected by tides, currents, and storms, and have traditionally garnered the most attention from photographers.

Ocean waves can be quite dynamic, evolving through a series of well-defined phases that offer many photographic opportunities. This begins when the shape of a wave rises up from the surface into a peak form with a curl, to then crash onto the shore followed by a foamy withdrawal back into the sea. The photographer has the option to select the phase of motion in this cycle that will, for example, represent the energy of the wave or some other quality, such as the beauty of a momentary shape taken by the water.

The photographer's choice, however, must contend with several variables. Specifically, the direction and quality of the light on the wave, the position of the camera relative to the wave as well as the influence of the lens focal length and shutter speed. In addition, there is the character of the wave itself. While there are definable phases, there is also variation within each phase. In short, ocean waves as any surfer knows, will appear with both remarkable uniformity and considerable variation. They may come in well-spaced sets of three to five waves with fully developed phases and then fall into a less defined, even confused pattern. So how should one approach this dynamic but at times inconsistent subject?

Step One

There is a great temptation to begin photographing waves immediately when arriving at a location. A better approach is to take time to observe the wave patterns and try to get a sense of their frequency and structure. These observations should help form an idea for a picture and how to compose it. For example, if it is to capture the power of the wave then one could select either the maximum height of the wave, the full formation of the curl, or the chaos of the crash on the beach. Whatever the choice, there needs to be an awareness that only certain waves will probably show the particular phase desired, while others will run into each other preventing a complete development. Also, the size of the waves can vary and be interspersed with periods of reduced activity when the waves will not fully develop. So, in addition to taking the time to analyze the wave frequency and patterns, there is a need for patience to wait for the most desirable example and then be ready when it arrives.

You will need:

> A telephoto lens

> A sturdy tripod (for experimenting with various shutter speeds while keeping a constant composition)

> A waterproof DSLR, or adequate rain shield, to protect your gear from sprays of water

The most violent wave patterns come when a storm is off shore. Trying to photograph during a storm hitting the beach is not only very tough on equipment, but also the waves will often appear in a more disorganized form. Some of the best sources of information about waves in an area come from surfers, surf shop owners and local fishermen. As decisions are made about what part of the phase to photograph, choices in lens focal length will also have to be made. That is, a telephoto to isolate and compress, a wide angle to emphasize the near portion of the wave or a normal focal length for a more balanced rendering. More about this in step three. The most important outcome of step one is to decide what part of this dynamic subject is to be photographed.

Shooting Tips:

> It pays to patiently study the behavior of the waves ahead of time, and observe how they crash on the shore, if there are any particular groups of rocks that make impressive breaks in the water, etc.

> Don't be afraid of pushing saturation levels a bit further than usual in post-production.

Rhythmic ripples & repetitive textures

Progressive lines of small waves gently lapping on to a beach at sunset can appear as a rhythmic and peaceful representation of nature. Ripples across a lake or bay with the added wake of a boat will reflect the late afternoon sun in a repetitive texture. Both situations require a moderately fast shutter speed of 1/250 second or faster.

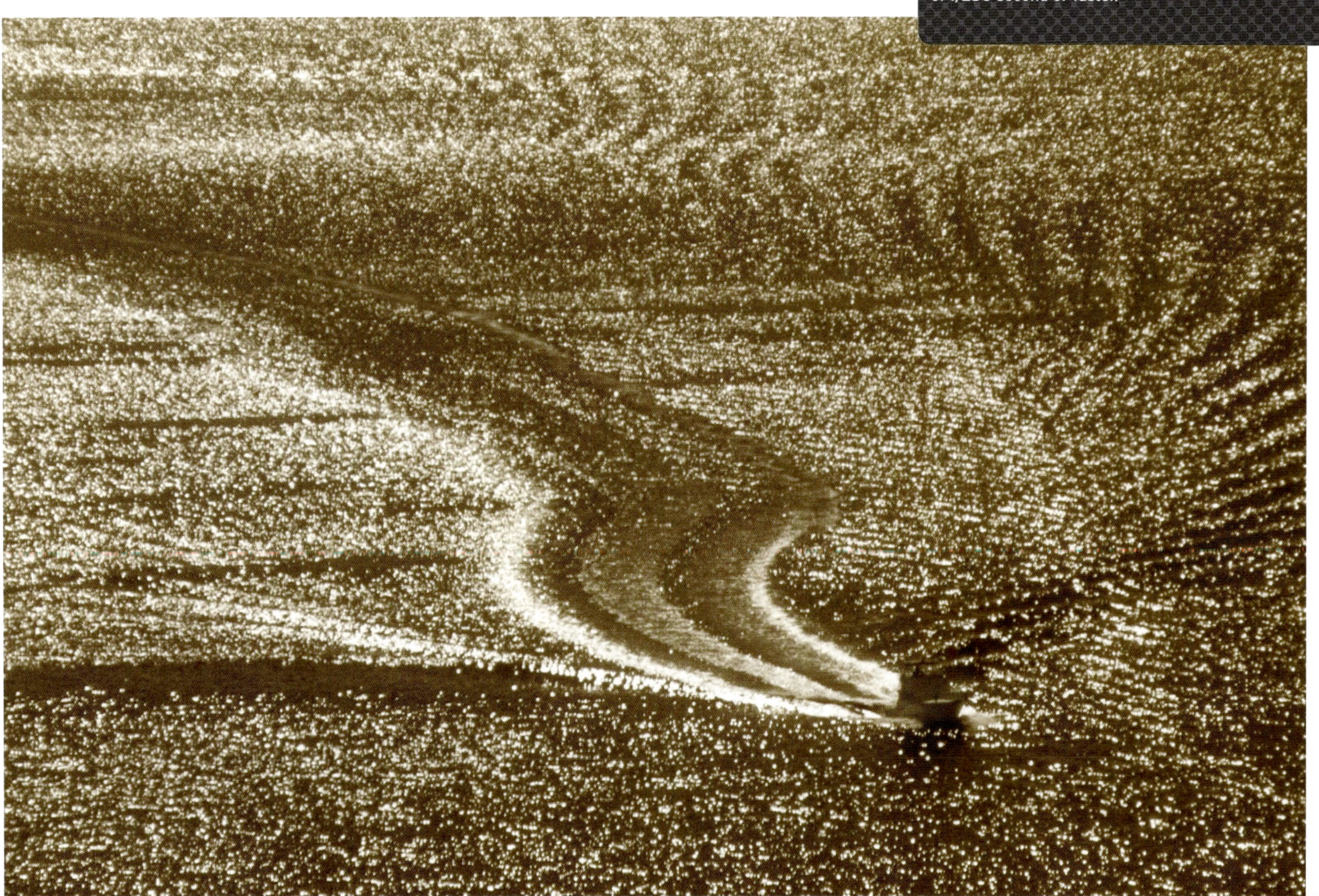

Step Two

An old saying in photography states that there is the light needed to take the picture and the light that makes the picture. In wave photography, it is very much the quality and direction of the light that will make the difference between a postcard rendering and something quite special. To be sure, some of the most dramatic representations of waves are in scenes where the light is at a low angle, as around sunrise and sunset, or is to the side or behind the wave. These periods are, however, short-lived, requiring the photographer to work quickly. Sunrise and sunset are also times when there is likely to be a pairing of the warm light of a low sun often reflected in the waves and a blue and magenta mix in the sky. As the sun moves higher in the sky, there is a reduction in this dramatic lighting, with the main part of the day producing a light with a more even coverage and neutral color balance. On the other hand, photographing waves during unsettled midday weather with dark threatening skies, high winds and unusual cloud formations can also make for very dramatic images.

The choice of white balance depends on the motives of the photographer. Automatic white balance (AWB) will tend to neutralize much of the warm coloration around sunrise and sunset. Placing the camera in daylight white balance will render these colors closer to what the eye sees. This distinction applies to a JPEG file capture where the effect of the specific white balance setting is recorded within the file. Changing the color balance later results in some degrading of the color file data. In a Raw file capture, the white balance can be changed during Raw processing without any degradation of the file data. Finally, using a polarizing filter may reduce some of the glare from the water, depending on the position of the sun. In general, on a clear day with the sun behind the camera position, a polarizer will darken the water and the sky. A graduated ND filter is helpful at reducing the brightness of the sky at sunrise and sunset so that this area falls within the latitude of the camera.

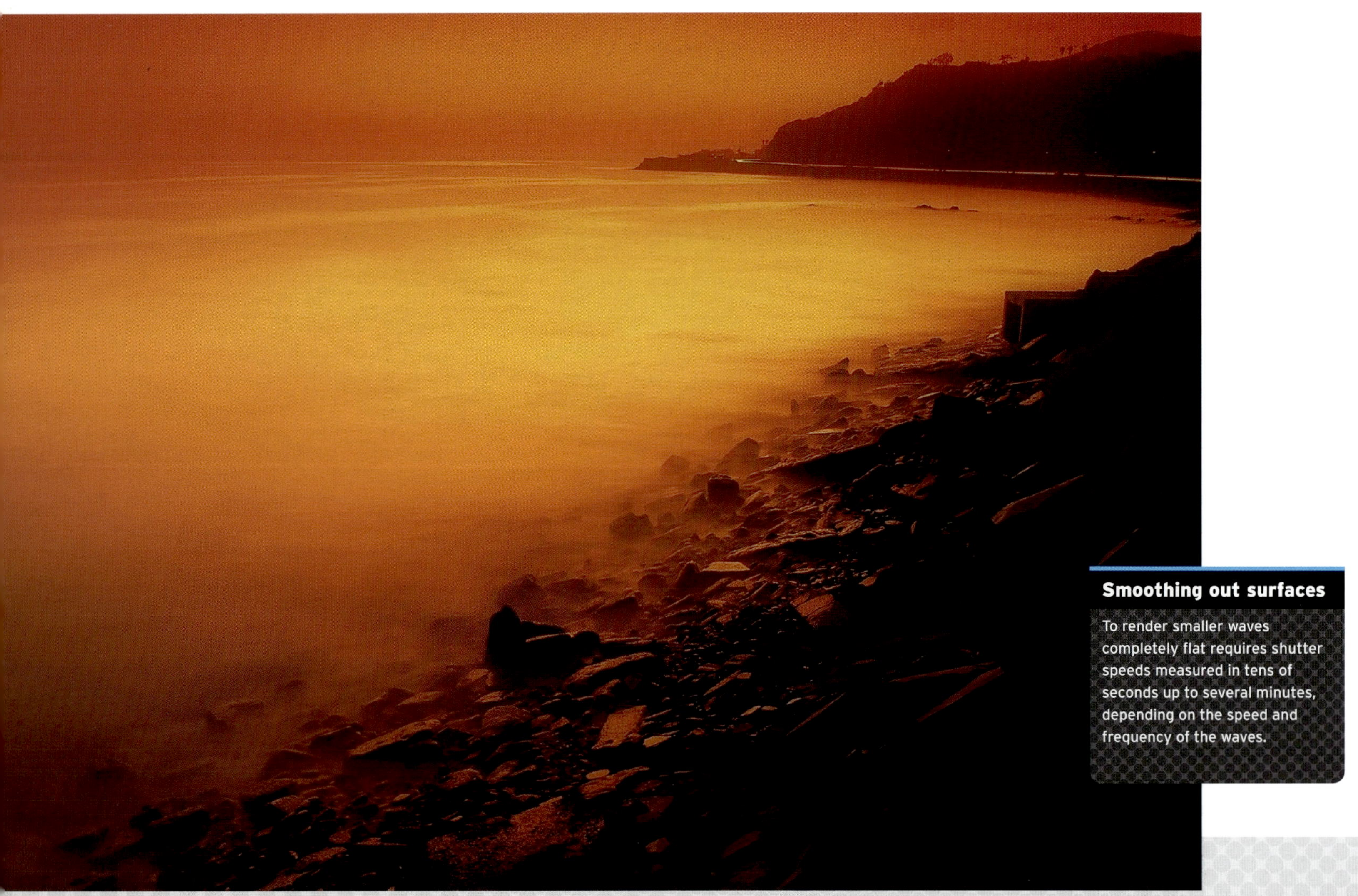

Smoothing out surfaces

To render smaller waves completely flat requires shutter speeds measured in tens of seconds up to several minutes, depending on the speed and frequency of the waves.

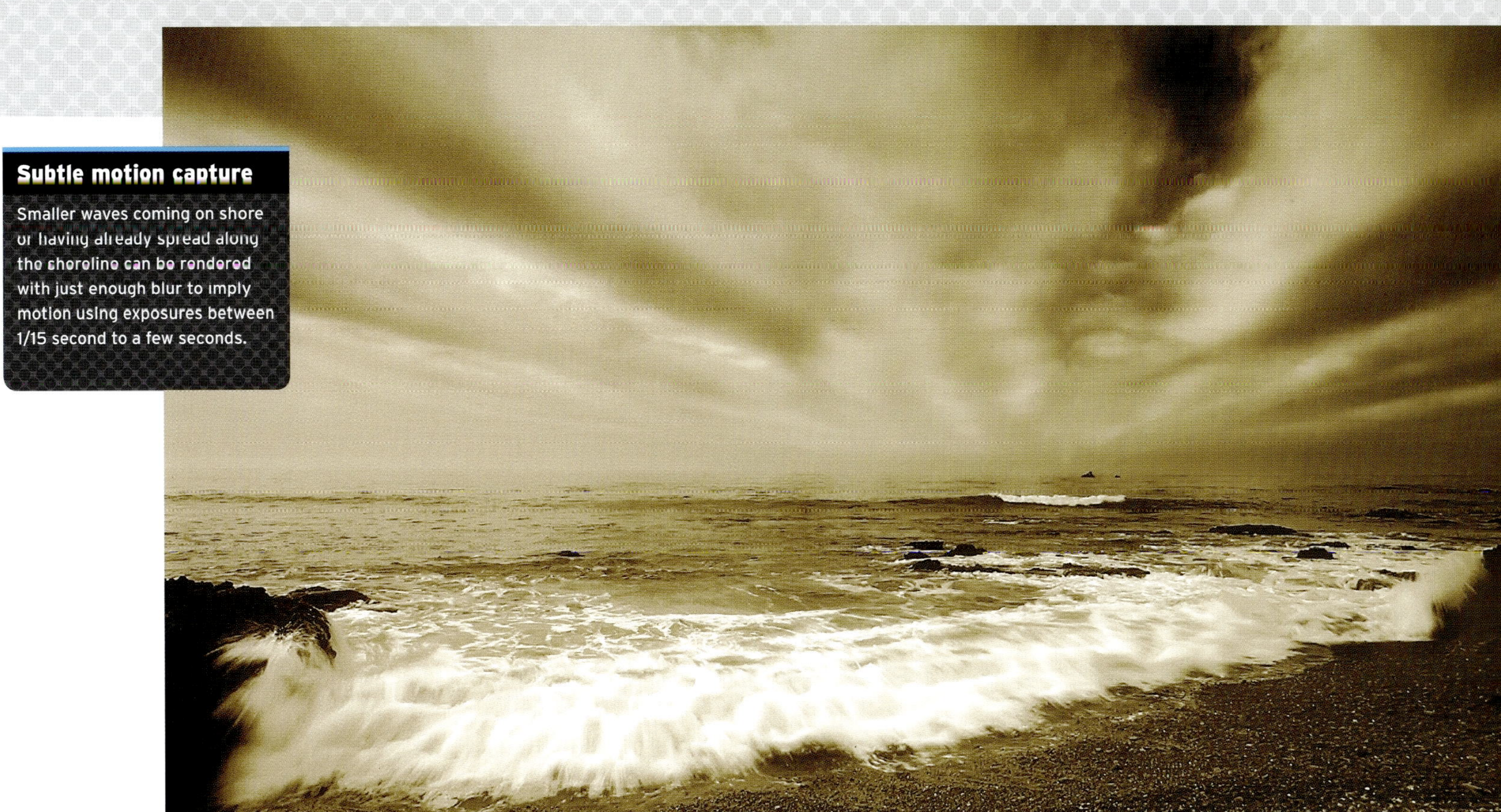

Step Three

How should the motion of the waves be rendered? Frozen in time, blurred over time or something in between. As a generalization, to freeze the wave in any phase will require a shutter speed of at least 1/500 second. To capture the fastest moving parts, such as the individual droplets in the wind-driven spray of a curl, requires even faster shutter speeds. That is, 1/1000 second in order to produce a razor sharp rendering of the droplets in the air. In most cases, the depth of field will be substantial to keep the whole wave in sharp focus and that means raising the ISO to compensate for the faster shutter speeds. Another situation when fast shutter speeds are needed is to produce a sharp rendering of the swirl patterns of a wave that is crashing on to the beach. The 1/500 second setting is minimal with 1/1000 second a better choice. Exposure rates of 3-6/fps are also very useful, since each wave can differ slightly as it quickly goes

through its phases. It will take a little practice to time the shots as these variations show up.

Another popular composition is to capture the wave with some blurred sections to imply motion. For example, frame the top section of a wave with a tight telephoto composition just as the curl begins to spray droplets of water before crashing downward. A moderate shutter speed between 1/60 second and 1/125 second is fast enough to render the body of the wave reasonably sharp while blurring the top of the wave where the wind is blowing off a section of spray. This can be especially dramatic if there is a strong wind. These shutter speeds are just suggestions, as the final effect will ultimately be determined by the force of the wind and how quickly the wave is moving to shore.

Using various slow shutter speed settings will render waves from just slightly blurred to something that looks like a silky smooth

almost creamy blanket spread out across the whole motion area of the wave. Just how slow to set the shutter speed depends on what the photographer is looking for as well as the speed at which the waves are moving. Unlike the fast shutter speed option, where a setting such as 1/1000 second guarantees freezing the action, the blurred motion approach offers a wide range of possible results. This is because slow shutter speeds are capturing a larger segment of time and all the motion is being compressed into a single frame. Humans cannot view the world in this cumulative way. Consequently, the recommendation is to experiment with different slow speeds to see what happens when the various phases of a wave are compressed over different lengths of time.

Extended Shutter Speeds

Long exposures require that the camera be placed on a solid tripod and preferably used with a cable release. Care should be taken to frame the entire area where the motion of the wave will occur. In general, the overall smooth creamy effect requires speeds measured in many seconds while just the soft blurring of the most active areas of the wave will result from speeds such as 1/4 second, 1/8 second up to 1 second. These speeds are particularly effective if the waves are hitting rocks, producing a spray that will be blurred taking on the shape of a soft fan radiating up from the rocks. These shutter speed settings are, however, just generalizations. Each situation will be different and influenced by many factors, such as where the camera is in relation to the motion of the wave and how fast the wave is moving. Again, the best approach is to experiment extensively with a variety of shutter speed settings, so that you can build up experiences and familiarity with their particular effects.

Most digital cameras will allow up to a 30-second exposure in shutter priority mode, and that will certainly produce the smooth, creamy effect. One useful method to determine what shutter speed to use is to count how many seconds the wave takes from curl to crash and use that as a starting point. Then take other exposures in which the time is doubled and doubled again. These slow settings will also mean using the lowest ISO setting as well as a very small aperture opening to obtain the long shutter speed settings. On brighter days, this combination of lowest ISO and smallest aperture opening may not be enough to gain access to very slow shutter speeds. A helpful accessory to reduce the amount of light is a neutral density (ND) filter that will block at least two stops of light. There are also special variable ND filters that can dial in densities over a continuous range from one to eight stops less light.

Using long exposures on moderate to small waves tends to yield a much more uniform smoothness than trying to blur very large

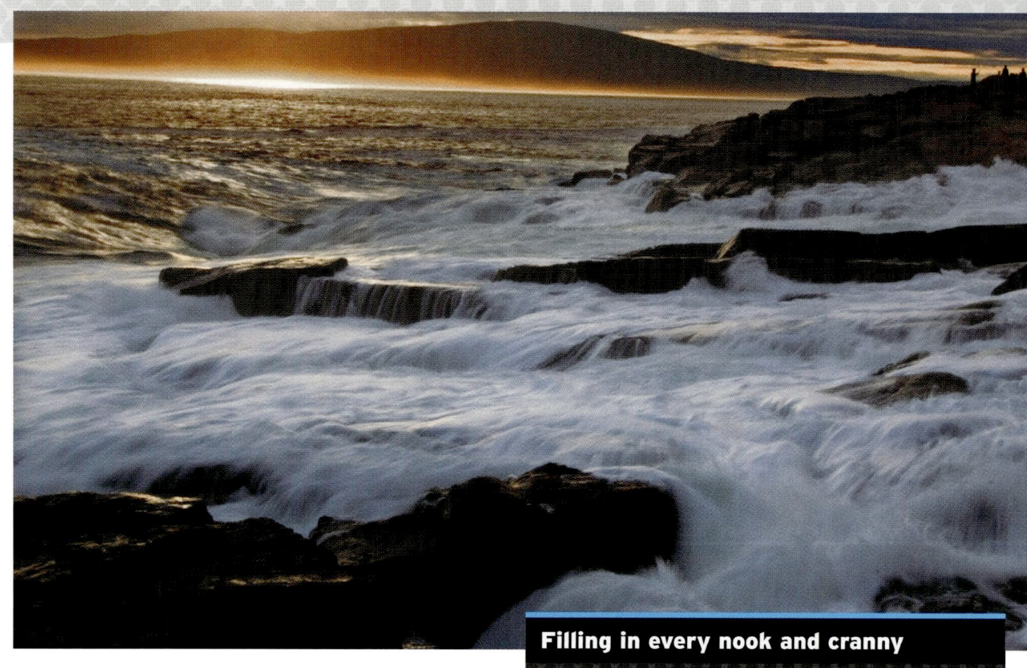

Whereas the long exposure for the waves on page 132 even out all the waves to a placid, flat surface, this equally long exposure paints together the multitudinous flows of the water among all the rocks along the shore, resulting in a wet-drapery effect that is quite elegant.

waves. A hazy layer of spray will tend to appear above the smoothed-out areas with big waves that may or may not appeal to the photographer. Long shutter speeds are also the way to smooth out any body of water with a rippled surface caused by a light wind. Because water reflects so much light, using slow shutter speeds at dawn and dusk produces interesting combinations of bright water within dark surroundings. Also, when composing, keep in mind that the areas of foam will add up and spread out over a much larger area during a long exposure and will therefore appear more prominent. Another technique is to take three long exposures at one-stop differences (e.g., indicated exposure, +1 stop and -1stop) of three different waves using very slow shutter speeds. Then use HDR software to combine the results. This is best done on a set of well-defined waves and the results can be very interesting.

Capturing motion will also be affected by the focal length of the lens. Combining a very slow shutter speed with a wide-angle lens set low on the beach is especially good at blurring the foam withdrawal back into the

sea, producing something that resembles a softly rendered fan. A fast shutter speed of 1/500 second will produce a sharp rendering of the foam right down to capturing plenty of foam bubbles. On the other hand, a fast shutter speed with a telephoto focal length enables one to move right into the wave itself capturing smaller details and specific areas, such as the inner portion of the curl. A normal focal length will deliver the overall structure of the wave within a beach setting. No matter what the composition and lens choice, be prepared to take many frames in order to capture that perfect moment. In point of fact, photographing waves is very much like photographing fast-moving team sports such as basketball and soccer. One has to not only be in the right position and ready to work quickly but also be able to anticipate the action that is about to happen.

A moderate approach

In between a shot of a wave just
beginning to curl, and one of
waves crashing into the shore,
is a shot like this, wherein the
wave that is just beginning to
crash, with the presence of wind
peeling off the tops of the waves
making for a more dramatic
capture and sense of movement.

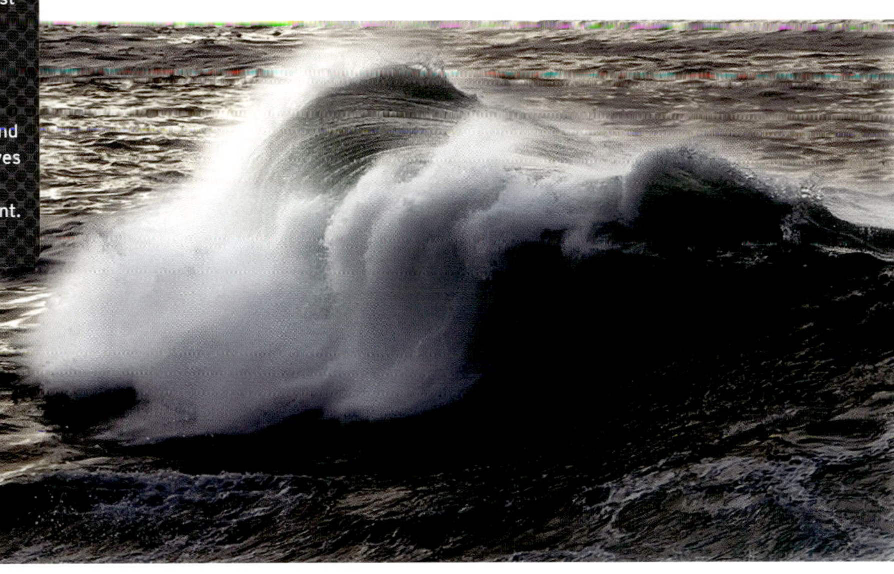

The final crash

The final crash onto rocks along
the shoreline can be dramatic
when backlit at sunset and
caught at its maximum height.
Take several shots until you are
confident you've caught the
waves at their most powerful.

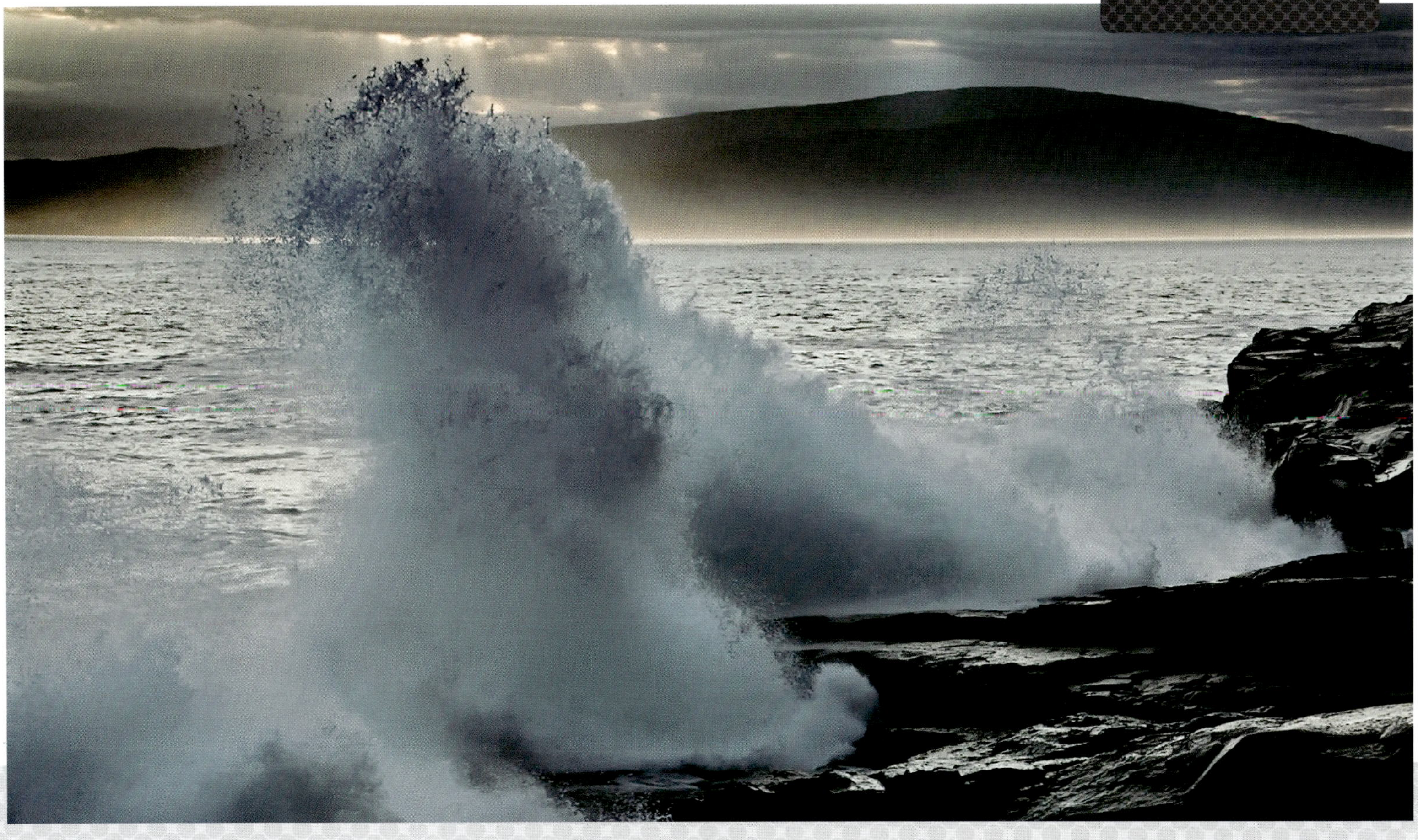

Tidal Bores

Few people have witnessed a tidal bore, let alone heard of one, which is a shame as they are spectacular natural events occurring regularly around the world. A tidal bore is a large, slow-moving wave caused by an unusually high tide, which is funneled down an increasingly narrow gap as it travels farther inland—like an estuary steadily thinning into a river. In some countries, bores resemble mini tidal waves and are engulfed with tradition, folklore, and festivities, adding to their photographic appeal.

The bore is essentially a surge wave occurring at predictable times of the year, as a result of exceptionally high tides, such as the spring and fall equinoxes. Bores will appear in specific estuaries and rivers according to the local marine geography. As the tide flows in, the leading wave is slowed by the river bed and constricted as the estuary funnels into a thinner gap. The rising flood tide becomes increasingly unstable and a bore forms at the leading edge, essentially forming a large wave that can continue for a number of hours along the path of a river and its increasingly thinning tributaries.

One of the best-known tidal bores occurs in the Severn Estuary in the UK. The estuary has the second widest tidal range (the

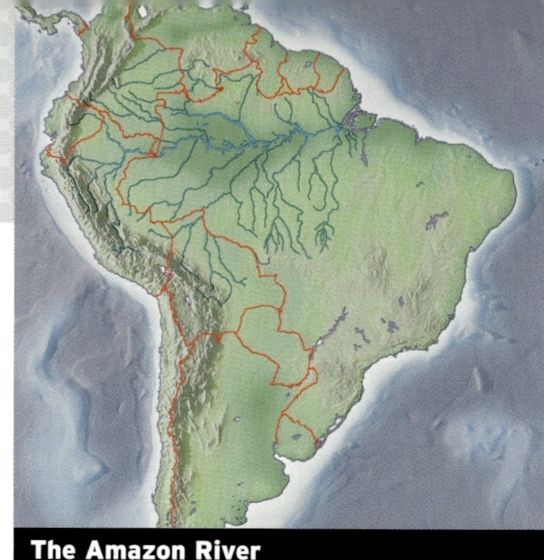

The Amazon River

difference between the lowest and highest tides) in the world at over 50 feet (15m). It narrows over the course of a few miles from 5 miles (8km) wide to just a 300 feet (100m) or so. The particular shape and topology of the Severn Estuary creates what is known as "The Severn Bore," which can be up to 7 feet (2m) in height and travels at around 9 miles per hour (15kph). Large crowds gather to watch the spectacle, with surfers often converging on the area en masse in order to ride the bore along the length of its journey. There are around 60 global locations for tidal bores, with eight of those in the UK.

With a bit of advanced planning the photographer can easily prepare dates, times and specific locations to witness and best capture a bore. The bore occurs several times on certain months of the year, when tides are particularly high. Consulting tide times and internet sources one can find out the best days and times/locations to visit a tidal bore location. High tides arrive twice a day (every 12 hours). So for example, the first tide/Bore can arrive very early (7AM) and repeat itself in the evening (11PM) on some days. Early morning events are particularly worthwhile as they coincide with sunrise. When the bore finally arrives it takes many hours to travel from the open sea up the river. The wave is continuous along its journey and takes on many shapes and forms over the changing topography of the narrowing river. This allows the photographer to pursue the moving wave, thereby choosing multiple locations along the riverbank in order to capture the event.

At times a bore is spectacular, and in some spots attracts many spectators to the banks of the river. Including watching spectators can add strength to the composition, as can

the surfers, who take great pride in riding the wave for as long as it allows. As well as an exciting subject, surfers on the bore wave gives good scale and perspective to a shot.

For photographers traveling long distances to witness and shoot a tidal bore, prior planning and accommodation booking is essential, as the event is likely to draw large crowds and other photographers.

On the day, the best option is to ensure some form of transport, such as a car or bicycle (although the latter may not keep pace with the wave), that allows the photographer to travel alongside—or rather ahead of—the tidal bore, visiting numerous locations along its path. It should be possible to take up to ten shots at each location.

If possible, travel the route of the tidal bore on the previous day, noting particularly strong locations and compositions for each shot—pre-planning not only allows the photographer to stay one step ahead of the bore, it also allows them to maximize the opportunities at each location. Remember, the wave will be traveling reasonably quickly, and the last thing a photographer wants is to miss the tidal bore while trying to decide on the best composition at a specific location. The result is not just a missed opportunity at that location but could also result in a domino effect, whereby the photographer falls behind the bore's progress and misses all further upstream opportunities.

For those without transport, or those who decide to stay put at a single spot, prior location scouting might be even more important—opportunities will be limited at a single location so nailing every shot is essential. Visit the chosen location beforehand and seek out a variety of the best viewpoints and compositions. The expected time of arrival of the bore will be known, so the photographer can assess the likely position of the sun and pre-formulate strong compositions, saving valuable time on the day of shooting.

Where possible, take along two DSLRs, mounting one with a high-quality wide- to mid-range zoom lens, and the other with a telephoto zoom lens (a 24-70mm and 70-200mm, respectively, would be ideal). Taking two sets of equipment not only significantly cuts the time required for changing lenses, it also means less weight to carry, and provides a combined focal length range that should cover most situations—from wide landscape views of the bore to close-ups of the crowd and surfers. Capturing a wide variety of shots also maximizes the opportunities of this relatively rare natural event. For those who cannot afford two sets of equipment it might be worth enquiring about the costs of equipment-hiring over a day or two. If not, pick one lens and stick to it (a 24-105mm, for example, or even a 50mm fixed focal length)—changing lenses wastes time and will not only increase the likelihood of missing the bore, but also make the experience a stressful one.

Where possible use the fastest lenses available. At sunrise, for example, ambient light levels will be low and, combined with the speed of the bore and the movement of surfers, will require wide apertures (low numbers), such as f/2.8. This avoids the need to crank up the ISO (which adds image noise) and reduces motion blur caused by slow shutter speeds. Any form of filter will only add to the shutter time required, so try to avoid them. For wide-angle shots, depth of field is more forgiving, so apertures of around f/5.6 make a good starting point and will help to get most points of

interest in acceptable focus. If in doubt, focus on the main subject matter in the shot, e.g. a row of surfers on the bow of the wave. In this case, it will not matter that the foreground riverbank is not in sharp focus. Check ambient light levels intermittently, as they are likely to change over the duration of the bore's journey.

Because of the speed of the bore, it is important not to hang around in each location for too long, which is where pre-planning and

prior scouting can reap rewards. Once the wave has passed, the chase is on. Stay calm and focused at each location. If you miss a shot at one location, forget about it, get back on schedule at the next location and make sure you nail the next shot!

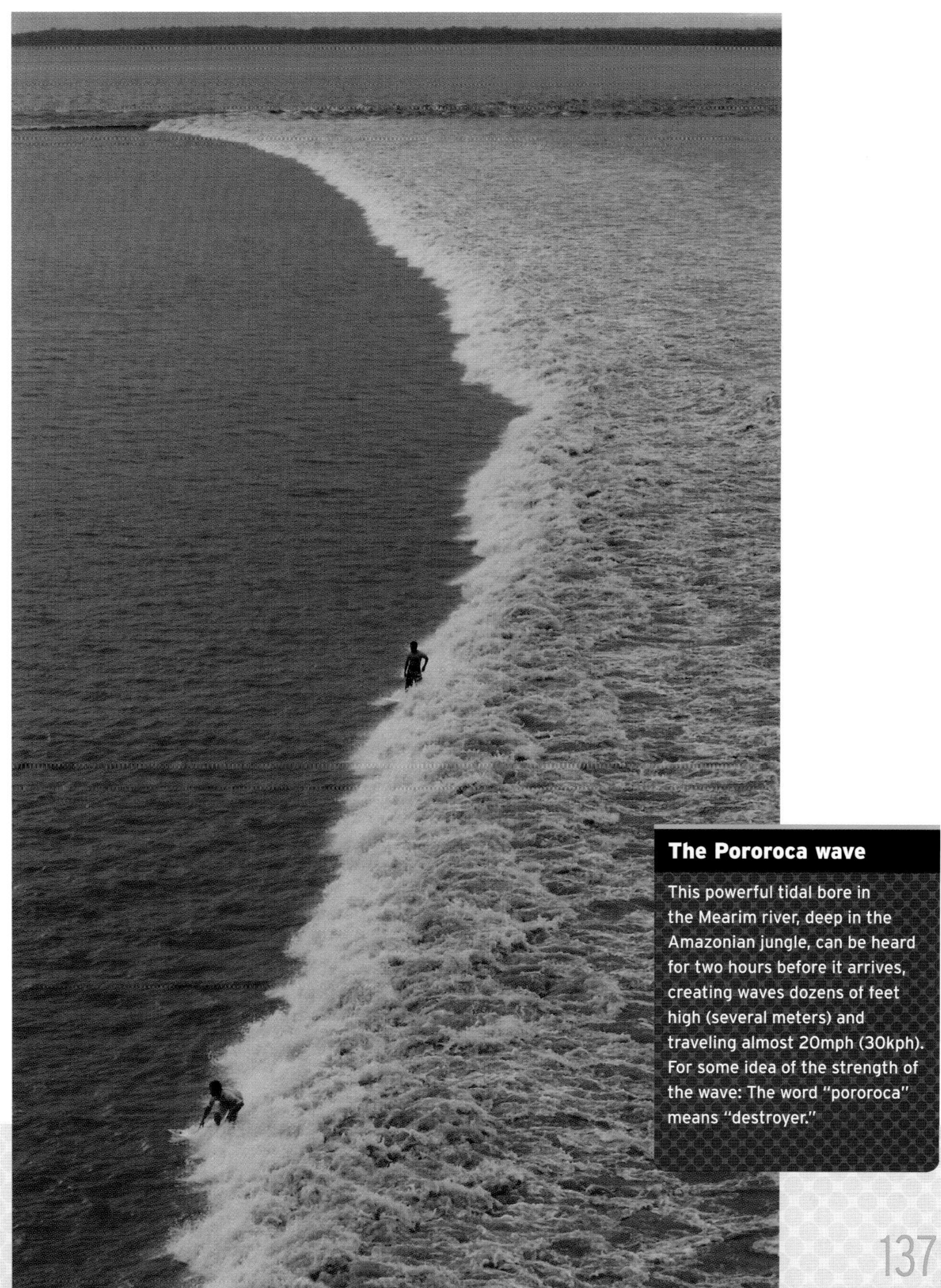

The Pororoca wave

This powerful tidal bore in the Mearim river, deep in the Amazonian jungle, can be heard for two hours before it arrives, creating waves dozens of feet high (several meters) and traveling almost 20mph (30kph). For some idea of the strength of the wave: The word "pororoca" means "destroyer."

Photographing in Extremely Cold Environments

Remote locations with extremely cold temperatures, such as the Arctic regions, attract photographers because of the unique wildlife in these areas as well as great expanses of austere and harsh landscapes. These places have a topography that is quite different from anywhere else in the world. But one does not have to travel to such remote locations to photograph the effects of freezing temperatures on an environment. Many places with moderate climates such as parts of Europe and North America have seasons of cold and snow. Consequently, while the thrust of this chapter is about photographing in the remote Arctic regions of Northern Canada and Greenland, most of the information also applies to photographing in any cold and snow-covered setting.

Planning the Trip

The previous chapter included information concerning the importance of careful planning for a trip to a remote area, with suggestions for backup cameras and lenses. This information applies as well to photographing in cold temperatures. In addition, there are some important dos and don'ts that should be considered when operating photographic equipment in such conditions.

(1) How low temperatures will fall, along with the multiplying effect of a wind-chill factor and the total time spent in cold temperatures are all very important variables to take into consideration. Accordingly, it is important to maintain a camera within it's working temperature range and with respect to its rating for moisture fit and robustness. Modern DSLRs and film SLRs perform quite well down to freezing temperatures and even a bit lower. Potential problems can arise,

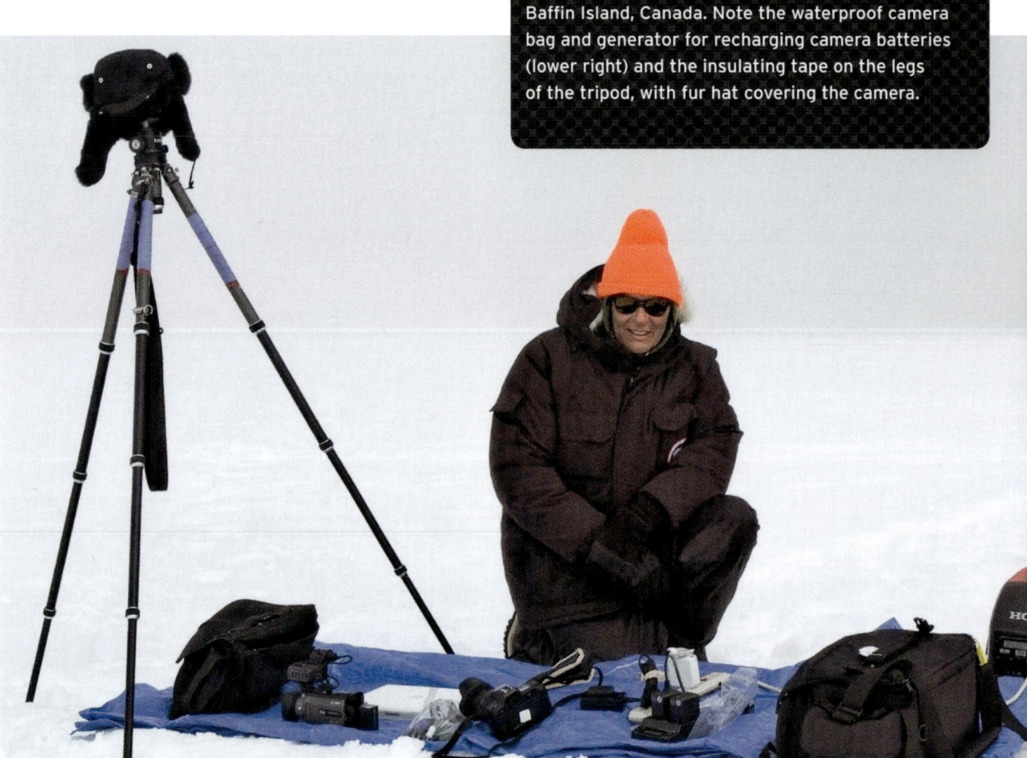

however, when the camera is left exposed for prolonged periods in sub-freezing temperatures. For example, a tripod-mounted camera exposed to strong wind-chill conditions. This is when some insulating cover should be used or the camera placed inside a camera bag until ready to use.

(2) All digital cameras and most film cameras operate on batteries. The simple fact is that all batteries lose their charge much faster in cold weather. The best way to deal with this is to recharge daily and to carry extra batteries. This is an appropriate strategy when on a photography tour from a ship or during daily trips on snow vehicles that return to a home base where electricity is available. When in the field, keep the extra batteries warm by placing them in a pocket next to the body. If the opportunity for re-charging is not available over several days then more thought needs to be given to maintaining battery power.

(3) Condensation will form on the surfaces of cold photographic equipment when moved into a warm setting. This thin coating can freeze when the equipment goes back out into the cold. If the camera is not well sealed against moisture and subjected to bitter cold and then suddenly moved into a warm environment, this condensation can form

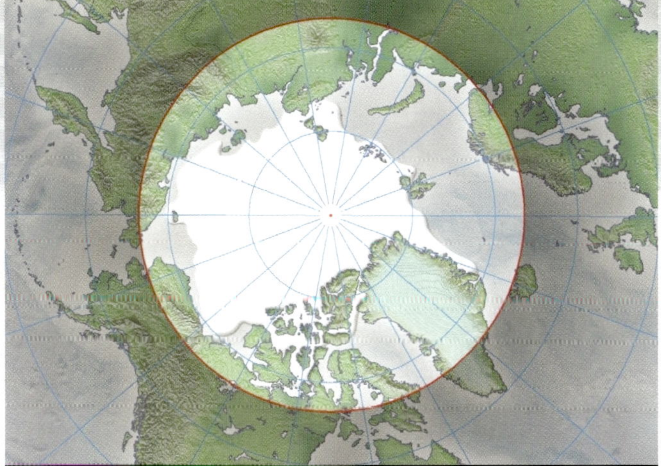

internally, and that can cause operational problems. When in the field, one should avoid breathing on a lens prior to wiping it with a cleaning cloth. In fact, the heat coming off a photographer's face can fog over a camera's viewfinder and then freeze in a matter of minutes. Carefully wipe this coating off with a soft cloth so as not to scratch the viewfinder glass. If condensation build up is an ongoing problem, seal the camera in a plastic freezer bag before going indoors.

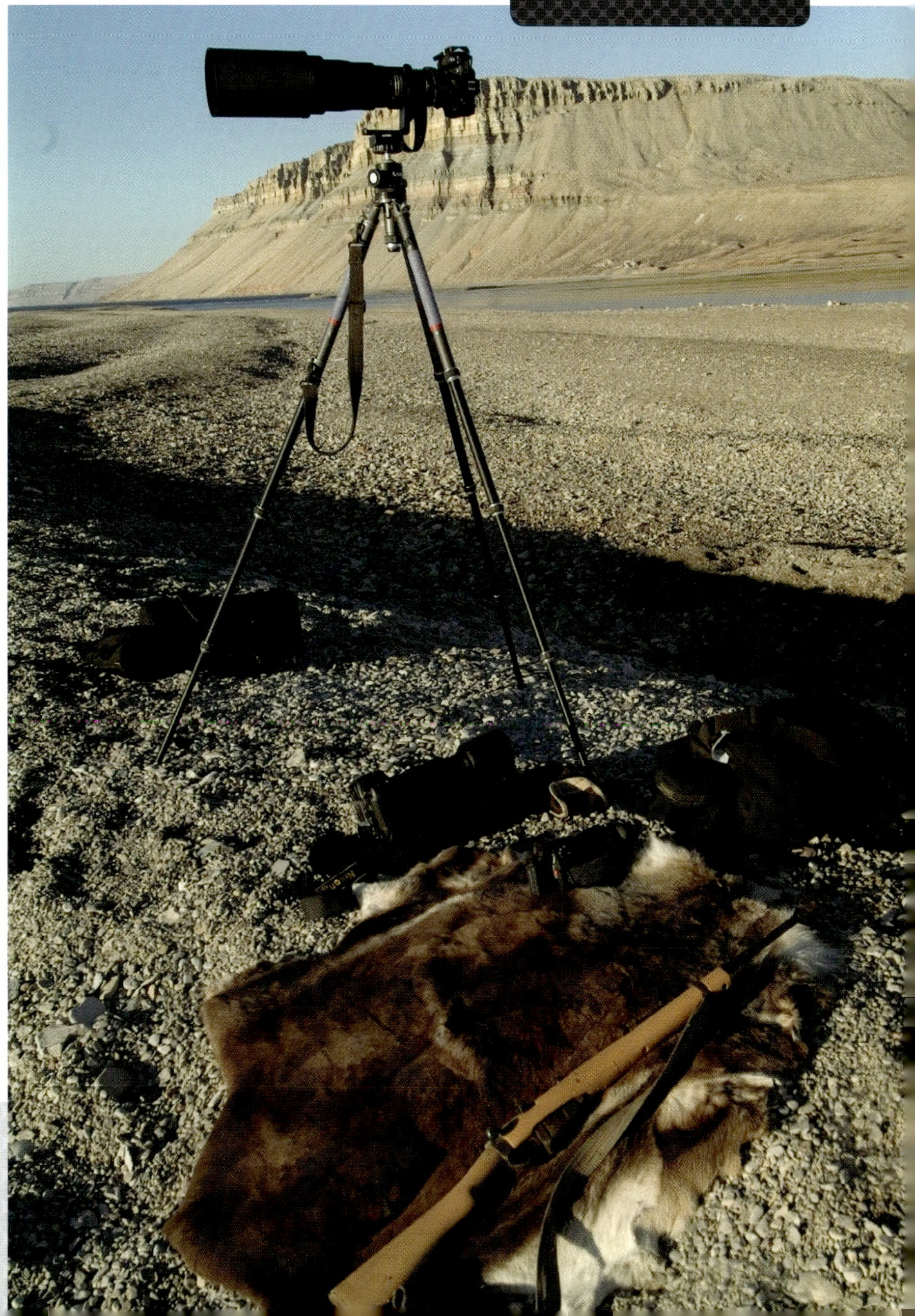

Another approach is to always keep the equipment from warming up to room temperature. For example, when camping keep the equipment in a camera bag on the tent floor near a wall and far away from any heater. Take the batteries out and keep them warm by the heater or in a pocket. A last alternative is to make the transition between cold and warm environments as gradual as possible so that significant condensation never forms in the first place.

Tips: Backup Battery Options

> If the time between recharging extends beyond a few days in a remote area, the photographer should consider using the largest camera battery option available. Many camera models will have an accessory battery pack/grip containing batteries significantly larger than the standard in-camera cell. Some cameras also provide an accessory AA holder to hold four batteries. Lithium batteries are superior to alkaline cells at holding a charge in the cold.

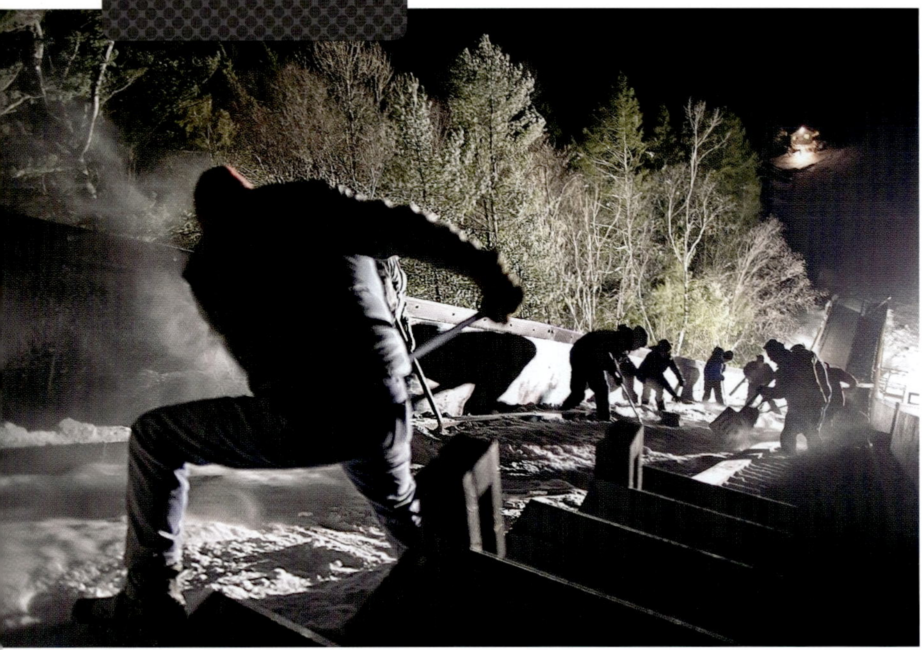

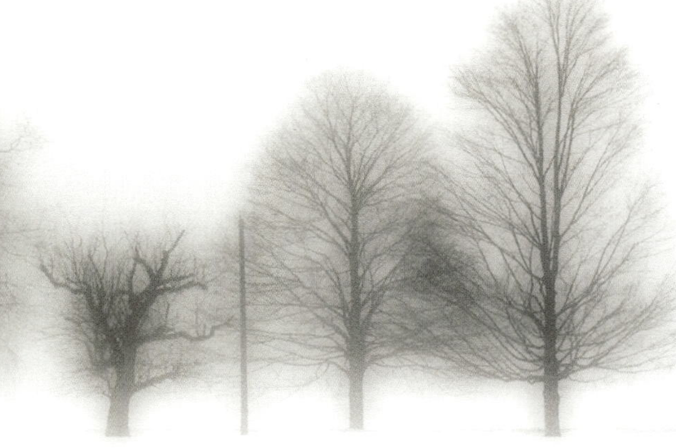

(4) The most challenging problem faced by cold-weather photographers is the need to stay warm and still be able to operate the small controls of cameras and lenses. Taking off gloves to press buttons and operate other controls will demonstrate how quickly the combination of cold metal and freezing temperatures can numb fingers. Needless to say, this makes even simple operations very difficult.

Backing Up Images in the Field

The options for backing up captured images while in the field will depend on two variables. The available recharging facilities and whether or not the photographer wants to see the images and edit the day's shoot while in the field. Here are a few options.

(1) Taking a laptop computer will provide the most complete backup option, since images can be seen and evaluated on a large screen and the day's session edited with standard software such as Photoshop or Lightroom. This is a good choice when on a ship or when each day ends with a return to lodgings with electricity. In a camping situation, where recharging will be a problem, additional backup batteries (kept warm like the camera batteries) are a must. Laptop batteries are just as susceptible as camera batteries to running down in the cold.

(2) Small battery operated portable hard drives with a view screen such as the Epson Multimedia Storage Viewer (www.epson.com) allow the photographer to see a picture approximately two to three times larger than the camera's LCD. The image also has more accurate color and contrast. Battery operated hard drives without screens are a third option. Portable hard drives are available in different storage sizes such as 40GB, 80GB and 160GB. Extra batteries are recommended if recharging facilities will not be available for several days.

(3) In-camera backup is also possible with those DSLR models that take two memory cards. The photographer has the option to program the camera to record each shot on both cards. In general, solid-state memory cards are far less prone to failure than laptop or portable hard drives but are much more expensive per MB of storage. Memory cards are now reasonably priced and some thought should be given to taking many, many cards. This allows the data to remain on the card until back at home rather than downloading and reusing the same cards when on the trip.

Accessories for Work in Remote Locations

Each trip to a remote location will require slightly different accessories to help the photographer deal with local conditions. Here is a general list of items to consider taking along.

(1) A small pop-out gobo held beyond the lens hood but still outside the capture frame is an excellent way of dealing with light in a scene that might cause flare.

(2) A set of warm gloves are a must for working in very cold temperatures.

(3) Lens cleaner and tissues will clean lenses and viewfinders, but in freezing temperatures a better choice is a lens cleaning cloth.

(4) Some waterproof materials should be taken when working around ocean spray, in wind-driven sand conditions as well as rain or snow. Shown here is a yellow poncho that can be used to almost completely cover a tripod with camera attached. Alternatively, a showercap or spare hat can also be used. Many camera bag manufacturers include a waterproof pouch that opens to fit over the bag.

(5) A few tools should be taken, including an all-purpose tool with a screwdriver head, pliers, knife, etc. Also, consider taking a small jeweler's screwdriver kit to deal with the tiny screws on lenses as well as a small blower brush or a small can of compressed air (not shown).

(6) Backup camera batteries are a must for remote locations. If a generator is available then add the camera battery charger. Don't forget at least one flashlight (two recommended) and batteries. Lithium batteries of all sizes are the most resistant to cold and will also hold a charge longer over time.

(7) UV or skylight filters for protection are recommended for all lenses as well as polarizing filters and ND filters.

(8) Plenty of camera memory cards are recommended stored in solid carry cases that stay shut to protect against sand, snow and rain. Ideally, these cards will not be used over and over while on location. Solid-state memory cards are among the safest form of image storage versus all forms of hard drives.

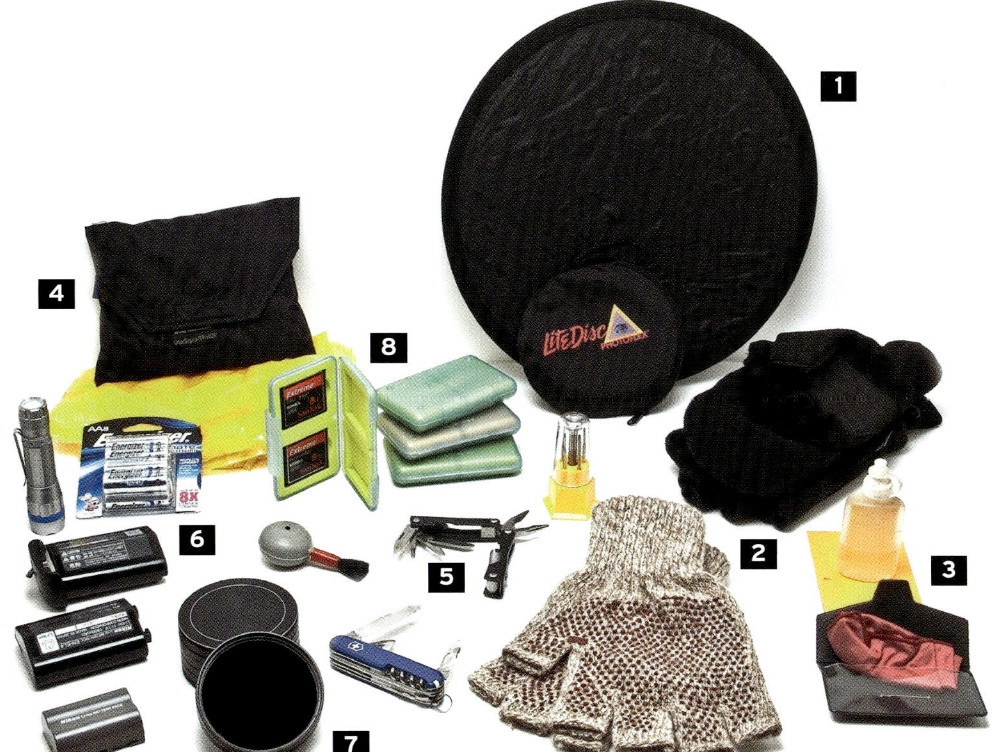

Snowscapes

Exposure for Snow Scenes

Photographing landscapes with large areas of snow and ice, especially in bright sunshine, requires that the photographer make three important adjustments. (1) The indicated camera meter reading will have to be adjusted to compensate for a setting dominated by very light tones. (2) Snow scenes may need specialized techniques to capture a brightness range that exceeds the camera's shadow to highlight recording latitude. (3) Care will have to be taken to protect the lens from very bright reflections that can cause image-degrading flare.

Exposure Compensation

Camera meters are designed to supply exposure settings that render the brightness of a scene as a middle gray tone. To illustrate this, imagine using a camera set on automatic exposure to photograph a medium gray wall, a black wall and a white wall. The camera will dial in a different exposure setting for each wall but the result will be the same: a middle gray wall. That is, the black wall will be overexposed, the white wall underexposed and the gray wall correctly exposed. The white wall can be thought of as representing a snow scene. If no exposure compensation is made, the automatic camera setting will underexpose a snow scene, producing gray snow. The general rule of thumb for such very light tonal scenes is to increase the indicated exposure by between 1-2 stops.

How does one know exactly how much to compensate? This will depend on the individual scene. For example, snow in bright sunshine versus the same scene with significant shadow areas formed by clouds. One approach to compensation is to take a series of different exposures. Most modern DSLR and film SLR cameras will have an auto bracketing function allowing the user to expose at the meter's indicated value, as well as different settings for under- or overexposures in a sequence. Since the camera's meter will give a setting that will underexpose a snow scene (as in the case of the white wall), more exposure is needed to place white snow in the brightest highlight areas. A bracketing sequence of between one to two additional stops provides a good range of compensation as in: +1 stop, +1 1/2 stop and +2 stops. This bracketing can also be done with the camera in the manual exposure mode, making changes manually to the shutter speed, aperture, ISO or combinations thereof. Bracketing is not only a way to get the right exposure; it can also instruct in how to handle difficult lighting situations

Another approach is to use the camera's exposure compensation dial that can be set for additional stops of exposure as well as underexposure. Once set, the camera will continue taking pictures at this compensated exposure setting. This works well when the light is constant and the photographer has determined the amount of compensation by checking the camera's LCD histogram. The optional shape for a snow scene would be one in which the areas of snow are skewed well into the highlight end but not so far as to greatly overexpose this area. If the peak of the curve representing the snow is in the middle or toward the shadow end of the histogram, the snow scene will appear overly dark and underexposed.

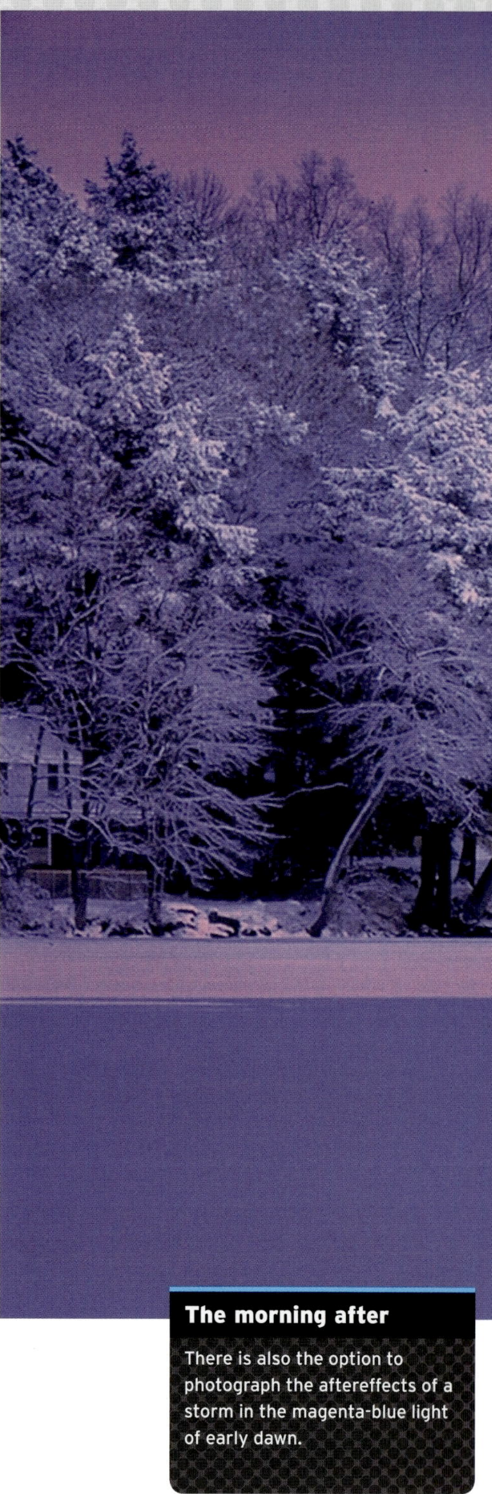

The morning after

There is also the option to photograph the aftereffects of a storm in the magenta-blue light of early dawn.

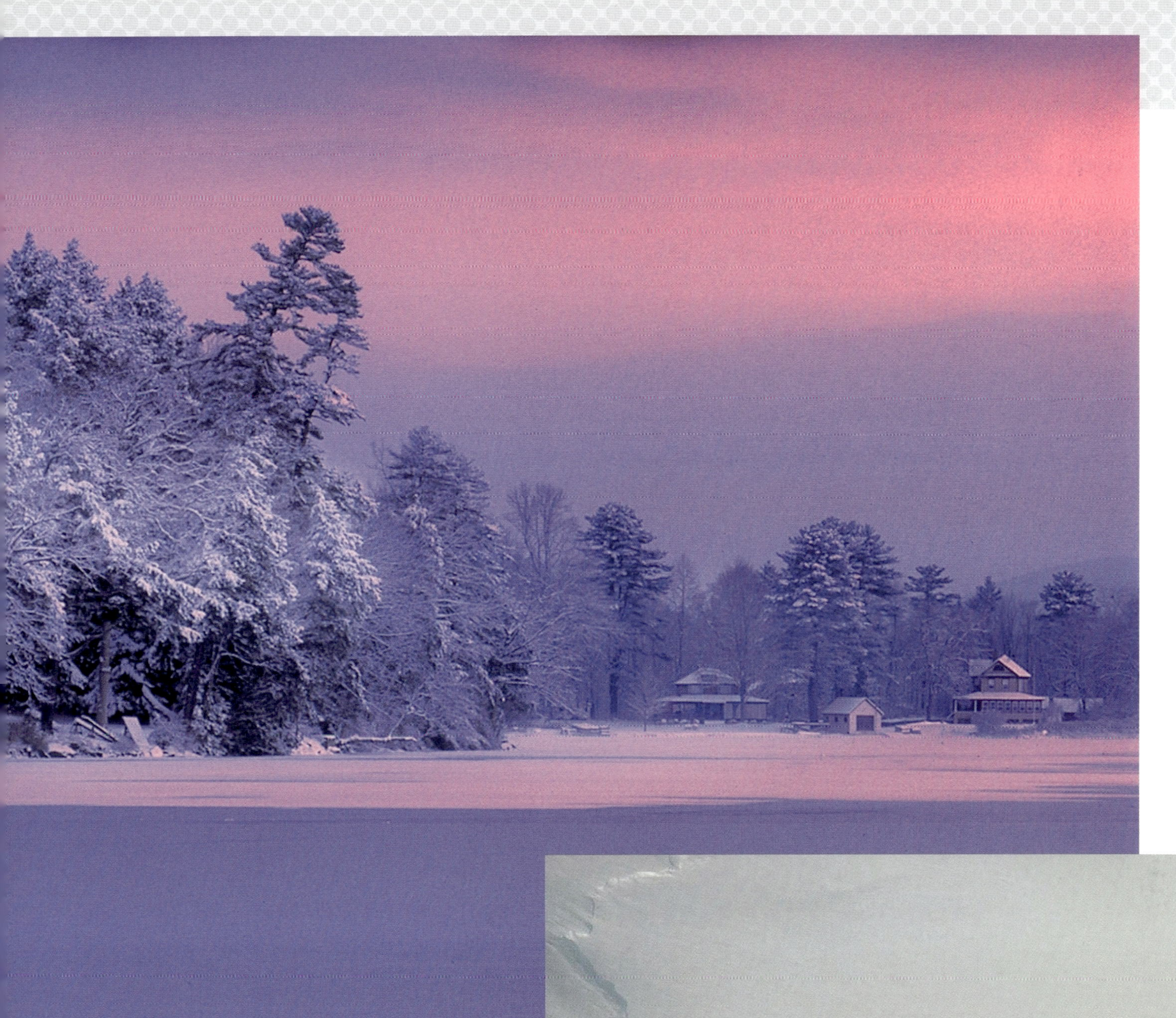

Not for the faint of heart

When working out of a campsite in a snow-covered Arctic environment in extremely cold temperatures, one must be willing to endure wind-driven cold conditions day in and day out, as well as a sense of isolation that can be unnerving.

Raw Files

Setting the camera to capture a Raw file will give the photographer a last chance to correct for an underexposed image. Capturing a Raw file means that virtually all the light the sensor "sees" is stored in the camera and then read in a Raw file reader software. A JPEG capture, on the other hand, processes and changes the original data to some degree before the file can be adjusted on the computer. It is thus possible to adjust the exposure using a Raw file reader program by one stop or even two full stops. The drawback here is that the original underexposed Raw file is likely to have recorded a higher proportion of noise relative to the picture data. The compensation methods mentioned earlier place the snow in the correct highlight areas at the time of exposure with comparatively lower levels of noise.

In addition to exposure adjustments, Raw files allow the photographer much more leeway in working with white balance, contrast, brightness, etc. Shown here is the Adobe Camera Raw (ACR) software in Adobe Photoshop that was used to correct for an underexposed original with an inappropriate white balance, plus other refinements using a whole range of basic and advanced controls.

Dealing with Excessive Ranges of Brightness

Regardless of how careful a photographer is in compensating for a correct exposure, there will be scenes whose total brightness range exceeds the camera's single-frame recording latitude. For example, a sunlit snow scene in which there are significant dark tonal values from a forest area. Such scenes can have a reflected brightness range as much as 8-10 stops or more between important dark and light areas. As a generalization, digital camera and transparency film have exposure latitudes that will record details in areas separated by 5-6 stops. To overcome this difference, many photographers use high dynamic range (HDR) exposure techniques as described below.

Flare Protection

Finally, there is the concern for lens flare caused by extremely bright reflections off shiny surfaces. Lenses are designed to optimally record diffused reflections as opposed to the bright light reflected from very shiny surfaces or a light source per se. If a lens is not protected from such strong sources outside the frame of the composition, this "stray" light will literally bounce around within the housing of the lens and off aperture blades. The result is lens flare whose effect can range from a general reduction in contrast to the appearance of flare spots. A lens hood is very helpful at blocking such strong light sources originating outside the composition. In addition, if the camera is tripod mounted, one can further shield against any light the lens hood does not block with a small gobo.

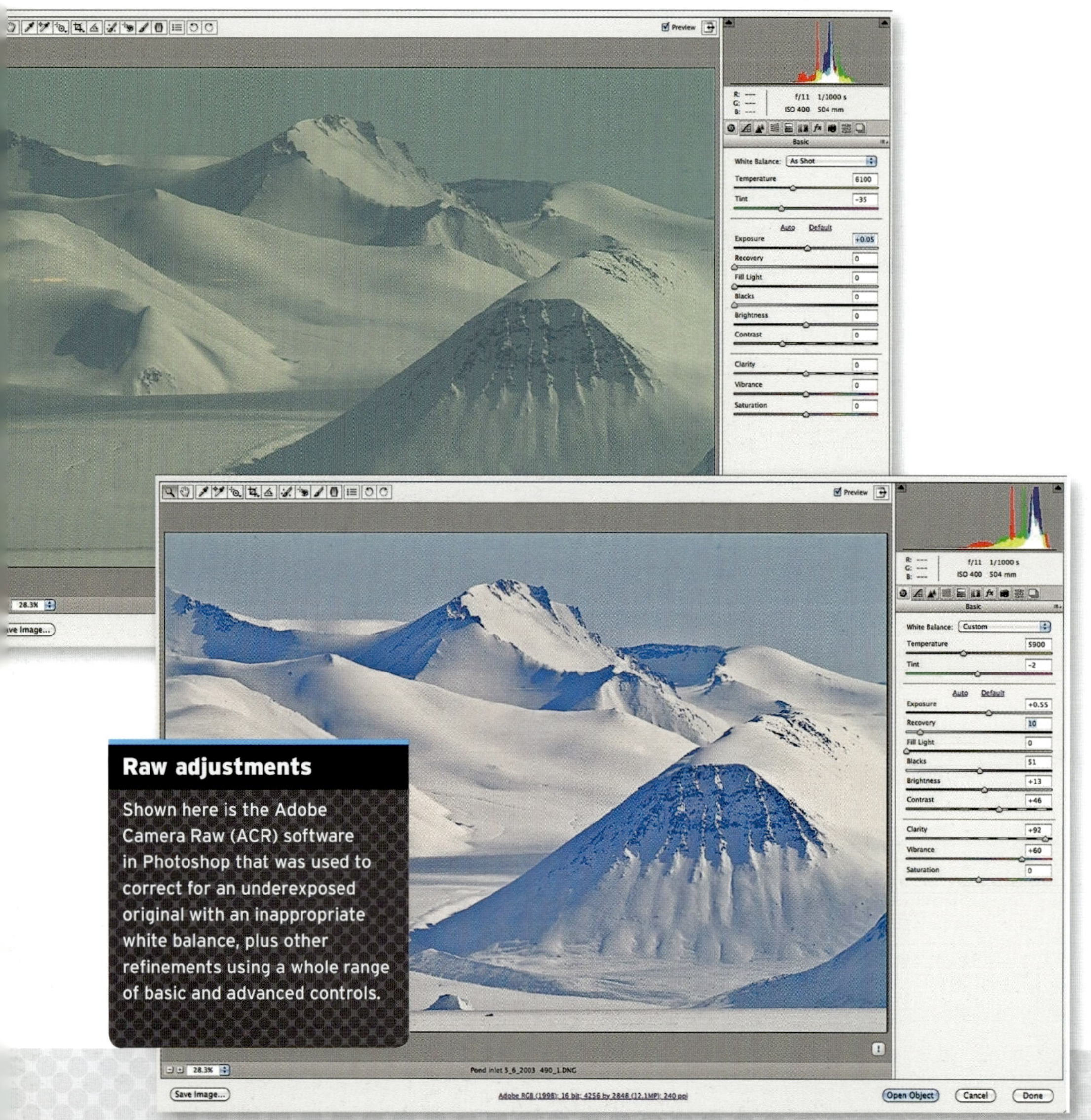

Raw adjustments

Shown here is the Adobe Camera Raw (ACR) software in Photoshop that was used to correct for an underexposed original with an inappropriate white balance, plus other refinements using a whole range of basic and advanced controls.

Cirrocumulus winters

You'll recognize this cloud
type from page 45, and here
it brilliantly contributes to
the scene by adding tons of
texture and contours that would
otherwise be completely absent
in this vast snowscape.

You will need:

> For extended expeditions, all the
essential cold-weather camping
gear (warm coats, sleeping bags,
tents, stoves, food, etc.)

> Plenty of extra batteries, kept warm
in your coat or sleeping bag

> Plenty of storage, spread out across
multiple memory cards (in case any
one should fail)

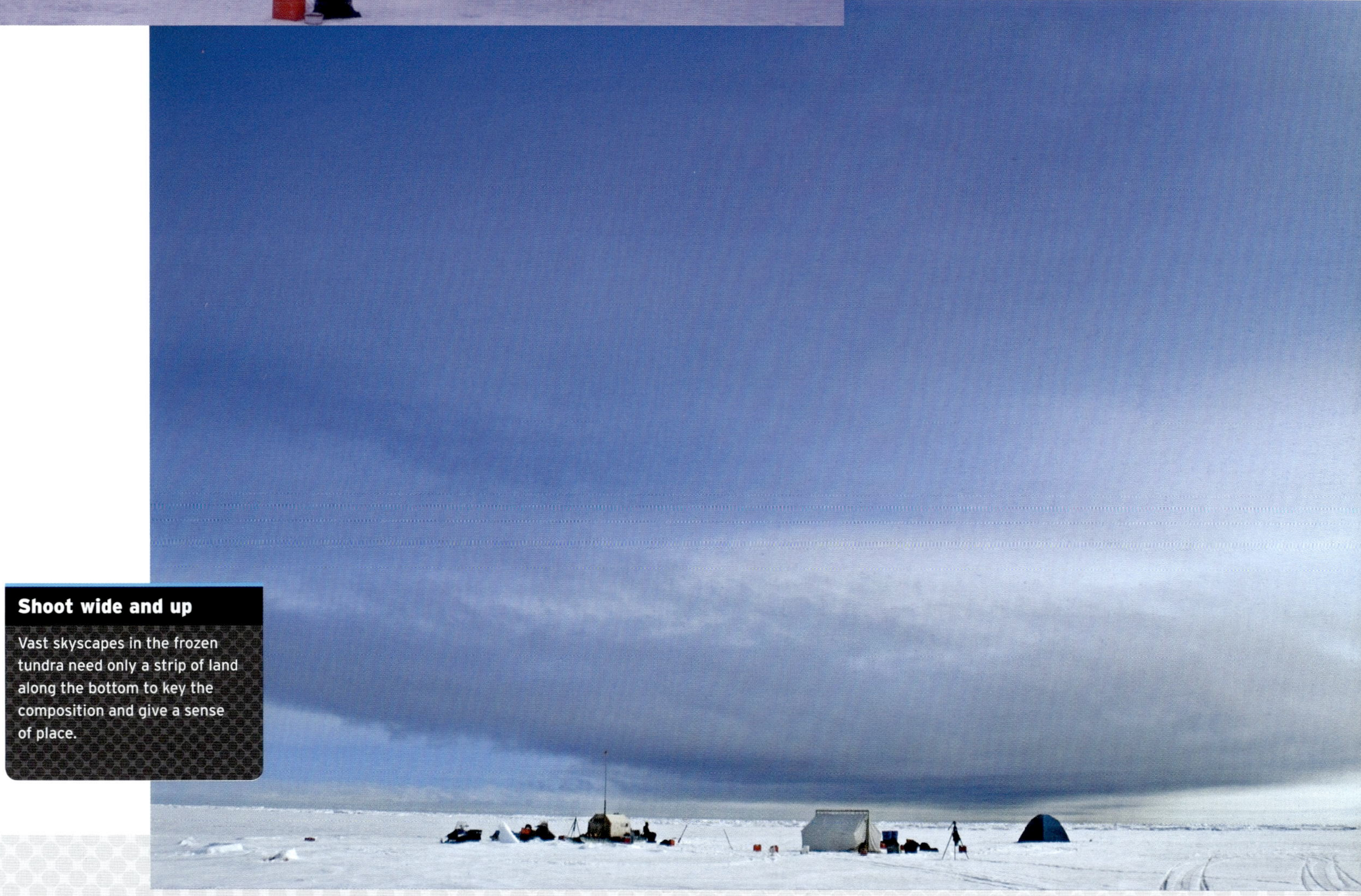

Shoot wide and up

Vast skyscapes in the frozen
tundra need only a strip of land
along the bottom to key the
composition and give a sense
of place.

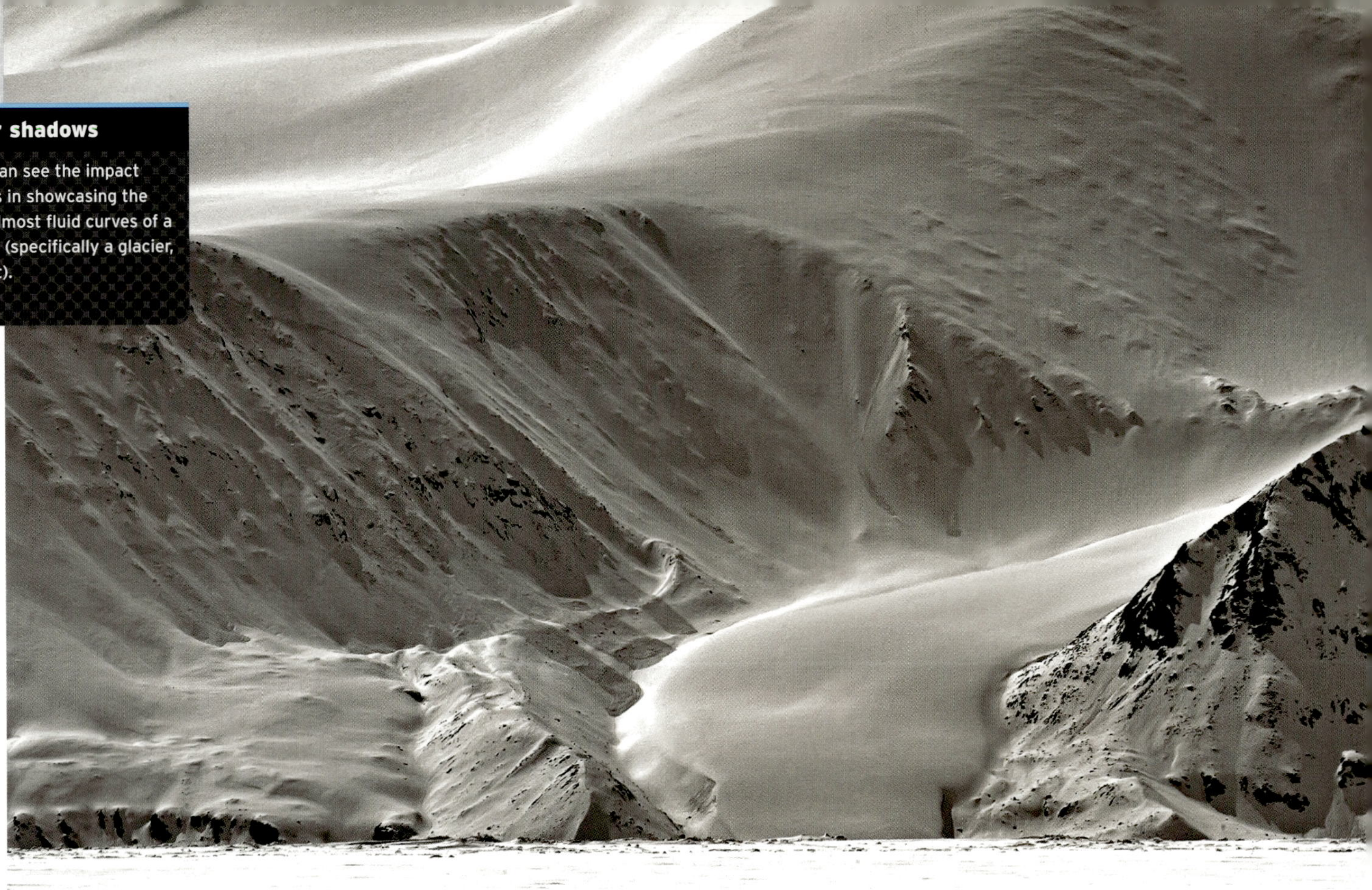

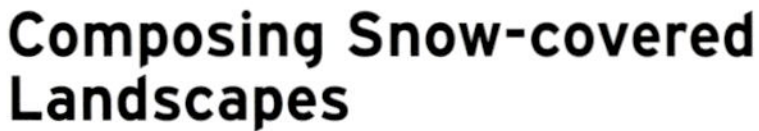

Composing Snow-covered Landscapes

As pointed out in the previous chapter, it is the individual photographer's preferences for subject matter and composition that will determine the makeup of the final image. What follows are suggestions designed to point out some of the opportunities found in the Arctic regions of Canada and Greenland, as well as in other frigid environments.

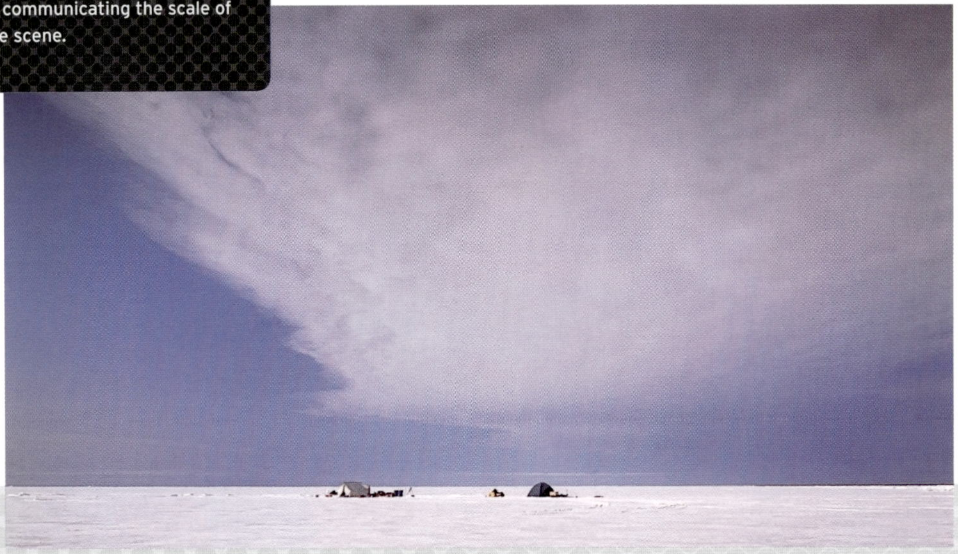

The Role of Shadows

The major visual characteristic of snow-covered environments is a softer look to those structures covered by the snow. This is somewhat similar to the appearance of sand dunes but with the starkness of white and more limited forms of surface textures. Thus, if the scene does not have a variety of structures such as mountains, trees and bodies of open water, the challenge will be to produce a photograph that has shapes and smaller forms as well as depth. Just as in the

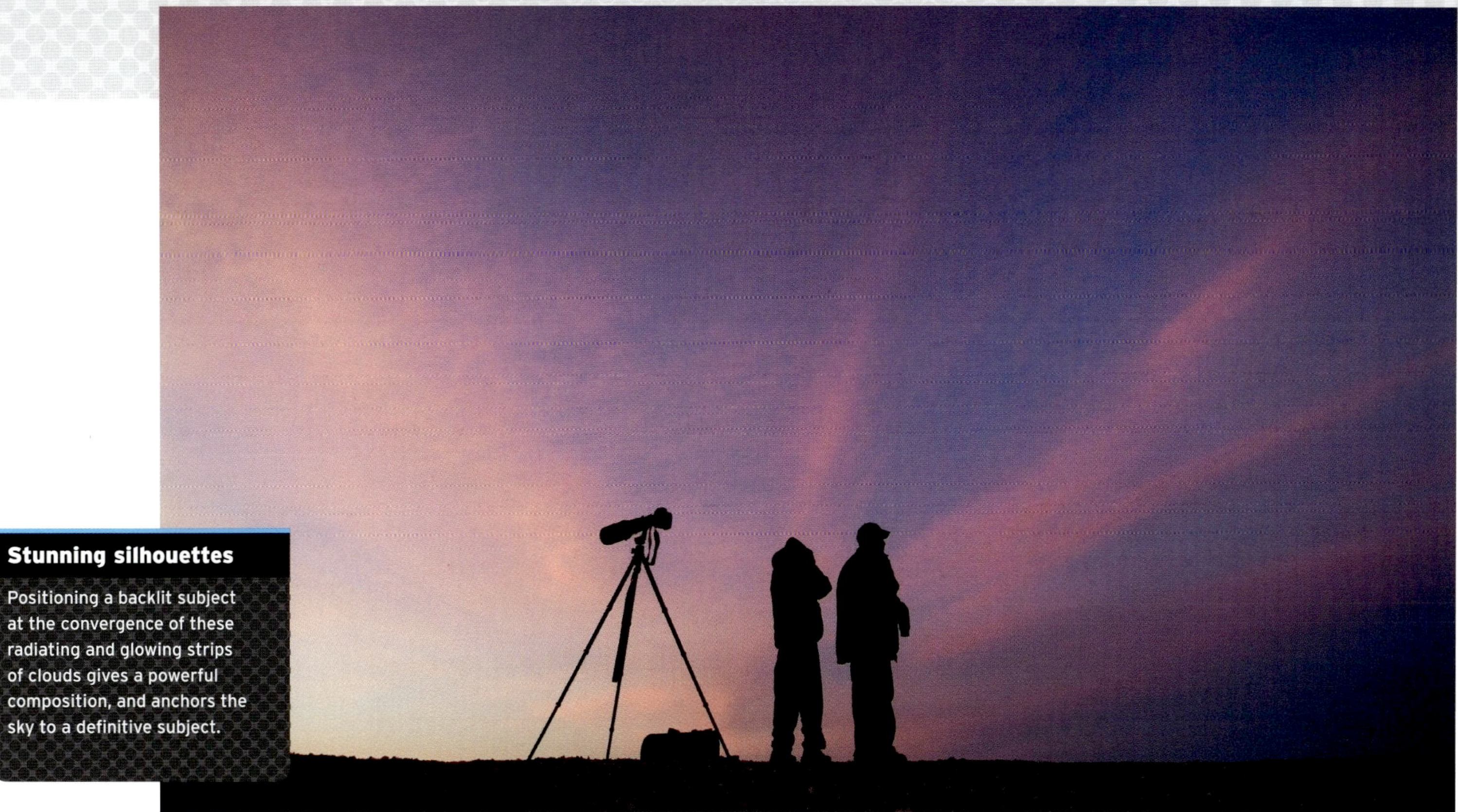

desert, it is the type of lighting that will play a key role in bringing out these qualities. That is, it will be shadow areas that define shapes and forms, and the best time is when the sun is low in the sky.

Capturing the Expanse

As illustrated in several of the images in this chapter, the one quality that is common to Arctic regions is the vastness and scale of the topography. This includes the ocean areas often filled with endless scatterings of ice flows and icebergs that surround and inundate Arctic land areas. Other settings, such as snow-covered farmland or beach areas in winter, will also convey such an impression. Typically using a wide-angle lens or composing a stitched panorama works quite well in capturing such vistas. While they both will pull in a large area, they do so differently and therefore can provide vastly different looks to a final image.

As pointed out in the previous chapter, wide-angle lenses will reduce the relative size of the background while exaggerating subject matter in foreground areas. This is an effective way of also homing in on some local quality of the scene. For example, emphasizing the unique structure of floating ice framed by the expanse of the ocean and a distant shoreline in the background. On the other hand, a panoramic view derives its power from being able to capture a much wider view horizontally. For example, sprawling areas of tundra or an expanse of frozen ocean. In addition, because there is the option to use a telephoto compression in a stitched panorama, a better size balance between foreground and background can be achieved relative to what happens with wide-angle lenses. See "Producing Stitched Panoramas" on the following page.

The Importance of the Sky

Another consideration is the role the sky will play in the final image. Unlike deserts, where weather systems tend to be rather stable, Arctic regions are notorious for quick and dramatic changes in the weather—something the photographer should keep in mind when planning the day's activities. Sky areas are critical for helping to set the mood of a scene and that is especially true of snow-covered settings where the topography can be rather uniform. Thus, it is very often left to the sky to introduce or reinforce a variety of moods. For example, the brightness and sparkle of a clear blue sky, the depressing mood of a uniformly gray sky and the threatening feeling of an increasingly dark and stormy sky. Consequently, when composing, due consideration should be given to the role the sky area can play in whatever mood the photographer wishes to convey.

Producing Stitched Panoramas

Producing a panoramic image is relatively easy with today's stitching software if certain basic procedures are followed. Most important is that the camera be set level so that the top and bottom of each frame line up as close as possible. Otherwise, significant cropping down to the commonly shared areas for all frames will be necessary. This can make for a very skinny panoramic image. Using a tripod and one of several leveling-panoramic heads offered by companies such as Kirk Enterprises or The Really Right Stuff will yield the best frame-to-frame alignment.

It is difficult to obtain good frame-to-frame alignment using a handheld camera. Taking a slightly wider-angle view will provide more leeway when cropping down to the common shared areas in the frames. Using the camera in the portrait (vertical) position versus the landscape (horizontal) position results in a higher height-to-width ratio. To obtain uniform exposures and maintain a set focus, place the camera in Manual mode and the exposure and focus point as if the whole scene were to be taken in one composition. Take each of the 30–50% overlapping frames with this setting. Using autoexposure or focus may produce different results from frame to frame.

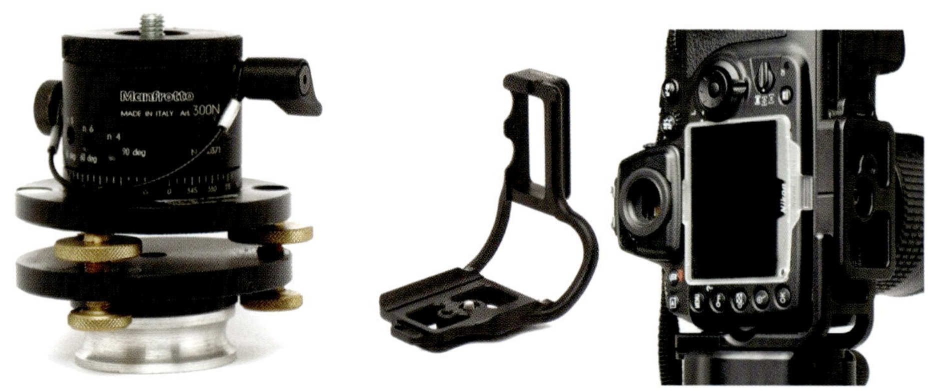

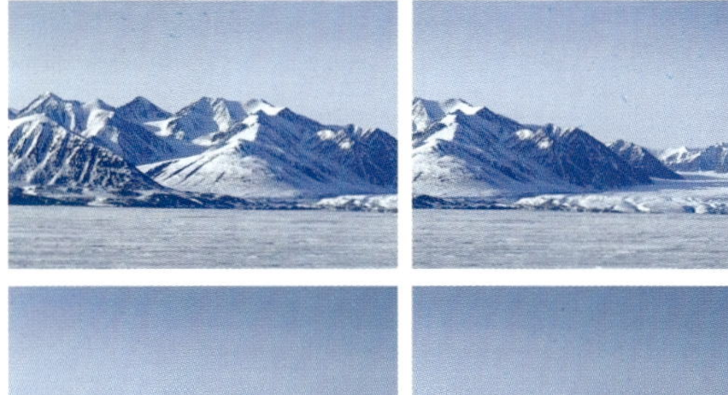

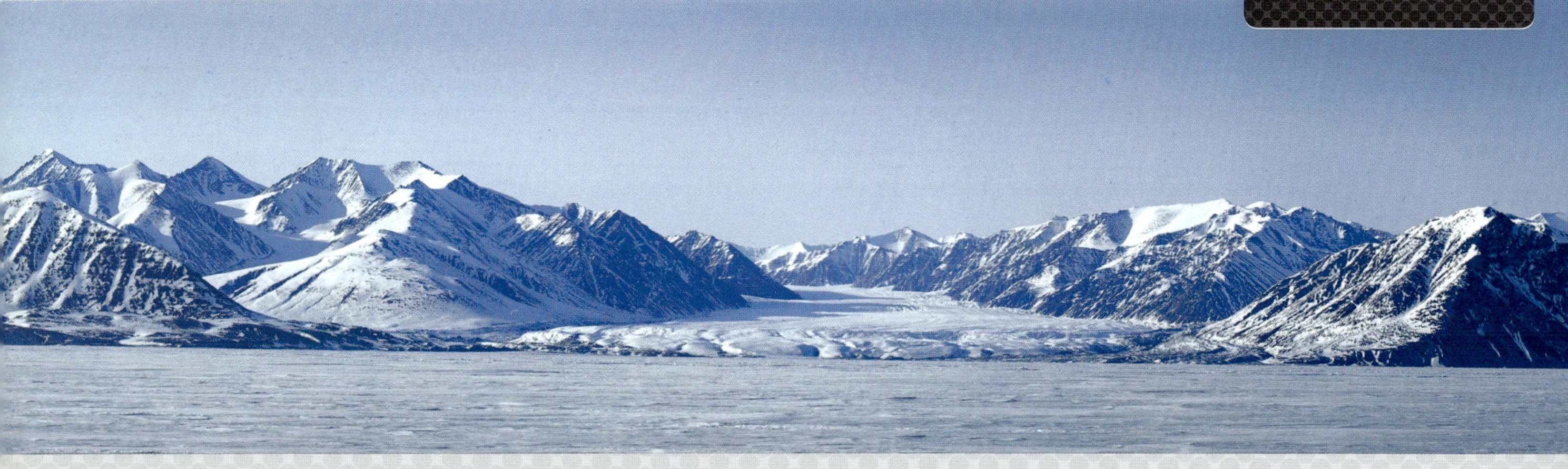

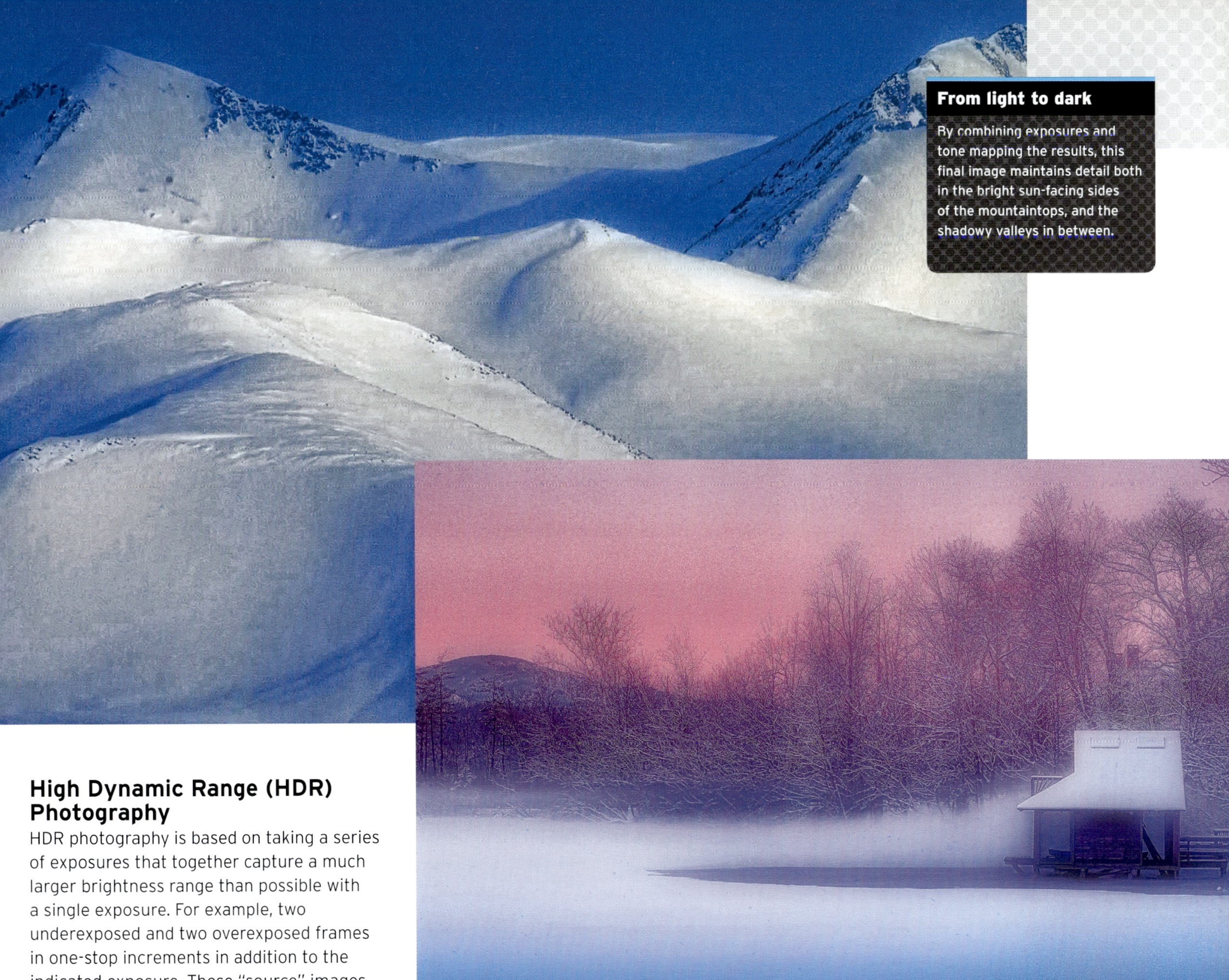

By combining exposures and tone mapping the results, this final image maintains detail both in the bright sun-facing sides of the mountaintops, and the shadowy valleys in between.

High Dynamic Range (HDR) Photography

HDR photography is based on taking a series of exposures that together capture a much larger brightness range than possible with a single exposure. For example, two underexposed and two overexposed frames in one-stop increments in addition to the indicated exposure. These "source" images are then processed into a final single image using one of two methods.

In the tone mapping method, all the captured brightness is treated using a set of tone mapping algorithms (mathematical instructions). The result is a compression of the extreme brightness range that was captured into an image that can be displayed on a monitor and printed. Results of tone mapping tend to have very strong saturated colors and high contrast levels resulting in what has been called the "HDR Look."

The second method, called exposure fusion, does not use tone mapping. Instead, different algorithms are used in which single pixels from each frame are selected to construct the final image. The degree of color saturation and contrast is less than with tone mapping, resulting in a more natural rendering but still with the extended brightness range.

The exotic environs of snow photography lend themselves well to HDR rendering, as they accommodate strong saturation levels that would be overkill on standard, commonplace scenes.

Snowstorms

Snowstorms are quite diverse events influenced by a set of variables that can play a role in the final appearance of a scene as well as determining how that scene might be photographed. Those variables are: (1) the diversity in the size of the flakes, (2) how fast they are falling and (3) the effect of wind altering the angle and uniformity of the falling snow. Depending on the rate of the snowfall and the size of the flakes, a snowstorm can reduce visibility to "white out" conditions or produce nothing more than a light dusting with plenty of variations in between. Thus, there is a range that can be exploited photographically using a number of different tools and techniques as guided by the intentions of the photographer.

Like the effect of fog and the light conditions of sunrise and sunset, falling snow can also produce its own unique atmospheric impressions in terms of mood and ambience. That is, imparting a soft look to the whole scene that reduces the saturation of colors and obscures fine details. This means large and well-defined subjects will tend to dominate as the snow is falling. The color balance of a snowy day will tend toward the blue end of the color scale reinforcing the feeling of cold temperatures.

One of the most powerful tools to control the appearance of falling snow and one that is often overlooked is the specific choice of a shutter speed. As a generalization, slow speeds will transform falling snow into blurred streaks while faster speeds will freeze individual flakes in mid air. The exact shutter speed effect will depend on how fast the snow is falling and the influence of wind. Thus, the best strategy is as with any situation in which motion is a key variable, to take a range of shutter speed exposures and build up experience with the results. A very intense storm can also act like fog to greatly reduce visibility, thus allowing subjects closer to the camera to be isolated from their background areas. Consequently, when snow is coming down heavy, one should think of minimalist compositions in which larger shapes such as trees, houses and fence lines in the foreground are the subjects enveloped in a mass of white.

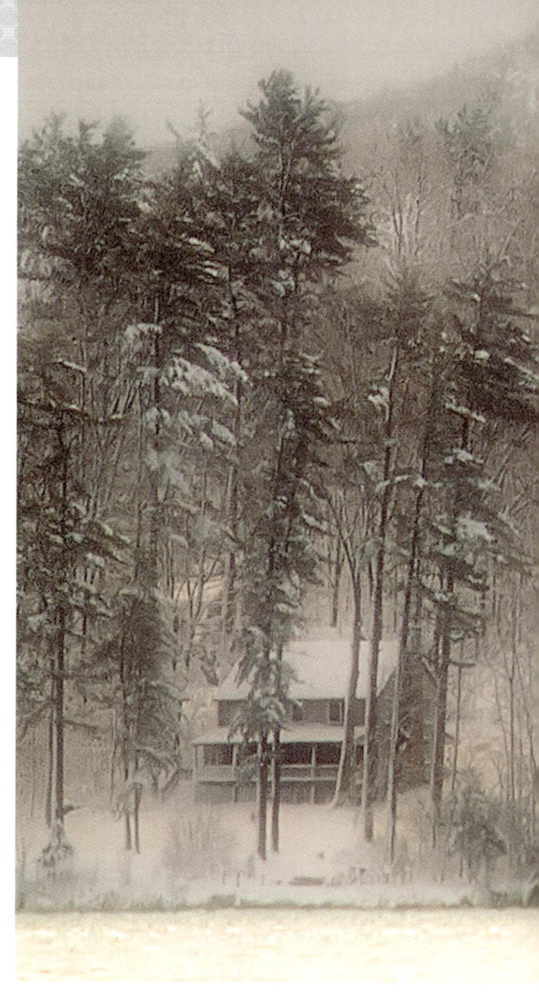

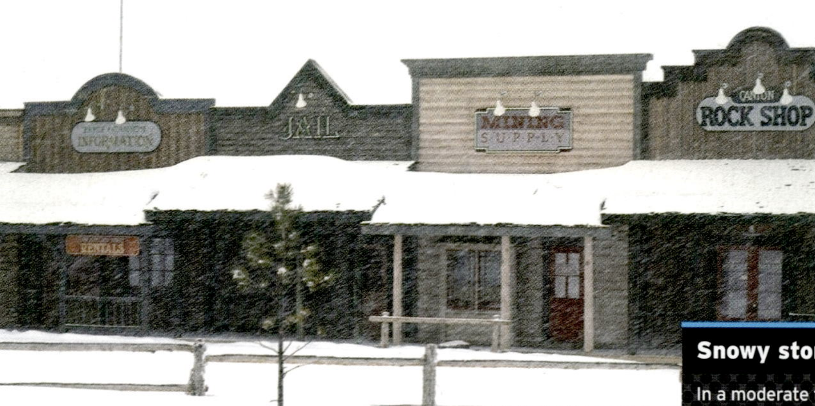

Shooting Tips:

> It's often hard to predict the full effects of your various shutter speeds on a snowstorm capture, so experiment and check your results along the way.

> A snowscape is far more effective when it is uncontaminated by tracks from vehicles and people— though these can be removed in post-production.

Snowy storefronts

In a moderate to heavy storm, using a fast shutter speed will produce very distinct snowflakes that can form a screen of white dots over the scene. But here, a slow shutter speed will reduce the appearance of individual flakes to streaks, and also diminish the wind's effect on the falling snow.

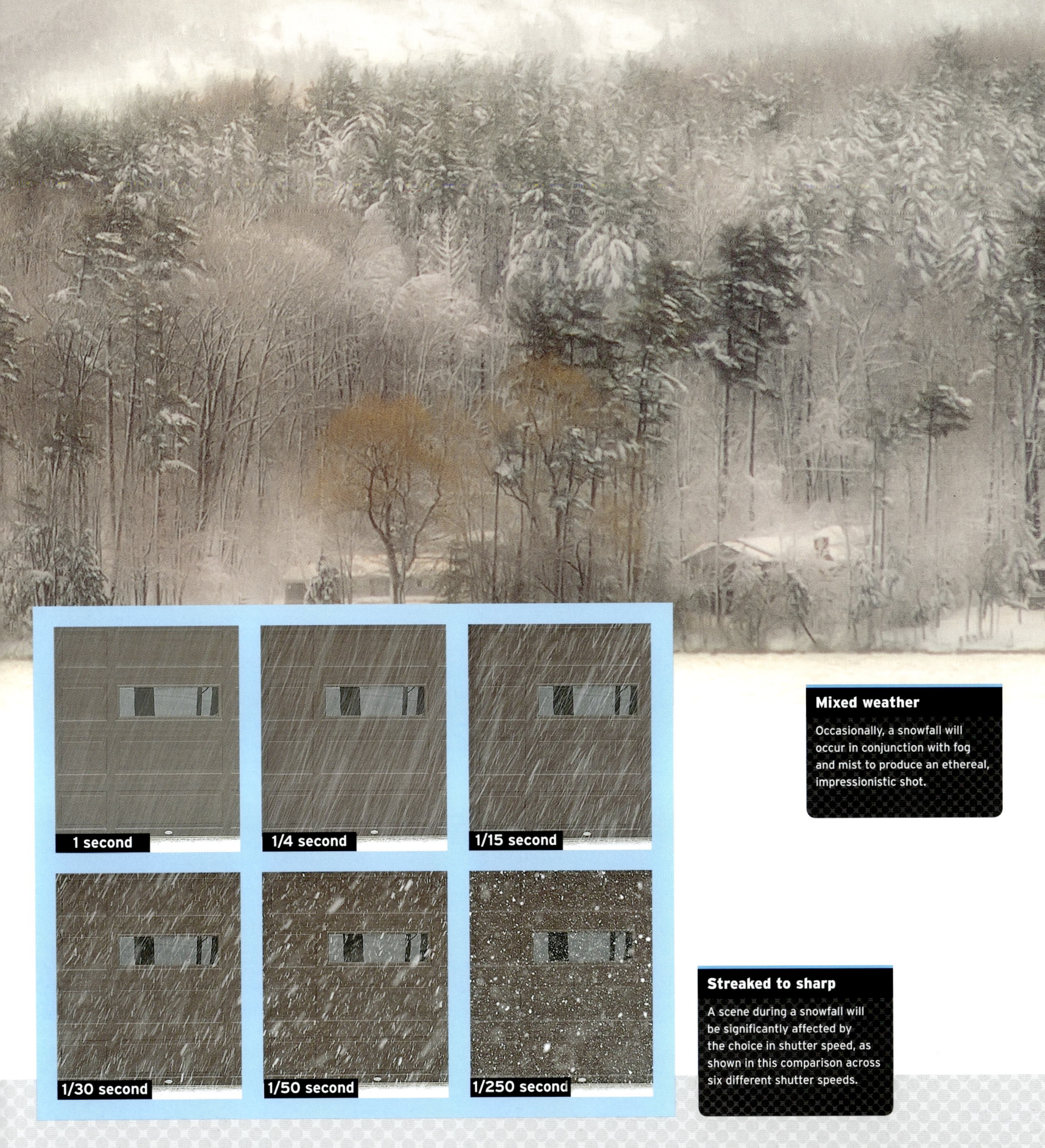

Mixed weather

Occasionally, a snowfall will occur in conjunction with fog and mist to produce an ethereal, impressionistic shot.

Streaked to sharp

A scene during a snowfall will be significantly affected by the choice in shutter speed, as shown in this comparison across six different shutter speeds.

Arctic Wildlife

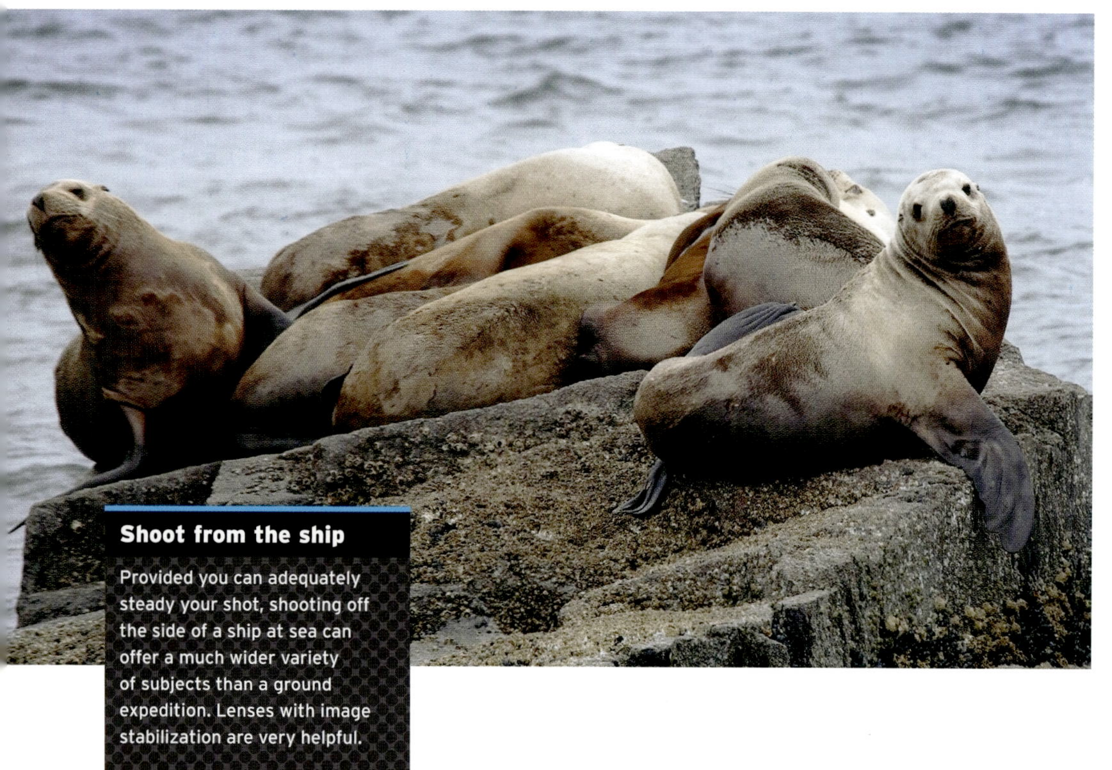

Shoot from the ship

Provided you can adequately steady your shot, shooting off the side of a ship at sea can offer a much wider variety of subjects than a ground expedition. Lenses with image stabilization are very helpful.

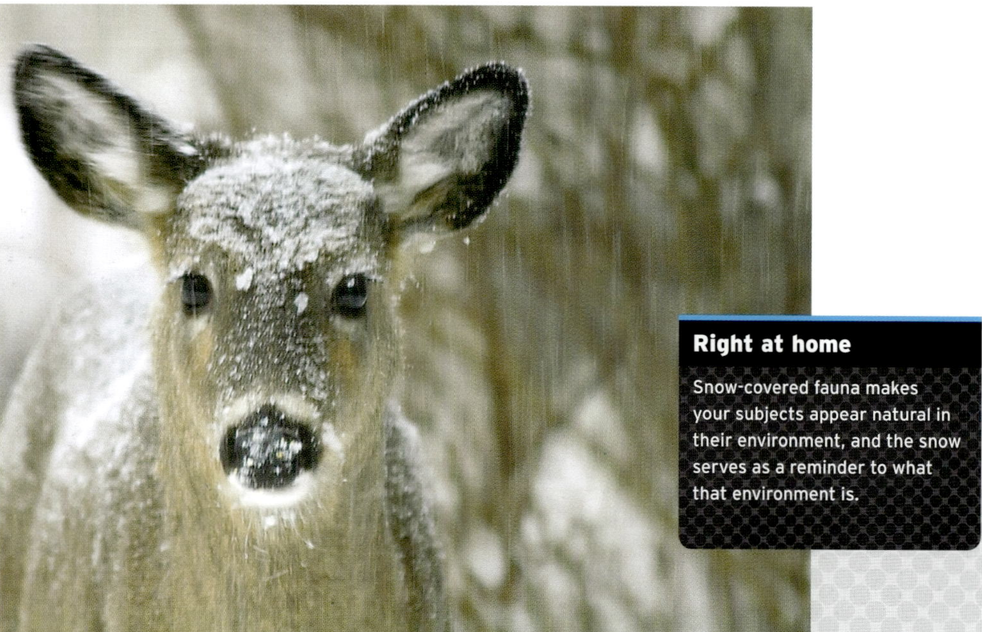

Right at home

Snow-covered fauna makes your subjects appear natural in their environment, and the snow serves as a reminder to what that environment is.

In the recommended lens kit covered in the last chapter, the telephoto focal lengths between 200-400mm can be used to capture wildlife in the Arctic under appropriate conditions. Photographic tours from snow vehicles usually will bring photographers quite close to the one animal everyone seems to want a picture of: polar bears. A telephoto zoom that goes up to 300mm or 400mm will be more than adequate when photographing from the safety of a tall snow buggy. Photographing these dangerous animals from a campsite requires the presence of armed guides who will keep a 24-hour polar-bear watch. They are responsible for the safety of tourists and, if necessary, keeping the bears at bay. Depending on the behavior of individual animals, one should be able to get some very good images with 300-400mm focal lengths, as these bears will tend to check out any campsite.

Waterfowl at the "flow edge" (where the ocean meets the ice or land) tend to be rather flighty if approached by a group. Patience and slow movements by an individual and staying very still once a position is reached are the best strategies. A simple snow blind that shields you from view and lots of patience will prove effective. Birds on the wing are much more difficult and require that the photographer have experience operating a long telephoto quickly on a moving target. The key is to get the autofocus point in the viewfinder on a single bird and keep it there. It is also important to use a very fast shutter speed such as 1/1000 second or faster to freeze the flapping wings.

Photographing wildlife from ships is very dependent on where the ship goes in Arctic regions. Most tours will indicate ahead of time what animals will likely be seen. These could be a variety of whales such as the Beluga, Narwhal and Bowhead as well as seals. Of the three whales, the Narwhal, with its characteristic tusk that can reach six to nine feet (two to three meters) in males, is the most striking but they are the most wary, whereas the Bowhead with its massive size is the most impressive. The longest telephoto focal lengths will be necessary to capture good compositions for all of these open-water animals.

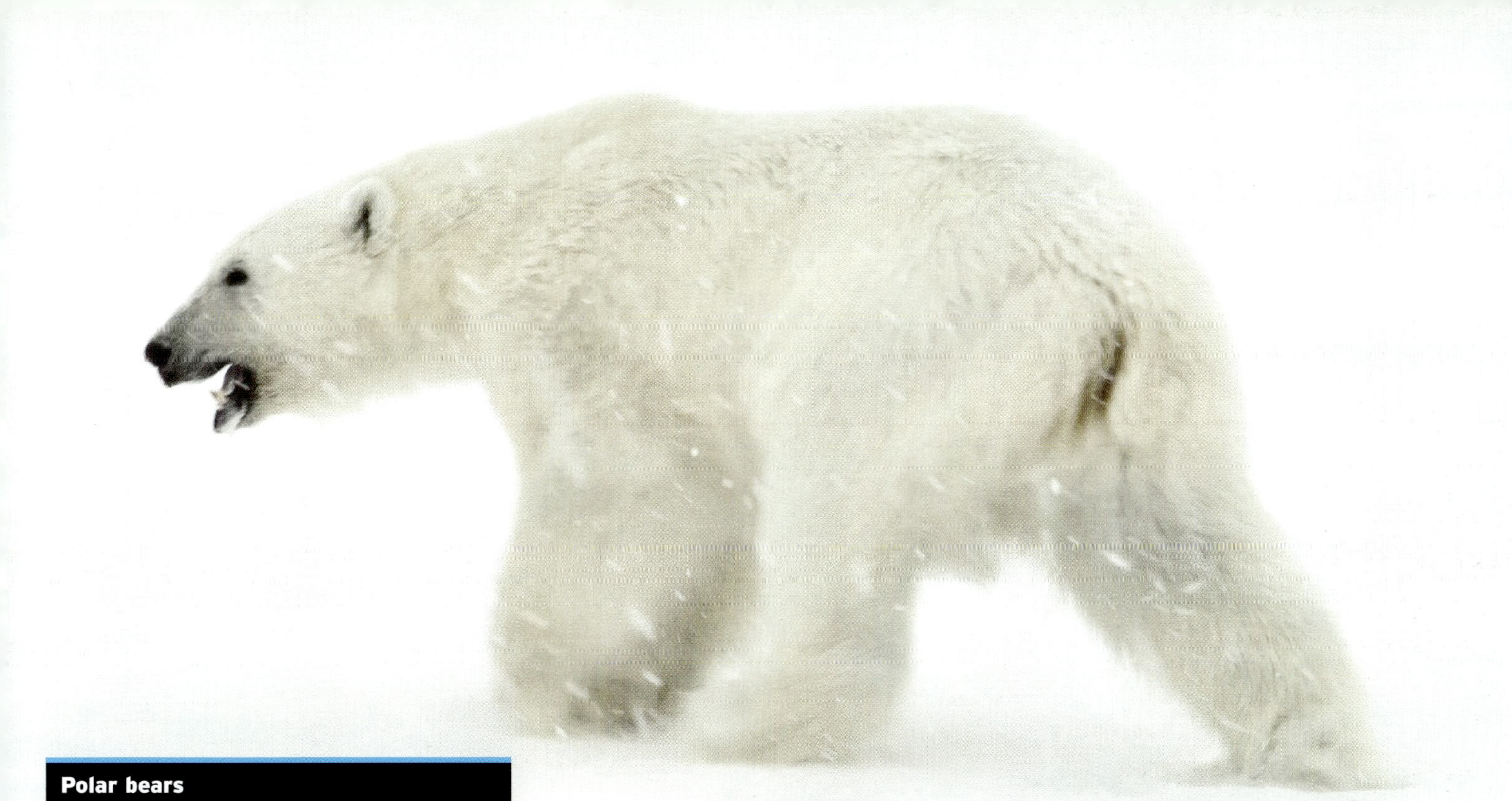

In summary, Arctic regions are among the most hostile places on earth to humans. Intensive cold, sudden storms, Polar Bears and unsafe ice conditions are real threats and one should never attempt to visit these areas unless on a tour or with experienced and armed guides.

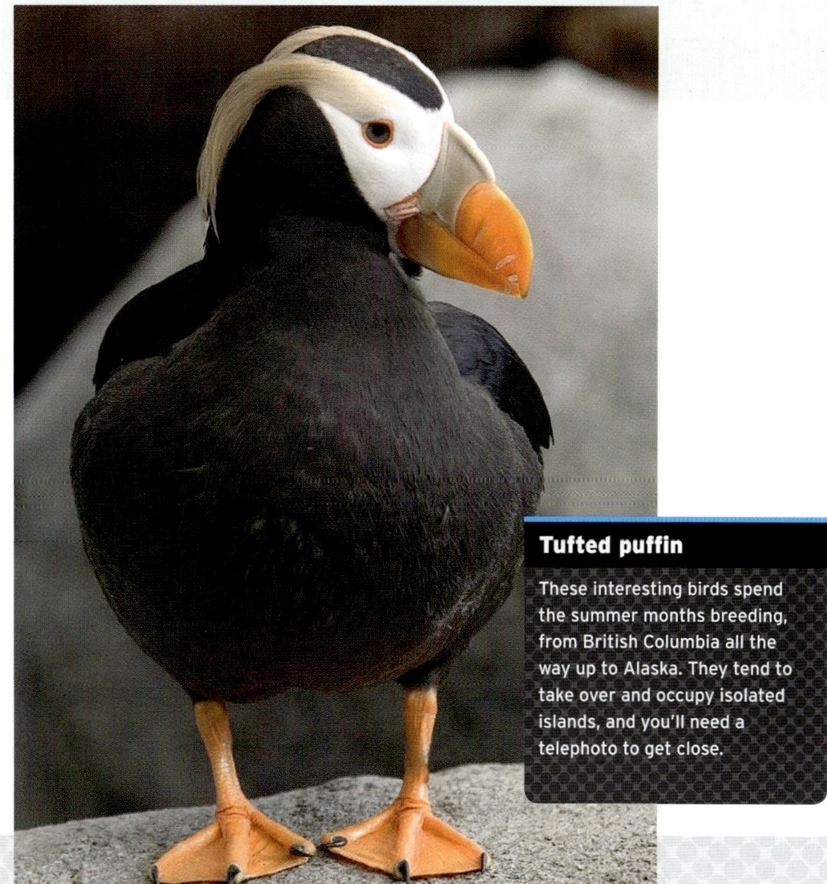

Glaciers

Glaciers are the product of successive accumulations of snow creating enormous pressure on previous snow layers over eons of time. This pressure produces "firn," a granular form of snow, and with more and more massive weight firn eventually becomes ice forming an ice field. This field becomes deeper and deeper with time as more snow is added. The colder portions in the higher elevations will tend to add more layers, while at the warmer end at lower elevations the ice is likely to break off in chunks ("calving") as the glacier moves ever so slowly toward its warmer end. If the glacier calves into a body of water, the result is an iceberg. Glaciers will also have rocks, dirt and other ground debris and therefore may appear quite dirty in places. These great masses of ice are common to both polar regions but may also appear in mountainous locations where there is significant snowfall and cold temperatures year after year.

Kenai Fjords, Alaska

For a smooth textural rendering, the best times are in the colder months when new snowfalls have coated the surface and filled-in ridges. This also makes glaciers an especially attractive black-and-white subject.

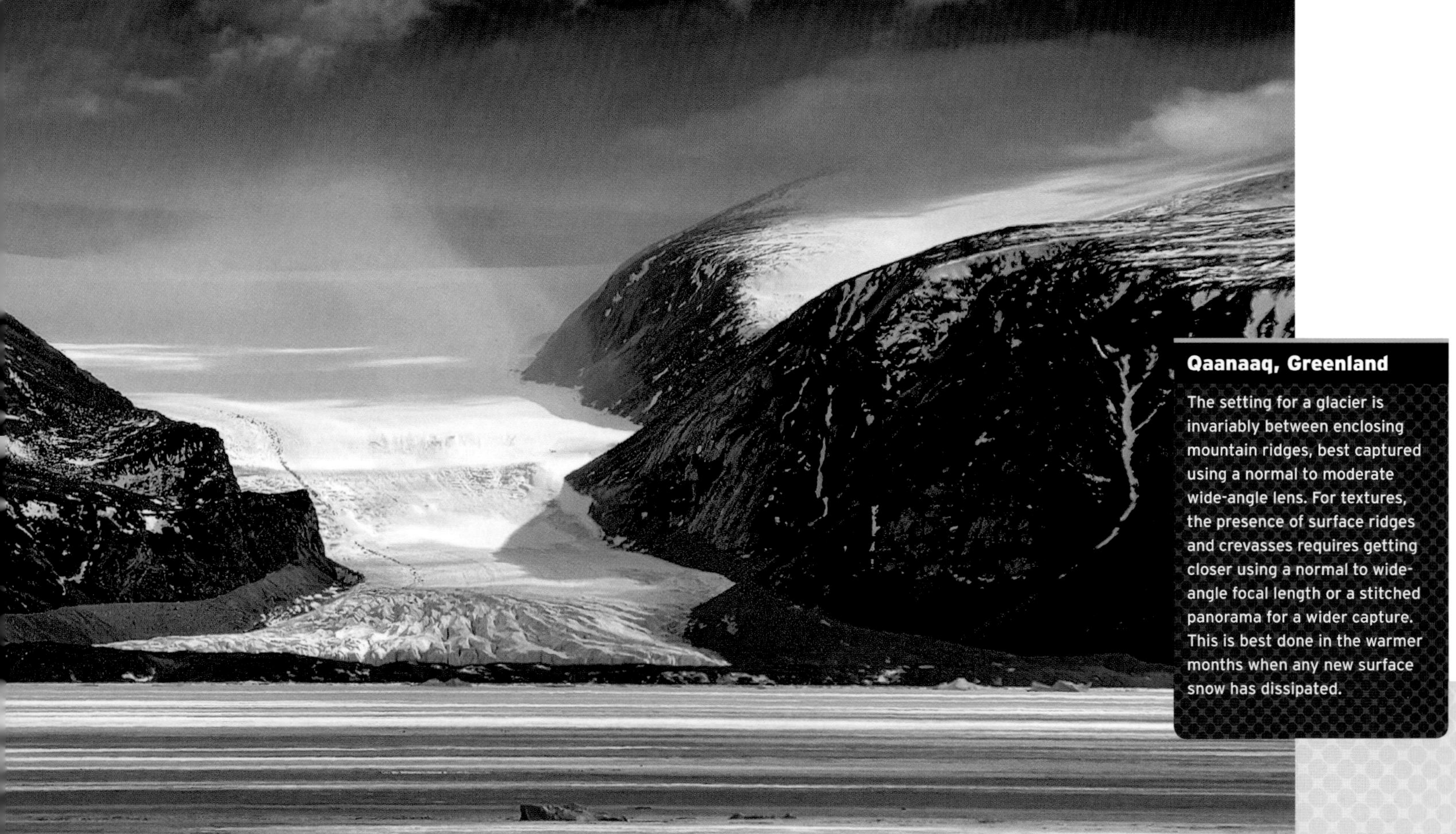

Qaanaaq, Greenland

The setting for a glacier is invariably between enclosing mountain ridges, best captured using a normal to moderate wide-angle lens. For textures, the presence of surface ridges and crevasses requires getting closer using a normal to wide-angle focal length or a stitched panorama for a wider capture. This is best done in the warmer months when any new surface snow has dissipated.

Photographically speaking, a glacier is a massive subject filling an entire valley between two mountain ranges like some great white river. On closer examination, however, a glacier typically has endless stress ridges and crevasses within its mass as well as different surface textures. But the overwhelming impression is one of great size and that fact invariably influences how it is photographed. The best perspective with which to capture the overall size and shape is from the air, typically using a moderate telephoto zoom and working to keep the plane's window frame out of the picture. It is strongly recommended to use a sufficiently

fast shutter speed of at least 1/500 second in an airliner, and 1/1000 second in a small plane or helicopter.

From the air, glaciers will appear smooth, while photographing from a closer distance on the ground gives the photographer the chance to reveal the irregular structure of ridges and crevasses. Its massive size usually requires the use of a wide-angle lens or taking a stitched panorama. If the image is going to be dominated by areas of white, then the adjustments in exposure will be necessary as explained on page 142.

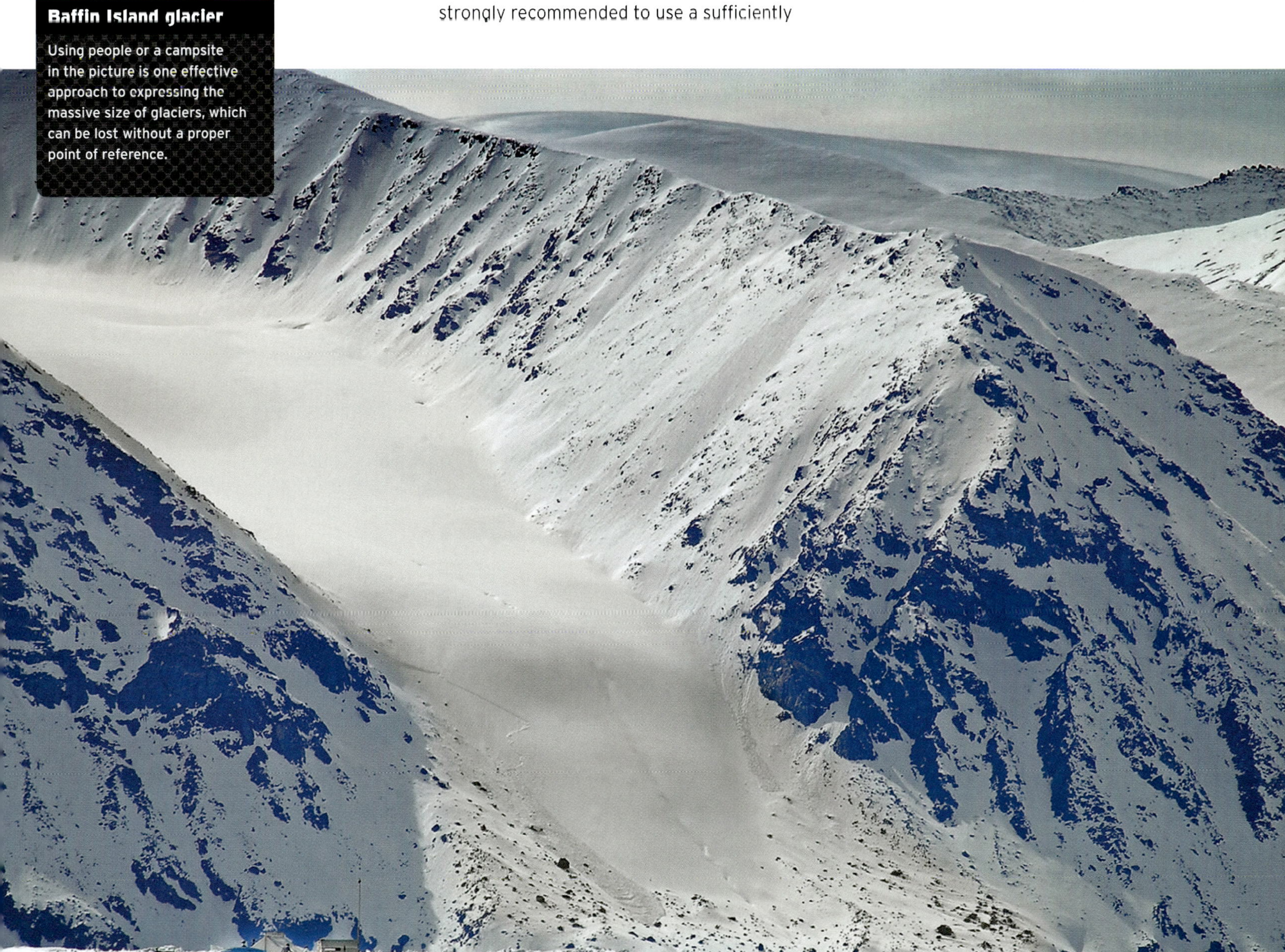

Icebergs

Icebergs born from glaciers are common in the waters near the two polar regions and can drift quite far south before melting completely. Their danger to shipping was forever established in 1912 by the sinking of the Titanic ocean liner when it struck an iceberg and sank, with the loss of more than 1,500 lives. The shape of an iceberg will vary greatly and there are actually categories established by the International Ice patrol to indicate the size of the berg as it appears above water. As much as 90% of an iceberg,

however, is below the water. This is because the fresh water that formed the iceberg in the glacier has a lower density than seawater and will sink until its mass is displaced. In addition, as the ice melts it changes the shape of the berg, often causing it to turn over in the water, and sometimes slowly rotating for hours until a new point of equilibrium is reached.

It is the endless variety of shapes that icebergs can take that make them such an interesting photographic subject. A berg can have deep cracks or concentric marbled strips throughout its surface, as well as arches and windows, to mention just a few variations. These come about because of different

conditions to which the iceberg was subjected while still in the glacier as well as the temperature and weather conditions when at sea. Icebergs can be photographed from land, as these floating masses of ice do tend to move near shorelines and often become trapped in harbors and inlets. The best perspectives, however, are obtained when one can photograph from a small boat that can take any position around the subject. In this approach, a fast shutter speed of at least 1/500 second is highly recommended.

Icebergs will tend to have different types of blue coloration that can be quite distinctive or an overall white appearance accented with ridges and sections showing a distinctive blue tint. In the case of a very warm sunset or sunrise, the white mass will also reflect some of this hue. Sidelighting is very effective at revealing the texture of an iceberg's surface. In the Antarctic regions, Adélie penguins will use icebergs as temporary rest areas while in the Arctic, a polar bear may occasionally be seen on a flatten berg that is in its final stages of melting.

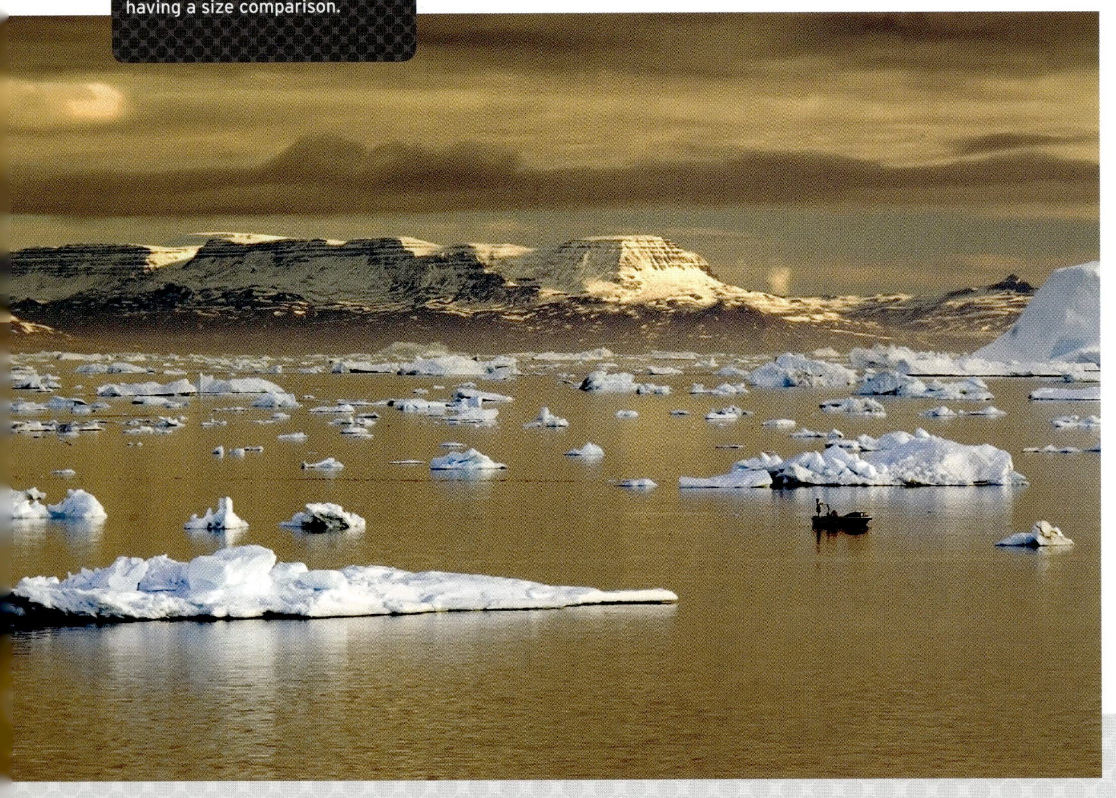

Shooting Tips:

> A guided boat tour is by far the best approach, and don't be too timid to request moving closer to certain subjects, or around them for a different angle.

> The golden hues of dawn and dusk work brilliantly with the cold blues typical of most icebergs.

> Consider abstract shapes and angles for a graphic shot.

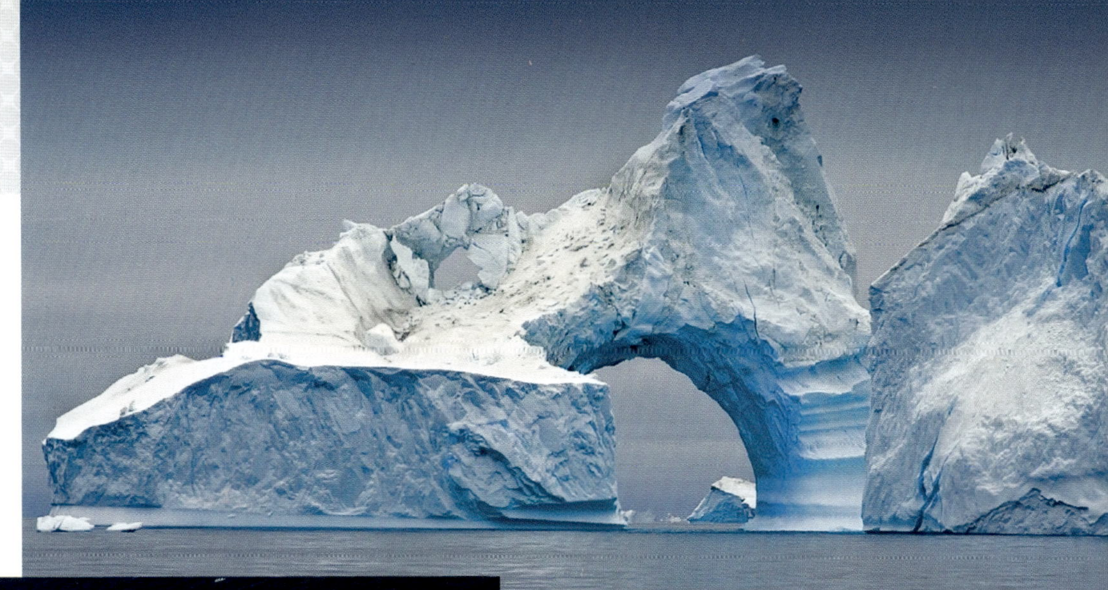

Arches in Greenland

The infinite variety of shapes invites taking a series of portraits as you circle the icebergs. This was one of several shots taken with moderate to long telephoto lenses.

Tip of the iceberg

The bulk of an iceberg is below the surface—a fact that can best be captured from a high vantage point, as in this aerial from a small plane that was shot with a moderate telephoto.

Ivittuut, Greenland

Icebergs vary greatly in size and shape, with a tendency to exhibit a blue coloration. This particular formation has a hole going clear through its center, which can be used as a frame-within-a-frame for subjects beyond.

Ice Storms

Ice storms are a beautiful, yet devastating, display of nature's power. Characterized by freezing rain, ice storms coat everything in their path with a thick layer of ice. The weight of this accumulated ice breaks tree branches, brings down power supplies, and incapacitates entire regions and cities, causing widespread disruption. For the photographer they offer great potential, including magical winter landscapes, photojournalist-style shots of the human devastation, and amazing macro shots of everyday objects encased in translucent ice.

Ice storms occur when a layer of warm air is caught between two layers of cold air. Frozen rain, in the form of hail or snow, falls from the highest layer of cold air down into the warm air. The warm air melts the frozen precipitation. Usually, the droplets continue to fall into the lowest layer of cold air, refreeze, and fall to the ground as sleet or snow. However, for reasons not fully understood, sometimes these thawed droplets fall into the lowest layer of cold air but do not refreeze, even if the temperature is under 0°C. This phenomenon is known as supercooling, whereby falling rain is at a temperature lower than freezing, but remains liquid. Some theories suggest that when the bottom layer of cold air is thin, the droplets do not have time to refreeze as they fall.

Either way, once these supercooled droplets hit any object under 0°C on the ground—such as pylons, branches, cars, roads etc.—they instantly freeze, forming a film of ice, or glaze ice, over everything they touch. The greater the precipitation, the thicker the glaze ice. This glaze can appear to drip over objects creating stunning and surreal crystal sculptures out of the most mundane subjects.

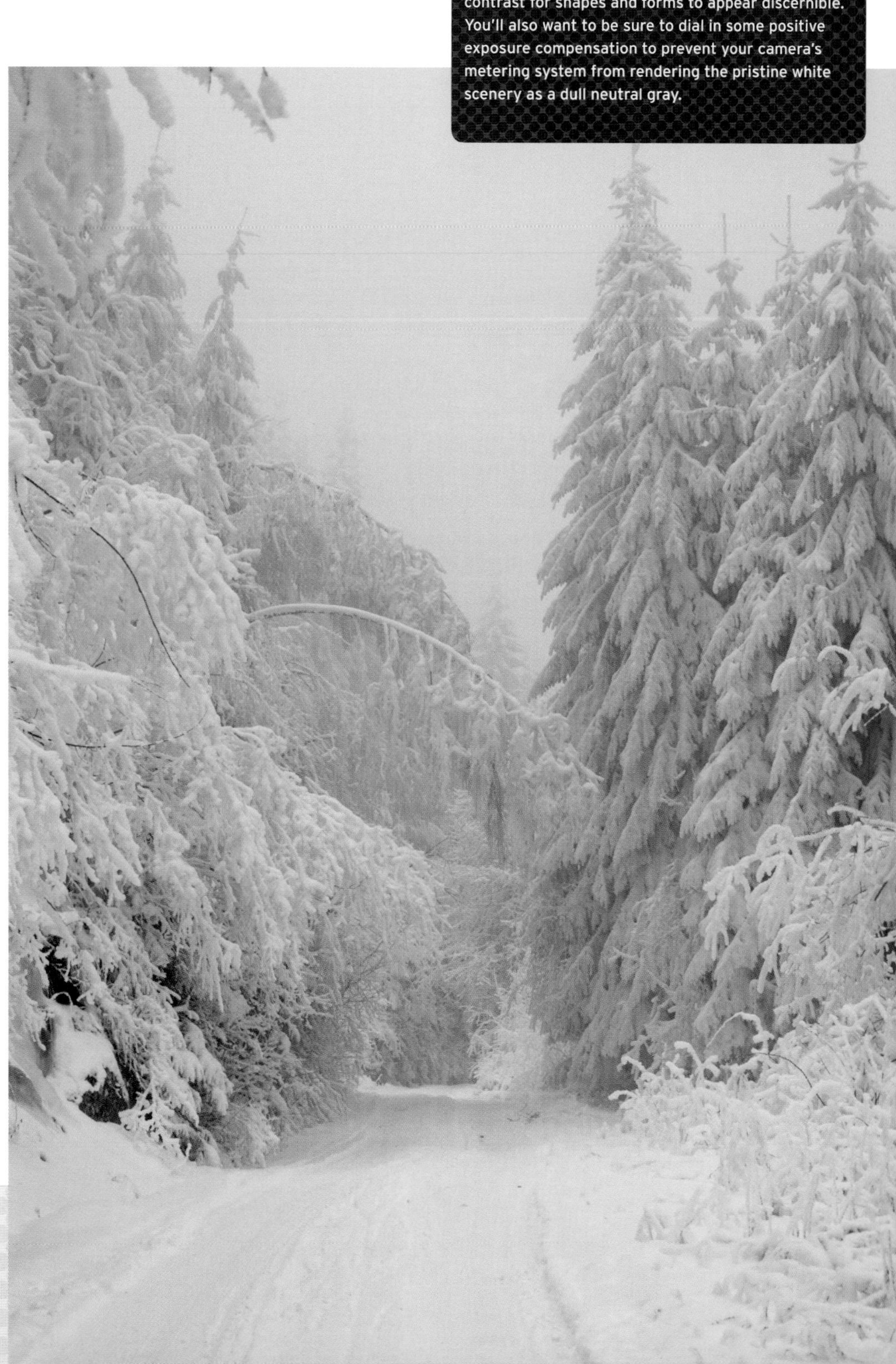

Cutting through the haze

Ice storms can make it a real challenge to get enough contrast for shapes and forms to appear discernible. You'll also want to be sure to dial in some positive exposure compensation to prevent your camera's metering system from rendering the pristine white scenery as a dull neutral gray.

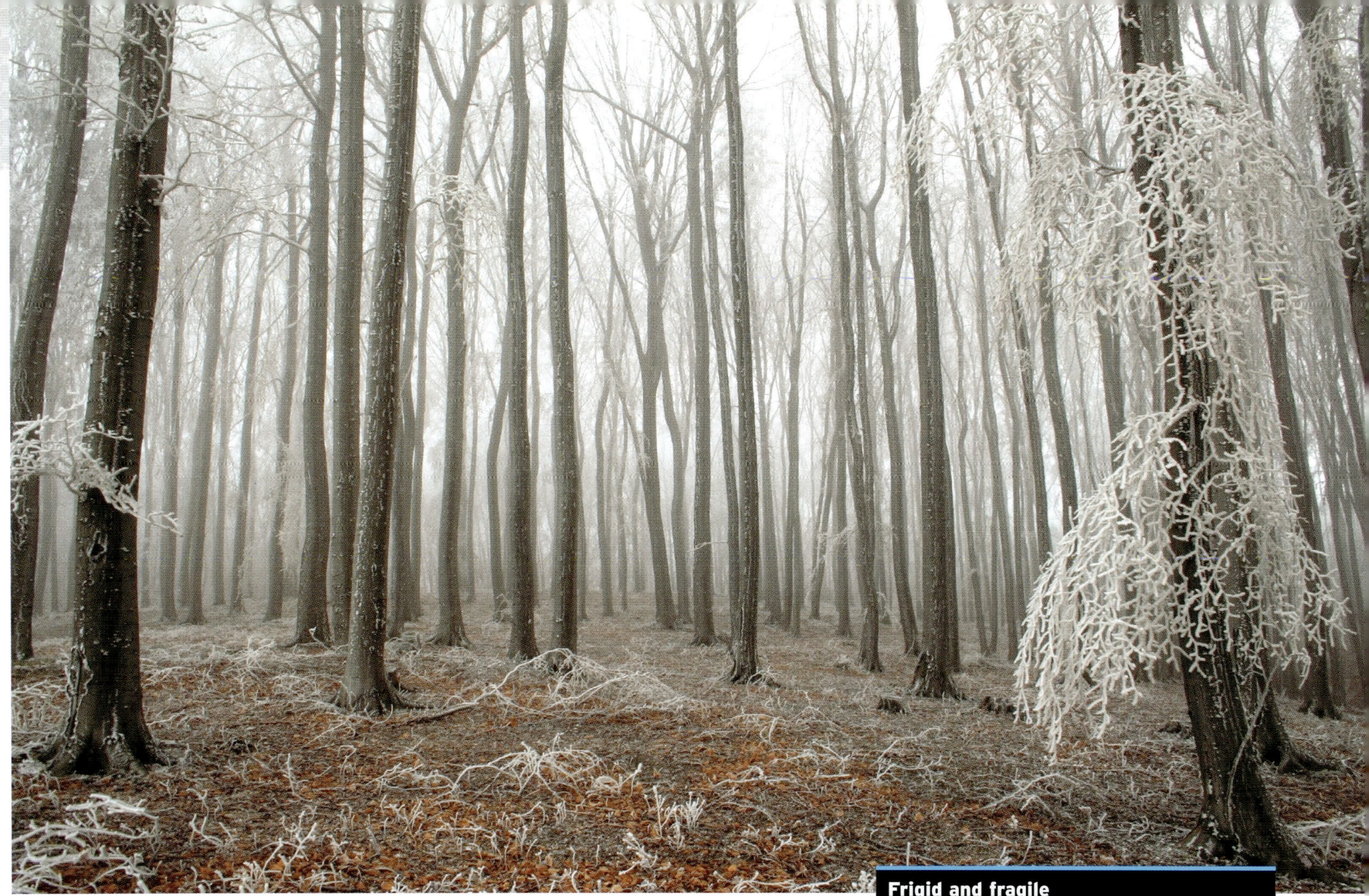

The weight of the glaze ice from a single storm—which has been known to form up to 8 inches in thickness in some of the worst—can weigh down branches, power lines, and other structures, which eventually buckle or snap, posing a real threat to human life, and causing millions of pounds worth of property damage. At first, ice storms can wreak havoc by stealth, because they appear to be harmless rain, yet instantly form treacherous black ice on any surface, which can be unseen by motorists and pedestrians alike.

Ice storms often occur inland where temperature extremes are greatest, with the US bearing many. However, in 2009-10 the north of the UK was brought to a standstill by a short-lived ice storm, and they can occur anywhere in the colder regions of our planet.

Ice storms can last several days, grounding air flights, crippling transport links, cutting power supplies and heating and closing schools, while the damage they cause to structures can last weeks or months.

An Ice Stormscape

One of the most striking aspects of the aftermath of an ice storm, however, is the stunning beauty of the transformed, glittering landscape. If the ice storm occurs overnight and the dawn is clear, the early photographer will be faced with a pristine landscape of frozen shapes and ice formations glistening like crystals in the glowing sunrise.

In this lucky scenario, the photographer must make the most of this rare treat before the

scene is spoiled by human activity, working quickly to shoot a variety of compositions. Wide vistas incorporating frozen trees, lakes, and towns, simple, graphical compositions using frozen fences or a line of telegraph poles and wires that shine like necklaces, and macro shots of as many details as possible. A budding branch or flower encased in ice, stalactites of ice crystals frozen mid-drip—the opportunities are almost endless. Just remember to press the shutter rather than stand in awe!

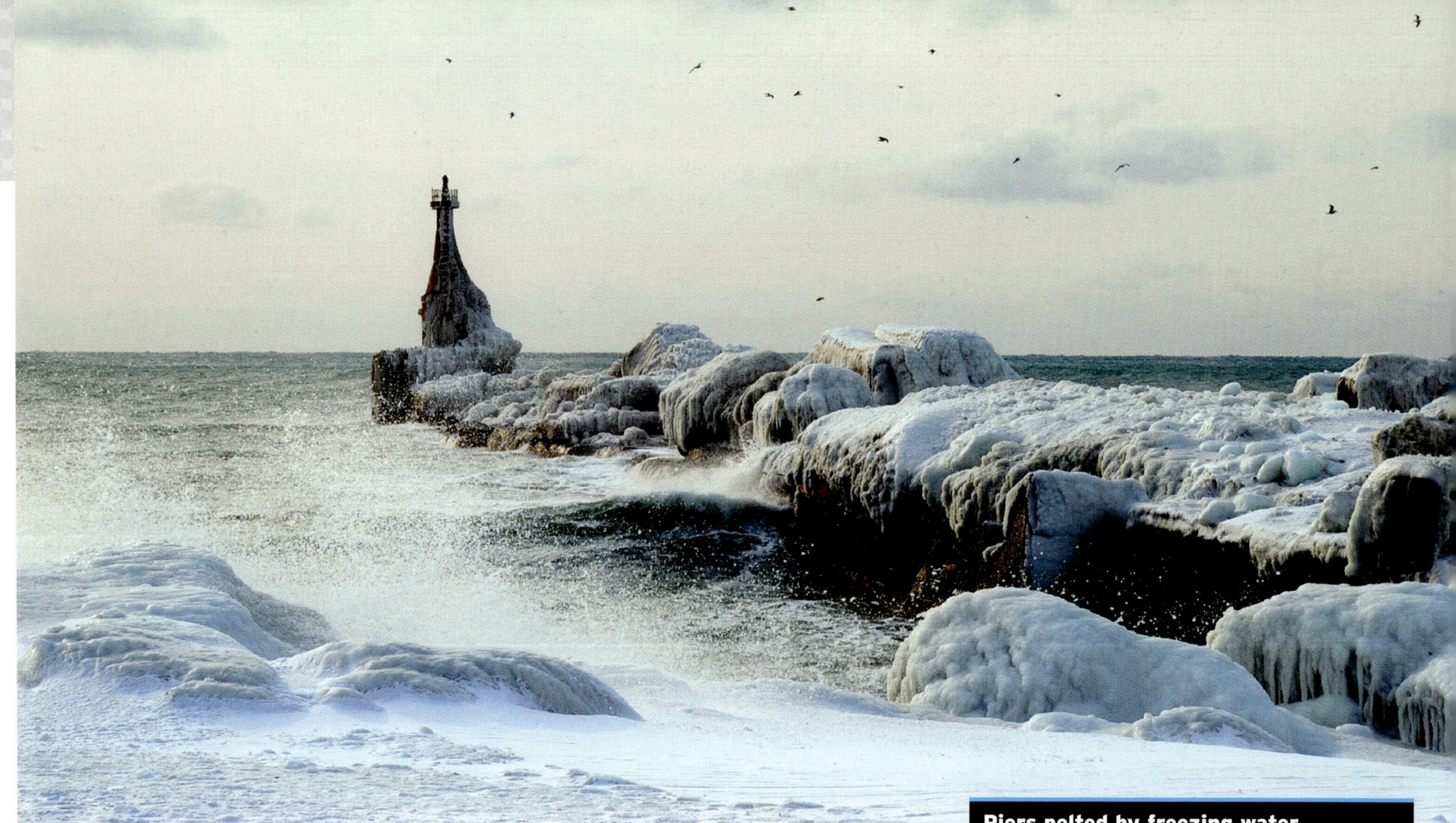

Nature versus Man

While wide landscapes will provide beautiful imagery, they will not tell the real story of an ice storm, and how it differs from, for example, a snowstorm. Details of frozen nature and man-made objects will differentiate it as an ice storm. At the same time, unlike other landscape or outdoor subjects, ice storm photography can be enhanced by the presence of human activity. So even when the rest of the world wakes up, there are still myriad photographic opportunities, particularly one that lend themselves to a photojournalistic take.

Try to catalog a range of images that convey the damage and destruction caused by the ice storm—fallen telegraph poles, tree branches fallen on roads and cars, structures that have buckled under the weight or temperature of the conditions, frozen everyday objects made surreal by their tomb of ice, or people pushing stuck vehicles. On a brighter note, record the more fun-filled side of the ice storm, such as children making the most of a day off school sledging along roads or in parks. In the UK ice storm in 2009, locals were reported to be going about their business on all fours—it was the only safe way to move around!

There is no single exposure that can be recommended for ice storms, as the sheer variety of shots will likely draw on all the experience and knowledge of the discerning photographer. Think about the requirements for each type of shot: a landscape is likely to require greater depth of field and so higher aperture numbers are more necessary, while

shutter speed may be less important in scenes without any movement—use a tripod, where possible, to avoid camera shake. Close-up and macro shots, meanwhile, will result in a thinner depth of field due to the close working distances—however, wide apertures (low numbers) at short distances can be desirable, throwing all but the main point of interest into a blurred abstract background of shapes and colors. The technical term for this out-of-focus effect is *bokeh*.

For shots containing people, shutter speed will be the most important setting in order to avoid motion blur and a stack of unusable images. A tripod is likely to be impractical for such shots, with the photographer needing to respond quickly to the activities unfolding. Lower aperture numbers, and therefore faster lenses, will be the order of the day for people and activity shots, while trying to keep ISO to reasonably low settings, say below ISO 800—although some of the newer, high-end DSLRs can produce perfectly acceptable results, in terms of image noise, up to ISO 1600. With the break of daylight, however, such high ISO levels are unlikely to be needed.

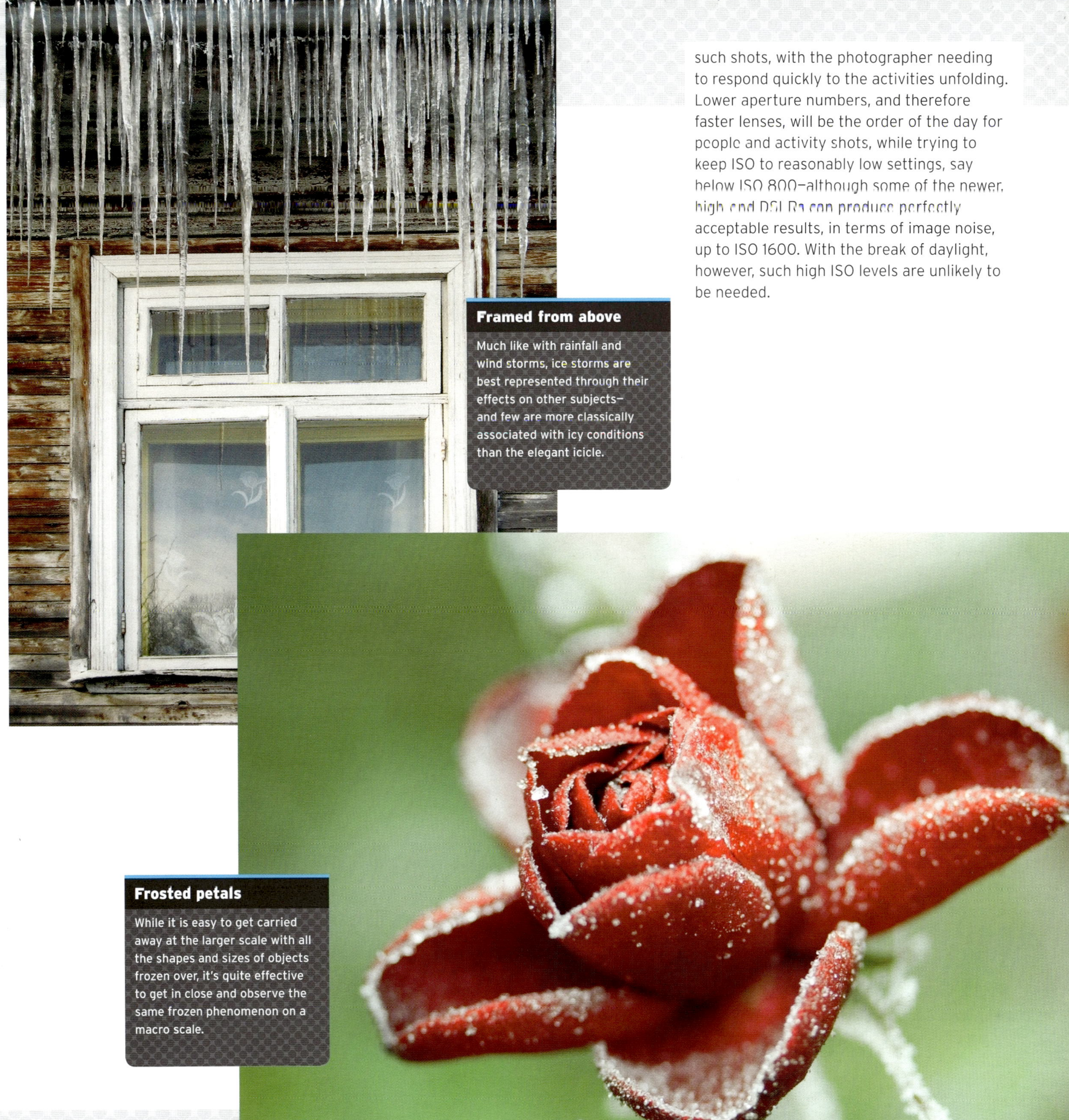

Framed from above

Much like with rainfall and wind storms, ice storms are best represented through their effects on other subjects— and few are more classically associated with icy conditions than the elegant icicle.

Frosted petals

While it is easy to get carried away at the larger scale with all the shapes and sizes of objects frozen over, it's quite effective to get in close and observe the same frozen phenomenon on a macro scale.

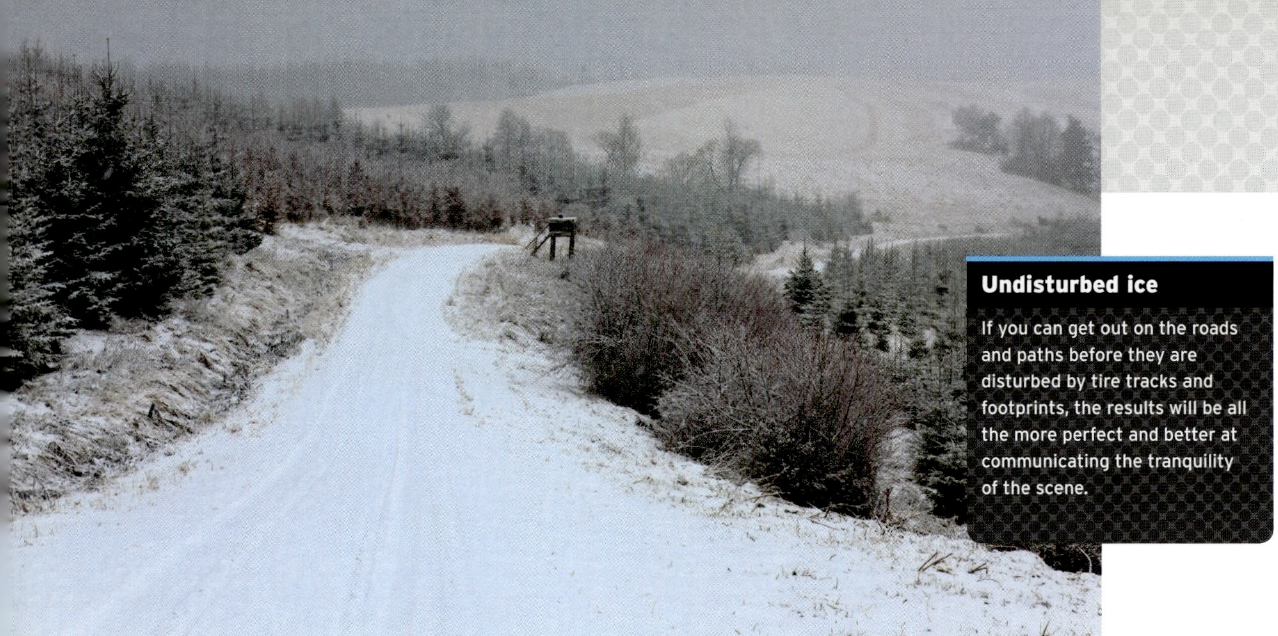

Exposing for Ice Storms

One important consideration, however, is metering. The bright, white and reflective nature of ice is likely to throw the camera's metering sensor running for the hills. Like snow, it may be that the photographer will have to dial in a stop or two of overexposure compensation in order to prevent the scenes in front of the camera appearing gray. Always check the histogram to avoid blowing out highlight details—however, in some cases, specular highlights (very bright points of blown-out detail, often caused by reflections) may be unavoidable, and as long as they are limited to tiny areas of reflected light are acceptable. Shooting in Raw mode will allow much more flexibility to pull and push exposure in post-processing (although even that will not recover lost highlights or shadow detail if they are extreme).

The use of a gray card can help for setting exposure (remember to dial in exposure compensation for the snow and ice), however, this may be impractical. Seek out neutral tones, where possible—such as the side of a gray or pale building, or blue sky away from the sun—and work from there, checking the histogram regularly. Another option, if the light levels are stable, is to meter once from a neutral tone (or gray card), dial in appropriate exposure compensation and shoot away until light levels drop or the photographer moves

to a different location. The ice and snow covering surfaces will provide a reasonable amount of reflected fill light, so the photographer may find that exposure settings remain stable in an open scene (i.e. no major areas of shadow).

Given such a wide range of potential shots it is important to ensure that lenses carried will cover an adequate focal length range. Wide-angle zooms will take in wider vistas and landscapes—and they can often double up as close-work lenses as many offer a short minimum focus distance. A telephoto zoom will also provide a range of focal lengths in a smaller package than numerous fixed length lenses. A macro lens will provide more impact for detail shots, providing 1:1 or greater magnification, but weigh up the pros and cons of carrying an extra lens and the time taken for changing lens, bearing in mind that temperatures are likely to be very low. Be aware that changing lenses will not only waste time, particularly during action shots, but that the photographer's fingers may be quite uncooperative and slow to respond in such extreme conditions!

With that in mind, ensure warm, waterproof clothing, utilizing numerous layers on every part of the body, particularly feet and head. Dedicated shoes, or boots with a strong grip are also essential for photographer safety—

black ice can be treacherous to both human bones and accompanying camera equipment. A pair of gloves that allows the photographer to maintain fine finger control for manipulating camera controls is also vital. One tip is to use a thin pair of fingerless gloves underneath a second pair of tougher, warmer gloves. If necessary, the photographer can quickly remove the top gloves in order to set camera controls with nimble fingers, and then re-glove until further camera changes are necessary.

In terms of equipment, cold temperatures will drain battery life, so carry enough fully charged batteries—always carry enough memory card storage (or a laptop or portable hard drive/card reader for transferring images) as there is nothing worse than running out of memory space in full creative flow. At the end of the day, or shoot, be careful to avoid condensation forming in the camera, as it is moved from very cold outdoor temperatures to warm indoor environs. Condensation can cause expensive damage to cameras, so to avoid this problem place the camera (and lenses) in sealed plastic bags as soon as they are taken into a warm area. This will act to buffer the extremes of temperature difference, warming the camera slowly, and such avoid the formation of condensation.

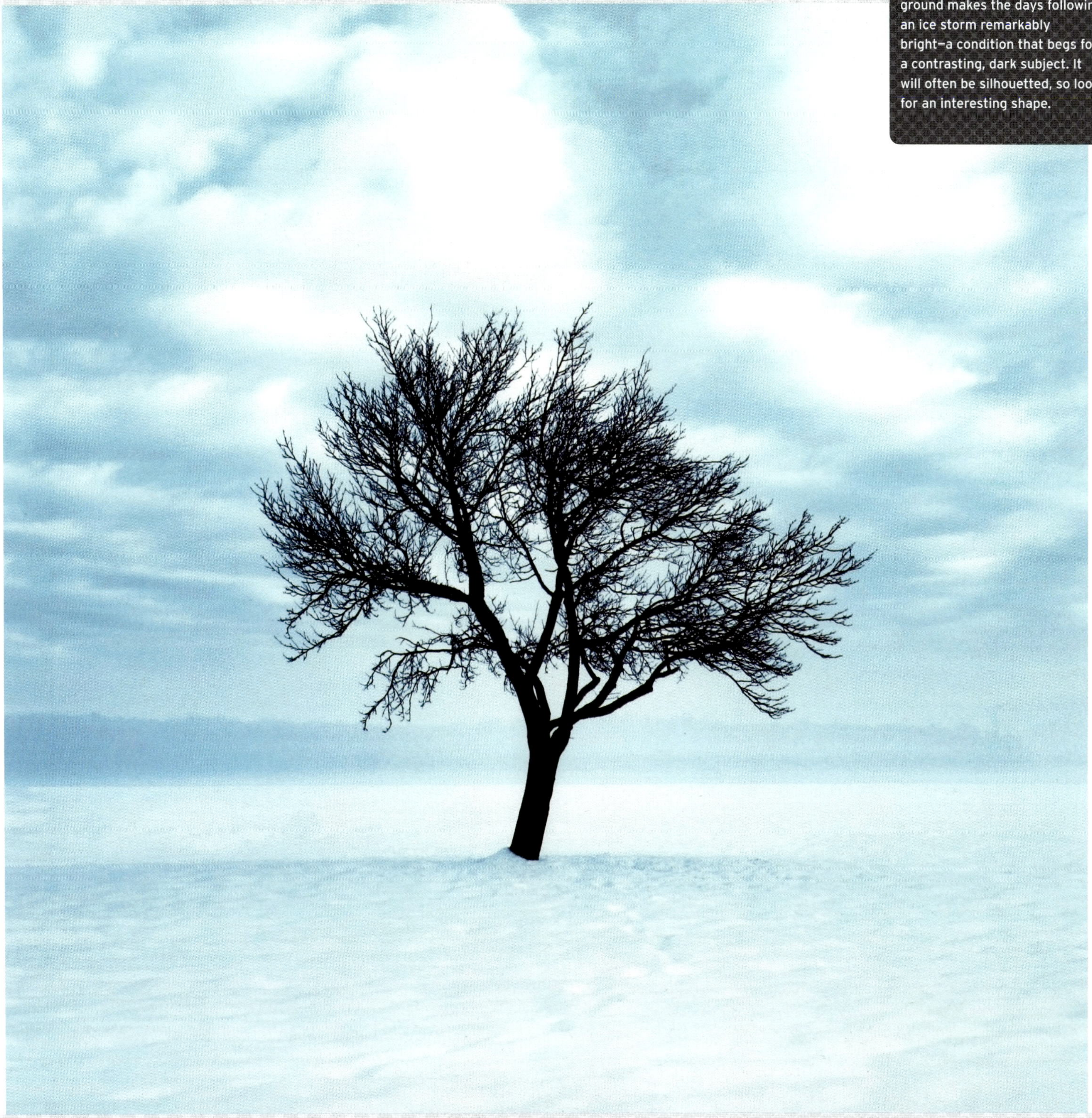

Centered silhouette

Being so reflective, ice along the
ground makes the days following
an ice storm remarkably
bright—a condition that begs for
a contrasting, dark subject. It
will often be silhouetted, so look
for an interesting shape.

Geysers

Tall erupting fountains of boiling water and hissing steam, set against a backdrop of bubbling, primordial pools and alien rock formations. Welcome to the world of geyser photography. When captured imaginatively, geysers can create images that transport the viewer into a different world, while the mineral-tinged pools and craters that surround them provide a glimpse into how the earth might have looked as it cooked up the recipe for organic life.

A geyser is a hot spring that intermittently erupts, sending water high into the air, followed by a vapor phase, in which a spout

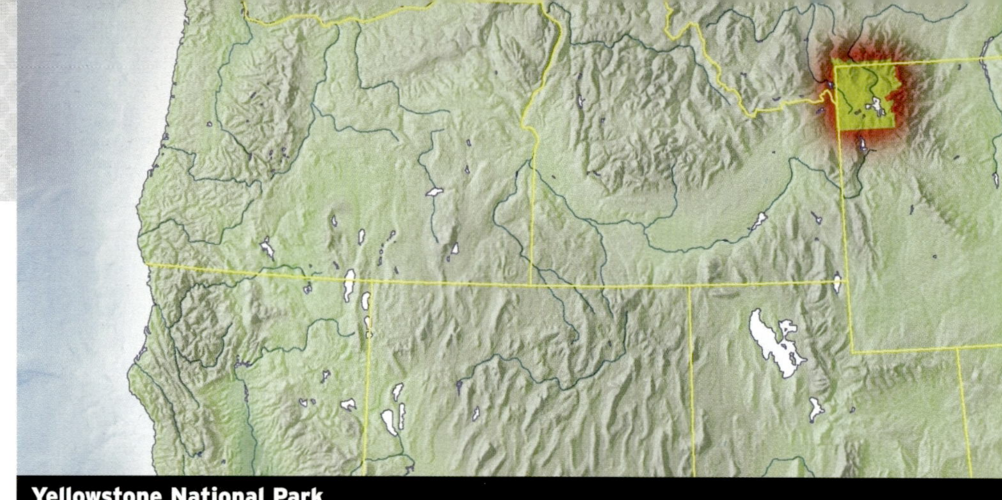

of steam is emitted. The word is derived from Geysir, one of the first historically recorded geysers in Haukadalur, Iceland. The word Geysir in turn comes from an Old Norse verb "geysa," meaning "to gush."

Geysers are relatively rare in the world as they require a specific set of hydrogeological conditions to exist. They erupt when water is heated rapidly by an underground heat source—usually magma which heats up the surrounding rock about 1.2 miles (2km) below

the ground. Geysers also require a water source, a fissure, crack, or hole in the earth's surface and a subterranean system of chambers and reservoirs in which the water can collect, heat and travel to the surface. As a result, they are usually located near volcanic regions.

What causes geyser eruptions? Over time, water in the ground drains into these chambers and reservoirs and eventually comes into contact with the heated rocks, whereby it is rapidly boiled. The resulting pressurization forces a superheated column of water and steam through the underground plumbing system and out of the geyser's surface vent or crater. Water and steam is forced violently into the air to heights of up to 165 feet (50m). Once the water and steam has been emitted, the cycle begins again. This process often occurs on a predictable basis, so the activity of some geysers can be forecast with reasonable accuracy.

There are around 1,000 active geysers around the world, 500 of which are found in Yellowstone National Park, Wyoming, United States. Old Faithful is perhaps the most famous, with eruptions occurring every 91 minutes or so. Geysers are either cone geysers, whereby the water erupts from a cone or mound of hardened siliceous rock in steady jets for up to several minutes at a time, or fountain geysers, which erupt from pools of water, often in intense bursts.

Old Faithful

During most days, Old Faithful is completely surrounded by tourists. While this can be frustrating, it's important to realize that such crowds can give a valuable sense of scale to the tall eruptions.

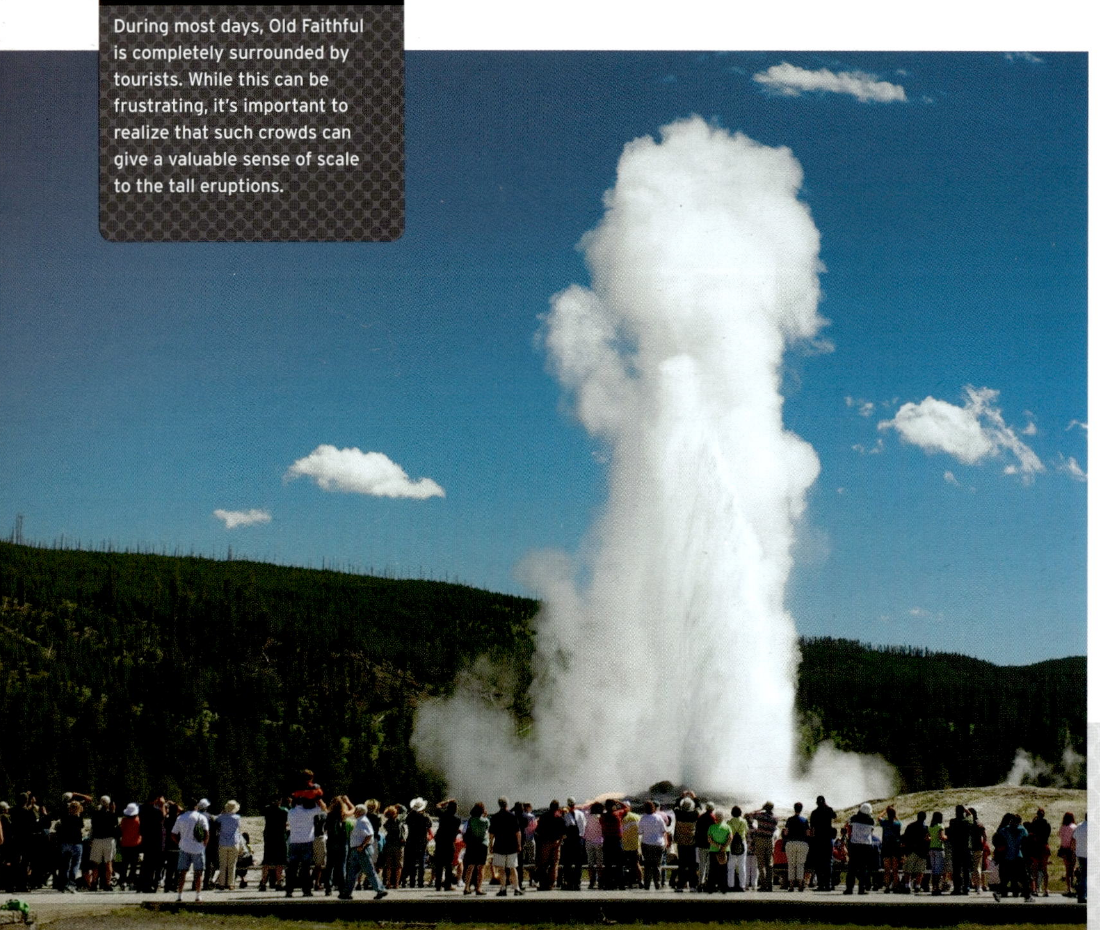

As well as Yellowstone, important locations include: Dolina Geiserov ("The Valley of Geysers") in Russia; El Tatio, high in the Chilean Andes: Taupo Volcanic Zone, on New Zealand's North Island; and, Haukadalur in Iceland.

Photographic Concerns

For the photographer, geyser fields offer a variety of compositions and shots: an erupting geyser set within a traditional landscape environment; close-up shots of the erupting column of steam and water; and shots of non-geyser features, such as steaming pools, hissing fumaroles, bubbling mudpools and warm seeps, which can often provide the chance to create abstract images of the highly colored patterns and shapes created by rich mineral deposits.

The shot that first hits the eye, of course, is that of an erupting geyser in a wide angle view incorporating the landscape environment as the backdrop. Many tourists and visitors are likely to have shots of erupting geysers, but there are numerous ways to make shots stand out.

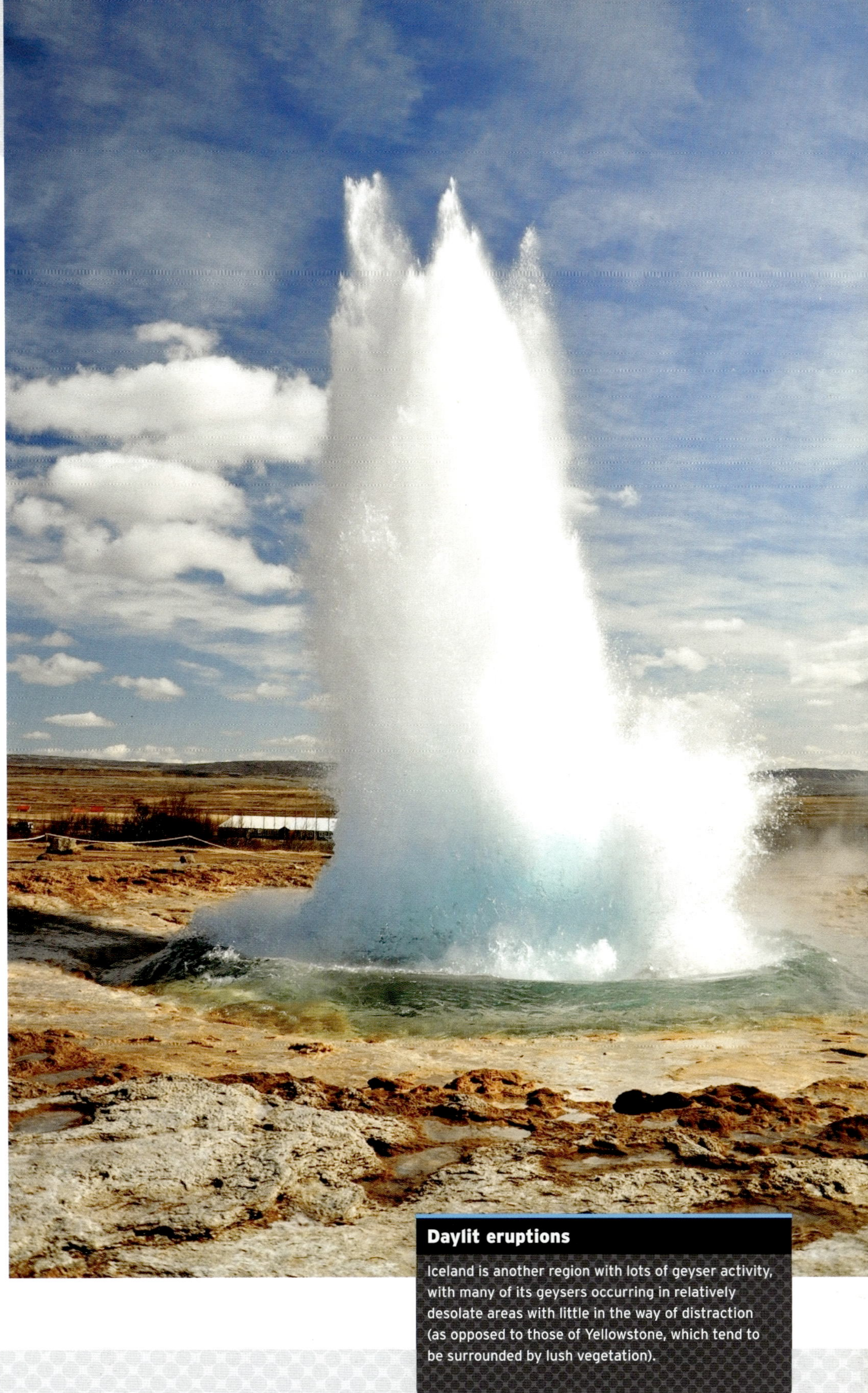

Daylit eruptions

Iceland is another region with lots of geyser activity, with many of its geysers occurring in relatively desolate areas with little in the way of distraction (as opposed to those of Yellowstone, which tend to be surrounded by lush vegetation).

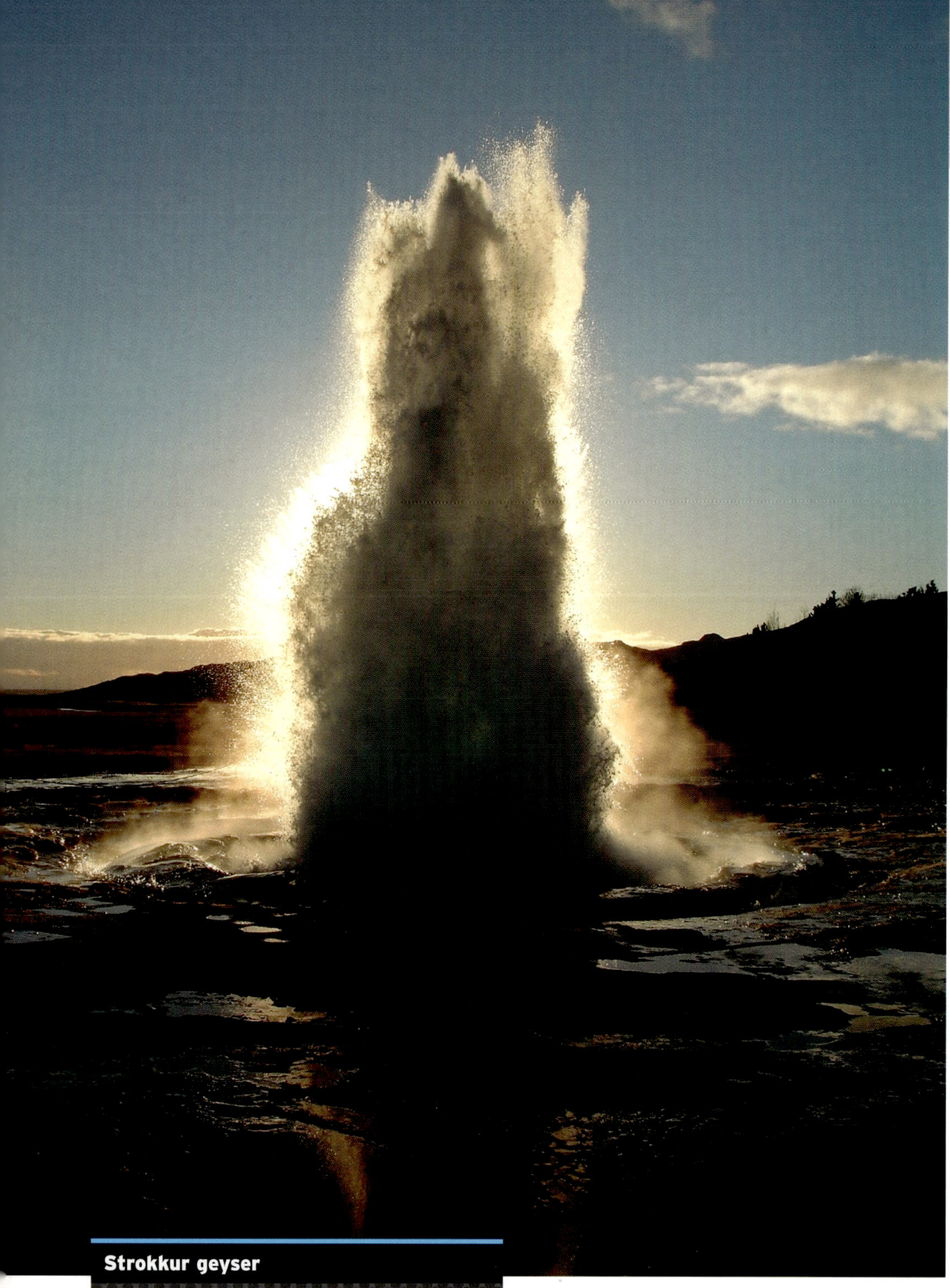

Strokkur geyser

Another Icelandic geyser, this famous formation erupts every 4-8 minutes, giving you plenty of chances for a winning shot. This particular image makes use of the sun as a rim-light to see the fine detail of droplets along the edge of the eruption.

First, do the research. If the geyser is frequent and predictable, it makes sense that the photographer ensures that its activity not only coincides with their visit, but also whether it will occur at the right time of day for the best lighting. The hours just after sunrise and before sunset—the so-called golden hours—are likely to provide the best quality of light. Not only to show off the geyser in the best light, but also help the photographer to compose, so that the fountain of water stands out from the background. Sidelighting and backlighting will have this effect, either modeling or rim-lighting the column of water so that its outline does not merge into the background, making it pop out from the backdrop and revealing highlight and shadow detail. For this type of lighting, only the golden hours will do.

Another important, and obvious, consideration is the direction of the wind at the location. If unlucky, the wind can blow boiling water over the photographer and equipment. Always position yourself and the camera upwind of the erupting geyser.

At the same time, dawn and dusk creates the appealing colors and glowing light associated with these times of the day, in turn adding drama and atmosphere to images. At midday on a clear day, the light will be flat or too contrasty resulting in dull or cluttered images. An added benefit is that in the morning, in particular, the air temperature is also likely to be cooler, which will create more steam and therefore more drama for the images. Low sunlight also offers the potential for rainbows created by reflections from the water droplets and steam—walk around a geyser to spot rainbows at specific angles to the sun.

Shooting geysers before sunrise and after sunset will require long exposure times, but the results can be exceptional. Arguably, the best lighting at this time of the day is front lighting, as the low glow from beyond the horizon should be enough to catch the white in the foaming water—again, the effect is to make the geyser subtly stand out from the background, even glow. Longer exposures will also add motion blur to the spouting water funnel, adding a dreamy or surreal feel to the shot. Coupled to a wide composition, and a low perspective that sets the geyser against a cool blue sky, this can add a real wow factor to the image.

An overcast sky will also kill any light modeling of the water fountain, as it creates flat and even lighting. If possible, try to coincide the following three factors for the best results: geyser activity; golden-hour lighting; and clear or partly cloudy weather conditions.

Don't forget to use the telephoto lens to add a real variety of images and help to capture the geyser in its many moods. Likewise, a macro lens can pick out details in the richly colored primordial pools surrounding a geyser field. The rich soup of minerals present create abstract patterns, reminiscent of cave paintings. Set the deep reds and browns of mineral deposits against the aquamarine blues of the water pools. Again, a circular polarizing filter will help to enhance the colors. Arguably, such photography is better served by overcast weather conditions—in this case, the flat, even lighting keeps colors saturated. Be wary of getting too close to the boiling, bubbling pools and, of course, always check beforehand that a geyser field is safe to visit, as toxic gases can sometimes be released.

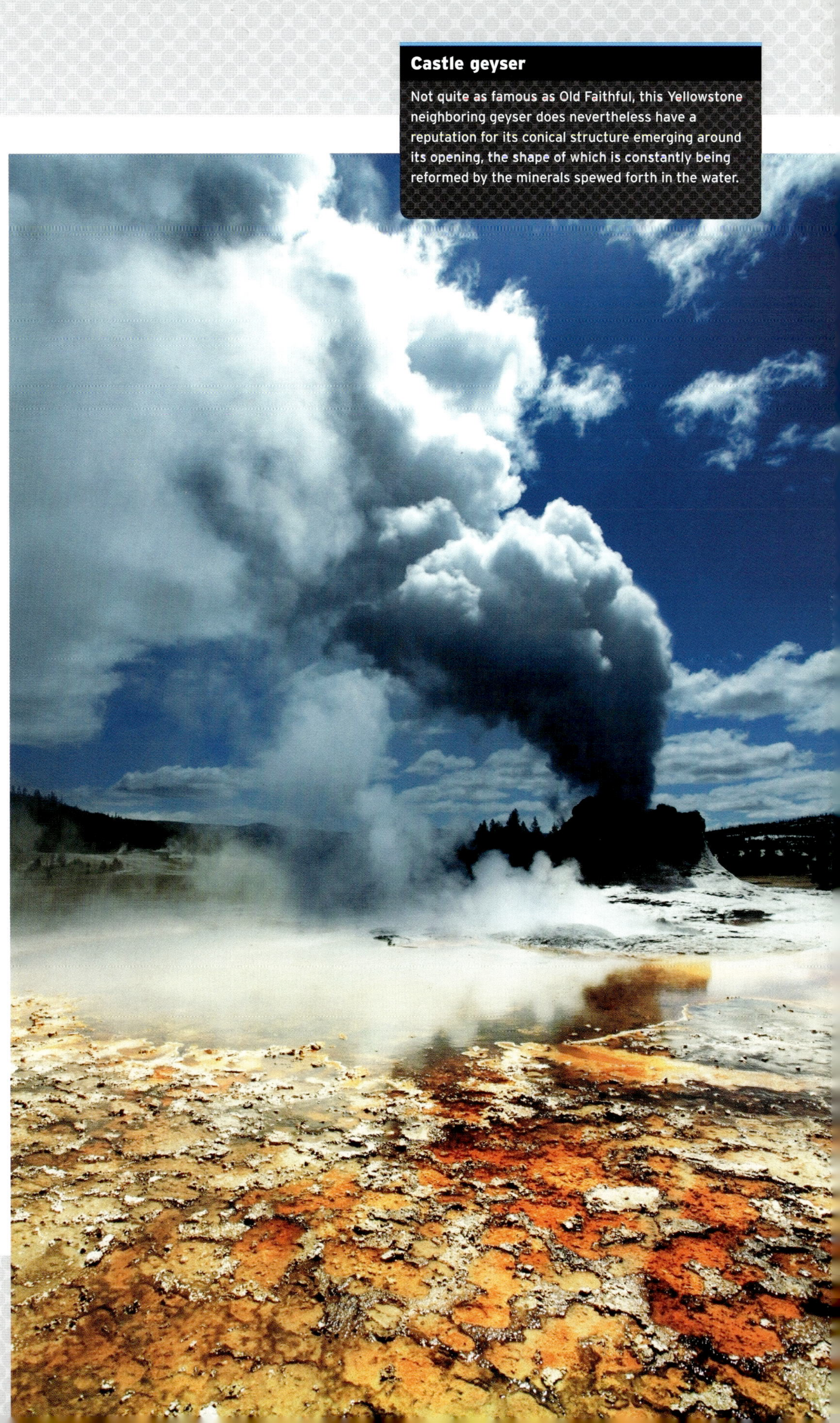

Castle geyser

Not quite as famous as Old Faithful, this Yellowstone neighboring geyser does nevertheless have a reputation for its conical structure emerging around its opening, the shape of which is constantly being reformed by the minerals spewed forth in the water.

From a photographic point of view, geysers can be captured as a single subject concentrating on the plume of shooting water or within an environment that can add its own unique features. This is particularly true of a geyser field that will often have a build up of colored mineral deposits on the ground. Like waves and waterfalls, the erupting water plumes also add the factor of motion that the photographer can work with in the composition.

Much of what was covered in the wave section (pages 130-135) concerning the effects of different types of natural light applies to photographing a geyser. Midday sun will give the most complete and even coverage especially if the objective is to document the whole geyser, including details within the spouting. That is, the layers of water within the plume caused by the pulsing action. On the other hand, dawn and dusk compositions combine the bright reflections of the water in the air and on the ground with darker shadow areas around the base.

The question of how to handle the motion of the plume tends to favor using a fast shutter speed of 1/500 second to 1/1000 second. This will freeze the patterns and layers within the spouting plume as well as sharply rendering the droplets in the spray. Slow shutter speeds will blur the spouting and thus prevent capturing these subtle details. It is also important to remember what goes up, will come down, so being too close to an erupting geyser can get equipment wet from spray that may also be blown around by the wind. Otherwise, there are no special precautions that have to be taken to protect equipment.

The choice of focal lengths will certainly have a significant impact on how a geyser or geyser field is rendered. Setting a camera low and in the portrait and especially the landscape orientation with a wide-angle lens will put more emphasis on the pools of water and mineral deposits and less on the shooting

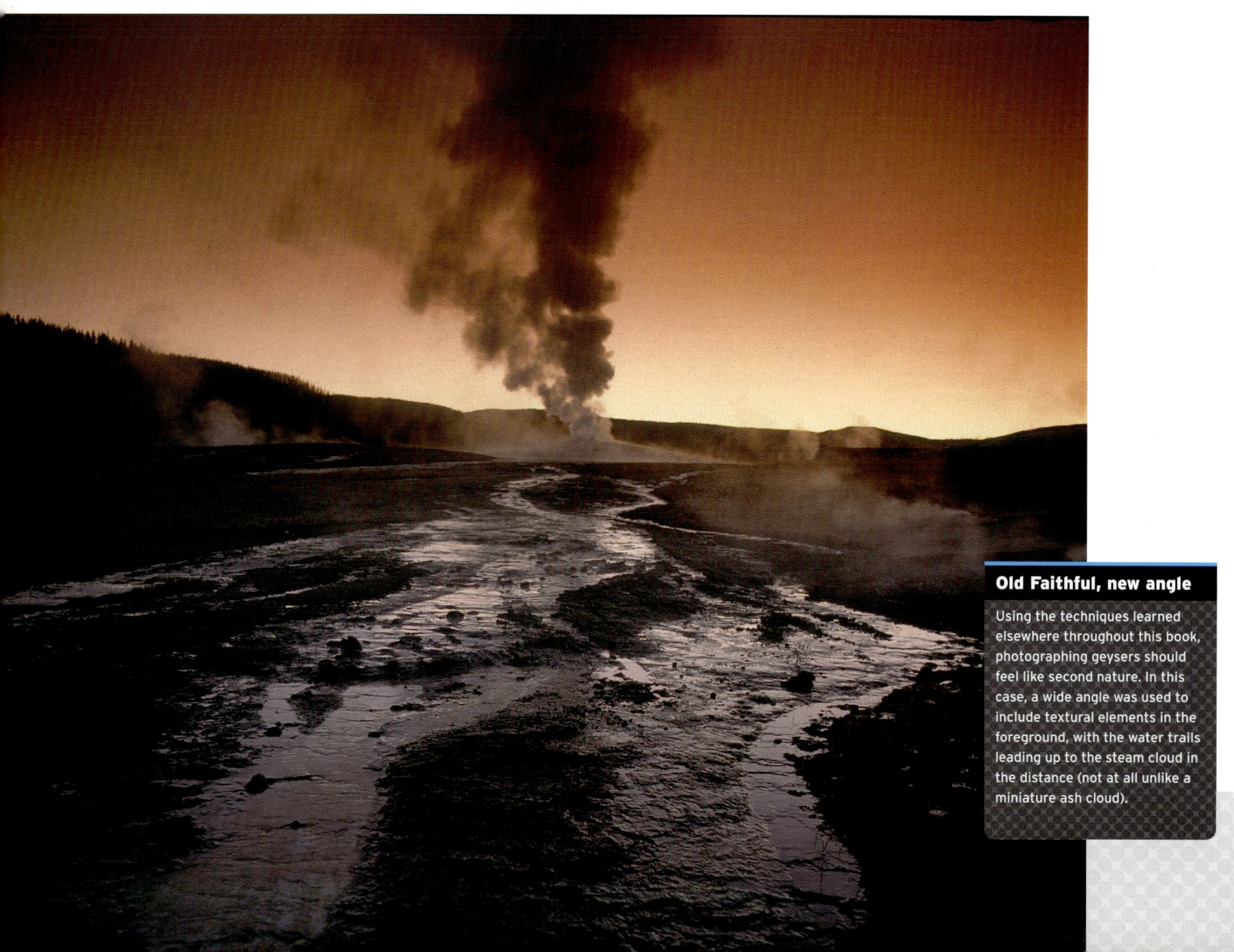

Old Faithful, new angle

Using the techniques learned elsewhere throughout this book, photographing geysers should feel like second nature. In this case, a wide angle was used to include textural elements in the foreground, with the water trails leading up to the steam cloud in the distance (not at all unlike a miniature ash cloud).

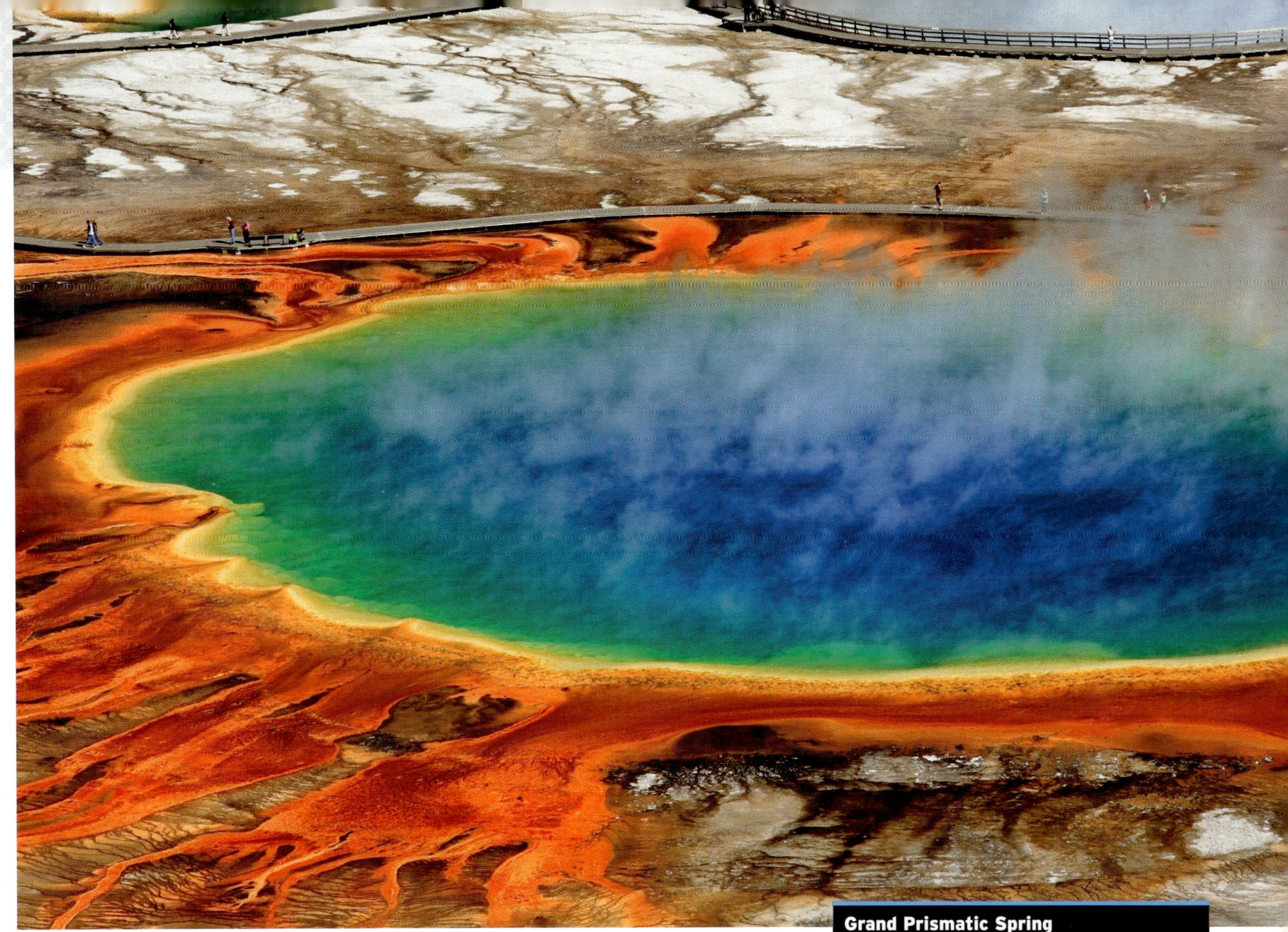

water. If the aim is to concentrate on the water patterns within an erupting geyser, then a moderate telephoto is a good choice while a normal focal length will give a more natural rendering of the whole setting. Many locations will have restrictions as to how close one can get to a geyser. Under these conditions, a longer lens will have to be used but this can bring backgrounds up into greater prominence via telephoto compression. Thus, one needs to pay attention to areas beyond the geyser and their possible impact.

Tip: Polarizers for Depth and Modeling

Polarizers reduce glare and reflections, and saturate colors. When used at 90 degrees to the angle of the sun, they will also render blue sky much darker than normal. If the photographer is shooting from a low vantage point, composing the column of white water against a polarized patch of blue sky will again make it stand out from the background, in turn creating a perception of depth to the image.

Grand Prismatic Spring

While this stunning geologic oddity is a hot spring (the third largest in the world) rather than a geyser, the two phenomena are closely related—with this particular spring occurring in the active Midway Geyser Basin of Yellowstone National Park. The vivid, saturated colors are the result of microbial bacteria growing in the mineral-rich water.

Capes

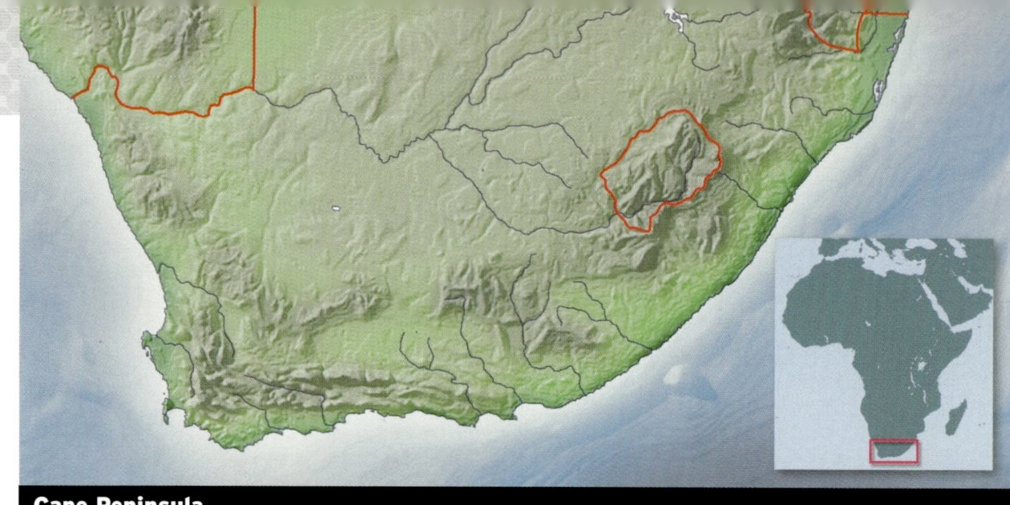

The mention of capes brings to mind the great Clipper Route of the nineteenth century, representing the fastest trade route for sailing ships between Europe and the Far East. The Cape of Horn, at the tip of South America, and the Cape of Good Hope at the extremes of South Africa, were notoriously dangerous sections of the route that claimed many ships and lives.

However, a cape is not always so grand and turbulent. A cape is any piece of land that is bounded on three sides by water—whether sea, ocean, river, or estuary—and extends out into a tip. The geological structure only differs from a peninsula by the fact that a peninsula is connected to the mainland via a very thin slip of land, whereas a cape is connected by land that shows no significant thinning along its length. Capes, then, can vary significantly in their scale and geology.

For the photographer, capes bring together some of the best elements of landscape work: interesting rock formations such as cliffs and pinnacles, sea and ocean, clear vistas, the opportunity for wide-angle and telephoto work, and often stunning and dramatic coastal locations. The Rumps in Cornwall, Cape Wrath in Scotland, Cape Tribulation in Australia, and

Cape Cod in the United States—just a few of the world's best-known capes.

Capes are often untouched and wild locations, hence their beauty, which is likely to mean long treks to reach appealing and quiet locations. With this in mind, the photographer needs to prepare, including appropriate clothing and footwear, weather protection for equipment and photographer, ample refreshment, and enough battery and memory as locations are often remote. Likewise, a torch can be a life-saver (sometimes literally!) as trekking to and from locations before sunrise and after sunset can be dangerous in the dark, given the exposed nature of capes.

Where a cape is prominent and coastal in nature, and the approach is elevated or provides vantage points—such as The Rumps in Cornwall—make the most of this opportunity to capture the entire cape using a wide-angle lens. Low side-lighting such as that occurring during the golden hours will provide very appealing light modeling of the contours and shape of a cape in this case. Set the DSLR on a tripod and compose a view looking along the length of the cape—that is, positioned at the base of the cape, or even on the mainland itself, looking across the cape out to sea.

Include interesting foreground subjects—such as rock formations and colorful flora, which will add depth to the image—and frame the

cape in a balanced composition that reveals its distinctive shape and form. Composing on the rule of thirds is a good starting point (of course, break the rules if the circumstances or creative intent dictates).

Choosing the right time of year to visit a cape can also make a significant difference to the final image. For example, The Rumps in Cornwall points in a north-west direction, which means that in early spring and late summer the sun will set at 90 degrees to the cape. This provides the required side-lighting that will produce soft and glowing sunlight, while highlighting the contours of the cape and any foreground subject matter. Conversely, in June the sun will set somewhere near the tip of the cape—while this can create dramatic images, it will also add challenges such as lens flare and high contrast exposures.

Another reason for choosing time of year wisely is that capes will often harbor abundant wild flowers at different times of the year. On the north coast of Cornwall, for example, in spring wild flowers blanket the cliff tops with glorious color, providing vivid foreground interest. Of course, every cape and location will be different so, as always, prior research and planning will yield the best results and help avoid potential disappointment on arrival.

A peninsula of capes

As the name might indicate, the Cape Peninsula is composed of many distinct capes, among the most famous being Cape Point and Cape of Good Hope. Boat trips around the peninsula offer no shortage of fantastic shots.

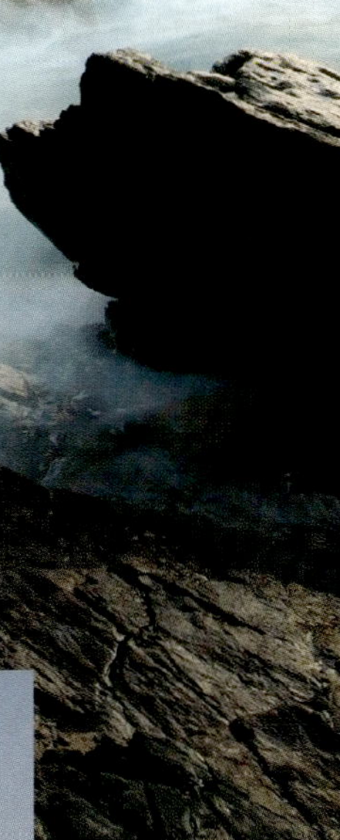

Cape Cornwall

Photographed from the nearby Porth Ledden Cove to include plenty of interesting foreground, the camera was set up on a (sturdy) tripod, allowing the nearby waves to blur into a nice, soft haze around the rocks.

Exposing for Capes

Exposure times will generally require the use of a tripod and remote shutter release: not only to avoid camera shake from handheld shooting and unnecessary vibrations, but also due to the use of low ISO settings (ISO 100 is said to provide greater dynamic range than ISO 50, but the lower the better) and small apertures to maximize depth of field. For example, during sunrise and sunset at ISO 100 and an aperture of f/16, exposure times are likely to be around a second as ambient light levels will be relatively low.

The reason for setting a small aperture in landscape photography is to maximize the depth of field—that is get as much subject matter in focus as possible, from very close to the lens to Infinity. The downside of small apertures is the effect of diffraction, an artifact that appears around f/16 and above and degrades edge sharpness, even in the most expensive lenses, so a balance is required. Otherwise, the use of hyperfocal distance charts for setting focus, which is outlined elsewhere in this book, offers an easy solution for overcoming this problem.

The use of a circular polarizing filter can deepen the color of blue skies, make clouds pop out from the background, and saturate colors. Particularly if the composition has sun at right angles to the direction of the camera (at which a polarizer is most effective), the understated use of a polarizer will add depth and contrast to the final image. Bear in mind, that a circular polarizer, when rotated fully, will reduce exposure by 1-2/3 f-stops.

If the photographer wants to blur the patterns of the waves crashing against the cape's rocks, for example, the use of a non-graduated ND filter (which are available in one f-stop increments) will increase exposure times and blur the waves into a swirl of surf. Good quality ND filters will not add any color cast (hence the "neutral" part of the name).

In most cases, the use of graduated neutral density filters will be required regardless of the creative filter techniques outlined above, in order to balance the exposure of the sky with that of the land and sea, and particularly foreground interest. The most likely requirement will be across the horizon of the sea. Take an exposure from a neutral tone in the sky (such as blue sky away from the sun, or a mid-gray cloud) and another exposure for a neutral-toned rock or patch of green grass in the foreground, and calculate the difference. If, for example, the sky exposures at f/16 is 1/30 second and the foreground is 1/2 second, the difference is 4 f-stops   (1 f-stop at 1/15 second, 2 at 1/8 second, 3 at 1/4 second, and 4 f-stops at 1/2 second)—therefore use a three-stop ND filter to bring the difference back to one f-stop (exposure levels between sky and land generally look more natural if some difference is retained—too little contrast and the image will feel flat and lifeless).

The choice of hard or soft graduation for the ND filter, here, will be dictated by the composition. If the horizon is visible, such as the sea's horizon, a hard graduated ND filter should be used, but where subjects block the view of the horizon or the horizon is uneven (that is, where the tip of the cape intersects the horizon of the sea, for example), then use a soft grad ND.

The variety of shots, of course, is not limited to the wide angle. Use a telephoto to capture interesting focal points of the cape, for example, a rocky pinnacle at its tip, or even the birds and wildlife that inhabit the area. Likewise, use a macro lens for the local flora.

Capes may also provide sand or beaches from which to shoot. Bear in mind that if the cape has steep sides, at certain times of the day, beaches or other sea-level photographic subjects could be in shadow, depending on the orientation of the cape and the direction of the sun. Compositions from lower levels are also unlikely to offer shots that frame the entire cape. Indeed, if the sides are steep then inherently only one side of the cape will be in view. If the sun is rising or setting on that side, however, there will still be opportunity to compose some great shots. Aerial photography, while expensive, can add to the variety and provide shots that stand out from the norm. A cheaper option may be to hire a local boat or guide and shoot the cape from opposite the normal viewpoint.

This smaller cape is much more easily fit into frame—indeed, you can see all three sides at once. It also slopes a bit more gently into the ocean, and the currents here aren't quite as dramatic as those around the Cape Peninsula. It's a tranquil, majestic setting, and the bright daylight makes the tones vibrant and inviting.

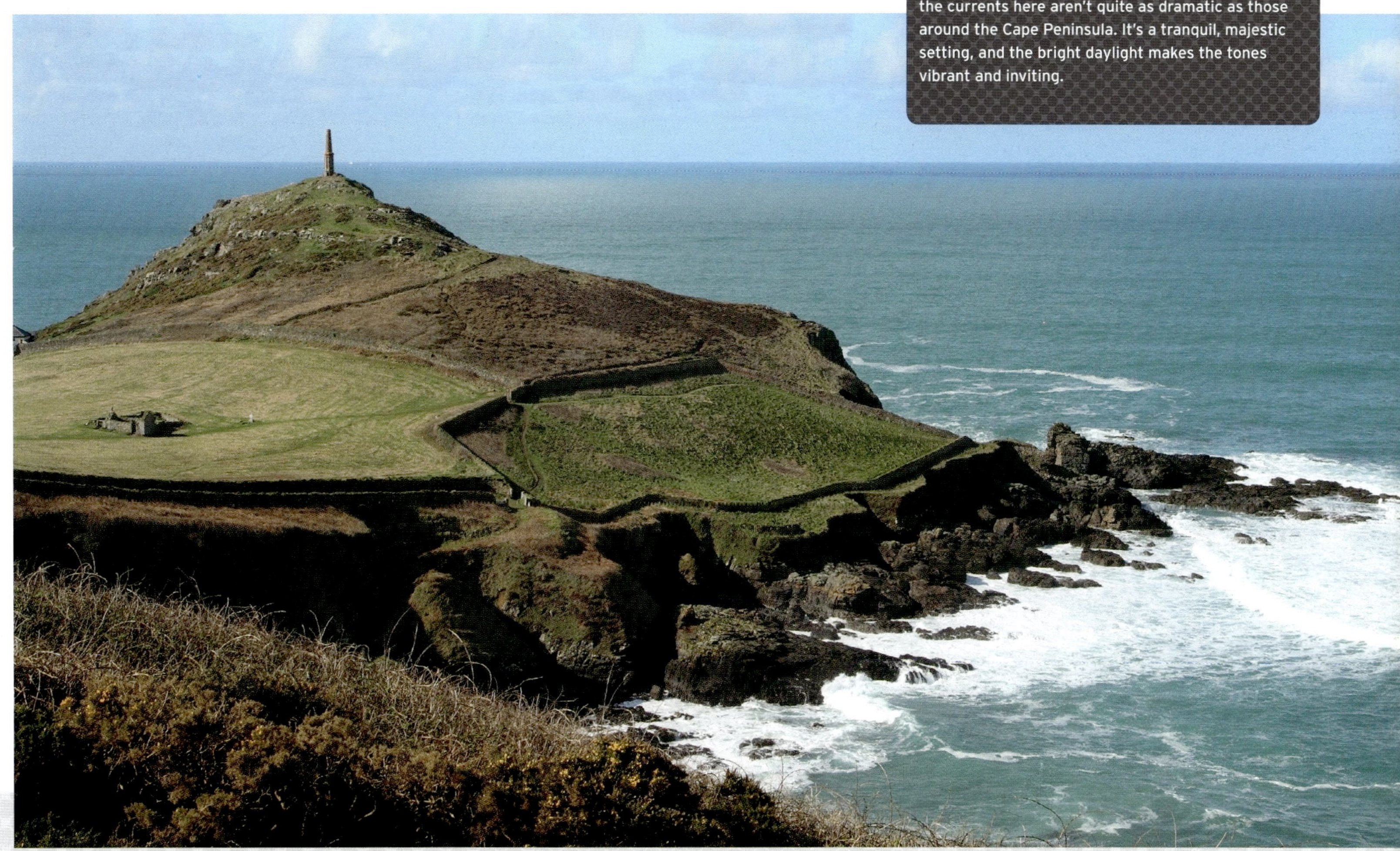

Rainbows

Rainbows are often described as one of the most beautiful light displays on earth. No matter how many times one sees them, they still have the ability to instill a childlike wonder at their appearance. Their elusive nature only adds to their allure, and their ability to transform a familiar scene means that many experienced landscape photographers have a dedicated folder on their hard drive, marked "Rainbows."

Rainbows are formed from a combination of water droplets or moisture in the earth's atmosphere and light—usually sunlight, but moonlight can also create moonbows, for example, around waterfalls at night. What causes a rainbow? White light is made up of all the colors of the light spectrum—specifically the primary colors red, yellow and blue, and the secondary colors their combinations create. When white light enters a raindrop, which acts like a prism, its direction of travel is bent, or refracted. But because each color has a slightly different wavelength, each color of light is refracted to a different degree by the droplet, essentially splitting white light into its component colors (in reality, the spectrum is continuous, rather than split into discrete colors).

Over millions of droplets, this effect appears as a rainbow, which arcs in a semicircle across the sky—blue colors always appear on the inner side of the rainbow arc with red (its opposite) on the outer side. Often a primary rainbow arc is accompanied by a secondary rainbow arc (and sometimes more) above it, albeit more faintly. A rainbow does not actually exist at a particular location in the sky, its apparent position depending on the observer's location and the position of the sun. Rainbows always appear in the region of the sky opposite the sun—and will be observed most intensely by an observer positioned 40-42 degrees away from the plane of the rainbow.

One of the trickiest aspects of rainbow photography is actually finding a rainbow. While they are elusive, particular weather conditions are conducive to creating rainbows. Rainbows are more likely to appear in summer or spring, but can appear anytime. The main meteorological condition in which they appear is when a shower or rain cloud is clearing, and is followed by a break in the clouds, i.e. sunshine. While showery

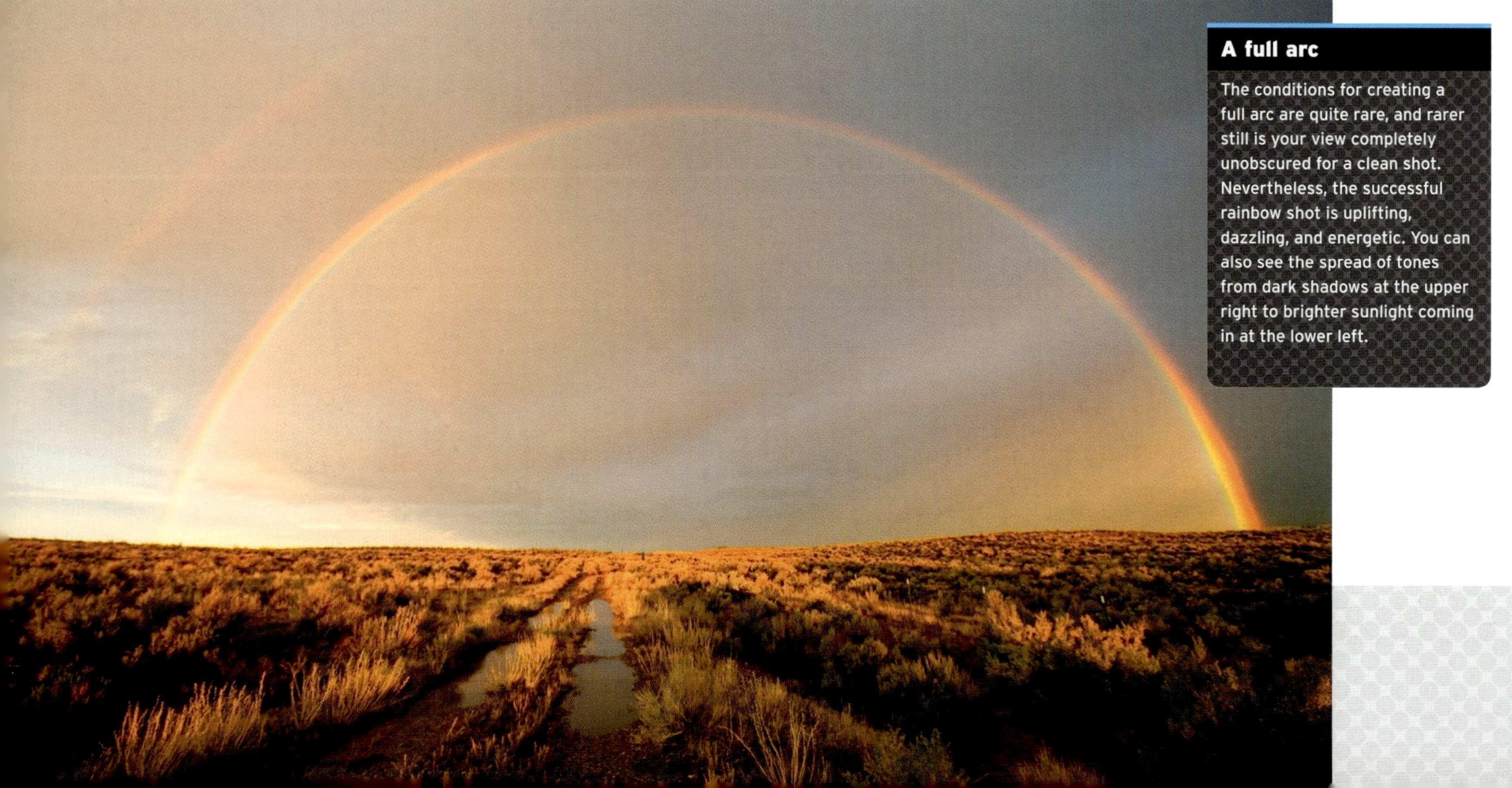

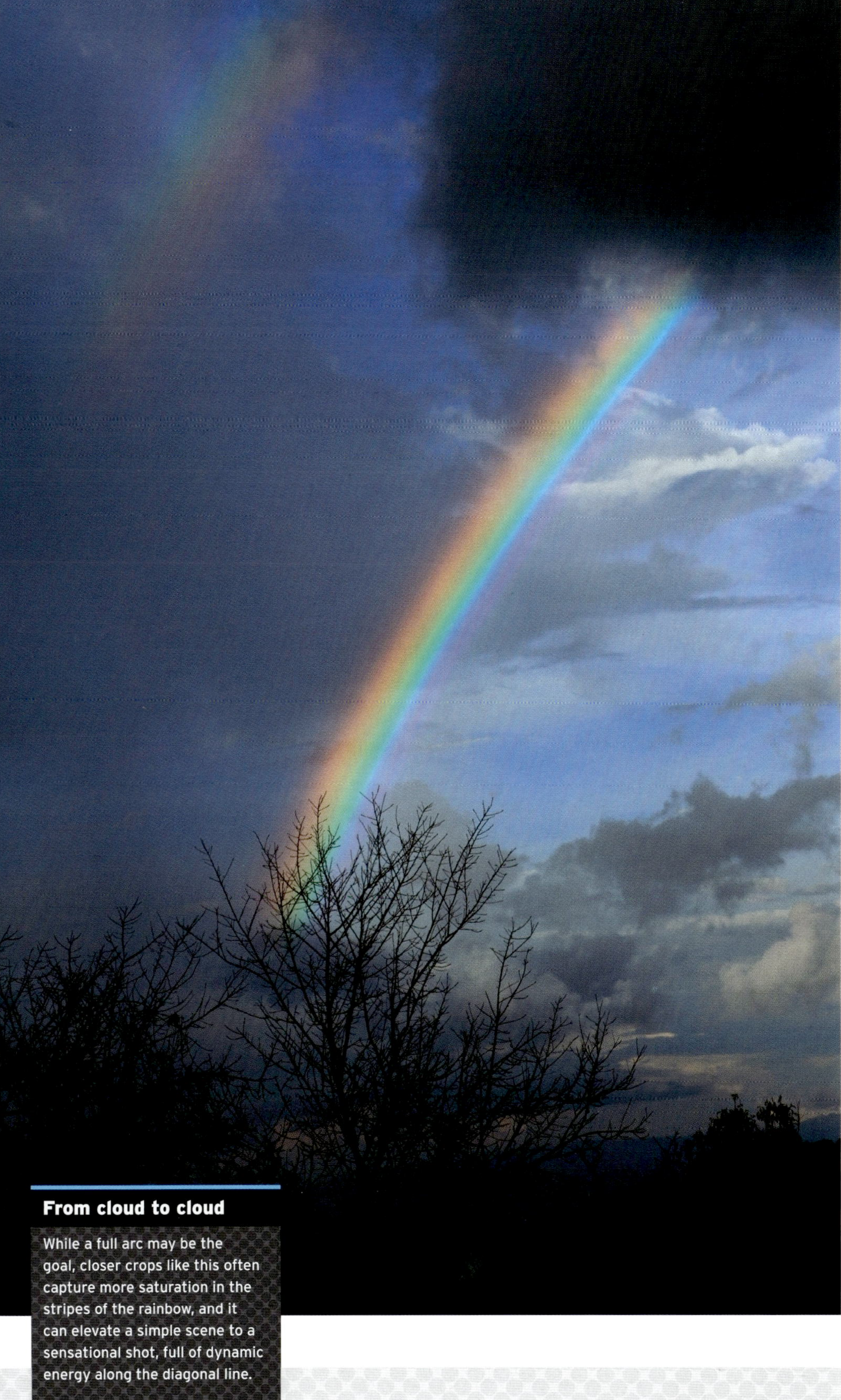

From cloud to cloud

While a full arc may be the goal, closer crops like this often capture more saturation in the stripes of the rainbow, and it can elevate a simple scene to a sensational shot, full of dynamic energy along the diagonal line.

conditions do not guarantee the appearance of a rainbow, they do make it more likely. As mentioned, rainbows most often occur in the early morning or late afternoon in summer or spring. However, the primary requirements are only moisture in the air along with sunlight, so their appearance is possible at any time when these two conditions are met.

A more predictable location for spotting rainbows is near fine mist or spray, such as that found in the vicinity of waterfalls or fountains. The mechanism is the same, but the compositional approach may differ slightly from those created in spacious, wide-open landscapes.

Unfortunately, due to the conditions that are needed for a rainbow to appear, you really do need to be in the right place at the right time. You also need to work quickly as they can appear and vanish within a matter of minutes. Don't fancy waiting for one to appear in the sky above you? You'll also find them in bubbles and near other water sources, such as fountains in town squares and around waterfalls.

If you do happen to stumble across one, position yourself so the rainbow can act as a frame for a building, interesting rock formation or whatever other photogenic subject you may find. If you don't, your shot will just look empty and boring. For added interest, position yourself so the rainbow intersects your subject, as this is where the eye will be drawn.

Tips: Metering

As rainbows need moisture and sunlight to appear, more often than not you'll have clouds full of rain lingering in the back of your shot—but this isn't a bad thing, as the dark colors of storm clouds will help enhance the vibrancy of the rainbow, making the colors really stand out. Just make sure you don't meter off this part of the sky, as your rainbow will end up losing some of its punch.

Maintaining Optimum Camera Performance

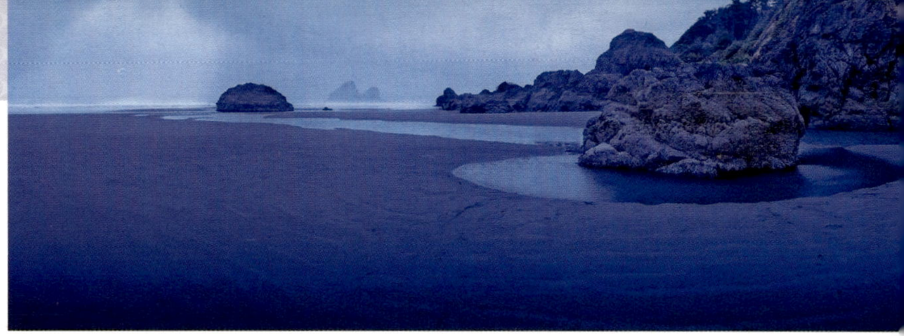

Most photographers quickly realize that getting the most from their digital equipment is about making sure that all the components are optimized as a system. Thus, the level of performance follows the old adage that a chain is only as strong as its weakest link. Most photographers also know that manufacturers are constantly improving the individual components in this digital chain. The implication here is that the photographer has to make sure that changing any single component does not produce a weak link somewhere in the system. So, for example, when making the decision to upgrade to a new camera model with a high frames/second rate and larger file captures, one also has to be sure that the memory card in that camera can deliver the goods.

The last few years have certainly seen a remarkable increase in the frame rates and file sizes captured by all types of digital cameras especially 35mm-type, full-frame digital SLRs. In particular, those models designed for fast action and commonly used in sports and wildlife photography now can take 8 frames per second with negligible shutter lag using large buffers. Even today's SLRs designed for general use are fast enough to capture fleeting moments at weddings, parties, in street photography setting, anytime with children or in any number of other spontaneous situations. In addition, many photographers are using their digital cameras in conditions considered quite harsh for film. For example, shooting for hours in the pounding sun of a 90-100-degree Fahrenheit (32-38-degree Celsius) day or in cold weather with the added stress of even lower wind chill temperatures. All of these considerations make it critical to select a memory card whose specifications can not only match the performance potential of the camera, but can also deliver in any environment in which the camera has to perform.

Know Your Gear

Most photographers will research a camera's capabilities before buying to make sure it meets their needs. Needless to say, the same attention to performance should be paid to the selection of a memory card. The three specifications that are most critical are: (1) the card's sequential write speed, (2) its sequential read speed and (3) the size of the card's total storage. For example, it is really counterproductive to have a camera with a great specs for frames per second speed and a large buffer if your memory card cannot write data into storage fastest enough so you can shoot at those speeds. Second, the card should also be capable of fast read speeds of the captured images as seen in the camera's LCD to be sure you have captured the moment you were after. And, of course, if the camera is generating large files, the card has to have enough storage so that you can concentrate on the situation and not have to keep stopping to change cards.

For expedition photography in such extreme environments as the 120-degree F (49-degree C) heat of California's Death Valley to the subzero wind chills of the high Canadian Arctic, top performance is absolutely required. With film, there was always a concern for such potential problems as the effects of heat on color or static marks in extreme dry cold, to say nothing of the constant worry about the effects of X-ray film inspections when traveling. The switch to digital and the use of high-speed cards such as the Ultra II and Extreme III cards by SanDisk have eliminated these concerns. Both cards have very fast write and read speeds as well as being available in sizes up to 8 gigabytes for the Ultra II and 4 gigabytes for the Extreme III cards. The Extreme III cards in particular are the best choice for tough environments in which high and low temperatures are a factor. They have been tested to perform between -13 to +185 degrees Fahrenheit (-25 to +83 degrees Celsius), which probably exceeds the safe working range of many cameras.

Fast Write Speed

When shooting in dynamic and rapdily changing, spontaneous situations, the 9mb/second write speed of both the Ultra II and the Extreme III cards allows the photographer to shoot fast enough to capture critical moments often too fast for the human eye to isolate. The gigabyte size of these cards has meant not having to stop so frequently and thereby possibly missing a great shot. For example, a 4-gigabyte card holds 523 images with a 6-megapixel camera and 1046 images with an 8-gigabyte card. That's about 14 and 29 36-exposure film rolls respectively which translates into the freedom to take chances and shoot extra frames. But in addition, the quick read speed of 10mb/second of the Ultra II and Extreme III gives the photographer the ability to edit on the spot during time-out periods, thus further extending the shooting time between card changes.

Travel Concerns

As far as the problem of x-ray inspection, tests carried out by the International Imaging Industry Association (I3A), the SanDisk Corporation and the U.S. Transportation Security Administration (TSA) indicated that there is " . . . no evidence of X-ray scanner damage to digital camera media cards or to the images they hold," (http://www.i3a.org). In addition, SanDisk cards are highly resistant to shock and vibration and come with a lifetime replacement warranty. In short, they are the best insurance for getting optimum performance from today's digital cameras.

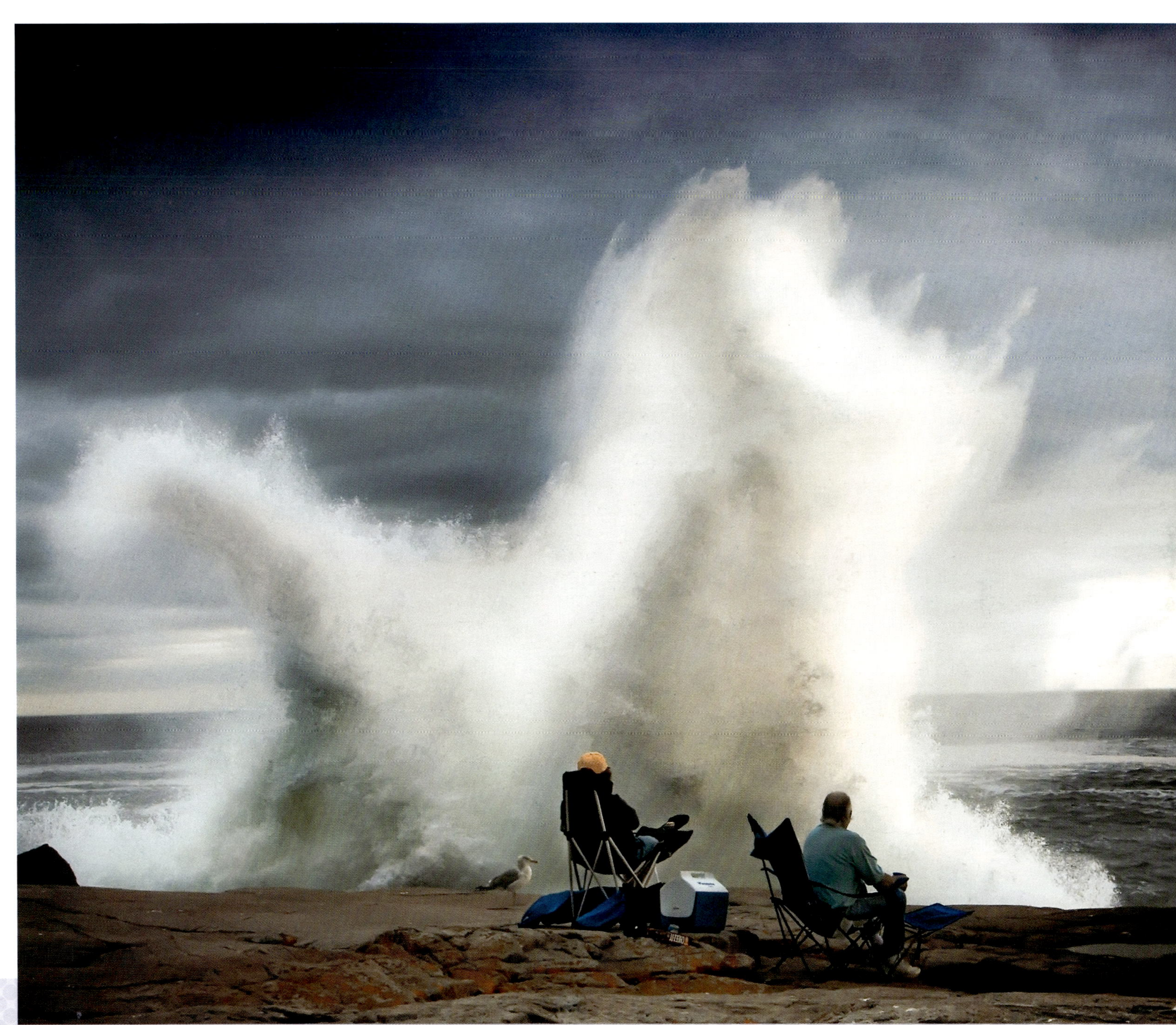

Sharpening

Many of the places and subjects discussed throughout this book offer precisely the kind of photography for which their is a large and consistent market, both in direct sales of prints and in licensing to stock agencies. Of course, capturing these elemental subjects in the first place is just the beginning, and while post-production is not firmly within the bounds of this book, it is well worth covering some tried-and-true approaches to optimizing your images, so your stunning subjects are shown off to the best of your ability. Specifically, the photographer should know how to output their final image, after all exposure and color adjustments have been satisfactorily made. Toward that end, let's take a look at some sharpening techniques.

Sharpening Workflow

It's generally an understood fact that digital images need to be sharpened before they can be considered finished. A large part of this necessity is the presence of an anti-aliasing filter on top of most imaging sensors that intentionally blurs fine detail as light passes through it, in order to mitigate the issues of moire. Another such necessitating factor is the sharpness of the lens itself (or rather, the lack thereof in cheaper samples). What is not so well understood about sharpening, however, is how best to perform it, and particularly what techniques to use for certain types of output. For instance, you should sharpen your images differently if they are to be displayed primarily on the Internet than you would if you plan on creating a full-sized, high-quality print.

First, it's best to understand the sharpening process in three distinct stages: capture sharpening, which takes place either as the JPEG file is being processed in-camera, or as the Raw file is processed in post-production; selective sharpening, in which the photographer applies sharpening to certain key areas of the image at their own creative discretion; and output sharpening, which is the final stage in any post-production workflow, and is customized for the specific display format.

Capture Sharpening

As frequently stated throughout this book, you are always better off shooting in your camera's Raw format. This gives you complete flexibility over the amount of capture sharpening to be applied in your Raw processing workflow. The key to this first step of sharpening is to zoom in to view your image at 100% and carefully adjust the sharpening controls until the inherent blur is removed. Note that at this first stage, it isn't even a matter of making your image stand out as sharp and crisp; rather, it is simply the process of removing the presence of blur induced by either a less-than-perfect lens or by the anti-aliasing filter.

Selective Sharpening

Next, isolate key areas in your image that could use a boost of fine detail. For instance, a shot of a forest need not have every single branch standing out in stark relief from the sky behind it, but perhaps a central tree trunk

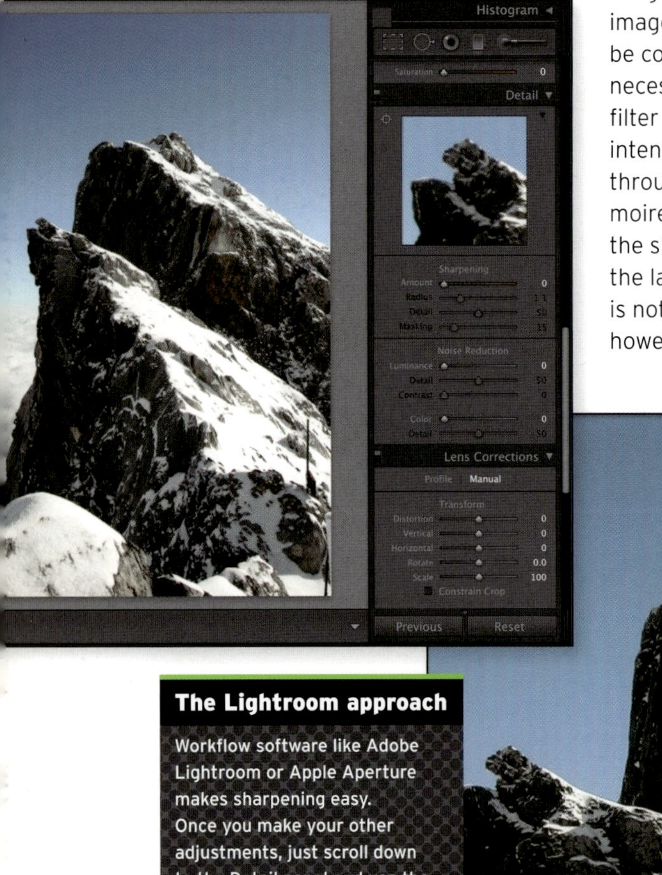

The Lightroom approach

Workflow software like Adobe Lightroom or Apple Aperture makes sharpening easy. Once you make your other adjustments, just scroll down to the Detail panel and use the sliders to set your Sharpening amount, radius, detail, and mask.

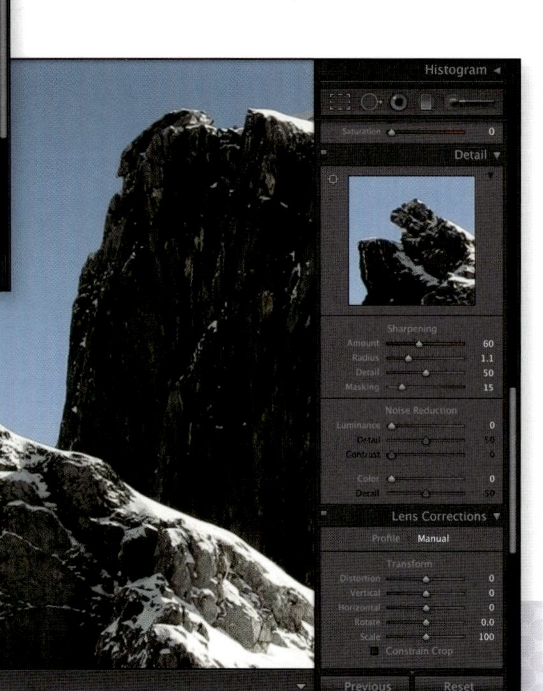

with a jagged outcropping would, if carefully sharpened, lift the entire image up by nature of its being the natural focal point of the image. Selective sharpening can be done using your image-editing programs paintbrush, set to Sharpen at the specific Amount and Brush Size levels appropriate for your subject.

Output Sharpening

In Adobe Lightroom and many other workflow-oriented image-editing programs, the final Output Sharpening stage is quite straightforward: You simply specify what type of display format the final file is to be presented in, and the software customizes one final sharpening pass specifically for that format. If you are working in a more intensive image-editing program like Photoshop, this manual final step will nevertheless be quite straightforward, so long as you know what the final display format is. But first, it's important to always keep in mind that this Output Sharpening is the absolute last step in any post-production workflow. As its effects are global (i.e., they affect not just one area of the image but rather the entire image simultaneously), they will interfere with other adjustments. In particular, you should always be sure to make any noise reductions you desire before the sharpening stage, as the sharpening process tends to exaggerate any noise present in the image.

Finally, if you are sending your image to an agency or repro house first, inquire as to their particular submissions standards, as they may in fact have their own sharpening workflow, or even want an unsharpened image from you initially.

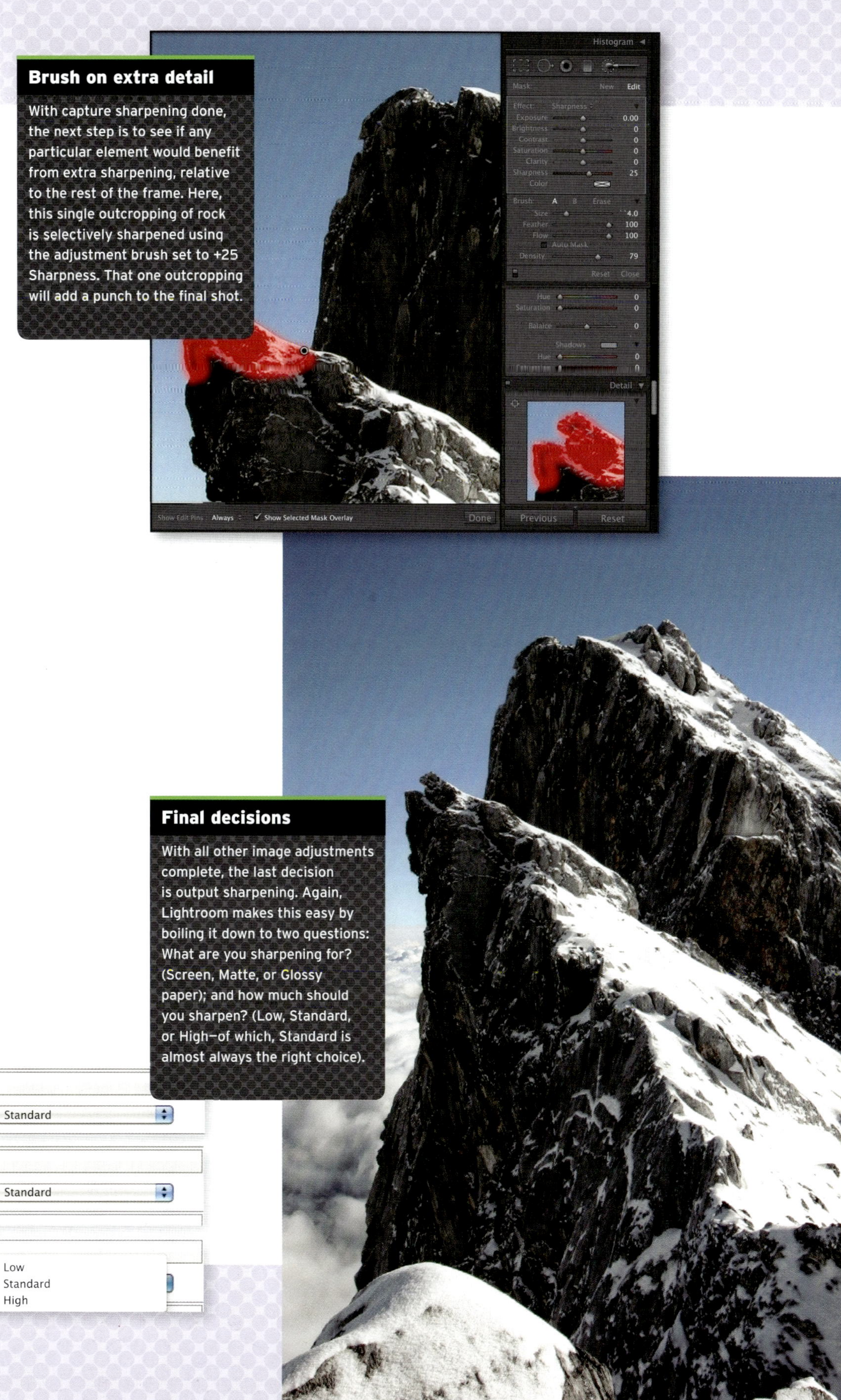

Brush on extra detail

With capture sharpening done, the next step is to see if any particular element would benefit from extra sharpening, relative to the rest of the frame. Here, this single outcropping of rock is selectively sharpened using the adjustment brush set to +25 Sharpness. That one outcropping will add a punch to the final shot.

Final decisions

With all other image adjustments complete, the last decision is output sharpening. Again, Lightroom makes this easy by boiling it down to two questions: What are you sharpening for? (Screen, Matte, or Glossy paper); and how much should you sharpen? (Low, Standard, or High—of which, Standard is almost always the right choice).

Alternative Sharpening Techniques

The sharpening workflow described on the previous pages is the simplest and most straightforward approach, designed to be an intuitive part of the workflow-oriented image-editing process. There are, however, many other possible methods of sharpening your images. Of course, assuming you are shooting Raw, these techniques would fall under the Selective and Output sharpening stages, as Capture sharpening will always be a part of the Raw-processing stage.

So, you've processed your Raw file, saved it as a 16-bit TIFF file, moved into Photoshop or some similar pixel editor, and made all your color adjustments, cropping decisions, exposure tweaks, and so on. The noise has been reduced as much as possible, and the image is ready for either selective or output sharpening.

First, you'll notice that Photoshop's Filter>Sharpen window offers you no fewer than five different options for sharpening your image. However, the first three are all similar, in that they are automated and don't offer you much in the way of control. Ignore them. Unsharp mask is the old industry standard, its counterintuitive name being derived from an old film sharpening technique. It offers the same controls as the Detail panel in Lightroom discussed previously. Smart Sharpen offers a few more interesting options, including the ability to sharpen highlights and shadows separately, and even a blur removal tool that can compensate for motion blur after you indicate the degree of movement in the shot. This is rather difficult to use precisely, but when it works, it can help save an otherwise blurry shot.

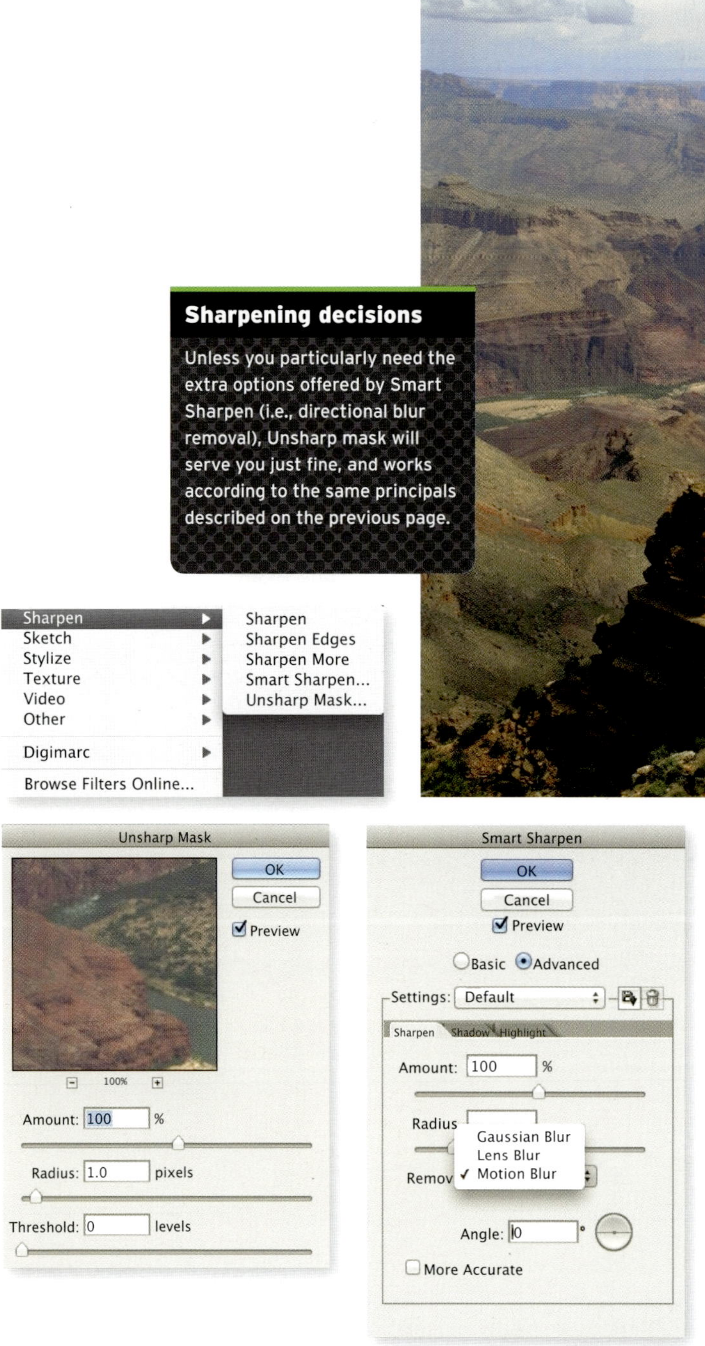

High-Pass Filters

Those Sharpen filters will take care of most sharpening needs, but it is worth pointing out that other, more elaborate options for sharpening your images do exist. In fact, so many exist that it is well outside the bounds of this book to discuss them all here, but one excellent and easy-to-learn example to get started with is the use of a high-pass filter. This process involves going "under the hood" of your image slightly more than a basic Sharpening adjustment, but the results can be well worth it.

First, a high-pass filter is applied to a duplicate layer placed above your main image. You control the intensity of the filter, which will bring out detail only in the edges of the image, leaving any open, empty spaces completely untouched. Most importantly, as this filter now sits on its own layer on top of your image, you can go back and adjust your sharpening layer at any point, or revert back to your unsharpened image with ease. Keep an eye out for halos around harsh edges—if you see them, it's a clear sign that you've gone overboard with your sharpening.

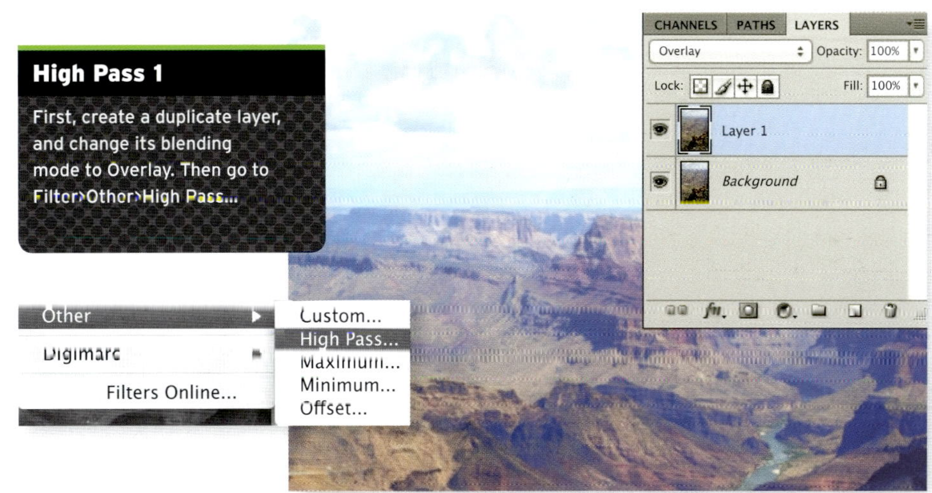

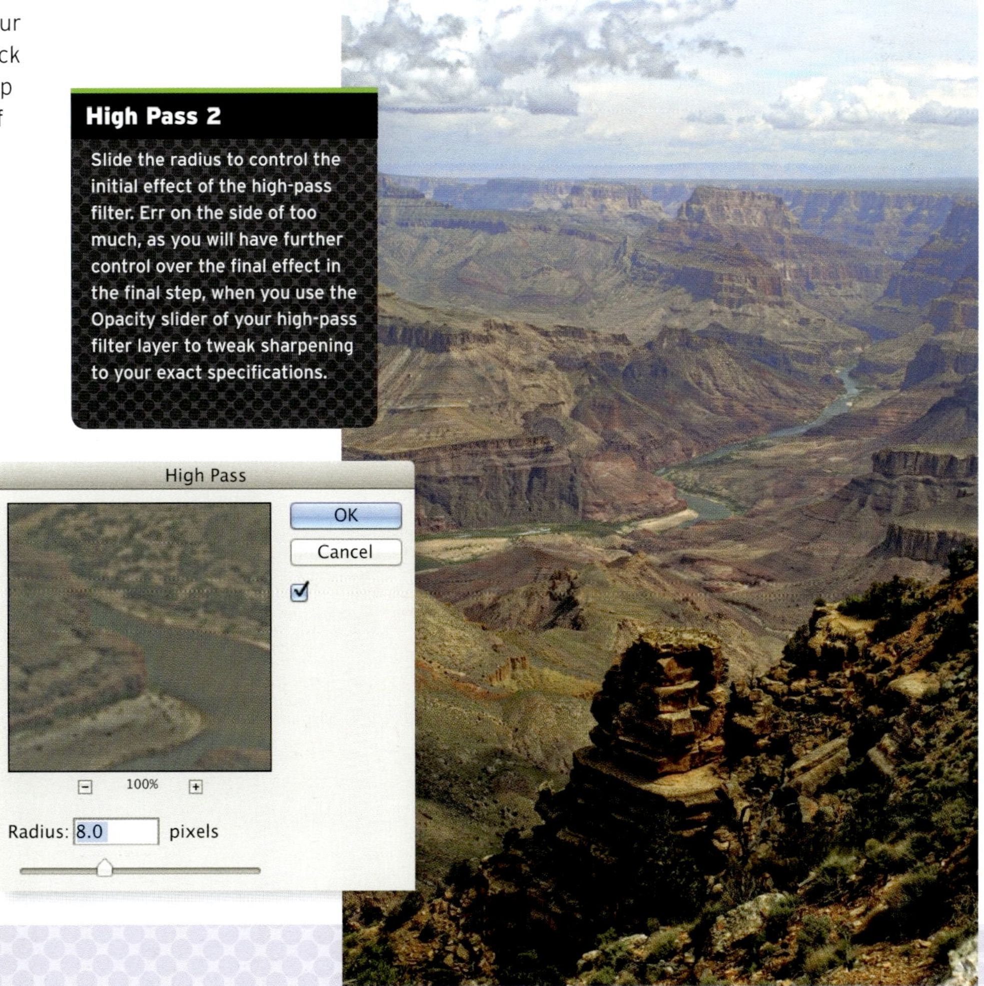

Photography Expeditions

While many of the subjects covered throughout this book are accessible by normal means (you don't need a paid guide to take you out to photograph a sunset, for example), many others are quite exotic, and you can benefit greatly from a knowledgeable guide and an organized tour. Indeed, extreme subjects like volcanoes and tornados almost require an expert guide, as they can be quite dangerous and it's not at all recommended that you undertake an excursion without adequate protection and planning. What follows is a directory of current popular photography-expedition websites, which range from smaller, informal photo walks to higher-end affairs (which are accordingly more expensive). Many of these expeditions are planned and organized months or even years ahead, but if you really want to get out there and explore the elements in all their natural glory, it's worth doing your research and planning a trip. Of course, this directory is only the beginning—new expeditions are organized every day, and if you are already planning on traveling to a certain area, it's probably worth doing some online research into what sort of guided photo tours are available to you once you reach your destination.

General Expedition Sites

www.nationalgeographicexpeditions.com/triptypes/photography

It's hard to find a better name brand in photography than *National Geographic*. Led by top *Nat Geo* photographers, they offer expeditions to every region of the world, ranging from two-week adventures to four-day weekend workshops.

www.photosafaris.com

Joseph Van Os Photo Safaris has a long history of organizing excursions led by a variety of established professionals. Each tour has a particular theme, and their website makes it easy to browse by either date or region.

www.naturalexposures.com/photography-tours-and-events

Led by Daniel J. Cox and supported by a select team of fellow professionals, Natural Exposure photography tours covers almost every region of the world, often with particular emphasis on wildlife. Their website features comprehensive itineraries for each day of the trip, so you know exactly what you're getting.

www.adventurephotoexpeditions.com

Run by Carole Devillers, whose impressive experience you can read about on the website, this expedition service covers all the basics, and also offers a customized expedition for you particular group—a rather unique perk worth checking out.

www.cuephoto.com

Standing for Close-Up Expeditions (CUE), they try to keep their expeditions quite a bit smaller—in groups of 6-7 as opposed to 20 or more—which can be a big help in getting personalized guidance if that's what you're looking for.

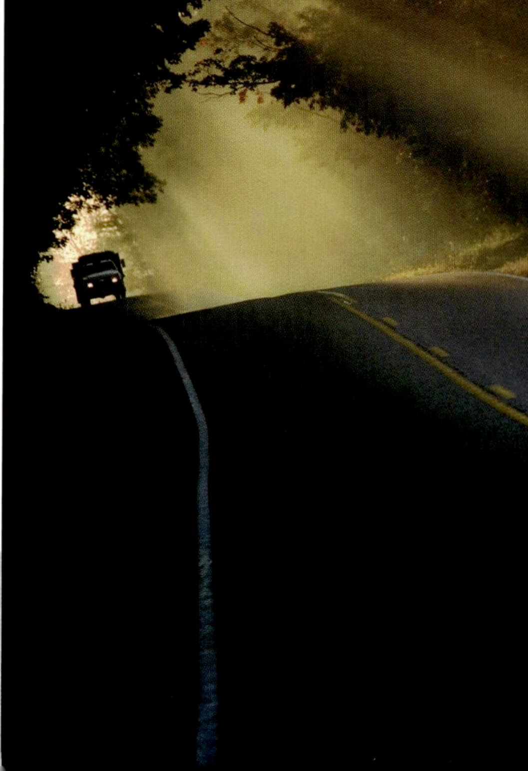

Earth

www.extremephotography.org.uk/guides-and-tours.php
A localized photo tour service, this particular group specializes in Scotland and the surrounding natural landscapes.

www.wild4photographicsafaris.com
Offering exclusively African safaris, they put a big emphasis on the wildlife, but if you read the descriptions, there are also plenty of opportunities for photographing the surrounding landscapes (e.g., the Serengeti).

www.adventurephototours.com
A much more low-key tour service based out of Las Vegas, this group offers affordable, one-day excursions to the surrounding area, including the Grand Canyon (by helicopter).

Fire

www.alaskaphotographics.com/northern_lights_photo_tour.shtml
The rest of the website features an abundance of cold-weather expedition options, but in particular they offer an extended and well-respected tour dedicated to capturing the Northern Lights (and, of course, plenty of the surrounding scenery along the way).

www.volcanodiscovery.com/photo-expeditions.html
This entire Volcano Discovery website is a fantastic resource on volcanic activity all across the globe, and their featured tours are just as comprehensive—easily sorted by either destination and/or category and theme. You can really feel this group's enthusiasm for volcano exploration.

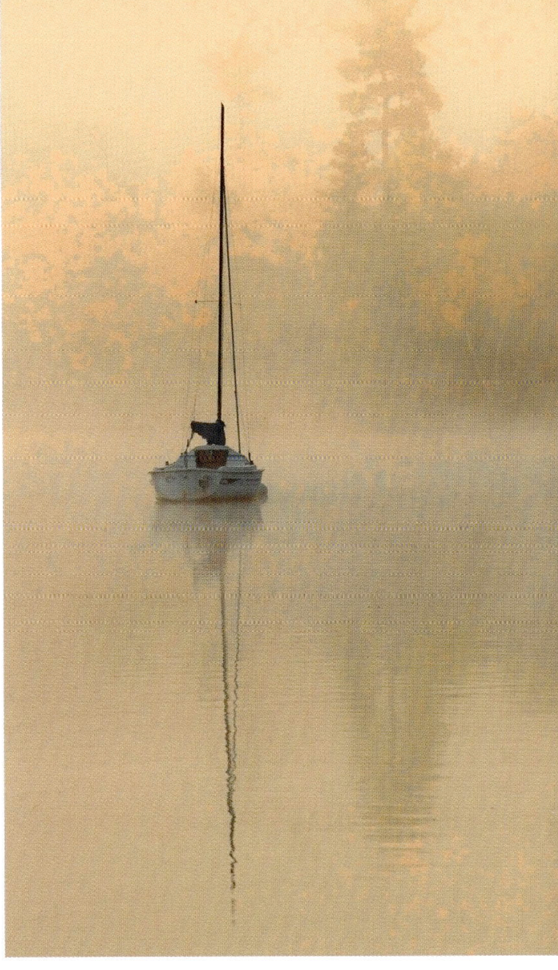

Air

www.stormchasing.com
Their website offers a ton of resources on storm-chasing, and their tour schedule focuses on the most active seasons, giving as close to a guarantee of results as is possible.

www.tempesttours.com
Offering comprehensive tour packages (with links to sample videos from the website), these storm chasers clearly have a lot of experience—which you can observe by browsing their extensive image galleries.

Water

www.icelandaurora.com/tours
Covering waterfalls, geysers, glaciers, and even volcanoes and the Northern Lights, the impressive lineup of tours offered here is testament to the photographic potential of the island of Iceland.

www.sunstonetours.com/photography-cruises/index.asp
While something of a luxury option due to the prices, if you want to explore Antarctica with a *Nat Geo* photographer, this service offer quite the incredible opportunity to do so.

Glossary

additive primary colors The three colors red, blue, and green, which can be combined to create any other color. When superimposed on each other they produce white. See also *rgb* and *subtractive primary colors*.

algorithm Mathematical procedure that allows the step-by-step solution of a problem.

aliasing The jagged appearance of diagonal lines in an image, caused by the square shape of pixels.

alpha channel A grayscale version of an image that can be used in conjunction with the other three color channels, such as for creating a mask.

anti-aliasing The smoothing of jagged edges on diagonal lines created in an imaging program, by giving intermediate values to pixels between the steps.

application (program) Software designed to make the computer perform a specific task. So, image-editing is an application, as is word-processing. System software, however, is not an application, as it controls the running of the computer.

artifact A flaw in a digital image.

ASIC (Application-Specific Integrated Circuit) A silicon chip that is dedicated to one particular function, such as to graphics processing, or to a specific program, such as Photoshop. Used in an accelerator board, this is a fast solution, but it has limited uses.

aspect ratio The ratio of the height to the width of an image, screen, or page.

backup A copy of either a file or a program, for safety reasons, in case the original becomes damaged or lost. The correct procedure for making backups is on a regular basis, while spending less time making each one than it would take to redo the work lost.

banding Unwanted effect in a tone or color gradient in which bands appear instead of a smooth transition. It can be corrected by higher resolution and more steps, and by adding noise to confuse that part of the image. See also *noise filter*

Bézier curve A curve described by a mathematical formula. In practice, it is produced by manipulating control handles on a line that is partly held in place by anchor points.

bit (binary digit) The basic data unit of binary computing. See also *byte*

bit depth The number of bits-per-pixel (usually per channel, sometimes for all the channels combined), which determines the number of colors it can display. Eight bits-per-channel are needed for photographic-quality imaging.

bitmap (bitmapped image) Image composed of a pattern of pixels, as opposed to a mathematically defined object (an object-oriented image). The more pixels used for one image, the higher its resolution. This is the normal form of a scanned photograph. See also *object-oriented (image)*

bits-per-second (bps) A way to measure communication speed.

BMP Image file format for bitmapped images used in Windows. Supports RGB, indexed color, grayscale and bitmap.

brightness The level of light intensity. One of the three dimensions of color. See also *hue* and *saturation*

buffer An area of temporary data storage, normally used to absorb differences in the speed of operation between devices. For instance, a file can usually be sent to an output device, such as a printer, faster than that device can work. A buffer stores the data so that the main program can continue operating.

byte Eight bits—the basic data unit of desktop computing. See also *bit*

cache An area of information storage set aside to keep frequently needed data readily available. This allocation speeds up operation.

cache card A card that can be added to a computer to increase its performance. It contains certain common instructions and data in a special form of memory that the computer's processor can access quickly. A cache card acts as a kind of acceleration, but is less expensive than an accelerator board.

calibration The process of adjusting a device, such as a monitor, so that it works consistently with others, such as scanners and film recorders.

CCD (Charge-Coupled Device) A tiny photocell, made more sensitive by carrying an electrical charge before it is exposed. Used in densely packed arrays, CCDs are the recording medium in low- to medium-resolution scanners and in digital cameras.

CD (Compact Disc) Optical storage medium originally developed by Philips.

CD-R (Compact Disc-Recordable) A writable cd-rom. Designed for desktop production using a relatively small recorder, CD R discs look like ordinary cd-roms and are compatible with cd-rom drives, but have a different internal structure. They can be used as high-volume removable storage (700MB), and for producing multimedia projects and portfolios.

CD-ROM (Compact Disc Read-Only Memory) A optical disc storage medium in which the information can only be read, not altered. The information is "written" onto the disc by a laser that creates small pits in the surface, and so cannot be changed.

CD-RW (Compact Disc Rewritable) A CD on which data can be rewritten any number of times. See also *cd* and *cd-r*

CGA (Color Graphics Adapter) A low-resolution color video card for PCs.

CGM (Computer Graphics Metafile) Image file format for both bitmapped and object-oriented images.

channel Part of an image as stored in the computer; similar to a layer. Commonly, a color image will have a channel allocated to each primary or process color, and sometimes one or more for a mask or other effect. See also *alpha channel*

clipboard Part of the memory used to store an item temporarily when being copied or moved. See also *cut-and-paste*

clip photography Photographs stored on disks or CDs that can be copied into an application.

cloning In an image-editing program, the process of duplicating pixels from one part of an image to another.

CMOS (Complementary Metal-Oxide Semiconductor) Energy-saving design of semiconductor that uses two circuits of opposite polarity. Pioneered in digital cameras by Canon.

CMS (Color Management System) Software (and sometimes hardware) that ensures color consistency between different devices, so that at all stages of image-editing, from input to output, the color balance stays the same. See also *pantone*

CMYK (Cyan, Magenta, Yellow, Key) The four process colors used for printing, including black (key).

color depth See *bit depth*

color gamut The range of color that can be produced by an output device, such as a printer, a monitor, or a film recorder.

color separation The process of separating an image into the process colors cyan, magenta, yellow, and black (CMYK), in preparation for printing.

color space A model for plotting the hue, brightness, and saturation of color.

Compact Flash card One of the two most widely used kinds of removable memory card in digital cameras. CF cards are used by Canon, Fuji, and others.

compression Technique for reducing the amount of space that a file occupies, by removing redundant data.

continuous-tone image An image, such as a photograph, in which there is a smooth progression of tones between black and white. See also *halftone image*

CPU (Central Processing Unit) The processing and control center of a computer.

cropping Delimiting an area of an image.

cursor Symbol with which the user selects and draws on-screen.

cut-and-paste Procedure in graphics for deleting part of one image and copying it into another.

database A collection of information stored in the computer in such a way that it can be retrieved to order—the electronic version of a card index kept in filing cabinets. Database programs are one of the main kinds of application software used in computers.

default The standard setting or action used by a computer unless deliberately changed by the operator.

densitometer Software tool for measuring the density (brightness/darkness) of small areas of an image, monitor or photograph.

desktop computer Computer small enough to fit on a normal desk. The two most common types are the PC and Macintosh.

dialog box An on-screen window, part of a program, for entering settings to complete a procedure.

digital A way of representing data as a number of distinct units. A digital image needs a very large number of units so that it appears as a continuous-tone image to the eye; when it is displayed these are in the form of pixels.

digital zoom A false zoom effect used in some cheaper digital cameras; information from the center of the CCD is enlarged with interpolation.

digitize To convert a continuous-tone image into digital form that a computer can read and work with. Performed by scanner.

DMax (Maximum Density) The maximum density—that is, the darkest tone—that can be recorded by a device.

DMin (Minimum Density) The minimum density—that is, the brightest tone—that can be recorded by a device.

dpi (dots-per-inch) A measure of resolution in halftone printing. See also *ppi*

drag Moving an icon or a selected image across the screen, normally by moving the mouse while keeping its button pressed.

drag-and-drop Moving an icon from one file to another by means of dragging and then dropping it at its destination by releasing the mouse button. See also *drag*

draw(ing) program Object-oriented program for creating artwork, as distinct from painting programs that are pixel-based.

drive Hardware device containing one or more disks.

driver Software that sends instructions to a device, such as a printer, connected to the computer.

DVD (Digital Versatile Disc) a storage disc similar to a CD-ROM on which a large amount of data can be stored (up to 17.08 gigabytes). See also *cd* and *cd-rom*

dye sublimation printer A color printer that works by transferring dye images to a substrate (paper, card, etc.) by heat, to give near photographic-quality prints.

dynamic range The range of tones that an imaging device can distinguish, measured as the difference between its dmin and dmax. It is affected by the sensitivity of the hardware and by the bit depth.

fade-out The extent of any graduated effect, such as blur or feather. With an airbrush tool, for example, the fade-out is the softness of the edges as you spray.

feathering Digital fading of the edge of an image.

file format The method of writing and storing a digital image. Formats commonly used for photographs include tiff, pict, bmp, and jpeg (the latter is also a means of compression).

filter Imaging software included in an image-editing program that alters some image quality of a selected area. Some filters, such as Diffuse, produce the same effect as the optical filters used in photography after which they are named; others create effects unique to electronic imaging.

FireWire The Apple bus that allows for high-speed transfer of data between the computer and peripheral devices. Data can travel up to 400 megabytes-per-second. See also *bus*

frame grab The electronic capture of a single frame from a video sequence. A way of acquiring low-resolution pictures for image-editing.

fringe A usually unwanted border effect to a selection, where the pixels combine some of the colors inside the selection and some from the background.

gamma A measure of the contrast of an image, expressed as the steepness of the characteristic curve of an image.

GB (GigaByte) Approximately one billion bytes (actually 1,073,741,824).

GIF (Graphics Interchange Format) Image file format developed by Compuserve for PCs and bitmapped images up to 256 colors (8-bit), commonly used for Web graphics.

global correction Color correction applied to the entire image.

graphics tablet A flat rectangular board with electronic circuitry that is sensitive to the pressure of a stylus. Connected to a computer, it can be configured to represent the screen area and can then be used for drawing.

grayscale A sequential series of tones, between black and white.

halftone image An image created for printing by converting a continuous-tone image into discrete dots of varying size. The number of lpi (lines-per-inch) of the dot pattern affects the detail of the printed image.

HDRi (High Dynamic Range imaging) Software-based process that combines a number of images taken at different exposure settings to produce an image with full shadow to highlight detail.

histogram A map of the distribution of tones in an image, arranged as a graph. The horizontal axis is in 256 steps from solid to empty, and the vertical axis is the number of pixels in each step.

HSB (Hue, Saturation and Brightness) The three dimensions of color. One of several kinds of color models.

hue A color defined by its spectral position; what is often meant by "color" in lay terms.

image compression A digital procedure in which the file size of an image is reduced by discarding less important data.

image-editing program Software that makes it possible to enhance and alter a scanned or captured digital image.

image file format The form in which an image is handled and stored electronically. There are many such formats, each developed by different manufacturers and with different advantages according to the type of image and how it is intended to be used, reproduced, or displayed.

indexed color A digital color mode in which the colors are restricted to 256, but are chosen for the closest reproduction of the image or display.

interface Circuit that enables two hardware devices to communicate. Also used for the screen display that allows the user to communicate with the computer.

interpolation Bitmapping procedure used in resizing an image to maintain resolution. When the number of pixels is increased, interpolation fills in the gaps by comparing the values of adjacent pixels.

inkjet Printing by spraying fine droplets of ink onto the page; by some distance the most common home printing technology.

ISDN (Integrated Services Digital Network) A digital telecoms technology for transmitting data faster than by traditional modem.

ISO (International Standards Organization) The body that defines design, photography, and publishing elements.

JPEG (Joint Photographic Experts Group) Pronounced "jay-peg," a system for compressing images, developed as an industry standard by the International Standards Organization. Compression ratios are typically between 10:1 and 20:1, although lossy (but not necessarily noticeable to the human eye).

KB (KiloByte) Approximately one thousand bytes (actually 1,024).

kilobyte See *kb*

Lab, L*a*b* A three-dimensional color model based on human perception, with a wide color gamut.

lasso A selection tool used to draw an outline around an area of the image.

lathing 3D technique in which a 2D image plane is rotated around one of the axes, like a piece of wood being turned on a lathe. The result is a 3D object which, viewed along the new axis, is a disc. Used for creating symmetrical objects.

layer One level of an image file, separate from the rest, allowing different elements to be edited separately.

LCD (Liquid Crystal Display) Flat screen display used in digital cameras and some monitors. A liquid crystal solution held between two clear polarizing sheets is subject to an electrical current, which alters the alignment of the crystals so that they either pass or block the light.

logic board The main circuit board in a computer that carries the cpu, other chips, ram, and expansion slots.

lossless Type of image compression in which no information is lost, and so most effective in images that have consistent areas of color and tone. For this reason, not so useful with a typical photograph.

lossy Type of image compression that involves loss of data, and therefore of image quality. The more compressed the image, the greater the loss.

lpi (lines-per-inch) Measure of screen and printing resolution. See also *ppi*

luminosity Brightness of color. This does not affect the hue or color saturation.

Mac OS X The standard operating system on Apple Macintosh computers. Different computers have either PowerPC or Intel processors, but the operating system remains—from the user's perspective—the same. Paid-for updates are often known by their pre-release codename (10.4 "Tiger," 10.5 "Leopard," 10.6 "Snow Leopard," etc.).

macro A single command, usually a combination of keystrokes, that sets in motion a string of operations. Used for convenience when the operations are run frequently.

mask A grayscale template that hides part of an image. One of the most important tools in editing an image, it is used to make changes to a limited area. A mask is created by using

one of the several selection tools in an image-editing program; these isolate a picture element from its surroundings, and this selection can then be moved or altered independently.

MB (MegaByte) Approximately one million bytes (actually 1,048,576).

menu An on-screen list of choices available to the user.

microdrive Miniature hard disk designed to fit in the memory-card slot of a digital camera and so increase the storage capacity.

midtone The parts of an image that are approximately average in tone, midway between the highlights and shadows.

mode One of a number of alternative operating conditions for a program. For instance, in an image-editing program, color and grayscale are two possible modes.

MS-DOS (Microsoft Disc Operating System) The old operating system used in IBM (and compatible) computers. Windows provided an easier-to-use front end for this text-based operating system, though later versions of Windows have moved away from direct compatibility.

noise Random pattern of small spots on a digital image that are generally unwanted, caused by non-image-forming signals.

noise filter Imaging software that adds noise for an effect, usually either a speckling or to conceal artifacts such as banding. See also *artifact* and *noise*

object-oriented (image, program) Software technology using mathematical equations rather than pixels to describe an image element. These are scalable, in contrast to bitmapped elements.

paint program A variety of pixel-based image-editing programs, with tools and features geared more toward illustration rather than photography.

parallel port A computer link-up in which various bits of data are transmitted at the same time in the same direction.

paste Placing a copied image or digital element into an open file.

PDF (Portable Document Format) An industry standard file type for page layouts including images. Can be compressed for Internet viewing or retain full press quality; in either case the software to view the files–Adobe Reader–is free.

peripheral An additional hardware device connected to and operated by the computer, such as a drive or printer.

Photo-CD A proprietary cd-rom format developed by Kodak for storing photographs.

photo-composition The traditional, non-electronic method of combining different picture elements into a single, new image, generally using physical film masks.

PICT A file format developed by Apple that supports RGB with a single alpha channel, and indexed color, grayscale and bitmap modes. Very effective at compressing areas of solid color.

pixel (PICture ELement) The smallest unit of a digitized image–the square screen dots that make up a bitmapped picture. Each pixel carries a specific tone and color.

plug-in module Software produced by a third party and intended to supplement a program's performance.

PNG (Portable Network Graphic) A file format designed for the web, offering compression or indexed color. Compression is not as effective as JPEG.

ppi (pixels-per-inch) A measure of resolution for a bitmapped image.

processor A silicon chip containing millions of micro-switches, designed for performing specific functions in a digital camera.

program A list of coded instructions that makes the computer perform a specific task. See also *software*

RAID (Redundant Array of Independent Disks) A stack of hard disks that function as one, but with greater capacity.

RAM (Random Access Memory) The working memory of a computer, to which the central processing unit (cpu) has direct, immediate access.

ramp Gradient, as in a smooth change of color or tone.

Res (RESolution) Abbreviation used for metric resolution. Thus, "Res 12" is 12 lines-per-millimeter.

resampling Changing the resolution of an image either by removing pixels (lowering resolution) or adding them by interpolation (increasing resolution).

resolution The level of detail in an image, measured in pixels (e.g. 1024 by 768 pixels), lines-per-inch (on a monitor) or dots-per-inch (in the halftone pattern produced by a printer, e.g. 1200 dpi).

RGB (Red, Green, Blue) The primary colors of the additive model, used in monitors and image-editing programs.

ROM (Read-Only Memory) Memory, such as on a cd-rom, that can only be read, not written to. It retains its contents without power, unlike ram.

rubber-stamp A paint tool in an image-editing program that is used to clone one selected area of the picture onto another. It allows painting with a texture rather than a single tone/color, and is particularly useful for extending complex textures such as vegetation, stone, and brickwork.

saturation The purity of a color; absence of gray, muddied tones.

scanner Device that digitizes an image or real object into a bitmapped image. Flatbed scanners accept flat artwork as originals; slide scanners accept 35mm transparencies and negatives; drum scanners accept either film or flat artwork.

selection A part of the on-screen image that is chosen and defined by a border, in preparation for making changes to it or moving it.

SLR (Single Lens Reflex) A camera which transmits the same image via a mirror to the film and viewfinder.

software Programs that enable a computer to perform tasks, from its operating system to job-specific applications such as image-editing programs and third-party filters.

stylus Penlike device used for drawing and selecting, instead of a mouse. Used with a graphics tablet.

subtractive primary colors The three colors cyan, magenta, and yellow, used in printing, which can be combined to create any other color. When superimposed on each other (subtracting), they produce black. In practice, a separate black ink is also used for higher print quality.

thumbnail Miniature on-screen representation of an image file.

TIFF (Tagged Image File Format) A file format for bitmapped images. It supports CMYK, RGB, and grayscale files with alpha channels, and lab, indexed-color, and it can use LZW lossless compression. It is now the most widely used standard for good-resolution digital photographic images.

tool A program specifically designed to produce a particular effect on-screen, activated by choosing an icon and using it as the cursor. In image-editing, many tools are the equivalents of traditional graphic ones, such as a paintbrush, pencil, or airbrush.

toolbox A set of programs available for the computer user, called tools, each of which creates a particular on-screen effect. See also tool

TTL (Through-The-Lens meter) A device that is built into a camera to calculate the correct exposure based on the amount of light coming through the lens.

upgrade Either a new version of a program or an enhancement of hardware by addition.

upload To send computer files, images, etc. to another computer. See also download

USB (Universal Serial Bus) In recent years this has become the standard interface for attaching devices to the computer, from mice and keyboards to printers and cameras. It allows "hot-swapping," in that devices can be plugged and unplugged while the computer is still switched on.

USM (Unsharp Mask) A sharpening technique achieved by combining a slightly blurred negative version of an image with its original positive.

WiFi A wireless connectivity standard, commonly used to connect computers to the Internet via a wireless modem or router.

wysiwyg (what you see is what you get) Pronounced "wizzywig," an acronym meaning what you see on-screen is what you get when you print the file.

Picture Credits

Joseph Meehan: 3TL, 3BL, 6-7, 9, 16-19, 36-41, 43, 52-55, 111, 124-135, 138-157, 168, 176-177, 182-183, 192

FLPA: Kevin Schafer/Minden Pictures: 35; Keith-Nels Swenson/Minden Pictures: 47C

iStock: Jay Lazarin: 68TL; Shaun Lowe: 70; Nicola Margaret: 71; John Kirk: 73BR; Nils Kahle: 99

Corbis: Bruno Domingos/Reuters: 137

Fotolia: Csourav: 10; Mykola Velychko: 11TR; S. Mohr Photography: 11BR; Paulus Nugroho R: 12; PhotoRomano: 13; Sam D'Cruz: 14; Oksix: 15; VLorzor: 21TL, 23; SeanPavonePhoto: 21BR; Magann: 22, 25; David Woods: 24; 00Ffilip: 26; Mammut Vision: 27; Sergey02: 28; Cmon: 3, 29; Kasto: 30; Olga Khoroshunova: 31; Alexey Stiop: 33BL; Yarden Tabori: 34; Hugh McKean: 44; Daniel Loretto: 45TR; Espion: 45TL; Nowhere: 45BL; Ulrike Steinbrenner: 46TL; ParadoksB: 46BL; David Ross: 47TR; S.T.A.R.S: 48-49; Nejron Photo: 56; Schachspieler: 57C; Demydenko Mykhailo: 57B; Stephen Bonk: 58BL; p0temkin: 58BR; Paul Moore: 59BL; DesertSolitaire: 59BR; Thierry Maffeis: 60T; Ronnortx: 61CB; Jason Branz: 62, 65; KoMa: 63TR; Georg Lehnerer: 67B; Erectus: 77CL, 77BR; RonniHauks: 78; James Thew: 79; Bocky: 81L; Valdezrl: 81R; Bastien Poux: 3, 84; James Steidl: 85; Beboy: 86; Tanguy de Saint Cyr: 89BR; Jochen Scheffl: 92; klikk: 93BL; Naeblys: 94; Satori: 95; Bill Gabbert: 108; Vaclav Janousek: 121; Erika8213: 158; Vladimír Radosa: 159; Divio: 161BR; Tosoth: 162; Bigshotd3: 164; J. W.Schaefer: 169; 1911: 179; Chee-Onn Leong: 180

Shutterstock: Ales Liska: 33TR; Ustyuzhanin Andrey Anatolyevitch: 45BR; kavram: 46C; Andrei Nekrassov: 47BR; Charles L Bolin: 60CT; Peter Wollinga: 60CB; Rene Hartmann: 60B; Niels Quist: 61T; John Wollwerth: 61CT; Todd Shoemake: 63B; Melanie Metz: 64; LAfoto: 66; Photobank.kiev.ua: 67TR; Caitlin Mirra: 68; Robert A. Mansker: 69; Vincent369: 73T; Roman Krochuk: 77TR; Melanie Metz: 2, 80; Kushch Dmitry: 82; Primož Cigler: 83; RZ_design: 87; Jerome Scholler: 88; Kamira: 89TL; Luigi Nifosi': 90BL; Celso Diniz: 90BR; Ollirg: 90T; Valeriy Poltorak: 91BR; Jejim: 91BL; PavelSvoboda: 93TR; Alin B.: 96, 98BR; Jon Beard: 97; PhotoSky 4t com: 98TL; Fel1ks: 100; Radu Razvan: 101; P.Schwarz: 102; Matt Tilghman: 103BL; Muzhik: 103TR; Mayovskyy Andrew: 104T; Patryk Kosmider: 104B; Vlue: 105; Kuttelvaserova: 112; Dmitry Naumov: 113; Andreiuc88: 114T; Daniel Petrescu: 114BR; Yegor Larin: 115; Janelle Lugge: 116; Christopher Meder: 117; Apple's Eyes Studio: 118; Eduardo Rivero: 119T; Luis Louro: 119B; MOSCHEN: 120; Lisa S.: 122L; Amnartk: 122TR; Elzbieta Sekowska: 123; RedTC: 160; Nadezda Boltaca: 161TL; OrionTrail: 163; PavelSvoboda: 165; Renewer: 166; Galyna Andrushko: 167; Ian Woolcock: 171TR; Matej Hudovernik: 171BL; David Steele: 172; Stephen Aaron Rees: 173; Galyna Andrushko: 174; Jamikorn Sooktaramorn: 175

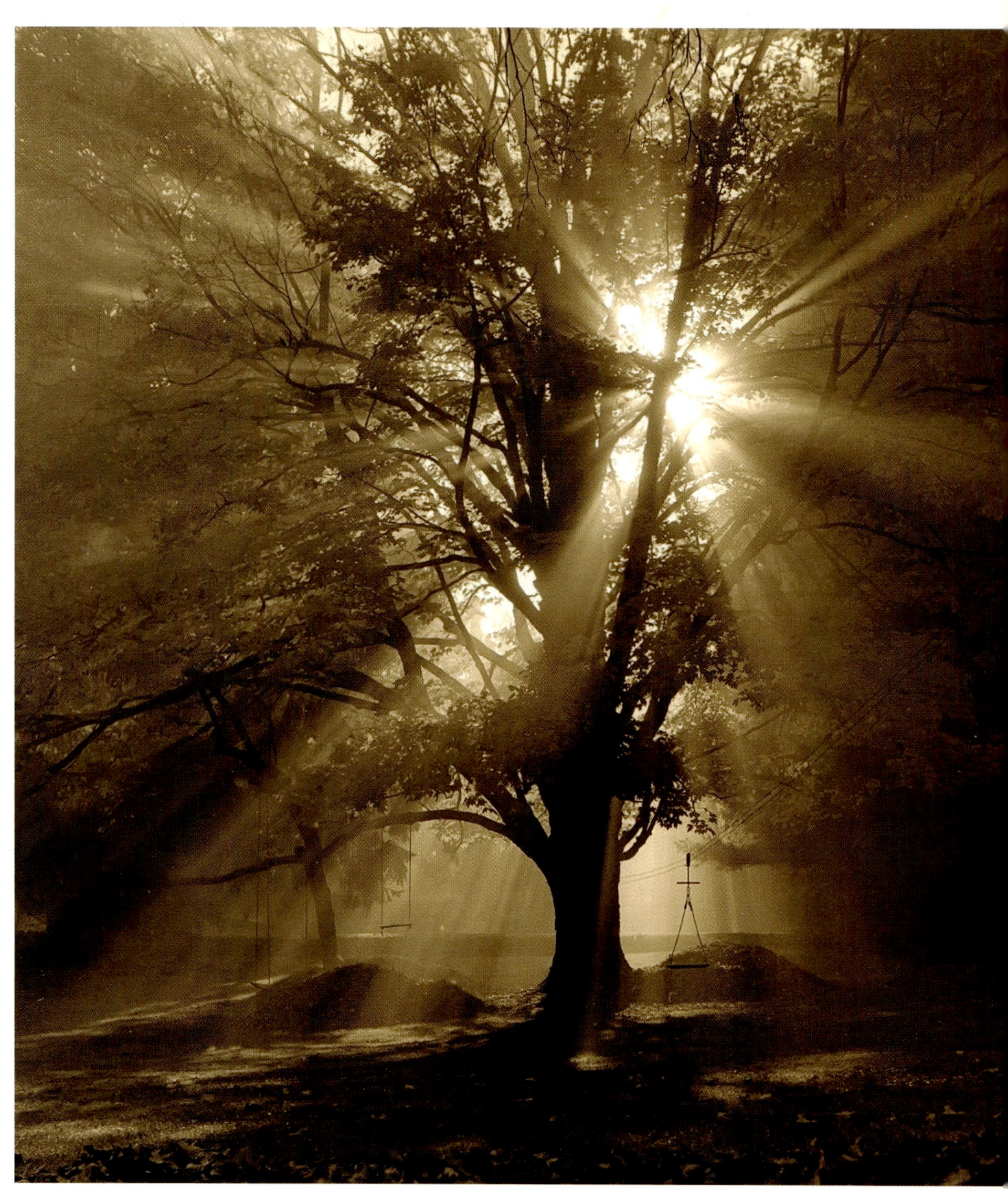

Reference